D0115523

On the Cusp

123
165

On the Cusp

The Yale College Class of 1960
and a World on the Verge
of Change

Daniel Horowitz

University of Massachusetts Press
Amherst & Boston

Copyright © 2015 by Daniel Horowitz
All rights reserved
Printed in the United States of America

ISBN 978-1-62534-145-7 (paperback); 144-0 (hardcover)

Designed by Jack Harrison
Set in Adobe Minion Pro with Quadraat display

Library of Congress Cataloging-in-Publication Data
Horowitz, Daniel, 1938–   author.
On the cusp : the Yale College class of 1960 and a world on the verge of change /
Daniel Horowitz.
pages cm
Includes bibliographical references and index.
ISBN 978-1-62534-145-7 (pbk. : alk. paper) —
ISBN 978-1-62534-144-0 (hardcover : alk. paper)
1. Horowitz, Daniel, 1938-2. Yale University—Students—Biography.
3. Yale College (1887-). Class of 1960—Biography.
4. Jewish college students—Connecticut—New Haven—Biography.
5. College students—Connecticut—New Haven—Biography.
6. Students—United States—Conduct of life. I. Title.
LD6343.H67 2015
378.746'809046—dc23
2014050123

British Library Cataloguing-in-Publication Data
A catalogue record for this book is available from the British Library.

To members of the Yale Class of 1960,
their friends and family, including
Helen L. Horowitz
Judy H. Katz and Len Katz
Sarah Horowitz and Brad Reichek
Ben Horowitz, Judy Liebman, and Aaron Levi Horowitz

CONTENTS

ACKNOWLEDGMENTS

In researching and writing this book I have benefited from a range of institutions. The libraries of Occidental College and Harvard University have given me access to published materials, while the Smith College library was my entry point to online sources. My endnotes reveal those who helped me carry out research in libraries I did not visit personally. More centrally, on visits to Yale, Jessica Becker, Michael Frost, William Massa, Stephen Ross, Judy Schiff, Claryn Spies, and Christine Weideman guided me through the riches of Manuscripts and Archives. Often after the library closed, I enjoyed the hospitality of Carol and Sandy Schreiber, and of Nora Ng and John Bullock. Smith College continues to fund the research of retired faculty members, something that has helped me considerably. While still president of Smith, Carol Christ suggested the title for the book.

Early on, in December 2012, at an informal meeting of Boston-area historians, Liz Cohen, David Engerman, Helen L. Horowitz, Julie Reuben, and Bruce Schulman offered especially helpful suggestions. Responses from more public audiences to "Think Yiddish" and "Dress British" helped me test drive my ideas. Deborah Dash Moore invited me and Jonathan Freedman hosted me for a week-long residency at the Frankel Center for Judaic Studies at University of Michigan, where I presented my work to a seminar and to a more public audience. Ellen C. DuBois arranged for me to talk at UCLA's Center for Jewish Studies. I gave talks and listened to responses twice at Brandeis University, once at a conference in honor of Steve Whitfield and then to an audience at the BOLLI program, which Beth Gordon Davis arranged. As I was finishing the book, Matt Jacobson arranged for me to give three talks at Yale.

The endnotes reveal how I relied on the recollections and suggestions of many classmates and near classmates. However, I want to single out several who were especially helpful: Steve Easter, Gary Gelber, Steve Johnson, Lew Lehrman, Lance Liebman, Jared Lobdell, Jesse Lemisch, Jeremy Nahum, Peter Parsons, Allan Rashba, Howard Richards, Robert Rifkind, Guy Stevens, and John Wilkinson. Even further beyond the call of duty are classmates (and sometimes their spouses) who have been interlocutors, in some cases over the decades and in others only since I began to work on this project. Among those who have spurred me on are John Bing, David and Mai Elliott, Len and Judy Katz, Edmund Leites, Tom and Nhu Miller, Monroe and Aimée Price, Ted Stebbins, Stuart Stoddard, and Kirke Wilson.

I have relied heavily on advice from a range of interested parties. Elise Capron of the Sandra Dijkstra Literary Agency offered useful suggestions about publishing. Those who read specific chapters or offered targeted suggestions are Paul Alpers, Ben Horowitz, Sarah Horowitz, Micah Kleit, Elizabeth G. Knoll, Heather Murray, Grey Osterud, Julie Reuben, Doug Rossinow, John Thelin, Steve Whitfield, and Leandra Zarnow. Pat Graham and Carole Turbin, who read an early version of the entire manuscript, saved me from mistakes and offered me invaluable suggestions. Above all, I relied heavily on the comments, proddings, suggestions (and sometimes even the phrases, concepts, and words) of scholars and friends who read the manuscript (sometimes multiple versions). Jerold Auerbach, Casey Blake MacKenzie, Brigham, Lynn Dumenil, Ruth Feldstein, Kimberly Marlowe Hartnett, Helen L. Horowitz, Maurice Isserman, Andrew Jewett, Wendy Kline, Edmund Leites, Julia Mickenberg, Carol Rigolot, Tony Rotundo, Diane Schuster, Jack Schuster, Judy Smith, Ted Stebbins, and one anonymous reader for a university press improved my prose, saved me from errors, sharpened my arguments, and suggested solutions to structural problems. Although in the end only I am responsible for what appears in print, their help transformed my manuscript into this book.

Once again, Clark Dougan of University of Massachusetts Press more than rose to the occasion, bringing to bear on my work the knowledge and skills of a historian, editor, and someone familiar with Yale—both from his years as a Yale graduate student and over the longer term from his marriage to Yale Drama School alum Suzanne P. Dougan, who has deep family roots in New Haven. From start to finish he understood, often better than I did, how to write this book. Carol Betsch, Jack Harrison, and Jim O'Brien did superb jobs, respectively copyediting the manuscript, designing, and indexing the book.

PREFACE

Directly, clearly visualized, he perceived, for the first time, what he was to perceive in every side of his college career, that a standard had been fashioned to which, irresistibly, subtly, he would have to conform; only here, in the free domain of combat, the standard that imposed itself upon him was something bigger than his own.

OWEN JOHNSON, *Stover at Yale* (1912)

On April 9, 1940, census taker Mary E. Ek walked down Colony Road in New Haven, Connecticut. Had she followed the news, she would have learned of the Germans marching across Europe: on that day Denmark surrendered and the Nazis conquered Oslo. Before approaching where my family lived, she carefully recorded information on our neighbors—Pinkus, Feinberg, Wallack, Teitleman, Feinstein, Brodsky, Goldberg. All of them were Jews. With the exception of one couple and one grandfather born in Russia, one wife in South Africa, and one servant in Hungary, all residents were American-born, mostly in Connecticut or adjoining states. The parents in every household, most in their forties, had two children, always a son and a daughter, who varied in age from three to seventeen. Only one house had a grandparent living in and almost all had a servant. The fathers worked as managers, engineers, merchants, salesmen, insurance agents, and dentists—but Ek listed no occupation for any of the mothers.[1]

200 Colony Road, New Haven, Connecticut, 1940

When she came to the house where we lived, Ek carefully wrote down what she found. She estimated its value at $10,000. Its inhabitants were five. My father, William, born in Missouri in 1907, had completed four years of college. Ek noted that he worked fifty-two weeks a year. The household's total income came from the $5,000 (roughly comparable to $80,000 in 2014) he earned as an executive at a "machinery manufacturing" company. His wife and my mother, Miriam Botwinik Horowitz, born in Connecticut in 1912, had also

xi

completed four years of college. Then there were the two children—my sister Judy, born in 1936 and me, born two years later. Finally, the servant, twenty-four-year-old Gladys Boyd, an African American born in Connecticut who had completed four years of high school and earned $520 a year by working in our home seventy hours per week for fifty-two weeks.

The census revealed some things but not others. My father grew up in Kansas City, Missouri, and came to New Haven for his education at Yale, from which he graduated in 1929. While there, he met my mother when she was still in high school; she graduated from Smith College in 1933. Even before they married on June 25, 1933, my father had begun to work at Botwinik Brothers, founded by my maternal grandfather and his brother, a company that bought, refurbished, and sold machine tools. The house we lived in had a garage for one car, two stories, and what was then an unfinished basement, about twenty-two hundred square feet of livable space in all—three bedrooms and two baths on the second floor and on the first, a half bath, maid's room, living room, breakfast room, dining room, kitchen, and screened-in porch. My mother once hoped she would become a social worker, something that two children, World War II, and the priority of my father's career, connected as it was to male ambition and to national defense, prevented.

He arrived penniless at Yale in 1925: his natural gifts, hard work, and Yale degree helped elevate his class position, as did a marriage into one of New Haven's most prominent Russian Jewish families. It was not only origins and gender that distinguished my mother from my father. She was a secular Jew, while my father skillfully mediated between being an American and being a son of immigrants who retained the deep imprint of his early education in Yiddishkeit and Judaism. At five feet, ten inches he had a commanding physical presence that she, at four feet, eleven inches and barely one hundred pounds, lacked. They also wielded influence in distinctive manners: a reporter in the 1950s characterized my father as a man with an iron fist in a velvet glove, meaning that he gently interacted with others while carefully exercising his power only on those rare times when it was necessary. My mother was more consistently indirect in how she prodded and persuaded. If my mother sustained a certain skepticism about democracy and capitalism, my father embraced both zestfully.

His self-assurance stood in contrast to her less-sure sense of herself. This stemmed from a number of things—the balance between motherhood and career that she could never quite achieve; the death of her father, Hyman Botwinik, at age fifty, less than two months after the visit of the census taker; the presence in her life of her mother, Esther Hirschberg Botwinik, who remained a powerful if often negative model. Matronly, demanding, old-fashioned, she favored my mother's two younger brothers, Norman and Stanley, more than she did my mother.

On Hyman's death, my father assumed his mantle in business and civic life. My father was gaining in social status while my mother was consolidating hers. Gendered expectations and aspirations governed their lives. Relying on what his father-in-law, peers, Yale, and American culture taught, my father easily pursued a model of what a man like himself could aspire to and accomplish. While at Smith, my mother studied with highly accomplished professional women, but her New Haven world offered few if any models of what she might do outside the home as a professional.

200 Colony Road, New Haven, Connecticut, 1956

Fast forward sixteen years, to March 23, 1956—the date of my eighteenth birthday and about the time I learned that in the fall I would begin four years as a Yale undergraduate. On that day the *New York Times* reported the conviction of Martin Luther King Jr. for leading a bus boycott in Montgomery, Alabama. The front page also recorded the uneven progress of the Cold War—the Kremlin restored to a museum a portrait of one of Stalin's opponents while Western leaders struggled to find common ground with the Soviets on issues ranging from conflicts in the Middle East to disarmament.

By the spring of 1956 life had changed at 200 Colony Road. My sister was in her sophomore year at Sarah Lawrence College, though she was often back home on weekends, especially after my junior year in high school when she started dating Len Katz, Yale class of 1957. I benefited from going to Hillhouse High School after her capacity for friendship, sociability, and leadership eased the way for me. By the mid-1950s, Botwinik Brothers was no longer my father's principal employment—now he was building small businesses with his own and Botwinik family funding and emerging as a major figure locally in civic life and the Jewish community.

His confidence, along with his focus on worlds outside the house, shaped the lives of my mother, sister, and me—even though the implications of his far-flung commitments played out differently in the lives of each of us. In the mid-1950s, partly as a stand-in for my father, my mother was elected treasurer of the city of New Haven, the only paid work she ever did. In the same years she fully if ambivalently worked as a volunteer in Jewish and secular worlds. In Judy's and my high school years, Mamie, the live-in African American maid whose last name I am embarrassed to say I cannot remember, prepared us for school in the morning while our mother remained lounging in bed. Our father had time to focus on us only for an hour or so around dinner and on the weekends.

All these differences reflected and reinforced the temperaments of my parents. My father knew who he was and where he was going. In sharp contrast, my mother had unfulfilled longings: inspired at Smith to make something professionally of her life, at 200 Colony Road she experienced her own version of what her fellow alumna Betty Friedan would describe in 1963 as "The Problem That Has No Name." On strike against domesticity, my mother could nonetheless not move from subterfuge to explicit solution. Although she was unsure of what she wanted, in the 1950s she wanted more than what she had. Her husband's ambition and careers, both in business and in public life, commanded a tremendous amount of attention and emotional space. In the neighborhood, civic, and religious worlds she inhabited, to say nothing of what the TV shows *I Love Lucy* and *Ozzie and Harriet* seemed to represent, she encountered few positive alternatives to running a household, raising two children, and doing important volunteer work. Nonetheless, our parents created a secure, protected household; opened our eyes to the wider worlds of politics and culture; imparted to us commitments to liberalism and interracial work; conveyed different meanings of what being a Jew involved; and watched our lives without being hovering helicopters. Whatever tensions there were between my parents and within me, I grew up in a privileged and protected world.

Yale College, Fall 1956: A Strange, New World

In September 1956, that sense of privilege and protection was suddenly threatened when my parents drove me a mile and a half from 200 Colony Road to Yale's Old Campus, where all freshmen lived. A short distance geographically but a long one emotionally. I was no longer at a coed, racially and ethnically diverse public high school that had virtually no well-to-do Protestants. In high school, being Jewish was just one possibility among many, no stronger than any other. And there I carried the personal heritage of my family's economic security and social position. In stepping into Yale, I entered a world where I was unsure whether I belonged or how I might fit in—let alone whether I could measure up to the expectations my parents had for me.

Yale seemed like foreign territory, even though my father was an alumnus. Now in a Protestant world, it meant something completely different to be a Jew. Moreover, I was a townie, a pejorative designation for local students. My background hardly resembled that of classmates who possessed more privilege than I had ever imagined. To a considerable extent, these young men of wealth and social prestige established the tone of college life. The faculty set academic standards and intellectual challenges for which public high school had inadequately prepared me. Yale also presented a masculine, at times even hyper-masculine environment where toughness seemed to matter more than caring or friendliness. Then there were imposing and mysterious buildings that, without words, said "keep out" or "enter at your own peril." For those peers who had encountered a demanding academic regimen at St. Grottlesex (handy shorthand that combined parts of the names of many elite prep schools) and known one another at debutante parties and summer homes, adjusting to Yale seemed to come more easily than it did for me. They had already learned how to play academic and social games whose rules I could hardly fathom.

It may seem strange, given my father's status as an alum and my family's prominence in the local community, that I should have felt like an outsider when I entered Yale. In part this is because both elite universities and the position of Jews in American life have changed significantly since the fall of 1956, making it hard to recapture an earlier time when places like Yale were in many ways unwelcoming to Jews and others. Even though I was a legacy—a term for young men whose relatives had preceded them to Yale—and grew up in New Haven, I had rarely if ever been inside a building on campus before my freshman year. In fact, once during high school, as I was walking in front of one of the residential colleges, a Yale student menacingly warned me never to come on campus again.

Then there was the complicated meaning of following in my father's footsteps. While I was growing up, he communicated relatively little about his own experiences at Yale. But when he did, he focused mainly on two themes: the financial difficulties and pain of exclusion he experienced at the time, and the gratitude he felt on looking back. He was proud of being a Yale graduate, but knew he had not been able to take full advantage of the social and educational opportunities it offered. He wanted me to go to Yale so I could do what he had not been able to do—benefit from all that it might offer me. My father's successful career after leaving Yale provided me with more opportunities than he had had, but he still could not avoid bequeathing to me his lingering sense of what it meant to be an outsider.

There Is Life after Yale College

A lot happened between my graduation in 1960 and 2011 when I began working on this book. Marriage, fatherhood, teaching, scholarly writing, and the passage of personal and historical time restored in me a sense of confidence that had suddenly eluded me in the fall of 1956. More than that, working on this book enabled me to come to terms more fully with the shock that I experienced then. When interviewing classmates, I learned that although many others experienced disruption on entering Yale, its nature and dynamics varied. Some of the more privileged ones, no longer at boarding schools where women and alcohol were banned and in loco parentis governed, now had to learn to navigate a world with fewer rules and more temptations. For others, disorientation came from being lost culturally and unprepared academically, suffering from a variant of what I later came to understand in some of my students as the "impostor syndrome"—the feeling that they did not belong because the college had mistakenly admitted them. Many peers—presidents of their high school class, star athletes, and high-achieving academics—at Yale felt like I did, overwhelmed, outclassed, terrified. We were now smaller fish in a bigger and less easily navigable pond. In September 1956 Mike Dickerson, a classmate who had earned every possible honor at his small-town New Jersey public high school, sat down next to a stranger. "What courses are you taking?" he asked. When the reply included a graduate seminar in math, the questioner remarked, "You must be a genius." The answer, "That's what they tell me," made a young man—who was the first graduate of his high school ever to attend an Ivy League school—realize the trouble he was in.[2]

Unlike most classmates, at Yale I was physically close to where I had grown up and emotionally in a liminal state between home and campus. Many peers were away from home for the first time. Those from South Africa, Norway, or Latvia were even farther away. To a student who came to Yale on scholarship from California, home was distant at a time when expensive long-distance phone calls and air travel intensified a sense of separation. In contrast, for four years I straddled the worlds of my family and of Yale. More so than almost any classmate, I remained in the orbit of my family, something that seemed natural to me at the time but has now struck some friends as unusual. I knew many of the merchants who catered to my peers. Indeed, when I entered Yale my father presided over a bank only two blocks from campus. He was trying to attract customers by persuading classmates to open accounts in exchange for a Yale tie and personal attention from a Yale graduate. My parents were already friends with one of the most prominent figures on campus, the philosopher Paul Weiss. While I was there they drew close to William Sloane Coffin Jr., who arrived as Yale's chaplain in the summer between my sophomore and junior years. I often returned home on weekends—to visit girlfriends who stayed in my sister's room, to eat home cooking or have laundry done, or to be at a Sunday brunch to which my parents invited classmates. In fact, a central dynamic of my undergraduate years was how I could remain close and loyal to my parents and yet emerge as a person on my own terms.

Working on this book complicated and even transformed my sense of what I encountered at Yale. When I entered college, and even after I left, I had a fairly simple sense of social hierarchies and divisions. There were outsiders and insiders; Jews and non-Jews; townies and outlanders; non-athletes and athletes; independents and those who joined fraternities such as DKE and senior societies such as Skull and Bones; graduates of public high schools and the products of prestigious prep schools; people in the middle and upper middle class and those out of reach above. Over time, but especially with the interviews for this book, I developed a richer sense of what I encountered. I began to understand not only how many of my peers struggled financially but also that there were subtle divisions among America's elites: between those on their way up and those on their way down; between those with more money than privileged pasts, and vice versa; between those whose families were prominent New Yorkers and those equally prominent but in parts of the hinterland like Minneapolis, Savannah, or Chicago's North Shore.

Above all, writing this book led me to better understand my own experiences and to find out what life was like at Yale for those who did not live in the more or less self-contained "silo" I inhabited. One classmate recently used the term, with only slight exaggeration, to designate the distinctive and often separate worlds of students.[3] At the time I assumed that the college men—and their local variant, the Yale men I recognized but almost never spoke to—were happy and well adjusted. Now I have discovered this simply was not true. I have talked with star athletes who were miserable and the playboy sons of America's elite who drank excessively and studied minimally. Becoming friends with people from more socially prominent backgrounds than mine helped me understand that my origins may have made it easier for me to navigate the changing world of the 1960s and 1970s than they—with homegrown prejudices and snobbishness—could.[4]

Getting to know people from other backgrounds was for me, as it was for many I talked to, a deeply moving experience. I realized that while an undergraduate I had taken too much to heart my father's conviction, conveyed to me as a child, that after five p.m. he could not leave the multiethnic world of politics or the Jewish world of his communal life to socialize with people from elite Protestant backgrounds. Communicating in writing this book with more than a hundred classmates, when we are older and perhaps wiser, helped me enjoy conversations that were emotional, complicated, and forgiving.

An Imagined Community: The Yale College Class of 1960

My ambivalence about my Yale experience takes many forms, none more apparent than the combination of absence from reunions in the last thirty years with lasting gratitude for the transformative quality of my Yale education. Writing this book has evoked both pleasure and pain. Pleasure when I relived moments of discovery, reconnected with old friends, or developed relationships with new ones, some of them with Yale experiences totally different from my own. Rereading the correspondence between Helen Lefkowitz and me from the spring and summer 1960, I experienced once again what it meant for the two of us to fall in love and quickly develop lifelong commitments to each other. Pain came in varied ways. As I researched and wrote about dead and dying classmates, I constantly confronted my own mortality, something not usually on my mind. My parents died in the 1990s, and writing about them reminded me of the loss I endured. I continually encountered friendships that had ended through drift, conflict, distance, or death. Again and again, I recalled hurting and being hurt, defenses built or resisted, failures to understand or be understood. Reading over what I wrote in the late 1950s, in both private letters and for class assignments, I revisited my life in slow motion. I faced how personally innocent and politically naïve I was. I also wondered how I might have lived my life differently. I sensed the contrast between my satisfaction with how my life has turned out and the struggles and uncertainty of my young adulthood.

My classmate and dear friend Monroe Price recently remarked that the real curriculum at Yale was not in the courses we took but on the fields of ambition in the extracurricular world. The goals of classmates in this dimension varied even more so than did the difference between majoring in physics, art history, economics, or industrial administration. Some wanted to get laid or drunk as often as possible; to win at poker or bridge; to make money selling newspaper subscriptions or laundry supplies; to garner letters as varsity athletes; to gain admission into a fraternity, senior society, or singing group; to make connections that would help after graduation; to earn a place on the masthead of the *New York Times* by building on experiences at the *Yale Daily News;* or to gain entry into medical, law, or business school. Remarkably few of us wanted to change the world, except as a by-product of our making money or succeeding professionally. I had my own ambitions, accomplishable both in the classroom and outside—to learn how to think and write; to balance the emotional and the intellectual; and to develop close friendships with classmates and girlfriends.

For most of us, this all played out against what author Owen Johnson in his 1912 classic *Stover at Yale* called "the standard that imposed itself upon" his hero, a standard that "was something bigger than his own." As a key to succeeding, Yale emphasized the importance of being "well-rounded"—of not focusing excessively on academics, but instead achieving success in the extracurricular world. Yale had its own version of the college man, a figure that dominated so much of undergraduate life across the nation. The Yale man was confident, poised, manly, smart but not intellectual. He was equally effective on the playing field and at a cocktail party, equally at ease among peers and college girls. "Boys go to Harvard for intellectual reasons," Harvard's president A. Lawrence Lowell supposedly said early in the twentieth century, and "they go to Princeton for social reasons." Anyone who went to Yale, remarked writers for the *Harvard Crimson* in 1950, did so to "become a Success." This involved "a four-year push to become a 'wheel,' to be socially acceptable, to approximate that archetype of merit, the Yale Man."[5]

Insider/Outsider

High school graduate, townie, Jew, budding intellectual, and incipient lefty, I had my own response to what I encountered at Yale. In high school I was the consummate insider—well-rounded with a perfect academic record and an impressive extracurricular one; the pet student of many teachers; friend of a wide variety of girls and boys in a world much more diverse economically and ethnically than Yale. As an undergraduate, I started on the outsider's path, but I worked to understand the world of insiders. This meant graduates of prep schools who competed on the athletic fields as well as for positions in singing groups, publications, fraternities, and senior societies. People like me could meld the perspectives of insiders and outsiders, trying to figure Yale out and to keep some distance from its norms. Negotiating the complex heritages my parents offered and the challenges Yale posed, I developed a skepticism, tinged with ambivalence, about much of what I encountered. In the late 1950s, without fully realizing what I was doing, much less able to articulate what it meant, I was seeking an alternative to both my parents' lives and the traditional version of the well-rounded Yale man.

What I encountered at Yale, without fully comprehending it, was the fundamental and provincial fabric of a particular slice of the nation's elite world. Senior administrators and many faculty members really believed in a life driven by the commitments "For God, For Country, and For Yale," the unofficial Yale anthem sung at football games while Yalies waved their white handkerchiefs in celebration of the university's mission and triumph. Upon entering Yale, I unwittingly joined a large club whose purpose was to help launch its members into the power elite. Now I was allowed to be in (or near) the inside, even if I had no idea of what it was or how it operated. The prospect of becoming a typical Yale man, or even a modified variant, at some deep level involved emotional puzzlement. Yale allowed me to enter and perhaps "join," even though I had almost no knowledge of what it was I was asked to join. There was remarkably little in the formal curriculum designed to teach me what Yale was. Official Yale presented a puzzle without providing much help in learning how to solve its riddles. Especially as a Jew, going from being one of us to one of them was bound to produce contradictory feelings, involving some sense of betrayal of my commitments to egalitarianism and authenticity.[6]

The Personal Is Historical

This book emerges not only from memory but also from my life as a historian and teacher. In biographies of Vance Packard and Betty Friedan, I gave attention to their collegiate educations in the 1930s and 1940s and their early careers as professional writers in the 1940s and 1950s, on the one hand, and the origins of protest movements of the 1960s, on the other. Starting with a lecture course in American history I first taught in 1966–67, I have continually explored the connections between the supposedly complacent 1950s and the insurgencies of the 1960s. For more than forty years I have talked to my students about how my experiences in college, and in the 1950s more generally, revealed the ways one era morphed into the next. Yet the meaning of my college experience and of the transition from one decade to another—however artificial such decennial markers are—by and large existed on separate tracks. With the coming of my fiftieth reunion, and especially as I sat down and read the book my classmates filled with reminiscences, I was struck by how many of them pondered the meaning of their own lives by placing them in the contexts of long-term historical change. It was then that I realized that I could merge my two concerns—an intense personal interest in my years in college with a historian's focus on how the 1960s emerged from the 1950s. If Betty Friedan began to imagine writing *The Feminine Mystique* in 1957 when she looked over how her classmates responded to a questionnaire as they neared their fifteenth Smith College reunion, I began *On the Cusp* as I ruminated over what my classmates wrote in anticipation of their fiftieth.

There are thus dual but interrelated origins of this book. I am a member of the class of 1960 at Yale and I am a historian who has studied, taught, and written about the postwar period for more than four decades. These two perspectives shape this book. I write about myself quite consciously. Despite how my teachers warned me to avoid the personal, I explore my own experiences and emotions. I link the recovery of my own past with research into the sources written at the time, join my life with those of my peers at Yale, and place the experiences of the class of 1960 in multiple historical contexts. As a historian I come close to approximating a truth (but not *the* truth) about both my own past and that of my college generation.

On the Cusp

INTRODUCTION
On the Cusp in 1960

For some time now a recurring thought has impressed itself on my mind about our class as the bearer of an era's values. Our adolescence spanned the decade of the fifties. We had the good fortune to pass through the turbulent growth of adolescence at a time of peace and quiet and innocence. Religious traditions and moral values carried weight in our thinking and behavior. There was direction and continuity in the lives of those to whom we looked for models. There was a coherence to our world. To graduate from Yale in 1960 was to stand on a boundary between that direction and continuity and coherence, on the one hand, and an incipient questioning and change and disorder on the other.

JIM KARAMBELAS, *30th Reunion Directory,* 1990

The late 1950s were a complex time, with changes afoot that were not always apparent in the moment. In this book I examine issues that are both time-bound and enduring, including the tension between privilege and merit in American society; the nation's role in a rapidly transforming global world; how politics and ideologies shift over the years; changes in the meanings of race, class, ethnicity, sexuality, and gender; the nature of a liberal arts education, as well as the unpredictability of its impact; and the sources of leadership. I look at a series of interrelated shifts in the world, the nation, Yale, among my peers, and in myself. In my college years, with people in Africa and Asia fighting for independence from colonial rule, the globe was less clearly divided between Communist and Western powers. At home, the United States was awakening from the Cold War and McCarthyism. Simultaneously, Yale was changing from being a provincial university to a more cosmopolitan one, with admissions policies that were about to reshape the meaning of elitism and social class in America. Transformations in the lives of my peers and in my own life reveal how our collegiate experiences served

1

as a bridge not only between adolescence and adulthood but also between one period and another. They did this for other generations but in distinctive ways for ours.[1]

I ponder the dynamics of the transition from the 1950s to the 1960s by looking at a microcosm—the world of the one thousand or so members of Yale's undergraduate class of 1960.[2] Historians distinguish between the 1960s, which had many characteristics of the late 1950s, and the more tumultuous Sixties. The change came somewhere between the assassination of JFK in November 1963 and the shift soon after from civil rights to Black Power, the dramatic escalation of the war in Vietnam, and the emergence of identity politics. By the mid-1960s, American politics were becoming more fractiously ideological, the nation's role in the world more problematically expansive. Jews, women, African Americans, Asian Americans, Latinos, homosexuals, and others who had once tried not to call attention to themselves began to name and explore their distinctiveness. As I researched and wrote the book, I changed my mind about the pace and predictability of what happened. At the outset I assumed that what some of my classmates and I had experienced amply and consistently foreshadowed the Sixties. However, I came to see change in more complicated, less linear ways.[3] I have learned from the lives of my peers that the connections between past and present are messy, with elements of the familiar, strange, foreseen, and surprising existing simultaneously. Now I understand how complicated are the arcs of our stories.

Yale Class of 1960 as a Case Study

The Yale class of 1960 is simultaneously exceptional and ordinary. There were no female undergraduates, and a quota system restricted the number of Jews and Roman Catholics, to say nothing of how admissions policies and procedures kept exceedingly low the number of African Americans, Asian Americans, Latinos, and young men from the working class. Academically talented Jews were more likely to gain admission to Harvard, Cornell, Columbia, Penn, NYU, and City College of New York than to Yale, Princeton, or Dartmouth. Of its peers, Yale was probably the most masculine of environments, something perceived to be connected to its commitment to recruit youths who came from socially and economically prominent backgrounds and to launch them into success. Yale had a weaker tradition of progressive undergraduate politics than Columbia and Harvard, but a stronger one than Princeton. Rereading *The Unsilent Generation: An Anonymous Symposium in Which Eleven College Seniors Look at Themselves and Their World* (1958) reminds me that its editor, Otto Butz, not only unwittingly reinforced how people thought of college students in the late 1950s, but also revealed how a handful of Princeton men in the class of 1957 seemed to live in an even more stereotypically conformist world than I did.[4]

The composition of the class of 1960 was hardly stable and its distinctiveness hardly conclusive. Some entered in September 1956 but left, in many cases sustaining their connections with the class. Some changed their affiliation because they accelerated or took time off. At several points, I explore the lives of contemporaries at Yale who were not members of the class. Another focus would have pointed in distinctive directions. Concentrating on the class of 1957 would have driven me to different conclusions as I examined a group of Yalies who powerfully shaped American culture: two *New Yorker* writers (Calvin Trillin and Gerald Jonas), the playwright and HIV/AIDS activist Larry Kramer, the publisher André Schiffrin, the art curator Henry Geldzahler, the author and activist Joel Kovel, and the transformative Yale admissions dean R. Inslee Clark.[5] Alternatively, had I turned my attention to the class of 1968, the contrast between Oliver Stone and George W. Bush might have driven my narrative.

Jim Karambelas, with his talk of the contrast between coherence and disorder, pondered the meaning of the shift from one decade to another. Unlike his emphasis on a "boundary" between decades, I emphasize "cusp" as marking liminal spaces, points where transitions begin, locations of awakenings where dawning consciousness was often unformed. Others have examined our class in different terms. "A reasonable argument can be made," wrote our class secretary in early 2013, "that we are an exceptional class, from an exceptional university, in an exceptional country. The outstanding accomplishments of class members," he remarked, include "United States Senator Jack Heinz, Secretary of Defense Les Aspin, President of Yale Bart Giamatti, and Secretary of Yale John Wilkinson." Every class at Yale (and surely Princeton, Harvard, Smith, and Wellesley) thinks it is exceptional, just as does every college and university, along with every nation. This particular star-chasing list is impressive. Yet it is also parochial, including two who achieved high positions at Yale, one of whom, Giamatti, also did so nationally as Commissioner of Major League Baseball. But it is also incomplete, as any such list would be—in this case leaving off two classmates who rose to prominence in the world of national security (Porter Goss and John Negroponte), as well as the scores and scores and scores of classmates who achieved prominence in their fields. What is exceptional about my class is not the prestige gained by its most famous graduates, but, along with other classes, its location on the cusp.[6]

In writing this book, I encountered the challenge of emphasizing how clubby Yale was in the late 1950s without becoming implicated in the university's often self-satisfied pride and exclusiveness. The elitism of Yale (and of comparable schools), by no means unchanging, remains a powerful force in America. I focus so much on backgrounds and markers of social location at Yale because this is how many of us viewed the world, supported by the campus newspaper and the class book that reinforced the importance of these referents. We thought about ourselves in terms of ethnicity and religion but rarely in terms of sexuality or whiteness. This differs from how later generations of students viewed their peers through the lenses of sexual, racial, ethnic, and stylistic orientations. The importance of social class came through to me at the beginning of a three-hour lunch in San Francisco in February 2013 when Kirke Wilson, a classmate I came to know only when working on this book, responded to my description of what I was writing by looking directly at me and asking where was social class in my analysis. I repeat now what I said in response, social class (crosscut by other aspects of our identities) suffused our experiences, shaping as it did how we thought of ourselves and each other, what activities we pursued, what friendships we developed, and what we planned to do after graduation.[7]

By their processes of inclusion and exclusion, the *Yale Alumni Magazine*, reunion books, and reunions themselves help every class develop a sense of itself and of who matters. Like other elite college and universities, Yale did its best to serve an elite (those already within such ranks and those it admitted who aspired for inclusion), to bring them together, to mold them into a self-conscious group that would identify with Yale and with the class of 1960, and to offer them experiences and organizations that would enable them to operate as leaders after they graduated.

Presenting such details as the schools from which members of our class came to Yale from and the organizations they joined once there drives home my point about the exclusivity and insularity of Yale in the 1950s, characteristics by which a social elite tried to affirm and reproduce its own and its progeny's social hegemony. As the director of undergraduate admissions said in 1957, being admitted to Yale was one of the best ways for "those who have enjoyed the privileges of cultural opportunities, wealth, and social standing, . . . to preserve the same for their children."[8] However, things did not always work out as planned for those who came from or aspired to lives of privilege. A focus on dramatic stories of individual and collective success overlooks scores if not hundreds of us whose lives undermine the assumption that Yale launched us all into brilliant careers. Some classmates dropped out and never returned; others died tragically, in some cases because of AIDS, suicide, or alcoholism. Some classmates with storied pasts and legendary careers at Yale have been unemployed or underemployed most of their lives. There were the disaffected who did not write to the alumni magazine or come to reunions; those who never accomplished what they expected of themselves or others expected of them; and those with workaday jobs. Career trajectories that once seemed assured turned out not to be. Dross overcame some golden Yale men. Divorce, illness, and accidents interrupted the expected paths to success. A wife might discover she preferred a woman to a Yale man. The stories of my classmates chronicle the making and unmaking of the American upper middle class.

If I do not wish to exaggerate the exceptional nature of my Yale class, I do wish to point out some distinctive aspects of this book, which combines genres often kept apart. Historians rarely deploy in their autobiographies the tools of analysis and research they use in other kinds of historical writing. There is no deeply researched history of the collegiate experiences of a class that relies on original research and places the author in the midst of a larger story. I am a historian watching myself as I write about my own life and draw on my command of history and historical method to place myself and my classmates in multiple contexts. This is not a conventional memoir, though I speak in the first person and incorporate personal, sometimes highly personal, materials. I rarely reconstruct long-ago conversations, relying more on historical research than memory.[9] To achieve this multifaceted analysis, I draw on a wide range of sources, including oral histories, personal letters, undergraduate publications, student papers, yearbooks and reunion books, memoirs, novels, faculty publications, and administrative records. I use a series of mini-biographies to illustrate points and give flesh and blood to my analysis. The narrative moves from stories of individuals to group experiences and larger contexts, with material on my own life providing one thread in a complicated tapestry.

A Guide to the World of Yale Men

Sons of alums in my class stood at just above 22 percent, a figure that would rise to 30 percent if I counted those who had other family members associated with Yale. Graduates of St. Grottlesex knew better than I and many others what to expect. Some of them felt they could cruise through courses and bring to Yale the mores and social skills of an elite world. If many from high schools were eager, many prep school graduates were cynical.

To understand the social order I encountered at Yale I turn to *Campus Life: Undergraduate Cultures from the End of the Eighteenth Century to the Present.* In this book published a quarter of a century after we married in 1963, Helen Lefkowitz Horowitz divided undergraduates into three ideal types even while recognizing that actual persons could blend aspects of more than one. First in order of appearance and prominence were College Men who "could fight for position on the playing field and in the newsroom and learn the manly arts of capitalism." They took inspiration not from faculty in the classroom but from peers in extra-curricular activities. They belonged to an elite, manly college culture that by the late nineteenth century dominated campus life at places like Yale. They exercised power not only over women but over men who because of their social origins, religion, political leanings, academic commitments, or sexual orientation did not fit the standard mold. The social networks developed at prep schools, debutante parties, and summer homes helped sustain them in college in ways not possible for students from more modest backgrounds. With family connections that they somewhat incorrectly believed would ensure their futures in the business or genteel professional worlds, they felt they need not concern themselves with grades. In their collegiate years trust funds and wealthy parents ensured that they did not have to earn money during semesters or summers. Avoiding demanding fields like math, science, engineering, and economics, they devoted just enough effort to their course work to remain in good academic standing. They turned their attention to participation in an extracurricular world where fraternities and senior societies played a central role. Here they rehearsed for their futures, built as they were on the joining of social power and private interests. The social class and organizational memberships of the most privileged students cemented the bonds that in the future might make Yale a focus of their loyalty.[10]

Historically, the ability of college men to live in the present and to fully express what Helen has called "their youthful high spirits and their hedonism" enabled them to indulge their appetites for manly activities such as gambling and drinking. Finding the right woman enhanced their pursuit of sexual satisfactions and social status. All this put them in opposition to faculty and to students committed to delaying gratification until they graduated. Activities in fraternities, singing groups, athletic teams, and senior societies created in college men a sense of loyalty and collective responsibility. By example, they taught that what was important was not what students studied in courses, but what they learned elsewhere about social networks, leadership, and proper forms of dress and behavior. Their values strongly influenced more modest middle-class students who hoped college would launch them into more elevated positions.

At Yale in the late 1950s the college men, especially classmates who came from private schools, played varsity athletics, joined fraternities and senior societies, and sang in a cappella groups, existed in significant numbers, nearly a majority of the class. Less visible and somewhat less numerous were the

Outsiders, mostly graduates of public high schools who focused on their studies; came from struggling families, the provinces, or small towns; and were marked as marginal by religion or ethnicity or both. At Yale many of these outsiders studied hard and stayed away from the major extracurricular organizations. As Helen has written, they "sought the approval of teachers, not of their peers" and "hoped, by dint of hard work, that achievement in the future would compensate for the trials of the present." Finally, smallest in number were the Rebels. In my class I could count their numbers on the fingers of one or two hands. Identifying "keenly with artists and writers breaking conventions and with the few iconoclastic professors moving into the academy," they "fought the social distinctions that sorted out college students and reveled in difference, not uniformity."[11]

As I look through my class book, it is not hard to find examples of these types. Gene Scott was a college man: he came to Yale from the prestigious prep school Lawrenceville and with multiple legacies. In college his not terribly distinguished academic record stood in contrast with membership in Fence Club, Skull and Bones, and an extraordinary career as an athlete—captain of the soccer team, major "Y" in a varsity sport on that and two other teams.[12] In the class book, outsider, high school graduate, and future Nobel Laureate in Economics Peter Diamond listed only academic achievements among his activities, though he did mention he played touch football on an intramural team for one season. Rebel Edmund Leites, who entered with us, graduated a year early because he felt Yale was an intellectual and artistic wasteland compared with the world he had known growing up in Manhattan, where he spent time with Paul Goodman, Dwight Macdonald, and the Beat poets. The categories of college men, outsiders, and rebels are both helpful and imperfect, with many of us representing more than one tradition. I myself was a cross between outsider and rebel. Many prep school graduates were nevertheless outsiders; some outsiders gravitated to major extracurricular activities, especially publications; scores of classmates excelled in both academic and extracurricular activities. Some undergraduates who fit easily into one category later crossed the boundaries into another. Later on, college men sometimes became outsiders or rebels, while some outsiders acted like grown-up college men once they were out in the world.

The notion of well-roundedness, fostered by admissions officers, residential counselors, college deans, and residential college masters, governed the view of the Yale man, the local variant of the college man. The well-rounded undergraduate, the psychiatrist Bryant M. Wedge and the sociologist James S. Davie remarked in 1958, as they viewed my world from the perspective of their roles at Yale's mental health program, "is characterized by a reasonable level of scholarship, a good degree of social competence, and an active involvement in campus activities." These were the "avenue to campus acceptance and prestige" that consumed "vast quantities of the time that is not spent on course work (and occasionally at the expense of course work)." Extracurricular activities, they asserted, promoted virtues no other focus did: they broadened and enriched students who experienced "the joys of comradeship and a sense of group identification and loyalty." An undergraduate should not merely join, but "be outstanding," and if he could "succeed in one of the more prestigeful activities . . . then so much the better as evidence of a man's intrinsic worth."[13]

At Yale, those who came from private schools and families with high incomes, their 1958 study found, were more satisfied with their Yale experience than their outsider peers. Upon entering Yale, the privileged undergraduate "had a somewhat clearer idea of what Yale is like" and once there was less lonely and nervous. The well-rounded man was also more successful in gaining highly prestigious positions in extracurricular activities. The adjectives they used to describe themselves, Davie remarked, were cheerful, contented, enthusiastic, genial, gregarious, happy, masculine, optimistic, poised, satisfied, sociable, and well balanced. The only things they disliked were key aspects of academic life such as graduation requirements and faculty members. As Helen noted, college men looked down on the studious and intellectually inclined as grinds.[14] Scorning or avoiding competition in the classroom, many of those who graduated from prep schools were more likely than others to cut academic corners—cheating on assignments, paying someone to write their papers, and cramming at the last minute. Even if they obeyed the rules, as many of them did, they had learned skills before coming to Yale that they might share with others. I remember walking to an exam with Lew Lehrman, a classmate who had gone to the Hill School. I listened intently while he told me that the way to handle an exam question was to focus an answer on the premises underlying the topic the professor asked us to explore.

News of the activities of college men and those who aspired to be like them filled the pages of the *Yale Daily News,* and not just in stories of the triumphs on athletic fields. To be sure, the campus paper prominently featured stories of faculty publishing books, giving talks, getting promoted, going on sabbatical, or leaving because tenure was not in the cards. Yet for most classmates (but not for me) professors were bit players who exemplified the adage "Those who can, do; those who can't, teach." Most classmates participated in an alternative, unofficial, and very visible curriculum located in social, athletic, and arts organizations and in undergraduate antics. Advertisements in the *Yale Daily News* for liquor stores stood alongside stories of drunken revelers and the administration's prohibiting delivery of booze to rooms in residential colleges when the drinking age was still eighteen. More than a handful of my peers learned skills later useful to them when they gambled with friends or with local bookies. Non-political riots continually broke out, as when students threw water bombs from dorm windows onto innocent bystanders below. Late at night the police arrested a student for driving his sports car on city streets with three or four friends hanging on. Campus police stopped a group of fraternity men walking down the street carrying a coffin in which a pledge was reclining. Deans cast a skeptical eye on a fraternity whose pledges were required to carry Linus blankets to class, where they had to sit sucking their thumbs.

Rituals marked the college year. Fraternities held their rushes in the fall and spring. Home football games provided moments for social encounters, none more humorous than on the Saturday morning before the Yale-Dartmouth game when students gathered on the Old Campus to watch the game of Bladderball, in which representatives of campus media outlets battled for control of a six-foot high inflated ball. Legend had it that the contest derived its name from an earlier use of an inflated animal bladder; likewise the Tang Cup—a competition to see which team could most rapidly drink glasses of beer—supposedly derived its name from the orangutan. During spring vacations I drove to Florida with friends, while less privileged students stayed on campus or went home, and more privileged ones went to Switzerland, Paris, Bermuda, or the Caribbean. On a spring evening representatives of senior societies enacted their rituals of selection.

Trumbull, the residential college where I lived for my final three years, had its own tradition, an annual Beer 'n' Bike Race when each member of a team rode several miles toward a women's college, chugged a significant amount of beer, and then turned the bicycle over to the next team member. In May of my senior year, Fritz Steele, with whom I had roomed during my first two years at Yale, pedaled skillfully even though his team, the Umbawas, lost to those on the Maidenform Five Plus One. Traditions change but never disappear, wrote David Gergen in spring 1960, as a member of the class of 1963 and well before he emerged as a presidential adviser and political commentator. "Surely as long as Yale exists, Bacchus will live behind the facades of ivy."[15]

Of course, life did not always work out the way classmates expected. Too much alcohol or partying, combined with miscalculation about the demands of academic work, might mean the deans forced a student to leave for a semester or longer, in some cases never to return. Unexpected financial reverses might undercut a family's ability to support a son in the style to which he was accustomed. Difficulty in meeting the standards of their social networks could mean disappointment when an aspirant did not gain admission into the fraternity, singing group, or senior society he had set his heart on. A young man's fancy might turn in socially unacceptable directions—toward another man or toward a girl with a less than ideal pedigree or none at all. Nonetheless, while still at Yale elite college men set the tone and expectations for many of the rest of us.

So it was no accident that when writing on the "Yale Man Image" in May 1960, an observer of the local scene talked of the "conception of a successful, socially ept, intelligent but not overly scholarly" student. He was "an enthusiastic follower of the success ethic" who was "confidentially secure" in the knowledge that "success breeds success." He was "quietly and graciously smooth; not a back slapper he is socially ept according to the rules of 'shoeness,'" a term denoting expert social skills by referring to the proper type of footwear. Extracurricular activities were an integral part of his life. "Because he ambitiously hopes for success in business or a profession, he tried to blend the intellectual and practical parts of his education, usually stressing the latter. . . . The Yale Man of the image is well-rounded, just as the catalogues advertise."[16]

Being a well-rounded Yale man meant making serious commitments of time, energy, and aspirations to extracurricular activities. Although there were class officers, Yale had no significant student government and prestige went elsewhere, to organizations that offered an enormous range of possibilities. But for college men the most important were fraternities, aboveground senior societies, singing groups, and varsity athletics.

Compared with many small colleges or state universities (or Princeton with its eating clubs), at Yale fraternities commanded the loyalties of a comparatively small percentage of undergraduates. Well under half of the class joined one of nine nonresidential frats. Each had its own style and constituency, with some more prestigious than others. In the fall of 1956 an insider's guide to Yale described Fence Club as "the most pretentiously snobbish organization at Yale." DKE's reputation, Calvin Trillin later remarked, was for "undergraduates whose enthusiasm for robust sport occasionally carried over from football and lacrosse to, say, furniture breaking." Except in a few cases where fraternities opened their membership and offered financial aid to talented athletes from modest backgrounds, membership came disproportionately from the ranks of legacies, graduates of private schools, and the wealthy. Eighty percent of all members of the most prestigious fraternities came to Yale from private schools, and 85 percent did not receive scholarship aid from Yale.[17]

For a price, fraternities offered a congenial atmosphere, models of collegiate behavior, lessons in how to achieve social success, a place to entertain dates, and, unlike the residential colleges, bars with ample supplies of liquor.

With Yale insisting that all students pay for twenty-one meals per week in residential colleges, the expensiveness of fraternities limited their membership, especially for the less prestigious houses, which struggled financially and even disappeared. Administrators worried a little about how fraternities discriminated against African Americans and a lot about how their members on average had less than ideal academic records. In the late 1950s, the university forced fraternities to eliminate or sharply curtail their pledge rituals and to lessen the number of weeks of rush. Two of them were closing down as we graduated, causing one classmate, who was a member of a surviving frat, to remark that the day was "imminent" when the residential colleges "would play a social as well as a leveling role."[18]

In my years at Yale, there was a fierce debate about whether fraternities provided something unavailable elsewhere. C. Howard Wilkins, a classmate and pledge master at DKE, insisted that Yale's fraternities fostered "a dynamic brotherhood among men of high character." By contrast, in the fall of our sophomore year, Jim Ottaway, on his way to the chairmanship of the *Yale Daily News*, remarked that "you do not know what 'brotherhood' means until you have sat on a piece of ice for 15 minutes or have not been allowed to stop drinking before you 'flash' or pass out."[19] As Monroe Price wrote in the *Yale Alumni Magazine* in the fall of our senior year, fraternity members "are grumbling, for with the abolition of pledging, they feel that slowly but surely the 'ideal of brotherhood' is falling into disuse and the old House will become just another club."[20]

In competition with fraternities for loyalty and identity were the ten residential colleges where all upperclassmen lived, except for the few who married before graduation. These colleges had splendid buildings with ample public rooms, and a staff that ranged from people who cleaned our rooms and prepared and served our meals in wood-paneled dining rooms, to a small number of professors who lived in their own suites, to a master who lived with his wife in a large house within the college's walls. These colleges had their own student government, athletic teams, traditions, social activities, and meeting spaces. Many of us strongly identified with our colleges. To a lesser extent, we identified with the field in which we majored, although my sense is that this affiliation did not stand near the center of our lives, myself and some peers excepted.

College men also gravitated to the prestigious, aboveground senior societies which publicly listed their membership. In many cases, they emphasized the social sorting that reinforced social stratification. Each had fifteen members who met twice a week. The most prestigious and mysterious of these "spooks" were those founded in the nineteenth century, housed in "tombs" located on or near campus. Listed in order of their founding they were Skull and Bones (whose members were Bonesmen), Scroll and Key, Berzelius, Book and Snake, and Wolf's Head. Of twentieth-century origin were Elihu and Manuscript, whose membership was more open to Jews, intellectuals, and the artistically inclined. In contrast were underground societies whose existence and membership were secret. They were markedly less prestigious or exclusive. I know of two of them because I joined one and had a good friend in another. They also met twice a week, but were housed in more ordinary spaces, were of more recent origin, and had an unstable existence.

Rumors abounded. Skull and Bones was Connecticut's second-wealthiest corporation; it guaranteed all members a substantial income; its sacred number (322) referred to the year the year Demosthenes died. Scroll and Key, whose building adjoined the one that housed the offices of Yale's president and trustees, ran the university. Wolf's Head had an enormous water bill. The selection processes were elaborate and mysterious. During the spring, a junior might be invited to lunch and receive phone calls at random hours as seniors considered whom to invite. This courtship period, remarked one classmate who was a member of Berzelius, was "a process combining the gay gun-happiness of Cuban politics with the solemn ritualism of electing a Pope." Then on Tap Day, or more precisely Tap evening, at 7:57 p.m. as the chapel bells struck eight, "dark-clad lemmings begin migrating violently in all directions." Rumor had it that at the appointed hour a senior from Skull and Bones knocked on a door where a junior lived and, once it was opened, shouted, "Bones, Bones, Bones, Do You Accept?"[21]

The rosters of aboveground senior societies included about 10 percent of a graduating class, a figure that hardly captured the notoriety and power they had for many classmates. Election to them, wrote Wedge and Davie, was "the highest honor that a student can receive from his fellow undergraduates," an honor "generally reserved for those who most closely approximate the Yale ideal, particularly for those who have been outstandingly successful in extra-curricular and athletic pursuits."[22] Such a statement overemphasizes their importance, meaningful to some but hardly to all of us. It also fails to recognize the substantial differences among societies. Leadership in athletics and in other traditional activities was most important in access to Skull and Bones as well as Book and Snake, both of which also recruited significantly from the ranks of students who came to Yale with legacies and from prestigious prep schools. Elihu was the one where I knew many members. Like the others its membership drew heavily on graduates of private schools; although it had its share of athletes, it included in its ranks peers with impressive undergraduate careers in the arts, politics, and religion.[23]

Administrators criticized fraternities but not senior societies, which they considered beyond reproach because of their importance among Yale leaders and because their practices, unlike those of fraternities, were truly secret. The *Yale Daily News* pronounced senior societies either beneficial or not especially objectionable, perhaps because although few from their staff joined fraternities, the campus paper was an important feeder for the societies, Elihu especially. In contrast, every year undergraduate leaders from the left—for example, André Schiffrin in 1957 and Sam Bowles in 1960—proudly turned down membership. Indeed in 1957 Schiffrin and his Afro-Caribbean classmate Michael Cooke joined with Professor Paul Weiss in denouncing the societies for their prejudices, secrecy, inwardness, and exclusivity. They made clear that collegiate fellowship was available without such hocus-pocus and elitism. William Sloane Coffin Jr. was the only senior Yale official who was both an alumnus of a senior society and a critic of some of what they represented. Although he applauded them for fostering a sense of fellowship, for promoting intellectual exchange, and for being more open to a varied membership than were fraternities, he nonetheless attacked them for their "tribalistic chauvinism," deleterious effect on social interactions, and opposition to change.[24]

When we shift attention to musical and athletic performances we enter realms more open to talent than fraternities and aboveground senior societies but still home to well-rounded college men. A cappella singing groups and sports teams commanded a tremendous amount of time and dedication of those involved. If fraternities were the recruiting grounds for some senior societies, then singing groups played the same role for membership in the seniors-only Whiffenpoofs, perhaps comparable to Skull and Bones in prestige, though not in mysteriousness.

Athletics were open to talent, although how significantly they were varied. Competitive sports commanded the attention of hundreds of undergrads who joined dozens of teams. Serving as a captain of a team or earning a major "Y" meant you were a big man on campus, at least in the eyes of some. Exceptional performance could open doors that social background might make impossible. There were limits, however. A southern member of DKE blackballed the African American football player Raleigh Davenport, and none of the five African American members of the class of 1960 made it into the ranks of a fraternity or aboveground senior society. Pre-collegiate opportunities, often shaped by culture and class, meant that some teams, such as golf, tennis, polo, or crew, created patterns of access. During my years, the swimming and tennis teams attained national standing, something amply recognized on campus. Yet despite the legendary athletic facilities, histories, and coaches, Yale, like other Ivy League institutions, did not take the steps necessary to produce highly ranked teams in football the way the University of Southern California, Notre Dame, and major state universities did.

Undergrads could join other groups: religious organizations, a military honor society, as well as clubs for outdoorsmen, bell ringers, sports car enthusiasts, and yachtsmen. Participation in arts organizations, publications, religious and political groups, ROTC and its variants involved a wider range of students than college men. The *Yale Daily News,* the *Yale Lit,* the class book *Yale Banner,* the radio station WYBC, the Yale Film Society, *Ivy Magazine,* and the *Yale Record* humor magazine commanded the attention of some of the most talented classmates. For those interested in the arts, there were the Yale Dramat and varied enough music organizations to satisfy almost any taste, except those interested in jazz, gospel, or rock 'n' roll. Bart Giamatti chaired Yale Charities Drive, although little did we realize that he would later put his fund-raising skills to good use as Yale's president. Members of Yale Key greeted visitors to the campus, while prom committees organized annual weekends.

Three important, high-prestige extracurricular activities deserve special attention: the *Yale Daily News,* student agencies, and honor societies. Of those prominent in campus organizations, I knew best many of those involved in the *News.* In my mind and for others as well, the *News* was the most influential and prestigious undergraduate organization. Its chairmanship, wrote Wedge and Davie, "has been one of the prize extracurricular plums for many decades."[25] Claiming to be the "Oldest College Daily," it included among those who had worked on it over the years Kingman Brewster, William F. and Christopher Buckley, David Gergen, Joe Lieberman, Adam Liptak, Henry Luce, Paul Mellon, Sargent Shriver, Strobe Talbott, Calvin Trillin, and Garry Trudeau. Its editors and writers had access to Yale's administrators and professors; its chairman met regularly with President A. Whitney Griswold. Its writers helped shape how undergraduates viewed the college and the world.

Student agencies produced the yearbook and sold refrigerators, beer mugs, magazines, newspapers, birthday cakes, caps and gowns, and laundry services. Supporters hailed them as offering business experience and income. Initially justified as providing self-help for scholarship students, by the late 1950s they were just as likely to attract men who did not receive financial aid. They came in for criticism for favoring well-to-do students over needy ones and for using their monopolistic position to compete unfairly with local merchants. In October 1956 Gerald Jonas, class of 1957, called their most successful leaders "Budding Barnums." They were often successful small businesses, run—if the laundry agency is any indication—by classmates who came to Yale from public high schools and without legacies. In the year before I entered Yale, their gross sales were $228,304 (or $1,963,380 in 2014 dollars) and profits reached $60,962. Some of their leaders took home, in 2014 dollars, more than $10,000 per year.[26]

If as an undergraduate I patronized student agencies when I subscribed to the *New York Times* and bought linens for my bed and a cap and gown for graduation, honor societies remained mysterious even though their membership was publicly known. Members of Torch, Aurelian, Linonia, and the Pundits met once a week over a meal and seemed to do little more than engage in witty conversation. By the time I graduated many classmates had come to feel that these groups, like class proms, represented an Old Yale and had outlived any raison d'être they might have once had.[27]

This discussion of the Yale man as a variant of the college man and of extracurricular paths to well-roundedness hardly captures the full range of undergraduate experiences. If many classmates chose bonhomie, partying, gambling, drinking, and joining, some of us buried ourselves in books. Membership in Phi Beta Kappa, Tau Beta Pi, and Alpha Chi Sigma came to those who excelled academically. The Elizabethan Club, located on campus in an unpretentious building that housed an extraordinary collection of sixteenth- and seventeenth-century books, provided a place for those interested in engaging in what one observer recalled as "repartee with the most imposing undergraduate intellectuals and the suavest faculty members." Many of us were thus what Wedge and Davie called "the intellectual or scholarly type" whom our peers "regarded somewhat askance." There were additional types who were not as well rounded as the college men. Separated from the mainstream by the location of their classes and by what many snobbishly considered their narrow intellectual perspectives, vocationally oriented premed students, as well as those who majored in science and engineering, spent hours in labs farther from the center of the campus than were Fence Club or Skull and Bones. As we were about to graduate, a philosophy major who was president of Aurelian and a member of Zeta Psi, the Elizabethan Club, Phi Beta Kappa, and Scroll and Key remarked that science majors seemed "out of the mainstream of Yale life. Certainly physically removed," he continued, "the scientists were often separated socially as well from the brotherly buzz of fraternity row by the exacting daily assignments and the specialized interests."[28]

Positioning Myself in a World of Well-Rounded Yale Men

Several things bound my world at Yale together, especially in my junior and senior years: intense friendships with a handful of peers; participation in political organizations; experiences in seminars in American studies; and work on the editorial board of a student publication. More so than in late-night bull sessions, in the Trumbull College dining hall I participated in discussions about politics, girlfriends, and life at Yale with several junior members of the faculty and a small band of friends. Those of us who studied hard and participated in liberal politics lived differently from those who stood at fraternity bars, remained uninterested in unconventional politics or politics at all, and looked forward to Tap Day, when they anticipated selection by a prestigious senior society.

The silo analogy may involve exaggeration, yet clear patterns kept most of us in different worlds. Some students were more successful than I in crossing boundaries that separated one silo from another—in fraternities, senior societies, singing groups, or more likely athletic teams that opened their membership to people who inhabited space outside their comfort zones. Chance meetings in the hall of a residential college or on a walk from class provided the opportunity to discover friends with unfamiliar backgrounds. While an undergraduate, with rare exceptions I had no friends or even close acquaintances who were members of fraternities, aboveground senior societies, a cappella groups, or major athletic teams. To some extent I knew classmates from other silos through extracurricular activities, especially in the underground senior society I joined. This protected me from becoming what Helen would later describe: a "nonconforming undergraduate" who "felt isolated, without mentors or allies on campus." They were "intense individualists," she wrote in *Campus Life,* "caught in the drama of their psyches" who played out their conflicts in personal relationships and in poetry."[29]

The Way We Were in the Fall of 1956

There were 1,033 of us who entered Yale, and about 940 graduated with our class, which means that the retention rate was lower than what Yale later achieved.[30] We were regionally less diverse than later classes, with slightly over 81 percent hailing from east of the Mississippi and only 1.5 percent from abroad. By later standards, we were both very privileged and not very diverse. It is easier to identify the considerable numbers who came from families with ample social backgrounds than the few who were working class. Names like Francis Rhett du Pont, H. J. Heinz III, Merrill Lynch Magowan, and John Sargent ("Jock") Pillsbury conveyed the pedigrees few of us could rely on. Slightly more that 40 percent of the class came to Yale from prep schools, more than half of them from ten: in descending numbers Andover, Exeter, Deerfield,

Hotchkiss, Lawrenceville, Taft, Choate, Hill, Loomis, and St. Paul's.[31] If we add those who went to private day schools and prestigious high schools (New Trier in Winnetka, Illinois, or Walnut Hills in Cincinnati) the figure of those who had elite educations grows to more than 70 percent.

When the admissions office thought about diversity, it typically did so not in terms of race, ethnicity, religion, social class, gender, and sexuality but of geography: classmates admitted from Norway, Iceland, or Russia—or from small towns like Tyler, Texas, or Columbus, Nebraska. There were no women and no homosexuals who were out of the closet in the late 1950s. Five African Americans. That I can determine, no native-born Latino as we understand that term, but some men with Hispanic names who listed their home addresses in a Latin American city and on Manhattan's Upper East Side. About 10 percent of us were Jews and a similar percentage Roman Catholic, although, as we will see later, even many members of those groups arrived at Yale with legacies from elite schools.

A handful came to Yale with Asian ancestry. Two (Dick Lee and Dana Young) had a Chinese grandparent and one (Ed Rhoads) had a Chinese mother, whom his father had married when he was teaching in Canton before the family moved to America in 1951. Lee did not find out about his Chinese heritage until after he graduated from Yale, a realization that impelled him to study and travel to Asia. Young cannot remember a time when he was not aware of his Chinese ancestry; as an adult he viewed himself as one-quarter Chinese but did not pause before checking "white" when a form asked about his racial identity. While Young embarked on a career in Japanese language and literature, Rhoads became a historian of China who neither considered himself Chinese nor denied his heritage. Ken Fujii, from an agricultural community in California's San Joaquin Valley, was the only native-born Asian American as we would now define that term. In addition, five classmates were born in China to Chinese families who migrated to America in the late 1940s and early 1950s. Four came to Yale from private schools; the exception was Larry Wan, one of two classmates who went to the legendary Bronx High School of Science.[32] In short, most of us were American, white, middle class or above, and at least publicly heterosexual.

The End of the Shortest, Gladdest Years of Life

Our plans for the future also lacked diversity. Some of us said we would enter active military service, while a few looked forward to study abroad. Most of us mentioned pursuing advanced degrees—especially in law, business, medicine, and academic fields. Harvard, Yale, MIT, Columbia, Stanford, and Berkeley were the universities most prominently featured. "Study of history and/or law" is what I listed in ways that hardly revealed the depth of my struggle to choose between a law degree that would enable me to pursue a life not unlike my father's and a PhD so I could follow where favorite professors led. I put off the decision by studying European history for a year in Cambridge, England. Letters I wrote to Helen in the summer after graduation show my own version of adolescent angst, how I hoped that going to England would provide me with a rebirth after feeling my years at Yale had confused and jaded me.

A handful of our classmates reported that they were returning home to attend a local professional school or to go into the family business. One example underscores the complexities of life choices and generational changes. After attending Greeley High School in Colorado, Bill Garnsey had come to Yale from Exeter with multiple legacies; at Yale he had joined DKE and Skull and Bones and earned a major "Y" in crew. In the spring of 1960 he announced that he would pursue "ranching or conservation, after agriculture course at Colorado State" in his home town. He may have done that initially, but he ended up serving as president and CEO of the Garnsey and Wheeler Ford auto dealership in Greeley; marrying a graduate of Wheaton College (MA); and having three children, two of whom went to Oral Roberts University and one to the University of Colorado. With no offspring going to Yale, a three-generation family tradition ended with him. An active Episcopalian as an undergraduate, on the occasion of our twenty-fifth reunion he spoke of how in 1960 he "had little direction" and then was born again. "Accepting Jesus Christ," he remarked, "is the most wonderful thing in my life; having a great wife who also loves Him is the next best thing."[33]

Finally, in what they wrote in the class book, several classmates captured the uncertainty and dark moods many of us felt that stood in stark contrast to the sunnier retrospective view of Karambelas quoted at the beginning of the chapter. Bill Lamb (legacy, Loomis, Zeta Psi, and Manuscript) remarked that "everyone had awareness, detachment." He then quoted a comment in the *Yale Daily News*: "We don't believe that group affirmations urged by the commitment slingers are going to help anyone toward the intelligent pursuit of a political, moral or intellectual goal." The Bomb hung over our lives, he remarked, "while opinions were disarmed, ideas were neutral. A cloud of unconcern more deadly (some would say) than fallout, hung on the intellectual horizon." When Jim Campbell (Lamb's roommate, Landon School, Zeta Psi, Phi Beta Kappa, Scroll and Key) offered the "Academic History" of the class, he spoke for many of us: "the matter of vocation became something other than a merely speculative question." When asked if he could predict what "the diffuse entity known as a liberal education will mean to us in later life," he insisted that the answer was "no—one can indeed only hope that it will mean something."[34]

As Class Orator, Angelo Bartlett Giamatti offered similarly skeptical even pessimistic remarks. Named Angelo after his paternal grandfather (who arrived at Ellis Island around 1900) and Bartlett after his mother's father (who went from Andover to Harvard in 1900), Giamatti could draw on this dual family heritage. He came to Yale from Andover, where in his only year there he had dramatically impressed his peers with his charm, humor, friendliness, and intelligence.[35] As an undergraduate he had a strong academic record and a spectacular, albeit nonathletic, extracurricular one as a member of the Pundits, Elizabethan Club, DKE, Aurelian, and Scroll and Key. In his speech Giamatti wondered "how many of us could get up and say that there is . . . no 'despair born of unbelief' within us." So many of our classmates, he observed, "do not even know what they would like to do, not to speak of those who do not care." The future Yale president held out the hope we would gradually develop "a noble and creative way of life." In the meantime, those of us who were not self-centered or apathetic instead made "a frantic effort to Be something."[36]

As class historian, Al Pergam offered similarly skeptical and ambiguous observations. The son of a father who had emigrated from Poland and an American-born mother, Albert grew up as a Jew in Flushing, New York, and came to Yale from Deerfield. As an undergraduate he had a remarkably successful academic and extracurricular career—junior Phi Beta Kappa, class officer, second in command of the *Yale Daily News*, Elihu. He described "our typical hero" as someone very unlike himself: "the well-rounded, best-prepared, geographically-distributed anonymity usually glimpsed modeling Madras jackets in the J. Press window." As we leave Yale, he intoned, "I only urge you to do your best for God, for country, and for . . . excuse me, I seem to have lost my place."[37]

Thus ended our "Bright College Years." Giamatti and Pergam underscored the effort it took to become a Yale man and how contingent that process was: Giamatti by acknowledging the tension between the everyday reality and the "noble and creative way of life," and Pergam by seeming to lose his way. When carrying out research for this book I thought I would find in the 1960 class book expressions of an exhilarating sense of being on the cusp if not of great historical change then of unbounded futures. In 1960 my classmates could hardly foretell what Karambelas later called the "incipient questioning and change and disorder" we were about to encounter.

The year we graduated from Yale College, 1960, was a momentous time.

On February 1, four African American students sat in at a Woolworth's lunch counter in Greensboro, North Carolina. In the calendar year 1960 seventeen African nations became independent, even as on March 21, police killed sixty-nine black South Africans in what became known as the Sharpeville Massacre. In September *Good Housekeeping* published "I Say: Women Are People Too!" by Betty Friedan, a prelude to her book *The Feminine Mystique* (1963). In the fall, the Student League for Industrial Democracy (SLID) changed its name to Students for a Democratic Society (SDS) and Young Americans for Freedom (YAF) held its first meeting, at the Connecticut home of William F. Buckley Jr. On October 30, John Kenneth Galbraith reviewed Paul Goodman's *Growing Up Absurd* in the *New York Times.* On November 8, Senator John F. Kennedy defeated Vice President Richard M. Nixon for the American presidency. I was an undergraduate between the publication of Henry Nash Smith's *Virgin Land* (1950) and Richard Slotkin's *Regeneration through Violence* (1973), the first highlighting the march by Americans across a supposedly empty land, the second emphasizing the violence of that march directed against Native Americans.

As I write this, I think of my undergraduate self as akin to Forrest Gump from the 1994 movie, an obscure person by chance present at major historical moments. A number of my friends picketed the New Haven Woolworth's, and a few weeks later I joined them in hosting a conference, "The Challenge of American Democracy," that featured speeches by Barry Goldwater, Thurgood Marshall, and A. Philip Randolph. In 1959, when I traveled to Africa, in Johannesburg I attended the treason trial of members of the African National Congress, including Nelson Mandela, and then visited Leopoldville right after riots led by Patrice Lumumba in the lead-up to independence from Belgium. In the spring of 1960 I chaired a panel at Yale on apartheid. Studying at the hyper-masculine Yale where there seemed to be few women my peers saw as people, little could I imagine that more than a third of a century later I would publish a book that connected Friedan's writing of the late 1950s and early 1960s with her radical journalism of the 1940s and early 1950s. In the second semester of my senior year, I participated in the activities of the John Dewey Society, Yale's chapter of SLID, and sat on the editorial board of a student publication that featured an article by a Yale Law School student who would soon become the first YAF president. I bought a copy of Paul Goodman's book as soon as it came out, feeling then as now how un-absurd my life was, even as I admired his critique of American society. In my mother's 1955 Chevrolet convertible during the summer of 1960 I drove across America with two Yale friends, ending up in Los Angeles, where I attended the Democratic National Convention and witnessed Kennedy's nomination. I had just graduated from

Yale as an American studies honors major, a program funded by an anticommunist donor but in which the professors suggested that life in the American West was not as virginal as Henry Nash Smith implied.

Map of the Road Ahead

Following this introduction, I begin with two chapters on Jews at Yale. In "Think Yiddish" and "Dress British" I explore changes from my father's experiences to mine, as well as those shifts in admissions policies and sartorial styles that marked the movement of Jews and others (my father and me included) from the margins to the mainstream of Yale and of American society. The phrase "Think Yiddish, Dress British" denotes how Jews chose to retain key aspects of their heritage while conforming outwardly to an Ivy League or preppy style. This involved complex processes of negotiating the finer elements a text or situation presents by using analytic powers, all the while looking and behaving like a gentleman. Thinking Yiddish also means approaching the world in ways that often involved no respect for borders between disciplines or conventional ways of thinking, and by deploying a sharp sense of shrewdness, melding a Talmudic attention to detail with an ability to think creatively. My most sustained friendship with a classmate reminds me of this every Sunday morning when Monroe Price and I go over the "Vows" and "Weddings" section of the *New York Times* and I listen to his ability to take an issue or question and turn it over, contradicting expectations, seeing connections or patterns not readily apparent.[38]

With chapter 3, "In White America," I look at the African American experience from a variety of perspectives: urban renewal in New Haven, the lives of my African American classmates, Yale faculty members' writings about African America, the coverage of African Americans in the U.S. history course I took in 1957–58, and the senior theses on African America by four classmates. With "Africa," chapter 4, I chart the shift of Western nations from the powerful triumphalism after World War II to decolonialization in the late 1950s. I focus on writings about Africa by one student and several faculty members, my two-month trip to that continent in the summer of 1959, and the postgraduate experiences in Africa of more than a dozen classmates. "Becoming an Academic Man," chapter 5, reveals the impact on me and a small group of peers in the American studies honors program of what our professors said, wrote, and assigned. If much of what they conveyed confirms the widely accepted picture of elitist and Cold War perspectives, there is also evidence that challenges a picture of 1950s complacency—visible in the course content and in the distance between professors' intentions and students' responses. Here is the place where I explore the profound impact that my formal education at Yale had on me, instilling a sense of what it means be a scholar and an intellectual, propelling me forward to becoming an academic man. In "Recasting Gender in a Masculine World," chapter 6, I explore how, coming from households dominated by powerful fathers and then living in such a hyper-masculine collegiate world, some of us, myself included, managed to develop into men quite unlike our fathers or professors. Especially revealing of this process are the wonderfully rich courtship letters that Helen and I wrote each other in the first months of 1960.

Chapter 7, "Political Engagement in an Apolitical World," focuses on how, against the background of a 1950s characterized by undergraduate political apathy, a small number of us, again myself included, challenged from the left and right the centrist focus so common in the late 1950s in the nation and on campuses. "It All Comes Together," chapter 8, explores how in my senior year, and especially in my final semester, political engagement increased significantly. Attention then shifts in chapter 9, "Postpartum Politics," to my classmates' political experiences after graduation—first in response to the Vietnam War and then more generally to the shifting tides of American public life. I discuss leading figures across the political spectrum, including a handful of classmates who had major public careers. The book concludes with "Looking Backward," where I ponder how the post-collegiate experiences of my peers illuminate issues that animate discussions of higher education today. Here I also explore the sometimes profound, often indirect impact that the years at Yale had on members of the class of 1960.

CHAPTER ONE
Think Yiddish

After being turned down for a summer job by the Wall Street firms, I went to see the dean of Yale Law School, Eugene Rostow. Rostow was Jewish but had managed to get a job at a Wall Street firm, and so he was called "Dean Gene, the white-shoe Jew." He explained that it was not impossible for an Eastern European Jew to break into Wall Street and that an important consideration was 'appearance.' He told me to "think Yiddish, but dress British," and he gave me $100 from the dean's fund to buy an appropriate 'interview suit' at J. Press, the local preppy store. I bought a blue blazer with brass buttons, a striped tie, and a pair of loafers. As my grandmother would have put it: S'gurnished helfen—"It didn't help." No Wall Street firm wanted me, blazer or not.

ALAN DERSHOWITZ, Yale Law School, class of 1962,
Taking the Stand: My Life in Law (2013)

Bill Horowitz, my father, came to Yale in the fall of 1925 from Kansas City, Missouri. Born in 1907, a little over a year after his parents and older siblings got off the boat at Ellis Island, he had not heard of Yale until he was a teenager, when his mother returned from a wedding in New Haven.[1] From a midwestern immigrant family, he arrived at an Ivy League university better known for its ability to turn privileged prep school graduates into Yale men primed for national leadership than for its friendliness to Jews from modest and provincial backgrounds. He later told the story that when he applied to Yale, he listed his mother's maiden name not as Pebovovich, which it was, but Peabody, an Anglicized version that unintentionally, I assume, referred to Groton's legendary headmaster Endicott Peabody. However, the change surely did not fool the admissions committee since his last name remained Horowitz. Indeed, not long before Yale let him in, alarm had grown among those at Yale involved in undergraduate admissions about the "Hebrew Invasion." In the fall of 1921 the percentage of Jews entering as freshmen reached an unprecedented and to them a frightening high of thirteen.[2]

Yale Men and American Jews

As it deliberated about which students to admit or reject, Yale relied on a restrictive sense of its mission. The chair of the undergraduate board of admissions beginning in 1920, Professor Robert Nelson Corwin, was emblematic of the university's insularity and prejudices. His family had come to Massachusetts in 1633. Arriving at Yale 250 years later from a prep school, he was, the sociologist Jerome Karabel has written in his compelling book on the history of Jews and admissions at Yale, Harvard, and Princeton, "a living embodiment of the Yale ideal of the all-around man." Corwin's Yale connections were ample: two brothers and his wife's father, grandfather, seven uncles, and five brothers. In his senior year Corwin captained the nation's championship football team, which led to his election to Skull and Bones. His anti-Semitism was typical for people with his background. The majority of Jews, he wrote in 1922, lacked "manliness, uprightness, cleanliness, native refinement." Jews were "an alien and unwashed element" who did not possess the ethical standards he believed characteristic of Yale men. Jews graduated "into the world as naked of all the attributes of refinement and honor as when born into it"; they took from Yale but gave nothing in return.[3]

Despite (or ironically perhaps owing to) the fact that Jewish students outperformed their peers academically, Yale took steps to reduce their numbers. It shrunk the size of the entering class, limited financial aid for Jewish students, and intensified the emphasis on character, a key concept that along with geographical distribution, personal promise, and leadership potential enabled admissions officers to deny entry to qualified children and grandchildren of immigrants. Aware of the adverse publicity that surrounded Harvard's move in the 1920s to a more restrictive admissions policy, Yale discreetly limited the number of Jewish students. There was thus a critically significant distance between how Yale saw what it had to offer and to whom, on the one hand, and, on the other, my father's way of looking at Yale as an opportunity for an ambitious son of immigrants to rely on merit, to benefit from an elite collegiate education, and then to rise in the world.

By the time my father entered Yale, the percentage of Jews among undergraduates had slipped to slightly more than ten, about where it remained for forty years—until the 1960s, when he played a key role in transforming admissions policies. Yale had a much smaller percentage of Jews than did Harvard or Columbia, but Yale's administrators worried that their excessive numbers would undermine the college's ability to attract the sons of America's elite. It was not only Jews Yale discriminated against: Yale College admitted no women and restricted the numbers of Latinos, Asian Americans, African Americans, and Roman Catholics, especially those whose families had come to America after 1880. Between 1924 and 1945 only seven African Americans had graduated from Yale College. In contrast, in the 1920s and 1930s, approximately one-third of college-age young men listed in New York's *Social Register* enrolled. Admissions policy favored graduates of prep schools and legacies. Only one in four of my father's classmates came to Yale from a public high school. Instead of what it saw as narrowly focused and socially awkward grinds, Yale wanted young men with leadership potential signaled by their athletic ability, social poise, and character. As Yale's president and my father's classmate A. Whitney Griswold remarked in the early 1950s, someone admitted to Yale would not be a "beetle-browed, highly specialized intellectual but a well-rounded man."[4]

In the spring of 1926, when my father was finishing his first year, a *Yale Daily News* editorial titled "Ellis Island for Yale" captured the implications of the admissions policy. The writer remarked that the university should "institute immigration laws more prohibitive than those of the United States government" by emphasizing not brains but "the character, personality, promise and background of the individual in question." These traits would make it more likely that sons of alumni would gain admission and then go on to leadership positions at Yale and, later, in the nation. "The survival of the fittest should yield men who are equipped to do more than pass scholastic examinations or earn money," the editorial remarked, using coded anti-Semitic language. Perhaps, the editorial suggested, Yale should require applicants to submit photographs of their fathers, upping the ante over Harvard, which had recently required that applications come with a picture of the student.[5] It was hardly coincidental that the U.S. government had passed a highly restrictive immigration law in 1924, the same year that Yale adopted a quota for Jews and others in undergraduate admissions. Likewise, American immigration policy became dramatically more welcoming in 1965, precisely the year that Yale opened up its undergraduate admissions policy.

Although my optimistic and ambitious father was clean and highly ethical, in many ways he did not fit Yale's stereotype. He was a Jew; from a family that had arrived on these shores in the twentieth century, not the seventeenth; with no Yale blue blood in his veins; un-athletic; and lacking in "native refinement." Though as an adult he was smoothly polished, young Bill Horowitz faced the ordeal of civility. As an undergraduate he had to learn codes of behavior that many of his peers knew practically from birth. To be sure, as he was graduating

from high school, his math teacher commented that a judge in a debate competition had described him as "a whole team in himself." My father was among
the minority of Yale undergraduates who attended a public high school; in 1930
almost a third of undergraduates came from one of eight prep schools, with
graduates of Andover, Exeter, and Hotchkiss alone comprising 20 percent of
the entering class. Seventeen percent of his classmates were alumni sons, many
subject to less demanding admissions standards than others. At a time when
almost 90 percent of students came from east of the Mississippi, his hometown was one thing that may have made his admission more likely. He was not
one of the supposedly great unwashed, smart Jews from public high schools
in New York City, Chicago, or Philadelphia. These three cities had about half
of the nation's Jewish population but in 1930 sent only thirteen graduates of
its public schools to Yale. In contrast, St. Paul's, a prestigious prep school with
only sixty-eight graduating seniors, sent twenty-four.[6]

Little could Corwin or his colleagues know that by admitting my father
they were letting in what in 1922 Corwin said was a student who would "profit
by the opportunities and advantages offered at Yale," would "be a credit to
the institution," and would give more to his alma mater than he took from
it. Totally beyond Corwin's imagination in 1922 (and surely my father's seven
years later when he graduated) was the possibility that he would be the first
"Hebrew" to sit on the Yale Corporation and would enthusiastically vote to
admit women as undergraduates.[7]

In 1931 Yale junior Eugene Rostow, whose background powerfully illuminates the complex dimensions of Yale's relationship to Jews, wrote of "The
Jew's Position" in an undergraduate publication. Early in the new century
Rostow's father, Victor Aaron Rostowsky, had migrated from Ukraine, aware
that his publishing a socialist newspaper in the old country would land him
in jail. His parents, a scholar recently remarked, had "an appreciation of high
culture, an unerring belief in the transcendent value of education, and a
shared commitment to socialism," a socialism more Tolstoyan than Marxist.
Appropriately, they named their children Eugene Victor (after Eugene Debs
and Victor Hugo), Walt Whitman, and Ralph Waldo. Their chemist father and
homemaker mother moved to New Haven in 1926 to be near relatives. They
were aware that the top graduates of New Haven public schools could benefit
from a Yale scholarship.[8]

Rostow graduated from New Haven (known after 1949 as James E. Hillhouse) High School with my mother in 1929. The high school, his brother
Walt later said (and I also learned), led him "to an abiding view of the American people as 'we' and not 'they.'" At Yale, Eugene Rostow excelled—Junior
Phi Beta Kappa, member of the water polo team (a distinctly un-Jewish sport

in early 1930s America), writer for student publications, and winner of a prize that used language normally reserved for non-Jewish students: for the senior who "had the combination of intellectual achievement, character and personality." Dershowitz encountered him when Rostow was dean of Yale Law School.[9]

Rostow's willingness to think the best about American institutions was clear in an essay he wrote as an undergraduate. Not long after the eminent linguist and anthropologist Edward Sapir had been the subject of a 1932 anti-Semitic blackballing from what served as Yale's faculty club, Rostow acknowledged that the professoriate of great American universities was "strictly sterilized against Hebrew contamination." But although the Ivies discriminated against Jews in undergraduate admissions, Yale, he reported naively, was "above callow prejudices." Little could he know that, less than a year later, Yale's president would write to Corwin concerning the fluctuations in the number of Jewish undergraduates at Yale, stating, "if we could have an Armenian massacre confined to the New Haven district, with occasional incursions into Bridgeport and Hartford, we might protect our Nordic stock almost completely." Yet Rostow's career validated Corwin's definition of character and citizenship. Both he and Walt (BA 1936, Rhodes Scholarship, PhD 1940), who had grown up in a socialist household, later became anticommunist defenders of American capitalism.[10]

William Horowitz, Yale Class of 1929

A pogrom drove my father's parents out of Russia. Arriving in New York in their early twenties, they eventually settled in Kansas City, Missouri. My paternal grandfather, Louis Horowitz, rose from cleaning train cars for the Missouri and Pacific Railroad, to working at a feed store in 1910, to managing a hay company in 1920, to being a roof jobber in 1930, to running a wholesale poultry business by the mid-1930s. By then he, his wife Esther Horowitz, and their children were living in a modest, respectable neighborhood in Kansas City, halfway between downtown and the affluent Ward Parkway area where family members would settle soon after World War II. My father's family was thus experiencing what Will Herberg in 1955 called the deproletarianizaton of Russian Jewish immigrants. Unlike his two older brothers, Sam and Morris, my father had a college education. After a year at the University of Kansas, in 1925 he left the Midwest for good to head east to Yale, but he carried with him the powerful imprint of his Jewish upbringing. In addition to public schools, he had attended an Orthodox Talmud Torah (or Cheder) at She'erith Israel D'Lubavitz. He also played crucial roles in the early history of the Jewish high school fraternity, AZA, which he helped form in his high school years in partnership with others, including Phil Klutznick, his roommate at University of Kansas and secretary of commerce under President Jimmy Carter. As Klutznick later said, AZA was a club that could enable its members to "fit comfortably into their American and Jewish environments."[11]

My father benefited from growing up in a deeply religious family, shaped by the combination of commitments to Zionism and a Lubavitcher faith, a version of Orthodox and Hasidic Judaism founded in Russia in the eighteenth century. He was unlike many other second-generation Jews whom Herberg described as "confused, anxious, and discontented" about their identity and overeager to turn against the culture and religion of their immigrant parents. From an early age, optimism (perhaps ebullience is the more appropriate word) and self-confidence characterized my father's life. Although he was not physically marked as Jewish in a clear manner, his commitment to Judaism sustained him through his life.[12]

As an undergraduate, my father earned only a slightly above average academic record as he struggled to stay afloat economically, which required him to devote limited time to his studies or to extracurricular activities. He continually borrowed money from his roommate and from family members including, as I wrote in my senior year at Yale, "an older brother whose winter coat was always in hock to pay my father's way through Yale."[13] He earned money by teaching Hebrew at a local synagogue (which is how he met my mother) and by working in the kitchens of fraternities. At a time when financial aid was less available than it is now, a dean gave him a check for $50, and on another occasion the university awarded him a $350 scholarship, which covered tuition.[14] The only teacher I recall his mentioning was William Lyon Phelps, the legendary English professor who attracted rapt audiences at Yale and in the wider world. My father remained very much an outsider to mainstream life at Yale, something reinforced even among his more assimilated Jewish classmates when he arranged for a talk by Chaim Weizmann, the head of the World Zionist Organization and, two decades hence, the first president of Israel.[15]

Reflections in a Silver Spoon: Paul Mellon, Yale Class of 1929

If my father was one of the least privileged members of his class, Paul Mellon was surely the most privileged. When he arrived in New Haven from the Choate School, Mellon did so as the grandson of the immensely wealthy industrialist and banker Thomas Mellon and son of Andrew Mellon, one of the richest men in America. Andrew Mellon was secretary of the treasury from 1921 to 1932 and founder in the late 1930s of the National Gallery of Art. The wealth and prominence of Paul Mellon's father eased his entry into Yale, something also made possible by the fact that the headmaster at Choate was the son-in-law of Yale's president. Skull and Bones himself, President Charles Seymour could count among those who preceded him at Yale an ancestor who had received one of the university's first honorary degrees, a father who taught classics at Yale, and two members of his family who had served as the university's presidents.

As an undergraduate, Mellon inhabited worlds my father had neither the time for nor access to: as vice chairman of the *Yale Daily News* (with his own father making it possible for him to interview President Calvin Coolidge), on the board of the *Yale Literary Magazine,* and a member of the crew team. Paul Mellon turned down Skull and Bones and instead joined the equally prestigious Scroll and Key. When he took an art history course, he remembered, it seemed pointless to look at reproductions "when I could see originals of similar quality" in two of his father's residences. At a time when his father oversaw offices charged with enforcing Prohibition, Mellon spent many a weekend in New York at speakeasies and nightclubs consuming abundant amounts of illegal liquor. Yet all the privileges of wealth and power did not guarantee him happiness. He suffered from the fallout of his parents' bitter divorce and from being shuttled between them. His "happiest days," he later reported, were with the servants, especially Irish American women. "They treated me seriously and talked to me as one human being to another," he remembered, something that stood in contrast to how his parents related to him.[16]

As an undergraduate, Mellon noted in his memoir, he fought "an inner battle" between being "a thoughtful scholar and a laughing hell-raiser." Stung by "occasional mild fits of depression and feeling of a lack of direction in my life," he faced graduation in 1929, just months before the crash of the stock market. As he later reported, "there would never be compelling financial reasons for me to have to take a regular job." After leaving Yale he went on to Clare College, Cambridge, and then to a career as an owner and breeder of thoroughbred horses (including Yale-referenced ones such as Branford Court, Arts and Letters, Chapel Street). He was a major art collector, some of which ended up in the Yale Center for British Art that he founded.[17]

For Mellon "thinking Yiddish" was impossible; "dressing British," easy. My father grew up speaking English, Hebrew, and Yiddish; as an adult he dressed British when useful. My father grew up in a tight knit, intact family; his classmate came of age in a fractured one. Nor did Mellon have religious rituals or beliefs to sustain him as my father did.

Through his relationship with my mother, my father entered a world of greater privilege than the one in which he had grown up. With the support of my mother's family, the newlyweds in 1933 took an extended honeymoon trip to Europe, Egypt, and Palestine. Nonetheless, Mellon worked for his father briefly after graduation; my father, after a year in graduate school at Yale, entered the family business of his future father-in-law. Botwinik Brothers, Inc., and a Jewish burial society hardly equaled Alcoa Aluminum and Mellon Bank. My maternal grandparents' collection of the fifty-one volumes of "Dr. Eliot's Five Foot Shelf," the books of literature and philosophy that Harvard's president in 1909 had first recommended as providing a liberal education, was not the equivalent of Andrew Mellon's purchasing more than a score of paintings from the Hermitage in the 1930s—including works by Botticelli and Rembrandt.

The World of Miriam Botwinik

The story of my mother's family is quite different from that of my father's. My maternal grandmother, Esther Hirschberg Botwinik, my only American-born grandparent, was born in 1890 and moved from Maxwell Street near Hull House in Chicago to New York's Lower East Side before her family settled in New Haven. She met her husband, Hyman Botwinik, when they were both working in the Strouse, Adler corset factory on Olive Street, and they married in 1911. Her experience as a factory worker helped turn her into a Debsian Socialist.[18]

Hyman Botwinik was born in 1888 and arrived in America in 1905 from Rakov, a shtetl or small town thirty miles east of Minsk in what is now Belarus. David Laskin's *The Family: Three Journeys into the Heart of the Twentieth Century* (2013) reveals how members of his family, like mine, remained in eastern Europe or migrated to Palestine and the United States. Hyman's sister Beyle married one of the six children whose lives Laskin chronicles. Among their relatives, Laskin writes, "there were scholars and Zionists, revolutionaries and philanthropists, even one young man who fought beside Trotsky during the Russian Revolution." In the Jewish world of Rakov, men worked as manufacturers, shop owners, and scholars while women both took care of the children and worked to bring in money. Yet in Europe there were limits to what family members could achieve: land ownership was impossible, as were government, professional, and academic jobs. Anti-Semitic threats were constant, whether in pogroms, boycotts, or daily acts of violence. Civil wars, the Russian Revolution, World Wars I and II, and the invasion by the Nazis meant that Rakov was a pawn in continual, violent struggles that ravaged territories and people, Jews especially.[19]

Shortly after his arrival in America, Hyman Botwinik left his job in the corset factory and joined his older brother Harris. They soon transformed their junk dealership, a typical and much maligned Jewish trade, into a more respectable machine tool dealership, initially located behind their house. They bought metalworking machine tools, repaired and painted them, and then sold them for a profit. By 1918 the enthusiastic author of a book titled *Eminent Jews of America* talked of how the Botwinik brothers "are not only very wealthy, but are conducting the largest business in their city." This was an exaggeration born out of ethnic pride and a desire to sell books to Jewish businessmen. In 1918 the company, with at most a dozen employees, paled in comparison to New Haven's Winchester Repeating Arms; the Botwinik brothers were hardly among the wealthier and long-established citizens of the city. Yet the book did capture the commitments of the brothers to Jewish charities in New Haven and elsewhere.[20]

Shortly after the end of World War I, my maternal grandparents moved a little more than a mile—out of a crowded, multi-ethnic neighborhood of tenements near the center of New Haven—to an eight-room house built in 1916, twenty-three hundred square feet in size, with a sprawling, terraced backyard. Most of those who lived nearby were Jews, though several doors away were two households of the Keyes family, who ran the city's leading African American funeral home. With more than a little pride, friends and relatives called my grandparents the Governor and the Duchess. In 1922 they had the Bachrach firm take their picture in their new home—my grandfather, age thirty-four, standing in a well-tailored suit and holding his fashionable straw hat and my grandmother, two years younger, seated and proudly looking matronly and handsome.

In 1938 Hyman and Esther traveled to Poland for the third time, where they tried, unsuccessfully because of American immigration policy, to help his relatives migrate to the United States, a project they were eager to support financially. When he died in 1940, Hyman could have no knowledge of what would become of his family in Poland. From 1941 to 1945, Laskin writes, the members of his family and mine who remained in eastern Europe died in gas chambers, "were shot over pits, lined up and machine-gunned, murdered by gentile neighbors, burned alive, worked almost to death, and then shot and incinerated." At the end of World War II, Uri Finkel, the son of Rakow's last rabbi, returned from the Soviet Union to record what had happened in his hometown. "On Yom Kippur of 1941," he wrote, "the fascist murderers drove the entire Jewish population of Rakow to the marketplace. They made them bring all the books, . . . along with the *sefer-toyres* [Torah scrolls], and burned them. . . . The Jews had to stand over the bonfire, dance, jump, and sing; those who could not do this were shot on the spot." Later the Nazis, with the help of Polish Catholics, wiped out almost all of the local Jewish population that remained. While working on this book I discovered the website my Israeli relatives developed that contained these horrific stories. Only then did I realize the fate that family members who remained in eastern Europe suffered in the Shoah. I doubt whether my parents knew the full extent of the devastation wrecked on family members. While growing up I heard no discussion at 200 Colony Road of the Holocaust. Yet I am confident that what my father did know of the fate of the family—their destruction in Europe, plus the saving remnants in Israel and America—strengthened his commitment both to Zionism and to being on guard against anti-Semitism in the United States.[21]

Growing Up Privileged and Unabsurdly

Born in 1938 as a third-generation Jewish American, I grew up in an upper-middle-class New Haven neighborhood inhabited almost exclusively by Jews. After my parents married, they moved into an apartment down the street from my grandparents, and then about the time my sister Judy was born in June 1936, they moved again, this time two blocks to 200 Colony Road, where they would stay until 1960. The nearby houses were from fifteen hundred to twenty-five hundred square feet, built on lots of about a fifth of an acre. Within a few blocks of where I grew up were five households of my relatives. The neighborhood had dozens of children my age, most all of whom went to nearby public schools. My high school, surrounded by Yale buildings, was a microcosm of New Haven's diverse population: classrooms filled with Jews, African Americans, Irish Americans, Polish Americans, Italian Americans, poor and working-class white Protestants, and a handful of upper-middle-class white Protestants, a few of them children of Yale faculty. Of course, to a considerable extent, class and race defined who our friends were and what classes we took, some of them from people who had earned PhDs at Yale. Most of the Jews and well-to-do white Protestants, along with some of Italian and Irish descent and fewer African Americans, went off to prestigious colleges. Most of those with dark skins and lower- or working-class backgrounds headed for technical education, state schools, the military, or into factories and offices.[22]

The dynamics of the household in which I grew up inevitably shaped who I became. The sense of continuity and constancy my parents offered was profoundly reassuring, giving me for much of my life a confidence that everything would work out for the best. I entered adulthood assured of their support and love. Yet the contrasts they offered profoundly influenced how I saw the world. They opened up for me multiple possibilities of what it meant to be a Jew and a citizen. They imparted to me two powerful tensions—one about politics and the other about gender. When I had to present my autobiography to my underground senior society at Yale, I focused on how I looked at the world as both an insider and an outsider, someone who simultaneously chafed against and accepted the limits of what was politically possible. I was a legacy from a prominent family but as a townie and Jew felt closed off from mainstream Yale. Then there were the expectations about what men and women could achieve. My father helped me understand the challenges ambition imposed—to succeed in business involved frequent absences from family. During college I struggled with the implications of the particular choices he had made. I wanted to succeed and provide, but I also wanted a life that did not have the division I sensed in his between work, play, and family. At the same time, I somehow felt my mother's disquiet with the choices she faced as a woman. Deep, deep down I wanted to make possible something more, if not for her then for other women.

My parents remained united in marriage until they died, though tensions between them erupted in the late 1960s. During my childhood they rarely if ever fought in front of my sister or me. Whatever changes there were in their economic situation, I did not know about them—except indirectly through the trips we took, the country club membership we enjoyed, and the collection of fashionable clothing my mother assembled. My mother dressed carefully and elegantly. My father prided himself on dressing down, increasingly so as his socioeconomic status improved. He placed his Ivy League clothes in the back of his closet and dressed casually, even sloppily. My fondest memory of him, which captures his ease with himself and lack of guile, is this: at some point in the 1960s or 1970s, Helen and I, along with my sister and her husband, were sitting in the window having breakfast in a hotel in downtown New Haven. My father came and tapped on the window from outside. A waitress, seeing a man with somewhat unkempt clothing and hair, came over to us and said, "These bums are always coming around and bothering customers, so if you want me to call the police, I will."

The house at 200 Colony Road, hardly a little democratic commonwealth, was more like a benevolent monarchy with the king and queen having different spheres of influence and styles of exercising power. Our parents rarely if ever asked Judy and me how we might want to spend vacations or weekends or whom we would like to visit. They almost never discussed money, even though the choices they made left a deep imprint on me. As a child I had no direct knowledge of my family's income or wealth, although I was aware of how affluent we were. When I applied to graduate school in 1959, my father told me not to ask for financial aid because he wanted to protect his privacy and did not think the son of someone in his position should ask for or receive a fellowship. When researching this book, I did find a financial statement he prepared in 1955. It revealed that the household income was $36,000 (almost $300,000 in 2014). He claimed a net worth of $375,000, or about $3 million in 2014 dollars adjusted for inflation or more than $16 million had it been invested in the Dow Jones Industrials, which, alas, it was not.[23] With no mortgage on a house they bought in 1936 for less than $10,000, two kids in public school, minimal health care costs, and one of our cars supplied by Botwinik Brothers, my parents disbursed discretionary income in several ways. A live-in African American maid cleaned the house and cooked all the meals. My mother never prepared a meal on her own, though she assembled them on the maid's days off if we did not go out to eat. If Esther Botwinik kept Kosher and took cooking seriously, her daughter Miriam felt that domestic chores, food preparation included, were something a modern, privileged woman should not be bothered with.

Travel was the biggest splurge, representing as it did a central element in a cosmopolitan engagement with the world more compelling to my parents than a good life pursued through more routine rounds of consumption. Every few summers my parents took trips abroad—in 1948 to Israel just after it achieved its independence and again in the mid-1950s, and every so often to Paris, memories of which were kept alive by bottles of Perrier delivered to the house and songs of Edith Piaf played on a phonograph. Year in and year out, as a family we traveled within the United States—to Miami Beach during winter vacations, to Democratic National Conventions from 1948 to 1960, to historic sites in southern New England, and to Las Vegas, where my father loved to gamble and to watch watered-down versions of vaudeville shows. Twice my maternal grandmother took me on memorable trips: in 1952 to Alaska with my sister and in 1957, the summer between my first and second years of college, for eight weeks to France and Italy, where I drove and we stayed in grand hotels.

Closer to home, New York City was our destination during the late 1940s and throughout the 1950s. We saw Broadway shows and paid nostalgic visits to the Lower East Side, where Jewish merchants offered bargain basement clothes on pushcarts that spilled over into the streets. Botwinik Brothers had four box seats in the middle deck along the third base line at Yankee Stadium, and several times I was treated to their victorious seasons, something that intensified my sense of privilege. In many a late December we went to New York for a week, where we stayed in a suite at the Waldorf-Astoria.

Soon after the end of the war, in part so my parents were free to travel, I was shipped off every summer for eight weeks to Camp Adventure in Ridgefield, Connecticut, a secular, Jewish overnight camp run my parents' best friends. It was another marker of my family's arrival into an upper-middle-class world, for the campers were the children of Russian Jewish parents who had begun to benefit from substantial incomes in the 1920s and 1930s. When I was twelve or thirteen, I tried to run away from camp, setting out one day with three friends on the forty-one-mile route home. We did not get very far, with the camp director spotting us on the side of the road a mile or so from our starting point. After that almost until I was off to college, I went to day camp on the Connecticut shore near New Haven for eight weeks, this one also populated by children of backgrounds similar to mine and run by a different set of close family friends. Yet in other ways my parents inspired me to venture beyond the confines of home and family. Accompanied by a friend, on occasion in high school I would go into Manhattan by train to see a Broadway matinee and have an early supper at Gallagher's Steak House before returning home.

As I write all this I wonder if I am exaggerating the affluence of the regimen under which I grew up, though I must admit that putting together the story of all my travels makes me realize just how lucky I was. Yet I have to remind myself and my readers that my parents neither pursued an endless round of conspicuous consumption nor invested in lavish household goods as an expression of their personalities. Rather, by the mid 1950s they seemed quite satisfied with where they had arrived, using their money to build a comfortable life that allowed them to enjoy the experiences of friendship, civic life, and travel. They lived in the same house from 1936 until 1960 and did not alter it in any significant way. We had no second home—a choice I suspect my parents never even considered. We belonged to the all-Jewish Woodbridge Country Club, though neither of my parents displayed any interest in athletics, let alone expensive pursuits such as skiing, sailing, or golf.

Business, Culture, and Civic Engagement

In the mid-1950s my father, then in his late forties, made major shifts in his life—from Botwinik Brothers to a wider range of businesses and to an even fuller engagement in civic life. In 1954 the death of two Botwinik cousins, the sons of Harris, caused a crisis of succession in the family business. Passed over in favor of those with Botwinik blood, my father looked elsewhere. Turning down opportunities to join others in purchasing the American rights to the Japanese Godzilla movies, a National Football League franchise, or the license to a local television station, he put most of his money into shares of Connecticut bank stocks and old-line manufacturers, in some cases acting like a corporate raider. Sometimes he invested in my name and that of my sister: when I graduated from college, my father turned over to me a stock portfolio worth $50,000.

With family members and others, my father helped create and sustain *New Haven Info,* a local magazine, before there were glossy ones, on New Haven politics, restaurants, and cultural events. He was vice president of a local AM station, WELI, whose final three call letters, referring as they did to the first name of Yale's initial donor, Elihu Yale, signified one of his commitments. With family members he had a significant stake in a local FM station, WBIB, which he jokingly said stood for We're Botwiniks Including Bill. In time and money, however, his major business commitment was to General Industrial Bank, which my maternal grandfather had helped found as a Jewish burial society and my father ran starting in 1950. It was, one observer noted, "a small commercial bank established by Jewish families in New Haven in response to the systematic exclusion of Jews from other banks."[24] In the late 1950s my father had joined with other Jews from small New England cities in the take-overs of several national corporations, including Pyrene Fire Extinguisher Company and Detroit-based L. A. Young Spring and Wire, at the time an auto parts supplier and military contractor in the lowest ranks of the Fortune 500.[25]

My parents' commitment to the public sphere was extensive and long-standing, something deep in the Botwinik family specifically and Jewish traditions generally. My father took the lead in my parents' engagement in the Jewish world. He joined family members in playing a key role in founding the Woodbridge Country Club. Like his father-in-law he served as president of B'nai Jacob, the most prominent Conservative synagogue in the New Haven area. My mother was a secular Jew who went to synagogue out of a sense of obligation to the memory of her father and to the presence of her husband; my father felt his Judaism and Jewishness profoundly (although in culinary terms, he expressed his religious obligation only partially: no pork or shellfish at home but also no commitment to keeping a Kosher home and no restraints when eating out). Unlike many prosperous second-generation Jews, through-out his life my father never turned his back on his origins. He was fluent in Hebrew and Yiddish; put on tiffilin, small black leather boxes that contained verses of the Torah, especially when a representative of the Lubavitcher Rebbe visited him in his office; contributed generously to Jewish causes at home and in Israel; and was close friends with a succession of rabbis.[26]

Politics also engaged my parents. Blocked from advance at Botwinik Brothers, in the mid-1950s my father considered the offer of local Democratic Party bosses that he run for the U.S. House of Representatives in 1956. He did not let his name go forward and instead Robert Giaimo, after running unsuccessfully for the House seat in 1956, went on to serve ten terms beginning in 1959. My father accepted the appointment by Governor Abraham Ribicoff to the Connecticut State Board of Education, on which he served as a member from 1955 to 1973 and as its chair from 1959 to 1973. Gender shaped my parents' public lives. Described in a 1954 New Haven publication as "that little bundle of energy," my mother was more likely to work behind the scenes than, as my father did, appear on the bimah at B'nai Jacob Synagogue or a platform at a political rally. My father was treasurer of the local Democratic Party, and my mother got involved in politics as a surrogate for her busier and more outgoing husband. Elected treasurer of the city of New Haven in the mid-1950s, she was reportedly the first woman ever to hold a major position in New Haven's government. That same 1954 local publication remarked that she was proud of her election "not so much for the sense of fulfillment that it brings to herself, but as a representative of the womanhood in the area."[21]

Commitments to liberalism and civil rights suffused my political education. In the late 1940s, at a summer camp that was hardly socialist, I nonetheless learned songs that originated in political insurgencies of the 1930s. "As the peach pit said to the apple core, the color of your skin doesn't matter anymore" was one. Another was "Close your eyes and point your finger, on the map just let it linger, any place you point your finger to, there's someone with the same type blood as you." I can still sing many of the songs my father's Yale classmate Harold Rome had written for *Pins and Needles* (1937) that reflect 1930s labor unionism specifically and Popular Front commitments more generally. Among them were "Sing Me a Song with Social Significance," "Doing the Reactionary," and "One Big Union for Two." Soon after it premiered in 1949 in New Haven, I saw *South Pacific*, whose song, "You've Got to Be Carefully Taught," critiqued American race relations even as it focused on Southeast Asia.

My parents and friends exposed me to a wide variety of musical traditions that provided entry into and comfort with the diversity of American culture. On many a Sunday my father took me to New Haven's Schubert Theater, where I listened to jazz greats, including Louis Armstrong, whom I went backstage to meet. In addition, one of my best friends in high school was Jason Cutler, whose father's ownership of Cutler's Record Shop gave me access to original African American rock and roll music. In high school I drove with my buddies to the State Theater in Hartford, where we listened to the shows presented by the rock and roll impresario Alan Freed. Through my family's investments in local radio stations, I owned scores of long-playing records whose variety reflected the many musical tastes I had acquired: symphonies by Ludwig Beethoven, 1940s big band sounds of Benny Goodman, soothing 1950s melodies by Les Elgart, and jazz by Oscar Peterson and Louis Armstrong.

My parents involved themselves locally in interracial work and in the early 1950s became life members of the NAACP. What helped propel them was not only their sense of responsibility as a leading Jewish family involved in the Democratic Party but also their ongoing friendship with S. Ralph Harlow, my mother's religion professor at Smith. From a distinguished New England family and inspired as an undergraduate by William James to be open to new experiences, Harlow was active nationally in the NAACP. He was both a Christian socialist and a philo-Semite.[28] Early in the Depression he took my mother and her college peers to Manhattan to see how the other half lived. As did my New Haven grandmother, Harlow bequeathed to my mother a deeply engrained democratic socialism which stood in unarticulated contrast to her affluent way of life.[29]

If scholars from backgrounds like mine later agonized when they discovered they benefited from white privilege, I knew early on how privilege compounded and relied on the color of my skin. Once when I was in my early teens, my father was driving my sister and me in his new, air-conditioned Cadillac through the heart of an African American neighborhood. As a pregnant African American woman crossed in front of our car, a child or two in tow, he turned to us. "Don't ever forget," he said, "that only luck of birth had caused you to ride comfortably in this car, while she is sweltering as she walks across the street." Supported by my mother, he was conveying to me and my sister that although rewards came to those who worked hard, unexpected contingencies—like his going to Yale and marrying into my mother's family—could lead to privilege, even as for others chance led to less auspicious lives.

As part and parcel of my parents' broader set of commitments to communal, cosmopolitan values, they remained loyal to the Democratic Party of FDR and Truman, although here their orientations differed. My father was fiercely loyal to the Democratic Party and to the liberalism that originated with FDR's New Deal. My mother was farther to the left, influenced by Harlow and by a skepticism about whether America had really lived up to its commitments to democracy and equal opportunity. After the mid-1960s, feminism gave my mother ways of expressing herself both against my father and for her independence, making the 1960s more productive politically for her than for my father. Whatever the differences in their perspectives, from the 1930s until their deaths they shared a belief that federal intervention could enhance social welfare for the less privileged and provide greater equality of opportunity for African Americans. Unlike for many in their position, the turn from civil rights to Black Power, the war in Vietnam, and the rise of critiques of Zionism tested, but did not undermine, their politics.

Although clearly anti-Stalinists, my parents strongly opposed the way McCarthyism suppressed civil liberties. I remember my father bringing into the house in the mid-1950s a phonograph record, contained in a plain wrapper, that satirized the Wisconsin senator. My first sustained political memory came with the Army-McCarthy hearings in the spring of 1954. Watching them on television and listening to anticommunist commentators like Walter Winchell left a deep and lasting impression on me. Even in the twenty-first century, when I taught the writings of Karl Marx or Antonio Gramsci, I would half-jokingly tell my Smith College students that I wondered if any of them was going to report me to the FBI. An unlikely event, even though at Yale I was politically active on the left and later voiced my opposition to the war in Vietnam. I cannot overestimate how McCarthyism's impact, as viewed through my parents' eyes, instilled in me a sense of the dangers overly adversarial political commitments might bring.

When I left New Haven in 1960, I never again lived in or contributed to a world with the strong, focused, and local communal sense my parents fostered. They successfully balanced their commitments to ethnic particularism and to cosmopolitanism, the latter best expressed through travel and through their participation locally in an ethnically diverse Democratic Party. When researching and writing this section, I was awed by the depth and extensiveness of the civic commitments of my New Haven grandparents and my parents. My parents were proud of me, but I ended up teaching and writing about the public sphere instead of participating in it to the extent they did. Yet I found my own ways to contribute to the public sphere defined by the classroom and college. The trajectory of my life is from provincial Jew enmeshed in a dense local Jewish community to professional, secular, and more cosmopolitan Jew involved in networks that are far-flung nationally.

School Days

I do not want to leave the false impression that my life as a child and adolescent was without difficulty. Eating very selectively and idiosyncratically, I had what a later generation would call an eating disorder. I weighed so little that family members in the late 1940s called me the refugee from Buchenwald, the only reference to the Holocaust I can remember from my childhood. At several points, I rebelled against what was expected of me, with some of what felt comfortable for my parents feeling claustrophobic for me. I have already talked about running away from the overnight camp. Soon after my Bar Mitzvah,

I began acting out at Hebrew school, opening the window when it was freezing cold outside or throwing spitballs at my classmates. At a time when my father chaired the committee on religious education at the synagogue, I calculated that misbehaving at Hebrew school was not dangerous as long as I behaved perfectly in public school.

Then in high school, I rebelled by turning away from the friendship circle of socially prominent Jews and toward another one that was, in social class and ethnic terms, made up of male friends from more heterogeneous backgrounds. We called our group the United Nations because in our ranks were several Irish Americans, a German American, an Italian American, and a Greek American as well as several Jews. This group also included Leon Nelson Jr., an African American, high school basketball star, and class president who went on to Colby College and later to a career as a civil rights activist in Boston. Yet I was also aware that his father was a cook at Yale and at my summer overnight camp. To some extent he and I could bridge the gaps caused by race and class, but even as a child I was intensely aware that most African Americans lived in a different and less advantageous world than I did. My circle of female friends was diverse, but almost all of my girlfriends were Jews; when I lapsed and dated a non-Jew, my father made his displeasure clear by flexing his velvet glove. These relationships with girlfriends were not very deep or sustained, and certainly did not involve much sexual activity, given both my own personality and reigning notions of middle-class respectability. When we filled out questionnaires that circulated among us, I had no idea what "petting below the waist" meant.

Yet to all outward appearances, as an adolescent I was engaged, serious, outgoing, and popular. While my mother sat reading across the room, my father and I watched television together, competing with each other to answer quiz show questions. In other competitions, he was no match for me, in command as I was of baseball statistics, especially of the Yankees, and of information on the features of the latest automobiles. I read voraciously on my own. My favorite novels were C. S. Forester's stories of the naval exploits of Horatio Hornblower, a fictional officer for the Royal Navy during the Napoleonic wars. Reference books were to me what the internet would be for a later generation of youths determined to understand the world. I devoured volumes of the *World Book* encyclopedia, following leads one entry offered as I tracked down a related reference about geography, history, or current events. For school I studied hard, reading books assigned by teachers and those that my curiosity drove me to explore. Academic achievement followed suit; in addition, my extracurricular plate was full. My high school classmates voted me the male high school senior Most Likely to Succeed, an assessment that relied on both my capacity for diverse friendships and my role as heir to my parents' prominence.

Family and History

By and large, the story of my family goes against the grain of widely accepted pictures of American life in the 1950s and early 1960s. I begin locally, with Robert Dahl's *Who Governs: Democracy and Power in an American City* (1961). In opposition to C. Wright Mills's *The Power Elite* (1956), Dahl used his study of New Haven to support a pluralist view of American society and politics, one in which he distinguished between political, economic, and social realms to emphasize that the power of elites was dispersed and not cumulative.[30] At the time I found Dahl's picture of New Haven problematic. I understood intuitively in high school and soon embraced in college concepts that explained that power was more cumulative and intersecting than he envisioned. After all, my father was what Dahl called an Economic Notable by virtue of his bank presidency, a Political Notable married to another one, and a Social Notable, not as Dahl saw that in terms of membership in the exclusive Lawn Club, but in the world of local Jewish community.[31]

As I examine what writers say in the rich and abundant literature on the histories of the family, masculinity, and fatherhood, I realize how what they describe does not capture the distinctiveness of my family's life because scholars tend to focus on privatized cookie-cutter suburbs, organization men, and domestic women.[32] Unlike what happened in many other households, conditions in the Depression of the 1930s did not undermine my father's role as a provider. Moreover, during World War II, my father's work for a defense contractor exempted us from the trauma of an absent father and the gendered drama of his return. In the postwar world, as was true of many Jews, African Americans, and white ethnics, I was among those who benefited from being shaped by households distant from the world of organization men, housewives trapped by seemingly meaningless work, and families isolated from kinship networks and religious traditions.

Like many other children of immigrants, Bill Horowitz was finding spaces in the economy where his talents could flourish. My father's work in the 1940s and 1950s differed from that of William H. Whyte Jr.'s 1956 "organization man," who was employed by a large, bureaucratic corporation. Nor did my father fit the pattern of the politically indifferent, timid, and faceless cogs C. Wright Mills described in *White Collar* (1951). Indeed, if I applied the typology David Riesman offered in *The Lonely Crowd* (1950), I would describe my father as an autonomous, inner-directed man. Nor was there with him an indication of

male panic observers found in postwar America which, as the historian James
Gilbert has written, caused many men to "self-consciously rebel against real
or imagined 'feminization' developing within the workplace, public spheres,
and/or domestic relationships." Although my father's sense of himself as a
self-made man who had gone from rags to riches hardly hid the role his in-
laws played, his commitment to ambition, achievement, initiative, and mastery relied on character-based self-discipline rather than personality-oriented
self-realization.[33] By contemporary and even more so by current standards
my family did not resemble the "status seekers" Vance Packard described so
tellingly in his 1959 book. Within their community, my parents had a surfeit
of social status.[34]

The domesticity and sentimentality of the 1950s hardly suffused the household. Living in an almost entirely all Jewish neighborhood close to so many
relatives meant that the claims of kinship, along with the bonds of ethnic
communal life, structured social life. What Betty Friedan was to write about
in *The Feminine Mystique* (1963) did not adequately describe what trapped
my mother. Rather, she faced situations Friedan barely mentioned, especially
the contradictions between a significant career in public life and a husband
firmly in control of the household. Unable to counter my father's power
directly or openly, she explicitly passed on to my sister an awareness that she
had to establish her independence from the man she would marry by being
financially independent and to me, more implicitly, a commitment to build
a marriage with gender dynamics different from what confined her. If my
mother almost never cooked meals or cleaned rooms, my father had no interest in proving his manliness by carrying out home repairs, developing do-it-
yourself hobbies, or participating in athletics. His interest in playing sports,
by himself or with his son, was as close to zero as possible. So much so that
when I was almost twelve years old, I placed this letter in a sealed envelope:
"I Daniel Horowitz at the age of 38 will not be interested in any sleep after
I've had 8 hours of sleep on Sundays but will only play with my children (or
child)."[35]

Unlike what happened in many families, my parents relied little if at all on
the advice on experts even if consulting a psychologist might have helped.
Instead, my mother turned to friends and relatives, and my father, as far as I
can figure out, relied on his own sense of what was right. In a firm but non-
tyrannical manner, my father seemed in control, working with my mother
cooperatively and usually delegating to her the task of implementing decisions they together had agreed on. Our parents were not our friends and their
marriage was not a companionate one; absent was the soft comfort of togeth-
erness in family life. Rather, a certain order and mild decorousness was in

play. On the five nights when the maid cooked meals at home, we had dinners served for which my father dressed in coat and tie and my mother was clothed in a degree of formality to match.

Although Paul Goodman published *Growing Up Absurd: Problems of Youth in the Organized System* in 1960, my life then seemed and still seems not at all absurd. My parents offered to me and my sister a greater sense of possibilities than present in many similar households. When I read Goodman's book soon after its publication, I sensed that its picture of society's failure to provide meaningful work, leisure, and civic engagement might apply to American society but not to me. I was not living in what contemporary critics and social scientists described as a mass society that undermined individualism, one built on anxiety over gender roles and the diminution of family authority by outside forces. I knew political engagement imparted meaning to life even as I carefully balanced commitment and spectatorship. What shaped my world were elaborate networks of family, kin, and religious and civic communities, rather than consumer culture, domesticity, and a pursuit of therapeutic self-realization. Much more than my mother did, my father modeled what it meant to be an observant Jew proud of his heritage. As was true for others, my family passed on to me commitments to civil rights for African Americans and a politics that stood on the border between New Deal liberalism and social democracy.

My father's experiences before, during, and after he went to college, along with my mother's yearnings and commitments, made sure that when I entered Yale, compared with many peers, I was better, albeit imperfectly, prepared to navigate the strange world of undergraduate life dominated by Yale men. Growing up in Kansas City, my dad learned what American citizenship meant, even though while at Yale financial hardships and his outsider status made this a dream hard for him to realize. At the same time, what my mother learned from her parents and from her Smith professor Ralph Harlow provided ideals that both dovetailed and qualified what her husband represented. Beginning in the 1940s, my parents, taking over the civic commitments my maternal grandfather exemplified, began to make their mark in public life— in New Haven's Jewish community, political, and philanthropic arenas—and by the mid-1960s at Yale as well. The commitments of my parents to vibrant worlds where culture and politics intersected was a powerful example to me, which I strove to follow in my own ways.

By the time entered Yale in 1956, my parents had passed on to me a degree of social and economic privilege that, though less than that of many of my classmates, helped make my life easier than it was for my father in the late 1920s. If his struggle to fund his education made strong academic achievement difficult, what my parents provided in the way of economic resources, models of engagement, and emotional support freed me to concentrate on my studies. Yale presented to me formidable traditions and cultural expectations that initially threatened to erode self-confidence. Yet over time the sense of security and privilege my parents gave me growing up helped ensure I could learn to navigate a Yale that still had much of the elitism and self-satisfaction he encountered in 1925.

CHAPTER TWO

Dress British

George [Pierson] had more on his mind, however. "Leonard Krieger
is coming up for promotion to full professor," he said, "and I do not
want to see this department go the way of the law school." I was
stunned. Krieger was a deeply learned historian of ideas, most com-
fortable in the early modern period, and a talented teacher. He was
also Jewish. I made a quick decision to play dumb. I knew the law
professors described the rules of their special culture as "dress Brit-
ish; think Yiddish." But I said, "What do you mean about the law
school?" "All of its recent appointments," George replied, "have been
Jews." I paused before saying, "But I'm a Jew."

JOHN MORTON BLUM, *A Life with History* (2004)

In 2010, on the eve of Elena Kagan's confirmation as an associate justice of the
United States Supreme Court, Harvard law professor Noah Feldman wrote
an op-ed piece for the *New York Times* in which he praised the WASP elite
for having opened up premier institutions of higher education to students on
the basis of merit. What he said offers one perspective on changes at Yale that
began to take place when I was an undergraduate—and in which my father
played important roles.

With a title of "The Triumphant Decline of the WASP," Feldman celebrated
how Princeton in particular, but by extension other Ivy League universities,
had transformed their admissions policies. He noted that the new approach,
which weighed the achievements and promise of applicants more than their
pedigrees, had resulted in three Princeton undergraduates—the Jewish Kagan,
the Latina Sonia Sotomayor, and the Italian American Samuel Alito—ending
up on the Supreme Court. "Unlike almost every other dominant ethnic, racial
or religious group in world history," Feldman asserted, "the very Protestant
elite that founded and long dominated our nation's institutions of higher

45

education and government" had given up its "socioeconomic power by hewing voluntarily to the values of merit and inclusion, values now shared broadly by Americans of different backgrounds. The decline of the Protestant elite," he concluded confidently, "is actually its greatest triumph." Although Feldman recognized that the elite had not relinquished power quickly or without reservation, he insisted that "the inclusiveness of the last 50 years has been the product of sincerely held ideals put into action."

Feldman ended his op-ed on an intriguing sartorial note. He celebrated how inclusion "was accompanied by a corresponding diffusion of the distinctive fashion (or rather anti-fashion) of the Protestant elite class. The style now generically called 'prep,' originally known as 'Ivy League,'" he continued, "was long purveyed by Jewish and immigrant haberdashers (the 'J' in the New Haven store J. Press stands for Jacobi) and then taken global by Ralph Lauren, né Lifshitz." Thus the spread of the Ivy League way of dressing was "not a frivolous matter. Today the wearing of the tweed is not anachronism or assimilation, but a mark of respect for the distinctive ethnic group that opened its doors to all." Except, he failed to note, that J. Press did not carry women's clothes. Gender-neutral robes for justices covered some but hardly all differences.[1]

From the 'Hood: Jewish Merchants and the Ivy League Style

In the terms Feldman used to explore the social meaning of clothing, the most interesting thing about the neighborhood that I left in 1956 was that it was home to so many of the people who shaped and purveyed the Ivy League style. With its origins in British traditions, the American version of this men's style had developed early in the twentieth century and had its collegiate heyday from the 1920s until the late 1960s. What characterized it were fashions familiar to me but then and now unfamiliar to most Americans: tweed sport coats with three buttons and natural shoulders; cuffed unpleated pants (flannel, chino, or corduroy); penny loafers or white bucks; duffle coats for informal wear and Chesterfields for more formal occasions; button-down collars on Oxford cloth shirts; Repp or Foulard ties; gray flannel suits in the winter and seersucker ones in the summer; Shetland sweaters; Madras pants, shirts, and sport jackets.[2]

"American fashion as we know it today," remarks one observer, "is a Jewish creation," as she cites Levi Strauss, Hart, Schaffner and Marx, Hickey Freeman, and Ralph Lauren.[3] For me this is a neighborhood story. Over the back fence on Colony Road was a Gant (né Gantmacher, or glove maker) household; in the early 1940s a family member, after working as a stock boy for J. Press, began selling shirts to J. Press and Brooks Brothers before founding Gant Shirts.[4] Up the street and distantly related to me was the Shapiro family, purveyors of classic button-down shirts under the label Sero, like Gant an Anglicized version of their name. Two doors down from us was the house of Eva and Jack Feinstein. When I was about twelve and the Feinstein daughter, Betsy, was about thirteen, we "married" each other in the garage of a neighbor. Eva was my mother's closest friend. Jack, with his brother Bill Fenn (presumably né Feinstein, who lived three blocks away) owned Fenn-Feinstein, one of the leading competitors of J. Press.[5] Paul Press, one of two sons of Jacobi, lived one block from where I grew up, and as a child I knew his son Richard. Among the other Jewish-owned Ivy League haberdashers who lived nearby were the Isenbergs, who owned Gentree and whose son was my high school classmate and in my sophomore year my college roommate; Alan White of White's; Arthur M. Rosenberg of the store with the same name; the Isaacs family who owned the shoe emporium Barrie, Ltd. This company developed and sold the "white shoe," made of costly buckskin and heralding its wearer as someone from a patrician family. The word "shoe" or "white shoe" meant stylishly Ivy League.[6] I should also mention one more Jewish merchant in New Haven who sold Ivy clothes to undergraduates: Morris Widder helped in the circulation of goods, purchasing used clothing from wealthy students and then reselling it to less affluent ones. When he announced that his store was closed on Saturdays, he let knowledgeable people know he was an observant Jew.

In 1942 an author writing in the *Yale Alumni Magazine* humorously noted the importance of the Ivy style, pointing out that if you saw a white-shoe man, you knew he would go far. "Chances are," he asserted, "that the man hails from New York or out on the Island (the only *chic* island in the western hemisphere is Long Island), from Greenwich, Connecticut, or from such isolated outposts of culture as Grosse Point, Lake Forest, or Pasadena, with an occasional interloper from Dixie." Purveyors of the Ivy style did indeed set the sartorial standard among college students at elite institutions. Until the late 1960s, through traveling shows they also offered their wares to students at prep schools and to loyal customers in about thirty cities outside the realms of the Ivy League and the East Coast. For a longer period they sold men's clothing in Manhattan to graduates at their stores just to the west of Grand Central Station.[7]

The history of these merchants reflects the transformation of the nation itself. What always has interested me is the complex ethnic dynamics of shops owned by Jews—who purchased materials in Great Britain; had them turned into finished goods in small-scale factories in or near East Coast cities which relied on Jewish, Italian, and later Latino workers; and then sold them to a range of customers—from established members of the elite to students from modest backgrounds who had social and sartorial aspirations that the Ivy League style might help them realize. For the first group, salesmen acted like personal servants in an upper-class household when they carefully waited on their customers. Salesmen patiently taught their aspiring clients how to dress properly. In ways surely difficult for a younger generation to comprehend, students on Ivy League campuses in the late 1950s dressed more formally than now; clothing was a major marker of inclusion and exclusion. As high school graduates from the provinces and townies like me moved from our homes to the Old Campus, we quickly learned that what we wore helped define us as Yale men. As a classmate whose life paralleled mine remarked to me, the Ivy League style reflected "the classical (or stereotypical) Yankee WASP manner of modesty in speech and deportment—the vaguely 'aw shucks' bearing that both denoted and hid genuine wealth and class." Modesty is in the eyes of the beholder, and with clothing it hid the implication of what it meant for outsiders to measure up to an elite's powerful standards. As the story of Eugene Rostow giving Alan Dershowitz funds to dress British makes clear, shopping at J. Press involved both taste and money; aspiring Yale men could learn one but did not necessarily have the other.[8]

J. Press: "More of a Club than a Clothes Shop"

The history of J. Press provides a window into these dynamics, deserving of focus both because of its prominence and because Richard Press is a superb chronicler of the world his grandfather and father made. In 1896 Jacobi Press migrated from Latvia and, deeply learned in Talmudic studies, aspired to be a rabbi. Soon he made a different choice, following an uncle into custom tailoring. In 1902 Jacobi Press struck out on his own and soon after opened his first store, at 262 York Street across from what would soon become one of Yale's residential colleges. A few steps away was the corner of York and Elm, the crossroads of the campus near which so many of the local sellers of the Ivy League style eventually had their stores.

J. Press remained a custom tailor enterprise until the early 1940s. It suspended its retail operations during World War II when the federal government strictly regulated tens of thousands of enterprises so that business efficiency would help the United States lead the Allies to victory. As befitted the company's tradition, J. Press provisioned the military with uniforms for officers. After 1945, influenced by the wartime experience of production and distribution on a larger scale, the firm decided that the future was not in custom tailoring but in retail. When Jacobi Press died in 1951, he left the firm to his two sons. Then in 1960 third-generation Richard Press began to take over the New York operations from his uncle. In 1972 J. Press licensed its brand to one of Japan's major sellers of men's clothing, Onward Kashiyama, the first time an American men's clothing company had made such an arrangement. Then, in 1986, Kashiyama bought the company itself.

The author of a 1954 essay on the Ivy League style in *Life* magazine remarked, with some exaggeration, that the J. Press store, "sometimes regarded as more of a club than a clothes shop," was "a New Haven Institution which rivals Yale in some well-tailored hearts." Avoiding what it considered the capitulation to trendiness that Brooks Brothers was guilty of, aspects of which still elude me, J. Press stuck to its commitment to offer the most traditional version of the Ivy League style.[9] Writing in the campus humor magazine in fall 1956, a member of the class of 1957 captured the socially symbolic nature of proper dress in a way that mockingly made clear that access to the Ivy style was widely available. "The Haberdasherite" understood "the supreme importance of proper *dress* as a means to acceptance and success." If during the summer, home in Sunspot, Kansas, an undergraduate "wandered about in spread collars and flaming-colored ties," back in New Haven he "sneaks out the back of the railroad station and races wildly through deserted alleys until, huffing but happy, he finally reaches Upper York Street and finds out the proper width of lapels this season."[10]

In 1980 *The Official Preppy Handbook* captured the importance of the Ivy League look and of J. Press itself. Appropriately enough, it appeared from Workman Publishing, founded by Peter Workman, a member of the Yale class of 1960. Like Noah Feldman in his *New York Times* Op-Ed piece, but with a sense of irony Feldman lacked, the handbook's authors celebrated the egalitarian dynamics of the Preppy look. "It is the inalienable right of every man, woman, and child," its authors asserted, "to wear Khaki. . . . In a true democracy everyone can be upper class and live in Connecticut. It's only fair." The handbook emphasized the importance of details in clothing too subtle for me to recognize. Too much of artificial fabric, too wide a lapel, or an insufficient commitment to Anglophilia separated the proper from the meretricious, the Kosher from the *traif*. Although there were a number of the Right Stores, among the standouts was J. Press, which for decades had "catered . . . to the ultraconservatives of the Old Guard who feel Brooks Brothers is too trendy and women's departments are an abomination."[11]

The Press family's story recapitulates dimensions of Jewish American history: from the first-generation Jacobi with a Talmudic education outside formal American institutions, to Paul with his BA from University of Pittsburgh, to Richard with his degree from Dartmouth. The movement was from Jacobi as tailor-entrepreneur, to Paul as a major regional retailer, to Richard as the international conduit. The story of J. Press also illuminates the complicated mixture of international processes that resulted in the Ivy League style. J. Press imported much of its cloth, woolens especially, from Britain and relied on immigrants as factory workers and tailors. The eventual licensing and sale of the firm to the Japanese, and the way in which by the turn of the century many more Japanese men than American ones donned J. Press clothes, completes this cycle from Britain to the United States to Japan, and even from Japan back to the United States when Japanese renditions of the Ivy style returned across the Pacific to America.[12]

This history illuminates how in the 1960s the Ivy style spread off campus even as its influence diminished on campus. The market shifted from what Richard Press called the "campus aristocracy" at elite colleges to men in government and business interested in the "propriety of dress." On Ivy League campuses, as the historian James Axtell has pointed out, the combination in the 1960s of more diverse student bodies and broader cultural shifts ended the "single stereotype" based on what Owen Johnson's *Stover at Yale* in 1912 labeled "a standard" that "had been fashioned to which, irresistibly, subtly," college men "would have to conform." By the 1970s nothing could stop what Axtell describes as the "sartorial slide into eclecticism" many aspects of which were "guaranteed to annoy parents, alumni, and the tweedy gents" still dominant in Ivy League administrations.[13]

Paul Press and my father resembled other Jews in their generation who mediated between humble origins as children of immigrants and contacts with members of the nation's establishment. Paul Press, his son later reported as he referred to his father's special relationship to Dean Acheson in the 1940s, stood "in awe of the WASP aristocracy" and, using the term for a Jewish prayer ritual, "philosophically davened before them."[14] Such men aside, many of those who shopped in the New Haven or Cambridge stores worked at local universities as faculty or senior staff, were undergraduates getting ready for a special event such as a wedding or job interview, or grads returning for a reunion. To the Manhattan store near Grand Central Station, a stone's throw away from Brooks Brothers and from Abercrombie and Fitch (before it died as a sportsmen's store and was reborn for teens), came lawyers, bankers, and ad men traveling between their central city offices and their suburban homes.

The Ivy League Style and Jews as Yale Men

The Ivy League style had special meaning for Jewish men and other sons and grandsons of immigrants. Clothing, as well as other elements of style such as stance and speech, was the means by which an outsider could become an insider; clothing could transform us into Yale men. In his *Messages from My Father* (1997), the *New Yorker* writer Calvin Trillin recalled the tensions with his father over clothing styles. His father, "a strong believer in highly shined shoes and carefully folded pocket handkerchiefs," found his son back from Yale during vacations "only sporadically presentable." On their way home from shopping locally, "having bagged only a single shirt or a pair of trousers I knew I'd never wear, the silence in the car was" painfully uncomfortable.[15] The senior Trillin wanted his son to be well dressed, but there no way he could know the protocols reigning at Yale.

As a Jew from an immigrant family in Kansas City, Trillin followed the path my father had taken a quarter century earlier. In fact, my father interviewed Trillin on an informal basis, something he frequently did for Jewish boys considering going from the Paris of the Midwest to the City of Elms. According to the story my father told me, one that may well be apocryphal but which is too good to pass up, he told Trillin that his admission to Yale was unlikely because he had received a near failing grade in a high school chemistry class after he lowered a stink bomb into an air shaft in a classroom. My father's ability to predict accurately was lacking, but that did not prevent them from becoming friends.[16]

A set of articles published in 1957 in *Ivy Magazine* amplifies the sartorial differences between students who came from public high schools and prep schools. "The lone graduate of a high school from Broken Arrow, Oklahoma, or Snowflake, Arizona," an author asserted, "entering an Ivy League school is in no position to dictate to the multitudinous hordes" from leading prep schools who had grown up as "Toddlers in Tweeds." A graduate of a high school, especially a non-elite one, arrived on campus unaware that a knowledgeable Ivy League student "practices a kind of life and sets up ideals which are foreign to him." Compared with the prep school graduate, he was what one writer in 1957 mentioned as "likely to seem a creature of incomparable blandness and vulgarity. . . . His clothes betray his outlook," bespeaking "a complete lack of breeding, genetic or acquired," for he came from "a world of TV dinners and TV sex."[17] Codes of dress and behavior described in this article became clear to me when I entered Yale in September 1956. For a student at Hillhouse High School, dressing like a Yale man was not appropriate. Giving up wearing the hand-me-downs of my younger years that the Feinstein son Steve had worn, in high school I bought my clothes at a distinctly non-preppy store oriented to townspeople.

Sartorially Deficient, I Nonetheless Enter Yale

My going to Yale was inevitable, even though my transformation from out-sider to insider was more contingent and halting. Like "a rather intimidating foreign country," Trillin wrote, Yale "seemed very much like *their* place" as he referred to students from prestigious prep schools who seemed to dominate collegiate life.[18] To many of them, entering Yale confirmed their sense of privi-lege. To me, Yale represented a reward for how diligently I had studied, how I was following in my father's footsteps, and how I might become a different person, even though I could hardly figure out what that meant. The intimida-tion of a foreign country also had an architectural dimension. "Yale was about the ugliest place I had ever seen," a classmate from Kansas City remembered. The Old Campus, where all freshmen lived, "looked like grimy, Dickensian London." To me, the outsides of Yale buildings were strange and forbidding; the interior public areas replicated the muted and unfamiliar elegance of a gentleman's club.[19]

If the gritty city that surrounded Yale was familiar to me, for those who hailed from prep schools or suburban high schools Yale's urban location might well have been threatening—something made clear when the *Yale Daily News* carried stories of locals assaulting interlopers. Once on campus those from elite prep schools were on familiar territory—green lawns, buildings whose outsides and insides were reassuringly familiar in their poshness. In contrast, I found Yale forbidding.

At some point in high school, my father, feeling that there was no college better than Yale and that as patriarch he had the right to tell me what to do, informed me that only if I went to Yale would he pay my way. Having internal-ized from a young age that I would go to Yale, I neither challenged him nor seriously considered an alternative. Beyond his insisting I go to Yale, I never felt that, apart from a generalized set of expectations, he had a specific plan. He wanted me to succeed and achieve in the world, but neither he nor my mother pressured me toward specific career goals.

My father's comfort in his own skin and as a Jew was a great gift to me. It meant I never had to compromise my identity as I faced a powerful alternative set of choices. He provided a living example of how to resist calls for assimila-tion. He was a poor boy, and I was a legacy from a prominent, well-to-do local family. He faced a hostile non-Jewish world in the late 1920s that by the late 1950s, losing its confidence and coherence, had become somewhat more welcoming. Yet, I have come to think that I took too much to heart the impli-cations of his experience of exclusion for my own life at Yale.

In applying to Yale, I faced an undergraduate admissions regime that had changed somewhat from my father's day. Although at 10 percent the proportion of Jews in my class remained roughly similar to his and legacies accounted for one in five students, the proportion of those hailing from west of the Mississippi had more than doubled, from just under 10 to about 26 percent; the percentage of those entering from public high schools had increased from the 20s to the low 40s; and the number of those from abroad, though still small, had increased by more than 50 percent to a total of fifteen classmates.[20] Several factors worked against my admission to Yale. Like my father, I was conspicuously unathletic. In addition, in summer 1956, the dean of the freshman class reported to Yale's president that the public schools in the New Haven area were "relatively poor," leaving only Hopkins Grammar School, the local private day school for boys, as the one that adequately prepared men for Yale. The dean failed to acknowledge the fact, presented in the same report without comment, that, overall, high school graduates earned noticeably higher grades at Yale and were significantly less likely to flunk out than their prep school counterparts.[21]

Yet much was in my favor. I was a legacy courtesy not only of my father but because my uncle, Norman Botwinik, had gone to Yale in the 1930s. Despite its preference for students from private schools, for decades Yale sustained a commitment to enroll graduates of New Haven's public high schools. I needed no financial aid. I earned all As in high school. I won the Connecticut American Legion oratorical contest. I was well behaved if not civilized. Although I turned in an unimpressive performance on the SATs in my junior year, with private tutoring my scores jumped significantly to levels above the average for my Yale classmates. Getting into Yale was not as competitive as it would later become. For the class of 2018 Yale let in slightly more than 6 percent of the applicants; in the late 1950s it accepted about a third of those who applied. For those admitted in the mid-1950s, the 75th percentile on the aptitude section of the SATs was 650 verbal and 710 math compared with perfect 800s fifty-five years later.[22]

Shortly before the official letters went out, I learned of my admission in a way that marked my privileged status as I transitioned from townie to Yalie. Mayor Richard C. Lee came over to 200 Colony Road one evening to tell my parents and me the news, which he knew because he served on a committee that awarded prizes to local boys headed to Yale. The $50 was a token, at a time when room, board, and tuition were $2,000. The decision to admit me reverberated with what Robert N. Corwin, the chair of the undergraduate admissions committee, had written in 1929 to a Yale trustee about the problem the university faced in keeping down the number of Jewish students. "Some of our prominent local Jews," he noted, "hold key positions politically and financially." My family fit this category. A cousin, alas not a Yale graduate, had been treasurer of the local Republican Party; my father was president of the local Jewish bank and the head of the Connecticut Board of Education; and my mother was treasurer of the city.[23]

God and Men at a Protestant Yale

In going to Yale, I was entering a Protestant institution. In 1937 President Charles Seymour had remarked that the "the simple and direct way" to teach students "to appreciate spiritual values" was "through the maintenance and upbuilding of the Christian religion as a vital part of university life." When he used the word "Christian" he meant the brand of American Protestantism represented by the mainline denominations such as Presbyterian, Episcopalian, and Congregational. In my years, to a considerable extent Yale remained a Protestant institution in ways Seymour would have recognized, given its standards for admitting students and hiring faculty. I joined the local branch of Hillel, the national Jewish organization for university students, but rarely attended its events, which were more about Jewish thought than Judaism. Saint Thomas More, the Catholic campus organization, had an even smaller public presence than Hillel. In contrast, the Yale Christian Mission Committee sponsored a weeklong and well-attended visit by Billy Graham in February of 1957, and throughout the late 1950s the Christian theologian Paul Tillich often came to campus. Although in my last two years, through the social activism of the chaplain William Sloane Coffin Jr., I encountered one strand of American Protestantism, overall I experienced Yale as a Protestant institution principally through a general sense that Yale was a club in which I would never have full membership.[24]

Yale as a Protestant institution was one theme the Roman Catholic William F. Buckley Jr. explored in his 1951 *God and Man at Yale,* an immensely influential book written by a man who would become one of the nation's most prominent conservative writers and editors. Neither Catholics nor Jews, he asserted, had "social prestige of any sort" at Yale. Perhaps true in most cases but not for him; he was not like the Catholics with whom I went to high school, whose ancestors had come from Italy and Poland, and many of whose parents who were struggling to emerge from the lower middle class. To some extent Buckley's father's wealth, derived from Texas oil, overcame the stigma his Catholicism may have imposed on his son, who graduated from Yale in 1950 as chairman of the *Yale Daily News,* captain of the debate team, and member of Skull and Bones—before entering the crowded pipeline that went from Yale to the CIA.[25]

Buckley, by describing the university as offering undergraduates a godless and collectivist education, ran into a storm of criticism. The forceful reaction to Buckley's book should undermine the confidence of those who believe in a unified conspiracy of men from Skull and Bones. Bonesman Reuben ("Ben") Holden, assistant to President A. Whitney Griswold, helped coordinate the attack. One critique came from McGeorge Bundy, someone with impeccable credentials (Boston Brahmin ancestors, Groton, Yale 1940, and Skull and Bones) and a spectacular, if often problematic, career as dean of Harvard's Faculty of Arts and Sciences, National Security Advisor to President John F. Kennedy, and president of the Ford Foundation. Writing in the *Atlantic Monthly* in November 1951, Bundy remarked that "as a believer in God, a Republican, and a Yale graduate, I find the book is dishonest in its use of facts, false in its theory, and a discredit to its author." Buckley, he continued, had launched "a savage attack on that institution as a hotbed of 'atheism' and 'collectivism' " in a book that was "clearly an attempt to start an assault on the freedom of one of America's greatest and most conservative universities." A month later the *Atlantic* published an exchange between the two adversaries. Buckley attacked the "ascendancy of 'academic freedom' cherished by these haughty totalitarians" and called his opponent a "minor Court Hatchet-Man" who offered an "intemperate," "frantic and unreasoned apologia *pro alma matre sua.*" Bundy responded that his adversary was a "violent, unbalanced, and twisted . . . young man" whose rejoinder was "almost a complete fraud."[26]

The university asked Bonesman Rev. Henry Sloane Coffin to head a committee to look into Buckley's charges. Writing to a fellow alumnus, Coffin remarked that Buckley's Roman Catholicism "distorted" his outlook. Yale, he insisted, "is a Puritan and Protestant institution by its heritage and he should have attended Fordham or some similar institution." Bonesman, former chairman of the *Yale Daily News*, Rhodes Scholar, and prep school headmaster Frank Ashburn went further, saying with undue exaggeration that Buckley's book "has the glow and appeal of a fiery cross on a hillside," to which men would go at night dressed with hoods covering their faces and robes other than academic ones.[27]

Outsiders Go Inside

The outsider category included late adolescent young men who were first in their family to go to college; who grew up Jewish or Roman Catholic; who were from African American, working-class, and lower-middle-class families; who hailed from small towns or the provinces; who focused their energies on their studies, especially in the sciences and engineering; who were not politi-cally or religiously conventional; or who in some way sensed they were gay.[28]

I was surrounded by fewer Jews than at any time in my life until then, to say nothing of so few African Americans, Roman Catholics, and poor white Protestants. Even among Jews there was a wide range of experiences and stances. At one end stood two or three classmates, including fellow townie Fred Horowitz (no relation), who did their best to follow Jewish dietary laws by having the food servers in the dining rooms prepare special meals for breakfast and lunch and then eating most dinners at a local Kosher restaurant, with the university agreeing to lower board charges. Because the Hillel rabbi played no role in negotiating such an agreement and Yale did not inform all Jewish students of provisions for making Kosher food available, theirs remained a private arrangement. To the best of my knowledge no classmate fully followed Jewish religious customs, such as putting on teffilin or going to shul more than occasionally. Typical of those at the other end was Lew Lehr-man, a German Jew whose family had come to America in the middle of the nineteenth century, who went to the Hill School, and who at Yale joined both the fraternity Fence Club and the senior society Wolf's Head.

In terms of Jewish consciousness and practices, as well as insider/outsider position, I was in the middle of the spectrum—a member of Hillel, observant on the major holidays, and figuring out what it meant to be an outsider who was curious about the customs of insiders. None of my Jewish classmates could conceive of focusing their education in Jewish studies—only in 1958 did Judah Goldin arrive, a scholar of rabbinic texts and the first Yale professor to offer multiple courses on Jewish culture and religion. There was a course on Judaism, Protestantism, and Catholicism offered, naturally enough, by a pro-fessor whose last name was Christian. A full-blown program in Judaic studies would come later, in part as a result of a fund-raising drive chaired by my father and Professor Geoffrey Hartman, at a time when Yale joined a national movement to expand the curriculum's range.[29]

What is striking about my Jewish classmates, though hardly surprising given Yale's elitist culture, is how assimilated and well-to-do most of them were on arrival at Yale—and how fully most of them, like me, once at Yale marked their status by dressing British. Few if any were from families just emerging from the lower middle class; about 33 percent were legacies (a figure well above that for the class as a whole); 18 percent came from prep schools (a figure below the class generally), 26 from private day schools; and at least 22 percent from suburban high schools. There were eleven from Hillhouse High School and five from New York City public high schools (one each from Bronx High, Music and Arts, and Midwood, and two from Erasmus), but not a single Jew from a public high school in Boston, Philadelphia, Chicago, or Baltimore. Thus in deciding which Jews to admit, Yale could fill its quota without compromising what the admissions office saw as its standards.

Most of my Jewish peers had intensely mixed feelings about being Jews at Yale. We could not hide the fact that we were Jews or try to pass, though a few among us modified their names or with plastic surgery their physiognomy. Almost all of us were sensitive to expressions of anti-Semitism, even though some of us might privately express the thought that someone else was "too Jewish." Some of us stayed away from Hillel to avoid being marked as Jewish. Many of us focused our energies on our courses. In our extracurricular pursuits we gravitated toward where we were admitted or welcomed: academic honor societies, intramural sports, student publications, the film society, WYBC, the debate team, the Political Union, and student agencies—rather than fraternities, a cappella singing groups, most varsity athletic teams, or most aboveground senior societies.[30]

In at least one case neither the university nor a classmate himself realized that someone of Jewish ancestry was among us. When Philip (Phip) Hirsh Jr. came to Yale from Andover, as his grandfather and his father had, he was unaware of the family's fabricated past. His grandfather Allan (né Abraham) Hirsh had grown up in a wealthy German Jewish family in Richmond, Virginia, and graduated from Yale in 1901. Sensing that his rejection from Skull and Bones was due to his being a Jew, he buried his past after graduation, married a Protestant from a prominent family, and earned a fortune as an inventor and businessman who refused to hire Jews. Allan's son inherited some of his father's wealth and all of his prejudices.[31]

What helped separate my classmate from his progenitors were the summers he spent on the family's farm in Virginia, where his contact with white and African American servants opened him to a world of decency, kindness, and genuine work absent from his family's life. These summers, he wrote in *Voices from the Hollow: What Happened When Blue Bloods Met the Blue Ridge* (2005), were "the start of a cumulative process that ultimately saved me from becoming another vector in the family dysfunction, a kind of pathology based on elitism, intense prejudice, and an over-inflated sense of our importance." All this enabled him to veer from the path his father had chosen for him and instead become a psychiatrist. Hirsh uncovered his Jewish ancestry not long after finishing medical school, only later to discover documents that fully revealed the ironies of the family secret. In the 1990s, he found material in the attic of the family home that enabled him to figure out that, while still at Yale, his grandfather, with the unacknowledged help of earlier African American songsters and three classmates, had written the quintessentially Yale song

"Boola Boola." As was true of clothing from J. Press, Jews helped create for Yale men the external symbols that allowed students and alumni to engage in rituals of belonging.[32]

In contrast, Monroe Price was a classmate who understood from a very early age what it meant to be a Jew. I came to know Hirsh only when research-ing this book; Price I met in the fall of 1957. He is, as my daughter says with only partial accuracy, the only person she knows who is on five university fac-ulties (London School of Economics, Oxford, Yeshiva, Central European Uni-versity, and Penn) but teaches at none; in fact, he does teach at Penn, where he directs the Center for Global Communications Studies at the Annenberg School for Communication.

In his memoir, *Objects of Remembrance*(2009), Price explores what it means to have lived the first months of his life in post-Anschluss, German-occupied Austria. With his father jailed during Kristallnacht and then released, the family escaped to America. Monroe came to Yale from Cincinnati's public, selective Walnut Hills High School, whose principal, Harold Howe II, rec-ommended him to his brother, Yale's director of undergraduate admissions. Tall, ungainly, and without the polish of our prep school peers, Price arrived at Yale when his father, who in Austria had owned a large textile firm, was unemployed. Price more than fulfilled his promise: at Yale, senior editor of the *Yale Daily News* and editor in chief of the class book; at Yale Law School, executive editor of the *Yale Law Journal*; and at the Supreme Court, clerk for Associate Justice Potter Stewart. In his memoir Price mentions my father as an important mentor who adopted him because "he saw in me someone who was making a journey similar to his, from a protected but strong identity of the past that could survive and distinguish itself in the complexity of Yale."[33]

If, as Price says, the real undergraduate curriculum was ambition, Yale Col-lege provided multiple paths forward.[34] For me, gaining my intellectual foot-ing involved seeing grades as evidence of whether I was saved or damned as I struggled to learn from professors and peers how to think, write, and speak more effectively. My rise in the world would not be like my father's, from pov-erty to wealth, but like that of the teachers and friends on whom I modeled myself: from ignorance and naiveté to intellectual growth. In contrast, for most of my classmates the classroom and the life of the mind more generally were peripheral. They would get where they were going by garnering through extracurricular activities the skills and connections necessary to get ahead. Faculty and administrators often complained, reported Bryant Wedge and James Davie in 1958, "that campus life is too distressingly faithful a reproduc-tion of the intense competition of American business life." This undermined their "cherished conviction that the college years should be devoted to a life of quiet contemplation rather than one of frenetic activity." In contrast, most Yale students viewed joining a fraternity, playing on a varsity team, making money working for a student agency, or writing for a campus publication "as a practical preparation for later life." In Wedge and Davie's view, most Yale men did their best to "observe the adult world with all its competitiveness, commercialism and emphasis on action rather than thought, form their own conception of what constitutes success in adult life, and busy themselves accordingly."[35]

As a Yale undergraduate I did experience some combination of "feelings of envy, inadequacy, and outrage," that Lynda Glennon, a townie of my generation later felt about the university. Once I made the transition from Hillhouse High School to Yale College, I could begin to discover the qualities of America's elites previously hidden from me. Classmates from prep schools were initially better able than I to scope out how to read a book, write a paper, or take a test. As one classmate from a Kansas City high school later remarked, in our first year those who had gone to prep schools had a "huge head-start" academically.[36] Similarly, if Hillhouse had social and academic pecking orders that placed me at the top, Yale's social hierarchies placed me somewhere in the middle. Now I was surrounded by graduates of prestigious prep schools and scions of some of the nation's wealthiest and most prominent families. One of my classmates was a descendent of the entrepreneur and art collector H. O. Havemeyer, and one benefited from wealth derived from the discovery of the Comstock Lode in the 1860s. Another came to Yale with legacies that included his father, a brother, a grandfather, and seven uncles from both the Crosby and Pillsbury families that helped build General Mills into a prominent food-processing company. The roster of classmates also included Alfred Thayer Mahan Jr., whose name will be familiar to historians who know his ancestor's 1890 book on the importance of sea power, and Buck Schieffelin, a descendent of John Jay. At least one Jew came from a world I did not know: Conrad Cafritz, his father a Washington, DC, real estate magnate and his mother a convert to Judaism and prominent hostess in the nation's capital.

Only once, and then indirectly, did I hear an anti-Semitic slur, when a fellow Yalie mentioned "jewing" someone down in price. Yet in a profound way, like most of those from a background like mine, I knew both my own place and my inability, even had I wished to do so, to enter other worlds. One incident underscores my sense of boundaries I did not then wish to cross. In the spring of my junior year, Thomas Howard Fitchett Stick, who lived down the hall from me, graciously invited me to his wedding to Rosalie Wade Reynolds, a descendant of Maryland gentry. At the last minute, I turned down his invitation, for several reasons including a feeling that theirs was a world I did not belong in.

My one public effort to combat anti-Semitism at Yale came in my senior year. With Charlie Newman, I unsuccessfully protested to the class officers the plans to hold our senior prom at the New Haven Lawn Club (where his parents were members), at a time when it was not notably receptive to Jews as members. My parents had often talked of their disapproval of Eugene Rostow's joining the exclusive club as a token Jew rather than publicly challenging its restrictive policy. In early June 1960, just before I graduated, I wrote to Helen that behind our backs one of the Yale deans had earlier called Newman and me "blackmailers . . . for refusing to go to the senior prom because it was to be held at a club which had questionable membership policies."[37]

Conscience of a Christian: William Sloane Coffin Jr.

The issue found its way to William C. DeVane (Savannah-born, Yale BA, Phi Beta Kappa, and PhD), who had turned down a score of offers of college presidencies to stay at Yale, where he served as dean of Yale College for a quarter of a century beginning in 1938. DeVane, Coffin remembered, called Yale's newly installed chaplain. "Bill," DeVane said, "do we have to take this protest seriously?" "Dean DeVane, yes," Coffin responded. "Thank you," DeVane replied, "that's all I needed to hear from you." Newman and I had no sense of how to mobilize opposition and the class held the prom at the Lawn Club.[38]

At the time Coffin was determined to fight prejudice against Jews and African Americans as he looked for issues to wake students from political and social apathy. He simultaneously represented and reconfigured what the Yale man was: manly, tough, and aggressive. He had political commitments more typical of a rebel than a College man.

Coffin was a third-generation Bonesman and a third-generation Yale man but, as Helen recently remarked, a first-generation *mensch*. His uncle Henry, discussed above as a defender of Yale against the attack from Buckley, was president of Union Theological Seminary and a member of the Yale Corporation. Bill's father, William Sloane Coffin Sr., followed Henry and their father into Skull and Bones, and at Yale Bill headed, as had his brother, Dwight Hall, the campus branch of the YMCA. After Yale, Coffin Sr. returned to Manhattan, where he became a prominent businessman and philanthropist.

Yale's chaplain grew up in a two-story, seventeen-room penthouse on Manhattan's Upper East Side and on an eighty-acre estate in Oyster Bay, until the Depression and his father's death in 1933 undermined the family's position. He went to Deerfield and Andover, studied piano with a series of prominent teachers, and began at Yale in the Music School in 1942 before leaving to serve in World War II as a military intelligence officer.

He then returned to New Haven, this time to Yale College, and in his senior year to membership in Skull and Bones. After graduating in 1949 he spent a year at Union Theological, and then from 1950 to 1953 worked in the CIA, where he trained Soviet citizens as spies for the United States. He earned a BD at Yale Divinity School in 1956, the same year he married Eva Rubinstein, the daughter of the Jewish-born pianist Artur. Before coming to Yale in 1958 as chaplain, Coffin had served in the same position at Andover and then at Williams College—where students fired shots into his house after he criticized the privileges and exclusivity of fraternity life. By the time he returned to Yale he had commitments to what his biographer Warren Goldstein called "a left-liberal, social democratic internationalism" and neo-orthodox Protestantism based on the teachings of Reinhold Niebuhr. An antiwar and civil rights activist, he was, Goldstein asserted in 2004 "after Martin Luther King Jr., the most significant liberal religious voice in the United States for the past forty years." In the late 1950s Coffin dressed British and was a compelling wordsmith and speaker. Coffin, Goldstein noted, was "physically imposing, athletic, and trim into his fifties, a tough guy who could drink hard and face anyone down, and his powerful masculinity shone through in whatever he did."[39]

In many ways Coffin served me at Yale, as Ralph Harlow had my mother at Smith, as a model of a fighter for social justice, although it was not until later that I realized how fundamentally his Christianity undergirded his progressive politics. Aside from meeting over the protest against the location of the prom, our lives came together in other ways. In fall 1959, my father arranged for the two Bills (Horowitz and Coffin), Monroe Price, and me to go to a Lubavicher synagogue in Brooklyn where we celebrated Simchat Torah, the joyful ceremony at the end of a cycle of Torah reading. Dozens of bearded elders carried all four of us aloft until they delivered us to the bimah, the platform on which rabbis read the Torah. Then Coffin delivered the invocation at our commencement, reminding us of the importance of leading authentic lives. He passionately intoned against "the clamorous desires of self-preservation, the trivial, the superficial, and all the pervasive and powerful perversions of our time that would cheapen the humanity of human beings."[40]

Catalysts for Change from Privilege to Merit

In my senior year, their close friendship still in the future, the two Bills worked to change Yale's discriminatory admissions policies in an effort that marked a critical element in the shift from the 1950s to the 1960s. In September of 1957 the campus newspaper used the case of "Morris Ash," a fictional but identifiably Jewish name, from a public high school in Bridgeport as someone whom Yale accepted but denied financial aid. Despite "extremely high academic promise," he showed no evidence of participation in extracurricular activities or of popularity with peers.[41] Gatekeepers kept down the number of outsiders, Jews especially, because they assumed they would focus too much on academics and not contribute broadly to life at Yale. Reality challenged such claims. In 1953 Yale admitted Calvin Trillin, a graduate of a public high school who despite his first name was a Jew, and André Schiffrin, the son of Jewish refugees from France who came to Yale on a scholarship. At graduation, Trillin held the coveted positions of editor of the *Yale Daily News* and Class Historian and Schiffrin was Class Orator, all of which demonstrated that Jews could be well respected and even well rounded, that they could join the club and retain their identity as Jews.

Even under an Old Blue order, undergraduate admissions had begun to change in the 1940s. For decades some alumni, Jews especially, had urged Yale's presidents to emphasize merit more and pedigree less. Immediately after World War II, veterans came to Yale under the G.I. Bill and in the process helped transform the composition of the student body. Yet during and after World War II, as Yale looked more widely for applicants, it focused not on high schools in the Northeast, where Jews, ethnic Catholics, and African Americans were so numerous, but on public schools elsewhere: the Midwest, far West, and white South especially. In the late 1940s and 1950s, university officials fought pressure from civil rights groups working to persuade the Connecticut legislature to make it illegal to discriminate in undergraduate admissions. Competition with Harvard for talented students also played a major role in pushing Yale toward more emphasis on diversity and merit. In the 1930s, Harvard's president James Bryant Conant started the National Scholarship Program, an effort to develop a more diverse and talented student body by recruiting, among others, the children and grandchildren of immigrants. The stakes were considerable, involving much more than who went to Yale College. "The struggle over admissions," writes the historian Geoffrey Kabaservice, "was a small but significant part of a national debate over the structure of opportunity and social mobility in America. The admissions issue was inextricably bound up with thorny issues of race, class, the logic of meritocracy, the composition of the 'establishment,' and the nature of higher education and American society in the late 20th century."[42]

The campaign to change the situation at Yale intensified with the arrival of Hillel rabbi Richard J. Israel in 1959. He approached the dean of Undergraduate Admissions with his concerns. Israel then asked my father to join the effort. On April 5, 1960, my father met alone with his classmate, Yale's president A. Whitney Griswold—descended from Eli Whitney on his mother's side and from six governors of colonial Connecticut on his father's, a graduate of Hotchkiss, a member of Wolf's Head as an undergraduate, and awarded his Yale PhD in 1933, with the nation's first doctorate in American studies.[43]

Griswold represented and led a Yale in transition, in the process revealing that he was both a throwback and an innovator. In private he made clear his disdain for what he called "Bonesy bullshit" and "that Dink Stover crap." Yet as president he often took conservative positions, even as he insisted on the primacy of academics over athletics. In 1952 he supported the imposition of a coat-and-tie rule for undergraduates (which I resisted at Yale and then helped undermine in the late 1960s at Harvard) to help tame unruly students who came to Yale and were resistant to dressing British. He attacked public high schools as "rotten pilings" of the nation's education system and defended Yale for continuing to admit so many white Anglo-Saxon Protestant graduates of prep schools because immigrants and their progeny "through lack of previous opportunity, failed to comprehend [liberal education] and therefore failed to support it." African Americans were equally "beyond the pale, so to speak, of the liberal arts." Using coded language, he remarked that the ideal Yale man was well-rounded and not narrowly focused.[44]

The composition of the class of 1957 makes the results of admissions policies clear. Graduates of private schools comprised a majority of those enrolled. Trillin, who was a member of the class and a product of a midwestern public high school, remarked that to his father (and I might add that to my paternal grandfather and my father as well) the promise of Yale was that it would "turn the likes of us into the likes of them," not in terms of dress but of opportunity. They may have set the tone for social life, but, Trillin remarked, "there was widespread circumstantial evidence that, on the whole, we were smarter than they were." As he said about his arrival at Yale in 1953, "the appearance of the bright outsider was no longer accidental. There was a broad and conscious movement into the white middle class and toward the West, a sort of *apertura* to the yahoos."[45]

In asking to meet with Yale's president, my father made it clear that he was doing so as a loyal alumnus and not as chair of the Connecticut State Board of Education, although the polite assurance was reminder enough of his official position. Nor did he need to remind Yale's president that as governor of Connecticut another Jew, Abraham Ribicoff, had an ex officio seat on the Yale Corporation, as did the Irish American lieutenant governor John Dempsey. My father presented Griswold with statistics showing how constant during the 1950s the number of Jews entering Yale College and Yale School of Medicine was. With his usual politeness and diplomatic skill, Bill Horowitz remarked that the figures indicated the existence of a "quota," something "contrary to the spirit of a University," which he was bringing to Griswold's "attention for consideration." Soon after my father left his office, Griswold dictated a memo, which my father did not know about until Dan Oren did his research for his book on the history of Jews at Yale. In his memo, Griswold took my father's politeness for agreement and defended the university's record by noting "the tremendous improvement in the position of Jews at Yale" since he and my dad were undergraduates. He asserted that the most common complaints came not from Jews but from Gentiles who believed Yale was discriminating against their sons. The president "assured Mr. Horowitz" that he would bring the issue to the admissions committee. He "would make it my own duty" to pursue the criticisms my father had lodged, and he reaffirmed "that our aim would continue to be to find students of the proper qualities whether they were Jews or non-Jews." Griswold then moved quickly to investigate what my father had alleged but ran into resistance and reassurances from those involved in admissions.[46]

A September 1960 article in the *New Yorker* had publicly revealed the intricacies of admissions procedures at Yale, making clear just how much weight the office placed on manliness, physical appearance, family background, and personality and consequently how much brainy grinds were in disfavor. So in the fall of 1960 Rabbi Israel turned to Coffin, whom he had judged, Coffin later remarked, as "a goy for whom there is hope." Tough and skillful in his meeting with Griswold and cloaked in figurative if not literal clerical garb, Coffin told him that "the conscience of Yale" was not going to rest until Yale admitted more Jews. Griswold replied testily, asking the chaplain what he expected him to do. When Coffin responded that the president should investigate, Griswold answered "angrily," telling Coffin to do his own investigating. Fine, he replied, if the president would authorize him to do so in writing. "Go to hell, Coffin" was the immediate response, but within a day Coffin had his letter. The campaign that Israel (without access to Griswold) and my father (with access but an outsider to the Yale systems of governance) had started, Coffin intensified. After all, Coffin had social equality with Griswold, the chutzpah born of his religious authority, and his fiery and assertive masculinity. A skillful worker of the university's bureaucracy, in spring 1961 Coffin began to rely on his peers among the chaplains, the alumni Council on Religious Life and Study (headed by his legendary predecessor and fellow Bonesman Sidney Lovett), and the investigative authority Griswold granted him. Israel produced a study that revealed Yale had the lowest percentage of Jewish undergraduates in the Ivy League, lower even than Princeton or Dartmouth.[47]

Soon things began to move relatively quickly. In contrast to the continuing and powerful support for the status quo from most alumni, intensified pressure for change came from *Yale Daily News* and from many faculty members, including Paul Weiss, son of immigrants, high school dropout, City College BA, and Harvard PhD. In 1946 he had joined the faculty of Yale College as its only Jewish full professor, and his son Jonny was a member of the class of 1960. In 1961 Griswold appointed a committee that in the following year issued a report, named after its chair, Leonard Doob, and which Karabel has called "a watershed document" and "a meritocratic manifesto." Charged with focusing on the experience of undergraduates in their first year and aware of the challenges of Harvard to Yale and of the new importance of brains rather than pedigrees in winning the Cold War, the Doob Committee quickly broadened its scope to focus on the relationship between undergraduate admissions and intellectual life and on the shift from a college to a university model for undergraduate education. The committee included, among others, William C. DeVane and Eugene Rostow, then dean of the Yale Law School and wiser than he had been earlier about Yale's discriminatory policies.[48]

In its deliberations, members of the committee were especially concerned, Doob reported later in dismay, with "the fact that almost no students from the Bronx High School of Science were admitted, and that these were serious, lower-class New York boys, Jewish in many cases, who had a real interest in science, and they weren't the well-rounded types." The report, published in the *Yale Alumni Magazine* in June 1962, was discreet, making no mention of legacies, Jews, or other groups. Yet its meaning was clear. Because the university was "first and foremost an intellectual enterprise," the aim of undergraduate admissions, the report urged, should be to "attract students of intellectual distinction," admitting those who "demonstrate powerful intellectual interests and commitments." The class of 1967 was the first one in which the numbers of high school and prep school graduates were roughly equal, a goal Harvard had attained in the 1940s and Princeton in the mid-1950s. The result of Griswold's efforts, Oren has written, was that "training future Nobel prize winners and America's intellectual leaders was to be valued as highly as training the nation's social, political or business leadership long had been." In March 1962 Griswold issued a directive that began to reshape admissions policy.[49]

In focusing my discussion of admission on Jews, I do not mean to imply that they had an exclusive hold on merit, with no other group having a justifiable basis for feeling excluded. I concentrate on Jews for several reasons. To begin with, most of the historical scholarship focuses on them; there is, for example, hardly any scholarship on how elite, private colleges and universities discriminated against Roman Catholics. As we will see later, in the late

1950s there was some discussion about admitting women to Yale and about more systematically recruiting African Americans. However, it was not until well into the 1960s that these efforts bore much fruit. In the late 1950s there was also silence on the issue of broadening the scope of admissions in ways that would have brought to campus more Latino, Asian American, international, working-class, or truly poor students. Finally, historical circumstances made Jews stand-ins for a more capacious vision of whom Yale and similar institutions should admit. The history of anti-Semitism, knowledge of the Holocaust, the association of Jews with learning, the increasing importance of science, and greater mobilization of Jews among alumni all made Jews, for the time being, a leading indicator of broader changes.

Keeping a Secret

While advocating the entry of greater numbers of academically talented Jews, Doob kept a secret from his family and colleagues—that he was a Jew by birth, something his Christian wife accidently discovered in the late 1950s but that no one at Yale may have been aware of. When Doob got off the train in White River Junction in September 1925 to enter Dartmouth, he decided to put aside his origins as a Jew, responding with "Free Thinker" to the question on a form that asked for his "Church preference," even though while at Dartmouth he did not hide his political radicalism. As a senior majoring in psychology, he worked on a project researching the political attitudes of Dartmouth undergraduates, whose results his mentor Gordon Allport published in the *American Journal of Sociology*. Allport concluded that the most radical students, a high percentage of whom were Jews or Roman Catholics, had strong academic records, little social prejudice, and low levels of political misinformation. They were rebellious nonconformists; "*aggressive*," Allport insisted, because they broke the rules by refusing to answer the college's question about religious affiliation. As he graduated, Doob offered a summary of Allport's findings in a campus publication, with at least one difference: he did not mention Jews. Doob was saying goodbye to Dartmouth in a way that suggested his politics were radical, his academic performance high, his rebellion against his father in place, his prejudice minimal, and his Jewish identity a secret. A third of a century later, he advocated that Yale change its admissions policies to welcome the kind of students Allport and he admired.[50]

As a scholar who works hard to understand historical figures as they saw themselves and who remains very proud of being a Jew, I find the story of Doob's life haunting. Before World War II, writes Oren in his splendid *Joining the Club: A History of Jews and Yale,* "Jewish faculty existed in an intellectual and social demimonde." When he was deciding to join the Yale faculty, Doob most likely knew about the anti-Semitic treatment of Edward Sapir, a distinguished linguist and anthropologist who arrived at Yale in 1931 and soon experienced anti-Semitism. Doob doubtlessly understood that to have a professorial career worthy of his talents he would have to hide that he was a Jew. Until 1959, Oren notes, only one Jewish professor, the philosopher Paul Weiss, consistently and openly evidenced interest in Jewish issues. The news that Doob was a Jew, reported here for the first time in print, increases the number of Jewish full professors on the faculty of Yale College in 1950 when Yale promoted him to that rank. Perhaps President A. Whitney Griswold, surely unaware that Doob was a Jew, picked this very private but professionally accomplished professor to chair a major committee on undergraduate life and admissions because as a social psychologist he wrote extensively on how to change attitudes toward race and ethnicity. To Doob's credit, as a scholar and professor he fought racism and anti-Semitism.[51]

The Quickening Pace of Change

After my graduation, the transformation in Yale's undergraduate admissions accelerated. Elite members of the Yale community continued to play crucial roles: most notably, Kingman Brewster, a direct descendant of Elder Brewster who came to America on the *Mayflower* and who had turned down membership in Skull and Bones and who succeeded Griswold as president. In 1965 Brewster hired R. Inslee (Inky) Clark (Air Force ROTC, president of interfraternity council, Skull and Bones, editor of class book, major "Y" in golf) to transform undergraduate admissions. Also key was Brewster's special assistant Henry ("Sam") Chauncey Jr. (Groton, Yale 1957, Wolf's Head, major "Y" in hockey), who played a role in shaping admissions policy under Brewster, as his father had at Harvard under Conant.[52]

Events beyond New Haven also played crucial roles in fostering change. Anti-Semitism had declined dramatically from the 1930s to the 1960s. The 1964 Civil Rights Act denied federal funds to any academic institution that discriminated on the basis of race or national origins. Baby boomers swelled the ranks of college-bound students. Changes in media and transportation made it easier for some high school students to hear of Yale and then travel from their hometowns to New Haven. The insurgencies of African Americans, students, and feminists undermined traditional assumptions about whom to admit.

The result was dramatic changes in the composition of an entering class, the texture of life at Yale College, and the dynamics of the connections undergraduates could make. SAT scores soared. From 1960 to 1970, the percentage of African Americans increased from well under 1 to 9. Between 1960 and 1966, the percentage of Jews just about tripled from 11 to over 30. The numbers of Roman Catholics grew substantially but not as significantly. The numbers of graduates from public high schools rose while those from private schools fell. The percentage of legacies fell from close to 25 to just over 10. In 1969 Yale admitted women and in 1970 began to actively recruit Latinos.

The revolution was complete but partially reversible. The alumni reaction to what Brewster and Clark wrought was forceful. By 1969 Clark had moved on to become headmaster of the New York City private school Horace Mann. With the class of 1977 the percent of legacies returned to levels that had prevailed before 1962, although some of them were now daughters. Still, the changes that Griswold began and then Brewster intensified were not easily undone: by 1976, the class of 1980 contained 40 percent women, 13 percent people of color, and 33 percent Jews.[53]

The shift from inherited privilege to merit struck especially hard those who bemoaned the losses of the old boy Yale culture. Looking back on the Brewster years, in 2000 a member of the class of 1955 wrote the editor of the *Yale Alumni Magazine* that "like Lenin, Brewster was a social engineer who indeed changed the environment under his jurisdiction." He excoriated the president for denigrating fraternities "with meaningless pejoratives like 'elitist.'" Combining a focus on social class, manners, and dress with a fantasy of frat boys as connoisseurs, he went on to "compare nursing a fine brandy over billiards after a delicious steak at the DKE house to, in later times, dyspeptically wolfing deli lunch meat in a bleak activity room at a residential college" and then to "contrast the upbeat appearance created by the coat-and-tie dress code of the 1950s to the post-Brewster years, when campus fashions resemble casual day in a county jail." In the end what annoyed this alumnus the most was the disappearance from admissions decisions and from the college of what was actually a mythical past: the "happy, golden, bygone, non-ideological days, when individuals were just individuals and were not judged or classified in WASP or minority categories or by their socioeconomic status."[54]

"One Word: Harvard"

To understand what was on Griswold's mind when my father raised the issue of discrimination in undergraduate admissions, I turned to an experienced higher education administrator. "One word: Harvard," replied Mary Patterson McPherson, longtime president of Bryn Mawr and later vice president of the Mellon Foundation and executive officer of the American Philosophical Society.[55]

By the late 1940s, concerns were growing within the upper reaches of Yale's administration that the university's intellectual achievements and reputation were problematic. In his Annual Report to the President of 1947–48, DeVane wrote: "What I want for Yale College is an intellectual eminence that is as great as her athletic or her social. . . . For the man of intellectual achievement I am afraid we are surpassed by Harvard, Columbia, and Chicago." Yet any attempt to transform Yale into a place where among students ideas mattered more than breeding or manners was up against considerable odds. In 1951, at the time of the university's 250th anniversary, *Time* declared, "Yale is a dynasty, perhaps the most inbred of all ivy league colleges." Intellectually and academically motivated students headed to Cambridge, not New Haven.[56]

Griswold was aware of the competition. For the class of 1961, Harvard bested Yale by a ratio of four to one in the National Merit Scholarships.[57] In Griswold's graduating class of 1929, Yale had bested Harvard in the Rhodes competition and then continued to triumph over its rival. In 1955 and the following five years, Harvard did better than Yale every year except one, when they tied. In the fall of 1957 an editorial in the *Yale Daily News* remarked that Yale could win a greater share of Rhodes if the admissions office followed Harvard and redressed the balance between well-roundedness and distinctiveness. In my senior year five Yale men won Rhodes but, the *Yale Daily News* noted, there were seven from Harvard.[58] The profiles of my peers who won Rhodes scholarships that year reveals how the Rhodes committee was leading the way in reconfiguring the meanings of excellence and leadership— away from a reliance on athletic performance toward broader definitions of achievement. Of the five who earned Rhodes in late 1959, only two could have been seen as a traditional Yalie: Jonathan Dewey Blake (Deerfield Academy, captain of Yale's varsity cross country team) and Ralph C. Bryant III (son and grandson of alums, Exeter). Yet Blake was the son not of a famous member of the national elite but of a headmaster of a private school, and Bryant earned distinction at Yale through academic achievement and political activity on the left that stemmed in good measure from his being a Quaker.

Three others represented the Yale then birthing. Leslie Epstein (kicked out of the Webb School, a prep school in Southern California) was a Jew admitted to Yale only at the last minute. In our junior year, Yale suspended him temporarily for suggesting to the mayor of New Haven, as he was exiting Fenn-Feinstein, that he was there to collect a bribe. When Griswold learned the news of Epstein's Rhodes while skating at the Yale hockey rink, Epstein later reported, "He fell flat on his ass and cried out, 'What? That rude young man?!'" Epstein—whose father and uncle earned Oscars for the screenplay for *Casablanca* and whose son Theo at twenty-eight was hired as general manager of the Boston Red Sox, which he soon led to a World Series triumph—described himself as the inventor of the "only sandwich in the world that has meat on the outside," even though he himself had a distinguished career as a novelist and teacher.[59] The second of the new breed was Richard Celeste (class of 1959), an Italian American and high school graduate from Lakewood, Ohio. While at Yale he earned membership in Phi Beta Kappa and a major "Y" in fencing and was national president of the Methodist student movement. The third was Howard Kaslow, a Jew and graduate of a public high school in Omaha who excelled academically at Yale.

Thus, three graduates of prep schools, one of whom had been thrown out of both his prep school and Yale. Two Jews. Only two serious athletes, not hockey or football players but a cross country runner and a fencer, sports that often attracted students who were more academically oriented than the usual college man. Of the five, only two were members of aboveground senior societies—both Blake and Epstein joined Elihu, itself a relative parvenu and one of the two that chose creative and intellectual types in significant numbers. Equally significant, both Celeste and Bryant were active in Challenge, a political organization of the late 1950s that pointed forward to an even more engaged politics of the 1960s.

Ivory Tower in a Changing World

None of these Rhodes Scholars majored in the sciences, math, or engineering—and Yale's weakness in those fields concerned Griswold when he thought about attracting superb students and faculty outside the university's traditional strength in the humanities and, more unevenly, in the social sciences. Had Griswold been able to peer into the future, he would have learned that the six men who were undergraduates at Yale after World War II who went on to earn Nobel Prizes all had Jewish ancestors.[60] Moreover, in the late 1950s, there was no Nobel laureate on the Yale faculty, while Harvard had four. During World War II and in the immediate postwar world, Yale was not in a strong position—compared to its overall prestige born of its social cachet and its reputation for producing political and business leaders—in the quickly emerging competition for corporate, foundation, and government research funds for the sciences or even the social sciences.

Yale's disadvantages were many. Conant, Harvard's president from 1933 to 1953, was a chemist deeply involved in the development of federal support for science, whereas Yale's presidents from 1937 to 1963, Seymour and Griswold, were humanists and gentlemen scholars turned administrators. Indeed Griswold, a strong advocate of liberal arts education, opposed the university's support of institutes and applied research and remained distrustful of outside funding. In the key field of nuclear physics the university came late to the game. Students from prep schools avoided the sciences and instead flocked to philosophy, art history, English, history, and American studies. In sum, in critical ways Yale was too gentlemanly, too committed to the styles and manners evoked by dressing British. Policies governing undergraduate admissions and faculty hiring, to say nothing of campus culture, impeded the recruitment of first-rate scientists.[61]

The historian Roger Geiger has characterized postwar Yale as "an ivory tower aloof from the research economy" then rapidly in formation.[62] The results are clear from an examination of funding from the National Science Foundation (NSF).[63] Begun in 1950, the NSF came to play a key role in how university administrators thought about their institution's strengths and weaknesses. Its budget grew, especially with the Soviet launching of *Sputnik* in 1957. In the intensifying and momentous competition for funding and talent in the sciences, Yale was losing out—not only to Harvard but also to flagship public universities and even to some elite private colleges.[64] With relatively few wealthy alumni committed to the sciences as a high priority, a president and his development office faced a daunting if not impossible task of replacing NSF funding with endowment income.[65] By the end of the 1960s federal grants brought in more money than income from the endowment. Federal grants helped underwrite financial aid for undergraduates and enhanced the power of faculty who wanted new directions in admissions policy as opposed to those alumni satisfied with the status quo.[66] So when my father went to see Griswold in the spring of 1960, the president probably had on his mind the intersection of strength in the sciences, competition with Harvard, the admissions of talented Jews, and budgetary relief. With Brewster, the situation was clearer. He came to Yale from Harvard and for his inauguration he sponsored a symposium on the relationships between the federal government and the university.[67]

My Father Joins the Club

In 1964 my father ran by petition for a seat on the Yale Corporation. The victor, one of three officially nominated candidates, was John V. Lindsay (St. Paul's, Yale 1943, Scroll and Key), then a Republican member of the U.S. House of Representatives from Manhattan's Upper East Side and soon to be mayor of New York. Not to be deterred, backed by family, friends, and by his own chutzpah, Bill Horowitz ran by petition again a year later when he learned that the official nominees were three corporate executives with only moderately distinguished records, none of them as well known as Lindsay.[68] This time he was victorious, the first person to win a full term on the Corporation by petition. He defeated, among others, the president of the Missouri and Pacific Railroad, the very company my paternal grandfather had worked for as a laborer almost sixty years before. "Trustee of Yale Breaks Tradition" the *New York Times* headline remarked, pointing out that he would be the first non-Protestant to serve on the Corporation.[69] The board he joined included representatives of the nation's elite. In 1968 on it were six members of Skull and Bones, three of Scroll and Key, one each of Wolf's Head and Berzelius. Most of them had distinguished lineages and all of them had gone to prep schools. No wonder my father loved the way Harry Golden's 1958 book *Only in America* celebrated the fulfillment of the promise of American life, for Jews especially.[70]

My father talked little to family members about positions he took on the Corporation. Yet his elevation intensified rather than diminished his sense of himself as a Jew, precisely when Jewishness as ethnicity was growing in importance in the nation. Just as he brought a bit of Yale to an Orthodox community in New York City when he took Monroe Price, Bill Coffin, and me to a service, so he brought something of his religious and ethnic commitments to Yale. In 1971 when, serving as acting master of Branford, one of Yale's residential colleges, he placed a Mezuzah on the front doorpost of the master's residence, led the Orthodox celebration of Simchat Torah as it spilled over into the college's courtyard, distributed Hanukah gelt to undergraduates, hosted a Yiddish table in the dining hall, and transformed the annual Christmas dinner for students and staff to a Christmas-Hanukah party.[71] While on the Corporation, my father supported Brewster's effort to protect Coffin when he was under attack for his antiwar views. At the same time he was managing some of Coffin's investments and with my mother worked mightily, though unsuccessfully, to save Coffin's marriage to Eva Rubinstein. In 1968 he testified on Coffin's behalf in a federal court when he was on trial for supporting draft resisters. I also know my father was an enthusiastic supporter of Yale's admitting women. And in spring 1970, he responded to Vice President Spiro Agnew's criticism of Brewster by stating, "I frankly do not believe that your experience as a President of a PTA chapter qualifies you to evaluate the contributions to education by the most distinguished university president in the United States."[72]

Near my desk sits a reminder of my father's role in fostering changes at Yale. Next to a picture of my father, dressed in his best three-piece Fenn-Feinstein suit, is a note written at a meeting of the Yale Corporation on May 15, 1971. It was from William Scranton (scion of a family that has a Pennsylvania city named after it, Hotchkiss, Yale 1935, Berzelius), who wrote to A. Leon Higginbotham Jr. (son of a maid and factory worker, Antioch College, Yale Law School, NAACP activist, federal judge, and in 1969 Yale's first African American trustee). With tongue in cheek, Scranton remarked in private that "Bill [Horowitz] is one of the tellers for the election to the Corporation—Bribe him for Marian Wright Edelman!" This was the year that Edelman, a graduate of Spelman College and of Yale Law School and later founder of the Children's Defense Fund, became the first woman to serve on the Yale Corporation. "Après moi, le déluge," my father might have said with pride and humor.[73]

A Club That Changed Jews and Jews Who Changed the Club

How do we understand the story of the changes at Yale and the role that both Jews and elite Protestants played? Yale changed its admissions policies not because of sit-ins or marching protestors who challenged a frightened power elite. Things happened quietly in New Haven in the early 1960s, with pressures from Cambridge, state and federal governments, and a range of actors playing their parts. One source of change was the conscience and strategy of Yale elites.[74] Key insiders also played critical roles in transforming Yale: Weiss, Doob, and Coffin. Rabbi Israel and my father mediated between insider and outsider. However ambivalent I am about the elites who set the tone at Yale, I have tremendous admiration for the commitments of Brewster and especially Coffin. And for my father, someone who, unlike many of his generation, did not want to hide his Jewishness and instead taught me and others what it was like to use tensions productively. Nonetheless, this is not Whig history that reveals inevitable progress, as the departure of admissions director Inky Clark and the partial reversal of his policies remind us. It took a long time for Yale to admit women and then bring their numbers to 50 percent of the undergraduates. At Yale and elsewhere, the perplexing struggles over the role of merit, character, and diversity did not end in the 1960s.

Jews changed Yale and Yale changed Jews, revealing the dimensions of profound transformations afoot in America. Superficially, elites succeeded in changing some of us into them. It taught us how to dress British, even as some of us resisted the pressure to stop thinking Yiddish. However, as I show in later chapters on academics, gender, and politics, it also changed some of us into intellectuals and activists. Yale intensified my identity as a Jew even as my commitment to organized Judaism continued to wane. Yale also gave me a superb education, one that helped me develop an identity as a cosmopolitan

Jewish intellectual, even though I did not then have access to what that phrase signified. Yale helped me clarify my goals, in the process transforming me not into a well-rounded man but into someone who turned away from a career in business and toward both academic life and a reconstruction of what it meant to be a Yale man.

We return to where the chapter began, to Noah Feldman's 2010 celebration in the *New York Times* of the WASP elite for its beneficent and disinterested motives. Change did happen quickly in the 1960s but not without struggle. Members of Yale's elite did not shift simply out of goodness in their hearts or their meritocratic commitments, though the best among them had passion and conscience. In addition to exogenous forces, divisions within the northeastern Protestant establishment, as well as cultural and social changes in the nation, continued the process begun in World War II of undermining its power. This propelled the bold among them (Brewster and Coffin included) to commit the nation and Yale more fully to a meritocratic if not an egalitarian social order. In the late 1950s, as a separate, self-conscious, and largely coherent group, the East Coast elite that comprised the American establishment was on the cusp of moving into uncharted territory, in some ways breaking up and in others reconfiguring itself. The change in patterns of admissions, including recruitment from elite private schools that were themselves changing; the transition from privilege to merit; the shifts from old money to new, represented in part by Jews in the world of finance and later in technology; the mixing on campus of men and women, Jews and Gentiles, whites and African Americans, Anglos and new immigrants—all these factors meant that after the late 1950s Yale and the nation were markedly different from when I entered college in 1956.[75]

Without suggesting a causal relationship, I have to note the irony that the prominence on campus of the Ivy League style purveyed by Jewish merchants came at the same time, from the mid-1920s until the mid-1960s, that most of the Ivies imposed the greatest restrictions on the admission of Jewish men to undergraduate educations. As a collegiate style, Ivy clothing waned as proof of being a Yale man around when Ivy League universities opened their doors more widely. By the end of the decade the arrival of women, along with the influence of the counterculture and political insurgencies, would impel Yale students to dress more heterogeneously and casually than J. Press preferred.

However, clothing is only the external fabric and symbol of a complicated story. The late 1950s and early 1960s was a historically specific moment, when many Jews as outsiders worked to open up the university for their talented and ambitious landsmen, even as their success paved the way for the entry into the Ivies of public school graduates, women, African Americans, Latinos, and international students. Eventually Jews assumed presidencies of most Ivy League universities, with Yale having two in a row in the late twentieth and early twenty-first centuries. Affirmative action helped African Americans and other underrepresented minorities make way, with resistance from alumni eventually threatening their ability to gain fully their place in elite colleges and universities. Later Asian Americans would invoke the history of admissions of Jews in their own battles for recognition of merit. In all these battles, nothing less was at stake than the definition of America as a nation.

CHAPTER THREE

In White America

Too often the Northerner feels that his only responsibility in the seg-regation issue is to become "enlightened." . . . But segregation, like inflation, cannot be viewed as a problem too distant to affect our daily lives. Segregation not only affronts the principles of freedom and democracy, as situations do in Berlin and Hungary, but also distorts our practice of these principles at home. . . . Moreover, it is difficult for the Negro to sincerely internalize the spirit of the Yale "blue" when he is cheered on the basketball court or in the Yale Bowl and rejected as a possible member in fraternity houses.

RALEIGH DAVENPORT, class of 1960,
"Segregation, North and South," *Criterion*, April 1959

Before and during my college years, momentous events internationally, nationally, and locally began to reshape American race relations fundamentally—even as most students and faculty at Yale apparently remained blasé. In the spring of my sophomore year in high school, the Supreme Court handed down its landmark school desegregation decision and in December 1955, Rosa Parks refused to give up her seat on a Montgomery, Alabama, bus. Early in my sophomore year at Yale, the battle erupted over the integration of Central High School in Little Rock. As I began my final semester of col-lege in February 1960, Woolworth's in Greensboro, North Carolina, refused to serve four African American college students at a segregated lunch counter. Then in April, African American students formed the Student Nonviolent Coordinating Committee, challenging racial segregation in the South and the leadership of more moderate civil rights organizations. In New Haven, the migration of African Americans from the South was rapidly transforming the city's racial composition. At the same time, urban renewal, which destroyed the synagogue where my family had prayed for three generations, was chang-ing neighborhoods near Yale.

Times they were a-changin'—more at the Supreme Court, in the South, and in the university's surround than at Yale itself, even though there were hints of things to come even there. Few if any of us thought about what it meant to have an area of Pierson College called "Slave Quarters" or to have another of the ten residential colleges, Calhoun, named after an alumnus who owned slaves and defended slavery. The influential *Yale Daily News* focused only sporadically on the fights over segregation in the South, but in the spring of 1960 two of its journalists traveled to report on events there. The *News* usually saw urban renewal as the story of progress. The faculty who taught us wrote important books on race in America, even if they neither worked on African American topics with each other as scholars or teachers nor in most cases sustained a focus on race in their scholarship. The introductory course in American history I took in my sophomore year offered little help in understanding the connections between America's racial past and present, something amply reflected in my own confusion about Reconstruction. My five African American classmates remained isolated from one another, even as the least privileged among them, Raleigh Davenport, wrote compellingly in an undergraduate magazine of his experiences with segregation in the North and his hopes for change. A handful of white and black classmates chose to pay attention to race in America with words and deeds. Largely unprovoked by classes and professors, they acted because news from outside the university, Protestant ministers from within its walls, and their own histories, curiosities, and consciences drove them in new directions.

All this occurred against the background of the multiple privileges I and most of my classmates enjoyed. Local African Americans cooked and served our meals and cleaned the buildings we used—but we encountered them over what, if we even thought about it, were chasms of race and class. Yale's admissions policy afforded classmates few opportunities to interact with African American peers. Most of us remained isolated from the outside world where race was becoming increasingly important, as well as from changes in New Haven that might have made a difference in how we understood the world. As I discuss in a later chapter, this changed in early 1960, when responses to the sit-ins at southern lunch counters and the Sharpeville massacre in South Africa brought race to the fore for many of us.

Yale Daily News

On civil rights rarely did the *News* go beyond relaying what someone on campus said or national sources reported. A notable exception came in March 1960 when two reporters and a photographer traveled south to cover the rapidly emerging story of civil rights. The articles by Monroe Price, my close friend, and George A. Akerlof appeared right when the *News* was also covering protests at Yale against segregation and discrimination in New Haven and in the South. Akerlof, a member of the class of 1962, later married Janet Yellen (the future head of the Federal Reserve Board), and in 2001 won the Nobel Prize in Economics. Inspired by what Harrison Salisbury had written in the *New York Times* about how officials in a southern city used fire hoses on protesting students, Akerlof and Price approached William Sloane Coffin Jr., who offered encouragement and financial support. He also connected them with a local African American fraternal organization that helped underwrite their trip. They traveled first to Washington, D.C. They then headed farther south. They interviewed Martin Luther King Jr. They listened to Yale professor Liston Pope, speaking at Vanderbilt University, criticize whites. They attended a KKK meeting outside Macon, Georgia. They met with prominent white civil rights activists Virginia and Clifford Durr in Montgomery, Alabama. They observed a gathering of elite African American women at a meeting of their Jack and Jill organization in Atlanta. And they watched a Rock Hill, South Carolina, trial of African American students who had organized sit-ins at a lunch counter.

Akerlof and Price conveyed how polarized the situation was becoming, with the center not holding among whites. Before their reports, the dominant note in most stories and editorials in the *News* was that activists should not push desegregation too hard, for this would only intensify resistance by southern whites.[1] Instead, Akerlof and Price told stories of heroic protests by African Americans, college students especially, and racist resistance by southern whites. At the South Carolina trial, seventy African American college students, who stood accused of singing "The Star Spangled Banner" boisterously and disruptively, defended themselves by saying what they did "was like church music—sung sweet and low." Whites testified that African Americans expressed "an underlying sense of bitterness." When police arrested Alan Tuttle, the Yale photographer who accompanied Akerlof and Price, for taking pictures of an African American woman making a purchase in a store, he protested that America was "a free country"; "Oh, you think so, huh?" the arresting officer responded.[2]

Urban Renewal

The *News* devoted little attention to the significant changes taking place in New Haven itself. In 1940 African Americans were almost 4 percent of the city's 160,605 population; by the time I graduated in 1960 they were almost 16 percent of 152,048, the two sets of statistics reflecting migration of African Americans from the South and white flight to the suburbs. To many people in New Haven, but not to most of my classmates, the most visible drama in New Haven was urban renewal, which began with the 1953 election of Richard C. Lee as mayor. Once in office, he appointed George W. Crawford, Yale Law School's second African American graduate, as the city's lawyer and Ed Logue, the son-in-law of Dean William C. DeVane, as head of the city's redevelopment efforts. In our sophomore year, Lee predicted, as a classmate wrote soon after, "that New Haven would be the first slumless city in the country." Although they brought to New Haven the nation's highest per capita amount of federal funds, Lee and Logue faced an uphill battle against deindustrialization, the flight of white residents and stores to the suburbs, a decline in the tax base, and tensions between racial and ethnic groups.[3]

Because I had grown up in New Haven and my parents were so involved in local politics, I was especially attuned to what was happening to New Haven—massive reconstruction near the city's center that pitted those who saw urban blight against those who lived in long-established communities. My classmates were in Yale's bubble, while as a townie I knew the city well. During my college years, I saw the building of the Oak Street Connector, which made it possible to travel from the newly opened Interstate into the city but also destroyed a neighborhood, forcing residents to scramble for housing elsewhere. Urban renewal, part of a national effort in which New Haven pioneered, also attracted a major real estate developer who, supported by Yale financing, built a series of tall apartment buildings between the main Yale campus and the medical school. Right after I graduated from Yale, my parents moved into one of them.

What impact did all these changes in New Haven and the nation have on my peers? As one of the most politically aware classmates remarked at the time, New Haven was "redeveloping under our eyes," with "most of us blind to it." And to the extent that I and my politically conscious peers thought at all about urban renewal, like my parents we probably saw it as part of liberal progress. When the *News* covered the city's urban redevelopment, it typically treated it as a story of progress that revolved around local politics, commercial real estate, and the university's role in the city's affairs. The one piece of actual reporting came in the fall of 1959, when Herschel Post Jr. investigated what it meant to move 886 families out of the area being redeveloped. He too adopted the view that urban renewal really renewed. He pictured the old neighborhood as an area characterized by disease, poverty, racial and ethnic segregation, and exploitation by greedy and absentee landlords and treated by Yale researchers as a "teeming laboratory of human misery." Relocation, by moving "racial minorities, pensioners, indigents, and the outcasts of society," had "surmounted at least the worst set of problems" and provided everyone with a new home.[4]

In 1967 the feelings of those displaced by urban renewal came out fully into the open. Representatives of the National Commission on Civil Disorders visited New Haven, where they expected to hear praise for the city's efforts. Instead they listened as Fred Harris, my high school classmate and African American community organizer, denounced what he saw as the racism underlying the city's urban renewal. He thus revealed the dissonance between white liberals who expected appreciation and African Americans who offered a more critical perspective.

How the Yale Faculty Viewed African American Life

What Yale professors said in books about race reveals the state of scholarship in the field—at Yale and nationally. Each of those who wrote about race offers us retrospectively a different answer to the question of whether Yale in these years was on the cusp. What they published on race ranged widely, but in key cases they did not sustain a scholarly interest in race, precisely when the civil rights movement intensified. Although their books reveal cracks in the complacent consensus on race among Americans, most of the faculty who wrote about race could not or did not let their scholarship inflect their teaching. Thus to a considerable degree they failed to propel their students forward into new ways of thinking about race. To the extent that classmates themselves were edging closer to the cusp when it came to race, this happened despite what the formal curriculum offered.

In *Segregation: The Inner Conflict in the South* (1956) the Kentucky-born and Tennessee-raised Robert Penn Warren, who joined the Yale faculty in 1950, acted as a mediator between regions, explaining the South to skeptical northerners with a combination of sympathy and agony. Winner of the Pulitzer Prize in both fiction and poetry, here he turned to nonfiction reporting. He suggested that white southerners who remained in the South should rethink the meaning of race and white northerners should not intervene. The word "inner" in the book's subtitle referred not so much to what divided African Americans from whites, for which the book contained abundant evidence, but to the divisions within and among whites themselves. Prominent among the "many lines of fracture" he found were those between the "social idealism" some whites professed and their "anger at Yankee Phariseeism," intensified by memories of Reconstruction. Warren often talked of harmful clichés, but there were two he left unexamined: that outside agitators and even well-meaning northerners did not understand southern distinctiveness and that left alone the South might solve its own problems and provide a moral example for the nation.[5]

In contrast with what Warren wrote were the works of northern faculty. In *Romanticism and Nationalism in the Old South* (1949) Rollin G. Osterweis, a New Haven–born German Jew and Yale-educated historian, emphasized how central slavery was to the history of white southerners. "The civilization of the Old South," he remarked, "rested on a tripod": the cotton-based plantation system, the enslavement of African Americans, and southern romanticism. He probed the backstory to Warren's exploration of southern suspicion of interference by northerners. Although slavery made the romantic dreams of whites possible, his emphasis on chivalry, romanticism, and southern nationalism turned African Americans into bit players without agency in a white world. Osterweis also made clear that the cult of the Lost Cause rested on antebellum romanticism, a sentiment that we can see lay behind Warren's agony.[6]

John Dollard's *Caste and Class in a Southern Town* (1937) offered the most powerful critique of southern race relations. He had grown up in a small Wisconsin town and then earned his doctorate at the University of Chicago in sociology, a program known for its commitment to community studies. In this book he offered a powerful, no-holds-barred critique of race relations, one which remained influential in the late 1950s. Based on fieldwork carried out for five months in 1935–36 while he lived in a small town in Mississippi, Dollard examined how race and history profoundly shaped the South. He explored the conflict between dominant American beliefs and the mores of white southerners that underlay racist treatment of African Americans and squelched their aspirations for social mobility, personal dignity, and full citizenship. After the Civil War what replaced slavery was a harsh caste system that, he showed, wove together class, race, gender, and sexuality in a nearly totalizing manner. He emphasized how in their relationships with African Americans and poor whites, white middle-class southern men benefited from the privileges of whiteness, a phrase he used decades before it became commonly deployed. Whites exercised their power by avoiding manual work, sexually exploiting both African American and white women, and more generally relying on violence, intimidation, degradation, isolation, and self-righteousness. He took special care to lay out how African Americans responded, asserting that because direct challenges were dangerous, they chose "indirect, circuitous, and symbolic methods" of expressing their resentment toward whites by moving away, boycotting, gossiping, and sabotaging—or putting on the mask of Sambo. He insisted that more contact with and knowledge of life in the North would liberate African American "aggression" and result in "active demands for new opportunity."[7]

Robert A. Bone, the Yale faculty member most active in progressive causes, published a pathbreaking study of African American literature in 1958. Of Scottish descent, New Haven born, and Yale class of 1945, he embraced radicalism as early as his undergraduate days. It continued in the immediate postwar period when he served as National Secretary of the Young People's Socialist League, labored as a Michigan factory worker, and joined the United Auto Workers. At a time when labor militancy and the struggle for civil rights within unions were at their height and Cold War imperatives were beginning to take hold, he was in a perfect position to understand the relationships between race, class, and politics. His political activity continued during his years at Yale as a graduate student and instructor, when he organized the George Orwell Forum, the most left-wing organization on campus, and helped found local chapters of CORE and SANE.[8]

Bone's 1955 dissertation and his ensuing 1958 book *The Negro Novel in America* revealed that a white Yale professor saw this literature as worthy of serious consideration and offered a window into African American history. He placed his central focus on the traditions that shaped African American literature and, by implication, African American life. Ignoring the influence of an African heritage and of the slave narratives to which later generations would pay so much sympathetic attention, he located the emergence of an African American literary tradition after 1890. He had a low opinion of what African American writers published between then and 1920 because, too indebted to the Victorian Genteel Tradition and to anti-urban assumptions, they could not artfully resolve the tensions between utopian nationalism and sterile assimilation. All this began to change when Harlem Renaissance writers used literary modernism to mediate between what was racially distinctive and universally true.[9]

Bone saw World War II as a major turning point that had promising implications for African American writers and race relations. A series of presidential actions, state initiatives, and court decisions revealed how "the edifice of white supremacy is crumbling in every important cultural area." This helped underwrite "a wave of assimilationist sentiment" and cosmopolitanism among novelists. Yet aside from his reference to A. Philip Randolph and despite his own work organizing across racial lines, Bone gave little agency to African Americans, either to NAACP lawyers or to protestors who, precisely as Bone was transforming his dissertation into a book, were playing such critical roles in the fight for civil rights. Instead, as a good Marxist he saw the main impetus to change coming from the way modernization weakened the ancien régime in the South but more importantly from America's changing international position and the growth of "a permanent war economy." All this helped Bone herald the second great period of African American novels in the writings of Richard Wright, Ralph Ellison, and to a lesser extent Zora Neale Hurston. He emphasized how they fused race consciousness, a broad tradition of social protest, and an exploration of universal truths that approached "the Negro concretely as a human being rather than abstractly as a protagonist in the racial struggle." Antagonistic to both black nationalism and Stalinism, Bone cast his lot with broad, cross-class insurgencies and literary modernism.[10]

In his 1952 *Social Psychology: An Analysis of Human Behavior,* Leonard Doob exposed cracks in America's complacent picture of race and ethnicity. He emphasized the cultural nature of race, explored the dynamics of prejudice against a wide range of groups including African Americans and Jews, and wondered how to mitigate the power of racism. Unless the host group "hospitably" received immigrants and their descendants, he wrote, discrimination would drive them back into their ethnic enclaves and retard Americanization. His emphasis on the importance of acculturation, consonant with the melting pot ideology common in the 1950s, derived from social science research and personal experience. His life revealed what difference inclusion of an outsider meant: the more the host society, such as the dominant one at Yale, welcomed marginalized groups, the less threatening such groups would be and the more peaceful, less prejudiced American society would become.[11]

I wish I could say with any certainty that the writings or teaching of Warren, Osterweis, Dollard, Bone, and Doob influenced me, however important they are in showing the nature of contemporary scholarship on race. I did not know Warren, though by the summer of 1959 I had read *Segregation.* Late in my college career I came to know Osterweis through his daughter Ruth, whom I had fixed up with Monroe Price. I never met Bone, but my close friend Charlie Newman often talked of him. Nor did I ever encounter Dollard, although his son, also John, was a member of the class of 1959 and with me on the Trumbull College Marble Team. Soon after I entered Yale, I purchased a copy of the 1957 revised edition of Dollard's *Caste and Class.* In the preface, written as the civil rights movement was intensifying, Dollard did not see the pressures for change coming from grassroots action among African Americans. He insisted that little had changed since the 1930s, and cast American race relations in a Cold War framework. In my sophomore year I took Doob's social psychology course, and it is possible that his positions on race, prejudice, and assimilation spoke to me. Yet what I best remember from the course are two things. My roommate Fritz Steele and I gamed Doob's grading system by writing a somewhat mediocre optional paper on teenage gangs, the writing itself of which, rather than its quality, gave us a boost in our grades. This helped me earn a 95 in the course, at the time an extraordinarily high grade, especially for a sophomore. More vivid is the memory of sitting in my Trumbull College room going over what Doob taught about the metrics of social class in America and puzzling out my family's social position.[12]

As a historian now looking back, what strikes me is how to varying degrees these professors began piercing the armor of American racism. Yet, their isolation from one another speaks volumes for how far Yale as a scholarly community had to go before the arrival of a full-blown, focused consideration of race. One example suffices: Bone did not refer to the work of his Yale colleague E. David Cronon on Marcus Garvey (discussed below). Moreover, they did not provide a lasting campus presence of scholars to whom race was a central concern. The lives of African Americans, never at the center of Doob's scholarship, increasingly provided material for his more general concerns about propaganda, conflict resolution, and acculturation. By the late 1930s, Dollard focused on the study of fear, frustration, and aggression—which he sometimes but not centrally connected to race. As he wrote in the preface to the 1957 edition, he was "no longer up on Negro problems."[13] After Osterweis published the sequel to *Romanticism and Nationalism,* he turned to local history and Jewish history before they became respected topics. As a historian of the South, his presence was eclipsed by the arrival of C. Vann Woodward in 1961. Osterweis's renown came not from his historical scholarship but from his prominence as a teacher of the history of American oratory and Yale's debate coach from 1941 to 1979—positions in which he influenced generations of Yale men, including William F. Buckley Jr., John Kerry, and George W. Bush. In 1959, Bone left Yale. Given his radicalism, the lack of importance of race to the American studies program, and the dominance in the English department of New Criticism, much of it offered by southern whites, Bone's chances for staying on at Yale were limited. Although some of the scholarly components for a program in African American studies were in place, as a coordinated field that commanded attention and resources, its birth was more than a decade in the future.

My Introduction to the Study of the History of the United States

In my sophomore year, I took a two-semester survey of American history. Although it played a key role in my becoming a historian, reviewing it today makes clear how silences and stereotypes dominated the study of African

American life.[14] The first volume of the textbook emphasized the economic foundations of sectionalism and the political battles over slavery and its expansion more than the nature of slavery itself. One would not have known from reading it that white ownership of African Americans provided the basis for southern life. Although in one section the authors mentioned the violence inflicted on slaves, when they discussed how abolitionists turned increasingly "belligerent" after 1830, they referred to the "horrors of slavery" as "reputed." In contrast, they provided no critical evaluation when they described the views of those who defended slavery. Finally, like many historians of their era, they saw the Civil War caused not by the issue of slavery but by incompatible ways of living supported by politicians on both sides who were unwilling to compromise. The Civil War ended the "menace of disunion," but not, in their telling, the horrors of the enslavement of African Americans.[15]

In the second volume the only place where African Americans mattered was during the Reconstruction. Most historians now see this as a heroic and potentially transformative attempt to resolve the nation's racial problems, but the authors of the textbook focused on politically motivated northern do-gooders and on freedmen who were "illiterate, naïve, and susceptible to the influence of designing men." After 1877, African Americans virtually disappeared. They made cameo appearances as victims of discrimination and violence; agricultural laborers, strike breakers, and migrants to northern cities; leaders of institutions of higher education; the focus of civil rights legislation; and developers of jazz. Absent from America's past were Jim Crow, segregation, and the founding of the NAACP. The authors treated only four African Americans individually, not Frederick Douglass or W. E. B. Du Bois but Booker T. Washington, Louis Armstrong, Father Divine, and Ralph Bunche.[16]

In the survey course we also read two document books, notable for their conservatism on race—*Nationalism and Sectionalism in America, 1775–1877* and *Government and the American Economy, 1870—Present.*[17] In the first volume the editors called late eighteenth-century slaves "more or less savage." However, for the editors the real issue lay elsewhere. When they presented the call by W. E. B. Du Bois for expanded government action in Reconstruction, the editors remarked that "there would be today strong opposition to such participation in the individual's life."[18] Precisely when President Harry S. Truman was proposing an expansion of New Deal and civil rights legislation, they echoed what free market advocates and southern whites were increasingly articulating. Indeed, antipathy to expanded federal power linked the volumes, with Adam Smith's *The Wealth of Nations* (1776) and Friedrich Hayek's *Road to Serfdom* (1944) serving as the bookends to volume two. This common theme was no accident, given the key role Yale's historian David M. Potter played in shaping the series. Like Warren, Potter was a southerner in exile who, in response to Truman's proposed civil rights legislation, emphasized the advisability of incremental change in race relations and opposed government action he saw driven by pressure from African Americans and northern politicians beholden to racial militants.[19]

Looking at those who taught the survey, rather than the books assigned, offers a more mixed and promising picture of faculty members grappling with race. In the fall semester, the lecturer was Howard Lamar, who arrived at Yale in 1944 and remained there for almost his entire career, during which he and his students helped transform the field of Western history. Having paid relatively little attention to African Americans for the semester, at its end he portrayed Reconstruction as a lost opportunity, with southern African Americans failing to provide leadership and corrupt radicals "spouting wild equalitarian and agrarian theories." Then in his notes for the final lecture he remarked that the "Negro [was] forgotten until Sup. Ct. Decision of 1954. Election of 1956" indicated that "patterns of politics set by Civil War and Recon. are finally breaking up in a healthy manner, and the problems of recon are finally being honestly faced."[20]

In the second semester, the lecturer was E. David Cronon, who along with Bone was the Yale professor whose writing in the late 1950s most significantly focused on African American topics. In 1955, Cronon published *Black Moses: The Story of Marcus Garvey and the Universal Negro Improvement Association*. Drawing on "the fires that smolder in the Negro world" and appealing to "poorly educated, superstitious, and disillusioned Negroes," the Jamaican-born Garvey offered "an unrealistic escapist program of racial chauvinism," awakened a deep-seated African American nationalism, and instilled in his followers an enduring pride in their blackness, their African heritage, and their contribution as slaves to the nation's development. More than Bone, Cronon gave African Americans agency and emphasized the depth and power of their discontent. Cronon also offered readers lessons for contemporary Americans. He dated the preface May 23, 1954, six days after the Supreme Court handed down the *Brown v. Board of Education* decision. He called into question the judgment of "complacent Americans" who believed their nation was "the world's most successful democracy." You might think all is well in the 1950s, when many people celebrated the triumphs of democracy and capitalism, he was saying, but below the surface lay dissatisfaction among African Americans. Cronon, like Bone, left Yale in 1959.[21]

The man who led my discussion section was Martin Duberman, whose career offers an intriguing story of the relationships among a white scholar,

African American history, and homosexuality. As an adult Duberman saw himself as "Anglo-Saxon in appearance and manner," though when he taught me I was keenly aware that he was a Jew.[22] He graduated from Yale in 1952 and, after earning his doctorate at Harvard, joined the Yale faculty in fall 1957. At this time, he began to transform his dissertation into *Charles Francis Adams, 1807–1886* (1960), an award-winning biography of a statesman and writer who was a direct descendent of two presidents. Duberman remarked years later that with his personal life seemingly in "shambles," while working on the book he "never drew (at least not consciously) what would later seem the obvious analogy" between the fight by Adams to free slaves and "the need to struggle on behalf of my own liberation."[23]

Yet with hindsight it is possible to read what he said of Adams as what he might have said of himself in 1960. During the late 1950s and early 1960s, "locked in painful isolation" as he remarked later, he was struggling mightily with how to resolve the tensions between his mainline scholarship and his transgressive sexuality.[24] Like Adams in the early 1830s, Duberman encountered disappointment in his private life and the emergence of compelling national issues in his public one. Adams, he wrote, developed a "more active participation in public life" that helped him "break up his mood of discouragement and depression."[25] Duberman's own breakthrough came after we both left Yale, with his widely heralded off-Broadway 1963 play, *In White America*. Here he presented a very different picture from what the survey course offered, giving heroic African American men and women agency and letting them speak forcefully for themselves.[26]

I still have the early 1958 paper on Reconstruction that I submitted to Duberman. As I read it decades later with the benefit of hindsight, several things strike me. My prose is wooden and humorless. I gave no evidence of what it would mean to interrogate contradictory sources, instead taking at face value the judgments of observers and historians. On race issues I was confused. On the one hand, I wrote about "the reestablishment of order" in ways that permitted "the peaceful and beneficial operation of the South"; on the other, I discussed "the change, however gradual, in the status of the Negro until complete equality was attained as a necessary culmination of Reconstruction." I adopted a realpolitik stance that avoided moral commitments. I seemed hopelessly ignorant of the prejudices of southern whites, as well as of the talents, aspirations, and accomplishments of both northern Radicals and southern African Americans. Given what the textbook and reader said about Reconstruction, my response, though problematic, is hardly surprising.[27]

An examination of Duberman's reaction to my paper underscores my confusion. He openly questioned my judgments about the racial and ideological dynamics of Reconstruction. For example, when I said that northerners "rightly contended that immeidate [sic] suffrage for Southern Negroes would lead to persecution and corruption," after correcting my spelling and circling the word "persecution," he added "This is an open question—persecution would probably have come in any case—e.g. Black Codes *preceded* Radical Reconstr." Several times, he called into question how critical I was of Radicals. If I worried that Reconstruction "did not solve the question of the changed position of the poor white," he reminded me that neither did it begin the process of "*starting*" African Americans "on the road to equality." Then when I said that Reconstruction united "the Whites and thus created a realtively [sic] permanent color line," after correcting my spelling again, he underlined "and thus created" and asked in the margin, "Southern traditional prejudice played no part in this?"[28]

Of those who taught me in the course, I remember Duberman best. Although I recall little of the weekly section meetings he led, perhaps, as the historian Paul Robinson remarks of him in these years, in my class he was engaged in "cheerfully disabusing my classmates of their Republican prejudices." The one thing I do remember reveals something of my political quest. After a class in the second semester, when we were focusing on the role of the federal government in the economy, I ran up and asked him what he meant when he said there were only two alternatives, laissez-faire capitalism or socialism.[29]

Like Bone and Cronon, Duberman left Yale, in his case in 1962. In contrast, those who stayed—Osterweis, Warren, Dollard, Doob, and Lamar—did not make scholarship on African Americans central to their writing. In the late 1950s Yale, like most institutions other than historically black ones, did not think that studying the lives of African Americans, or hiring African Americans to teach, need command attention. In terms of their teaching and program development, and to some extent in their writing, Yale faculty who focused on African American life were far from going beyond the cusp.

African American Classmates

The lives of the five African Americans members of the class of 1960—Bruce Ballard, Raleigh Davenport, William H. Moses III, Al Puryear, and Greg Tignor—reveal just how Yale was stuck in the past, even as the futures of most of them make clear how Yale helped transform their lives.[30] In the mid-1950s Yale had begun to recruit small numbers of African Americans. For example, a white Yale undergraduate involved in Dwight Hall, Yale's principal Protestant organization, went to Ballard's high school to recruit an African American.[31] All five grew up below the Mason Dixon line, and all except Davenport were in families from the black bourgeoisie by virtue of their parents' educations and occupations.[32] None of them had a father or an uncle who preceded him to Yale.[33] Four of them came to Yale from segregated public high schools, while Moses arrived from Andover. It is hard not to be struck by the importance, except for Davenport, of historically black colleges and universities in the lives of their families. Two of them came from families associated with Hampton Institute: Moses, as son of two faculty members, and Puryear, the son of a Hampton graduate, had gone to a public high school located on its campus. Given the long association between Hampton and the family of Yale's director of admissions, Arthur Howe Jr., it is hard to imagine that this is mere coincidence, although Puryear came in part as a result of his promise as a football player. Surely in recruiting academically qualified African American football players, the admissions committee remembered that Levi Jackson, a graduate of Yale in 1950, was the first African American to captain a Yale football team.

The five led varied careers as undergraduates. They gained markers of academic success and decided on a variety of majors, in many cases through an honors track. Their participation in extracurricular activities ranged from minimal to extensive. Puryear and Davenport earned renown as football players. Several of them were active in religious organizations—Davenport as vice-chairman of the Undergraduate Board of Deacons—and in the lives of their residential colleges. Davenport was a member of Torch, an honorary society, but none of them joined a fraternity or an aboveground senior society. Although they were aware of one another as undergraduates, they did not meet as a group or in other ways associate, in part because only three graduated in 1960. Moses was more likely to hang out with his Andover friends, and the studious Ballard kept largely to himself. As was true with Jews who tried to observe dietary laws, and Asian Americans, so, too, with the African American classmates: it was as if they were all in a big room, milling about, at times aware of one another but not forming a cohesive or self-aware group.[34] If Tignor's experience is typical, then they experienced racist indignities. He squelched a peer trying to tell a joke using the "N" word but had to restrain himself when a faculty member, to whom he was turning in a term paper, told him he should make deliveries at the building's rear door.[35]

Yale transformed the lives of these five men. All earned advanced degrees and went on to professional careers. The three for whom there is sufficient information—Ballard, Puryear, and Tignor—married African American women who earned advanced degrees and themselves had successful professional careers. Their children followed in their paths when they graduated from Ivy League institutions and had professional careers. They focused significantly on African American issues in their careers. As an administrator, Ballard helped recruit minority students and taught medical doctors how to be more sensitive to distinctive issues African American patients faced. His PhD in business administration from Columbia in hand, Puryear joined the management faculty at Baruch College in 1970 and three years later published a major book, *Black Enterprise, Inc.: Case Studies of a New Experiment in Black Business Development*. He offered a careful study of the halting progress African American entrepreneurs made as they began "to cash in on the American dream" by moving "into the economic mainstream" of a capitalist economy.[36] Two remained within Yale's orbit: Puryear as a member of the Yale Corporation and Tignor as a professor at Yale's School of Medicine and president of the Connecticut Academy of Arts and Sciences. Moses graduated with the class of 1962 and died thirty years later. For reasons I do not know, Davenport cut himself off from all his classmates. In all the entries in their reunion books there is only one piece of evidence of how any of them thought of their years as African Americans at Yale. In our fiftieth reunion book Tignor remarked that he and his brother "were Black students at Yale long before affirmative action had been thought of," perhaps implying that his admission owed nothing to racial preference. He went on to say that he had recently talked to Ballard and Puryear about getting together. "Maybe one day," he remarked, "because we're unique survivors."[37]

Davenport's April 1959 essay "Segregation, North and South," which appeared in a student publication, is the only undergraduate writing I could locate by any of the five. He made clear that as an African American he was more intensely aware of America's racial dynamics than most white professors. As the title suggests, he insisted that northerners look in their own backyards. Like most southern African Americans who came north to college in the 1950s, his actual experiences challenged the widespread assumption among them and among northern white liberals that race relations were better where they went than from where they came.[38] Many a white northerner, he asserted, denied "his moral responsibility in a democratic society," rather than working to "uproot . . . vestiges of prejudice as irrational as that he decries in Southerners." It was also easier for them to criticize the repression of freedom in communist nations and live in "a detached niche of moral idealism" than to confront uncomfortable situations in "*his* club, *his* church, or *his* family." Greater "personal communication" across racial lines would erode fearful prejudice and make it possible "for an African American to get a job commensurate with his education, or move into an all-White neighborhood." That would be a hopeful sign of "a peaceful solution to the Negro problem" and the achievement of full citizenship for all, "whether they be Negro, Jew, Italian, Pole or otherwise."

Unlike most Yale professors, Davenport gave agency to African Americans. To be sure, he regretted "the inability of the core of the discontented to change deep-rooted prejudice based upon economic and sociological conditions of the past and irrational fears of the present." Yet he emphasized the role of African Americans who, "using passive resistance and perseverance before the courts," were determined "to change discriminatory attitudes through moral persuasion and to redefine or instigate the passage of anti-discriminatory laws through litigation." He hailed the "evolution of a new kind of Negro in America" who, countering "the early slave's pathos and the freedman's frustration," had embraced "a new militancy and a new sense of direction." He stressed the role of "colored peoples throughout the world" who were watching "critically" America's racial situation, which, if it improved, would place the nation in a stronger position in Africa and Asia.

Davenport also focused on the situation at Yale. Some of his friends had tried to get him into DKE. He made it clear that he had been blackballed and spoke more generally of how "legally sanctioned discrimination in fraternities" was "disillusioning to a Negro undergraduate at Yale." Those who condoned such a practice, whether from the North or the South, not only failed to uphold the university's values but also repudiated "people without giving them a chance to prove themselves." Although many classmates I interviewed said that it was a southerner in DKE who blackballed him, Davenport instead criticized "silent liberals" because "injustice sanctioned by reticence is no better than injustice upheld by irrational fears or faulty reasoning."[39]

What Davenport wrote attracted considerable attention on campus. Using "Negro" and "Colored" interchangeably, an editorial in the *News* emphasized that it was not necessary to go south to see prejudice, since Davenport had underscored its presence in Yale fraternities. At the same time, a Yale professor pointed to the "melancholy record of inaction and escapism" that Davenport found on campus and more generally in the North and also praised his critique of "the paralyzingly abstract quality of our liberalism."[40] Davenport's essay appeared in the April 1959 issue of *Criterion* edited by Pete Magee, class of 1959 and someone I knew well in Trumbull College. Perhaps Magee played a role in recruiting Davenport into the 1960 delegation of the underground senior society that I also joined. I would hope that his participation in that intimate group provided Davenport with what he called "the kind of close and lasting friendship and feeling of acceptance" he and others longed for.

Senior Theses on Civil Rights

Four classmates wrote senior papers on race relations. They took some inspiration from the formal curriculum, but it was news from outside the college gates that helped drive their curiosity. In three instances long-standing commitments as Protestant Christians inspired their work. The trajectories of their lives illuminates the divergent possibilities of life after Yale.

David George Ball wrote on resistance to school integration in the South. What moved him was reading Martin Luther King Jr.'s *Stride toward Freedom* in the fall of 1958 shortly after its publication. He played a key role in bringing King to campus, an act that turned him from an outsider into a Yale man. Ball grew up in an evangelical family in Britain and came to America to spend two years at the evangelical Moody Bible Institute College in Chicago. Once at Yale, as he figured out the stratified social structure of undergraduate life, he grew eager, he wrote in a memoir, "to escape the narrow social restraints of my childhood and become part of the larger world," an effort aided by a roommate—Henry Lawrence Blodgett III, who had come to Yale with multiple legacies, St. Paul's as his prep school, and Park Avenue as his family's address. Ball successfully rushed Fence Club, intentionally emphasizing for his future brothers that he played rugby but not that he came to Yale from a Bible college. Working against his social insecurity, he began to "savor the privileges" of his fraternity, such as meals a steward prepared and a club tie that made him "feel like one of the elite."[41]

An assistant chaplain, whom Ball met when he joined the evangelical Inter-Varsity Christian Fellowship, asked him to organize a lecture series to combat student apathy about national issues. So Ball formed the Undergraduate Lecture Committee and, prodded by the chaplain's office, invited King to speak at Yale. In his January 14, 1959, speech King connected biblical references, American dreams, and the pursuit of racial justice. He urged his audience of college students and townspeople to follow the example of Jesus by pursuing maladjustment rather than conformity. With his characteristic command of language, he called on the audience to join in the fight to help the nation "emerge from the bleak and desolate midnight of man's inhumanity to man into the bright and glittering daybreak of freedom and justice." The role Ball played in bringing King to Yale made him well known on campus, with a publisher of one student magazine, referring to a famous cultural impresario, calling him "the Sol Hurok of Yale University." Ball discovered that fame and achievement had its rewards when in the spring of his junior year he was tapped for Skull and Bones.[42]

Ball was jubilant, later remarking apparently without irony, "I sing the 'Hallelujah Chorus!'" "I'm an immigrant from England, the son of a humble nonconformist minister, who has just entered the inner circle at Yale, a world where everything seems possible." There followed in rapid order a dinner at the "manicured estate" of the parents of another new Bonesman and then a dinner at Manhattan's University Club, where Ball sat between Bonesmen Henry Luce, the founder of Time Inc., and W. Averell Harriman, a wealthy elder statesman and diplomat. All this prompted Ball to resolve the "tension between planning to be a minister and a new vague aspiration to be a leader in the establishment." Turning to Coffin for advice, someone who had earlier tried to persuade him to resign from Fence Club because it promoted the wrong values, he listened as the chaplain suggested that unless God had really called him to the ministry, he should choose another career.[43]

Ball wrote his thesis on integration under the direction of Louis Pollak, who had worked for the NAACP on the *Brown* case and in 1955 joined the faculty of the Yale Law School. What compelled Ball's attention was the way southern whites, without even mentioning race, used pupil placement with a hidden race bias as a way to avoid desegregation. Unlike Lamar, and surely guided by Pollak, Ball showed the roots of the struggle for civil rights well before the *Brown v. Board of Education* decision in actions by federal courts and administrative agencies and by African American and union activism. He insisted that the improving situation of African Americans came not only from their increased "bargaining power" but also from "a prevailing dissatisfaction in American society with a caste system that was totally inconsistent" with a modern constitutional democracy.

However, the main brunt of his thesis was sobering. Although he mentioned varied means of white resistance, including physical force and harassment of the NAACP, Ball carefully analyzed the legal, political, and administrative means that southern conservatives cleverly deployed even as they avoided any reference to race and the anti-democratic implications of their actions. With southern conservatives so effectively using pupil placement to extend the caste system and southern moderates seemingly satisfied with slow progress, African Americans faced an "uphill battle" and could "hope for little more than token integration." To be sure, inspired by King, he noted that African Americans were "breaking from their traditional apathy," as evidenced in "lunch counter demonstrations and mass protest meetings" and in "the new attitude amongst younger Negroes [that] may provide the energy for an accelerated drive for Negro rights." Still, he ended his essay by showing how pupil placement provided white southerners with "an effective device by which to avoid integration for some years to come."[44]

Ball's initial interest in race turned out to be an interlude in his long-term transformation. After graduation he knew he was "on a magic carpet . . . setting out with the rest of the class of 1960 to run the country." After Yale he worked as Wall Street lawyer, a senior officer of a large multinational company, and an assistant secretary of labor in the administration of fellow Bonesman George H. W. Bush, where he helped shift risk in retirements from employers to employees. Ball's life underscores how an elite college education fostered social mobility in America and how a clever and ambitious student learned to scope out paths to prominence. Civil rights never again commanded his attention as it had at Yale.[45]

John Bing wrote his thesis on fights over residential integration in Deerfield, Illinois, an affluent and racially exclusive North Shore suburb of Chicago. Striking is how as a then-closeted gay man he articulated his yearning for equal treatment by focusing on others whom class or race disenfranchised. He came to Yale from a public high school in Evanston, where his parents were moderate Republicans and where his father, Yale PhD in hand, had a successful career as a nutritionist. Two interwoven experiences growing up shaped him. One was his involvement in Social Gospel Protestantism, religious-based efforts to achieve social justice and peace. The other was his awareness that he was homosexual, though it would take him a while before he realized that this was more than a stage he would grow out of. As an undergraduate Bing sustained his pursuit of progressive politics through membership in campus and national Protestant organizations, influenced by his own commitments and by the presence of Coffin.

Bing framed his thesis as part of a long struggle of Negroes to fulfill "the hope of a truly pluralistic and integrated society" in which, unlike immigrants, they were still "alien to that which is his, by profession of law and profession of faith." In fall 1959, Morris Milgram, an Old Left activist turned developer of racially integrated housing, proposed building fifty-one new homes, with a dozen or so reserved for African Americans. The town responded by blocking the project. The dramatic story Bing told relied on an exploration of the tensions within American traditions—equal opportunity versus natural rights, communal obligations versus laissez-faire individualism, commitment to the rights of others versus selfish self-righteousness. Milgrim, Protestant ministers (and some parishioners), and the Urban League stood in opposition to foes of integration who used a "chorus of voices, some of bigotry, some of bewilderment, some of fear, raised in public and private." Although court decisions that gave victory to the opposition discouraged him, Bing found some "signs of health that may ultimately transcend the antagonisms and the anger that the controversy dislodged." Over time, he predicted in the final paragraph, the story of Deerfield was "a step in the slow, but real and forward movement toward solution" of the dilemmas of American race relations in the North.[46] Entering Yale as a Republican, he graduated as a Democrat. An American studies honors major, on graduation he headed for Africa and a career as a Protestant minister. However, his teaching in Africa instead impelled him into an academic life, one in which he sustained an engagement with race.

Of all my classmates, George McClain, who wrote on the struggles over racial integration in the United Methodist Church, developed the deepest and most sustained commitment to civil rights for African Americans.[47] He came to Yale on scholarship from a public high school in Fort Wayne, Indiana, having grown up in a Methodist and Republican household where his father was a teacher and principal in the local public schools and his mother taught Sunday school. At Yale, his extracurricular activities involved participation in Protestant organizations, most centrally Methodist youth groups—in New Haven, where he served as president of the Wesley Foundation in his junior year, and farther afield through his participation in national Methodist youth organizations. Connected with these activities and important in his political awakening was the mentorship of Dick Celeste, class of 1959, who headed the national Methodist student movement and preceded George as president at Yale's Wesley Foundation—and who recruited both of us into an underground senior society.

As an undergraduate, courses he took, books he read, and his work in the Methodist student movement inspired McClain to write his history honors thesis on the struggles to integrate the United Methodist Church. In a philosophy course during his first year, his teacher, aware of his interest in Christian theology, suggested he write a paper on Paul Tillich's *The Courage to Be* (1952). As a sophomore he read C. Vann Woodward's *The Strange Career of Jim Crow* (1955) in John Morton Blum's history course, a book that helped him understand that segregation and race relationships had a past and therefore were not immutable. In addition, Blum's course taught him about the liberal political tradition that stood in opposition to the midwestern Republicanism of his childhood. Soon after it appeared in 1958, McClain read Everett Tilson's *Segregation and the Bible,* a book that undercut segregationists' claims of biblical authority for their positions. In his senior year, he wrote a seminar paper on a late nineteenth-century Protestant minister in New Haven whose life, like Tillich's book, helped him move to a socially engaged Christian theology. McClain's work in the Methodist student movement was awakening him to issues of racial justice, and while at Yale he signed petitions calling for racial integration among Methodists. All of this helped lead him to delve into church debates and make the struggle over segregation among Methodists the subject of his honors thesis.[48]

As McClain wrote on the occasion of our fiftieth reunion, soon after graduating from Yale and while earning a masters of divinity at Union Theological Seminary, he "moved from writing about racial desegregation to active participation in the Civil Rights Movement."[49] Over the following decades, the religiously inspired fight for civil rights stood at the center of McClain's life, commitments he shared with his wife, also an activist and minister. McClain participated in many of the most important events of the movement. As minister, editor of the Methodist *Social Questions Bulletin,* executive director of the Methodist Federation for Social Action, teacher, writer, and activist he continued his work for racial justice in ways that drew on his commitments as a Christian.[50]

Although he was raised as a Protestant, it was John Train's identity as a highly privileged white son of the New South that inspired this fourth classmate to write on civil rights in a thesis on the NAACP leader Walter F. White. Affectionately known as Chooch, Train grew up in Savannah, Georgia, and came to Yale from Episcopal High School, a boarding school in Alexandria, Virginia. His grandfather built the fortune in railroads that in turn made it possible for Train to grow up in a household with four or five African American servants. His Yale father, known as Choo-choo, captained the lacrosse team, twice earning a place on the All-American team. After Yale he went on to a career in Savannah as a medical doctor and pillar of the Episcopal Church. At Yale, the son played varsity football and joined both DKE and the senior society Berzelius. Late in his years at Yale "to his family's horror," Train's widow remarked recently, he marched with Hosea Williams in a civil rights protest in his hometown.[51]

White, whose papers were at Yale, as the head of the NAACP for a quarter century until his death in 1955 was centrally involved in struggles for racial justice, from the anti-lynching campaign to the Supreme Court decision in *Brown v. Board of Education.* Train wrote sympathetically about him and drew on the best practices of contemporary American studies, stressing not only the importance of jazz as a genuine contribution to American culture but also relying on his extensive readings in African American history and literature. Unlike Lamar, he emphasized the sustained, transformative role played by African American protesters that preceded the *Brown v. Board of*

Education decision. Central to his essay was what he saw as an unresolved tension in African American history that White's life illustrated. Although Train decried African Americans who "lost their identity in a shrill fanaticism that expressed itself" in black nationalism, as he saw W. E. B. Du Bois doing late in his life, he nonetheless believed that White and Booker T. Washington surrendered too much in their drive to embrace "an American character so fully." In the most original section of the thesis, he compared drafts of White's autobiography with the published version, revealing that early on White emphasized race pride and even superiority but in the book focused on the aspiration to assimilate and the commonalities that united African Americans and whites. Train found powerfully meaningful White's struggle to resolve the tension-filled paradox of aspiration to fit in and commitment to assert distinctiveness. "The present has brought to the American Negro a gift from the past," Train remarked in the final sentence of his thesis, "a whole new set of 'circumstances,'" that made it possible for the African American finally to "be free to assert his identity as the unique individual and the singular part of America that he is."[52] Train graduated from Harvard Law School in 1963 and then worked for a major law firm in Atlanta. Although he struggled throughout his life with his heritage as a white southerner, from what I can tell civil rights did not play a significant role in his life after Yale. He died at age sixty-two.

These four classmates who wrote senior theses on African America were exceptional in their engagement with civil rights. They drew their inspiration from different strains of white Protestantism. Although courses they took and professors they worked with influenced them, more important was the impact of religious life at Yale and dramatic events beyond New Haven. Their engagement with African American life as undergraduates was an unreliable predictor of what they would do after leaving Yale, although both Bing and McClain sustained long-term commitment that their years at Yale fostered.

The Impact of Race

After graduation, most of us were largely unprepared for a world that stood somewhere between the early stirrings of the civil rights movement in one decade and the intensification of struggles in the next. Professors wrote extensively about race, but their work remained isolated from that of their colleagues, stood apart from the university's priorities and in some cases from their own careers, and only occasionally informed what they taught undergraduates. Thus most of the members of the class of 1960 were largely ignorant of what African Americans faced in the past and present. Even though the handful of African American classmates were isolated from one another and from most of their white peers, Yale transformed their lives. Given all this confusion, isolation, and marginality, it is striking that some classmates were ahead of most of our teachers in their views of a rapidly changing racial situation. By and large, it was not the classes we took but the distinctive backgrounds of classmates, the Protestant chaplaincy, and events in the nation that played a key role in inspiring the engagement of some classmates. For me, my formal education, family traditions, increasing political awareness, and more generally my openness to new ways of thinking helped me sustain, especially in my teaching, an engagement with African American history. Some essays in the *Yale Daily News,* an undergraduate piece by one African American, and the senior papers by a handful of whites made it clear that civil rights were more urgent to a new generation than to an older one.

CHAPTER FOUR

Africa

Being outside America is today like being born anew.

AL LEE, class of 1960,
"How I Joined the Peace Corps and Found Mao," c. 1966

From 1956 to 1960 more than a score of African nations gained freedom from colonial rule. Impelled by rising aspirations for independence, they were also responding to fundamental changes in the international political economy. World War II eroded the power of European imperialism, and the conflict between the United States and the USSR spurred competition for the allegiances of developing countries. Not every struggle ended triumphantly. Authoritarian regimes soon emerged in some of the newly independent nations. And in March of my senior year, the government of South Africa brutally countered the protests against apartheid by black Africans at Sharpeville. Yet to many of my classmates and me, independence movements, reverberating with the civil rights struggles at home, evoked excitement about events abroad.[1]

I begin this chapter with a discussion of the senior project of Richard Celeste, the only peer I can identify who wrote extensively on Africa while we were in college. I turn next to a consideration of what Yale faculty members wrote about Africa around the time of my graduation. The few of them who focused on the continent clung to older understandings. In the summer between my junior and senior years I went to Africa for two months, including four weeks in Johannesburg. There I lived with my cousins, who were determined to educate me about the evils of apartheid. In scores of letters home I pondered what I was experiencing. I conclude with a focus on a baker's dozen of classmates who went to Africa after graduation, inspired less by courses they had taken than by campus ministries, news from home and abroad, and their own histories. Their experiences and mine fostered a reconsideration of the meaning of America and its relationship to the world. My peers and I grew up with images of Africa as a place where naked natives dwelled, but our direct contacts with the continent challenged how we understood the world.

High Hopes

The senior essay on Pan-Africanism by Dick Celeste, class of 1959, offered an optimistic, even naïve discussion of changes in Africa. In my junior year he worked on this paper as a Scholar of the House, a program that every year freed a handful of seniors from the obligation to take courses so they could focus on a major project. In discussing him, I go outside the class of 1960 because of what he wrote, because he involved me and some other friends in this project, and because involvement in his project helped foster my interest in Africa. As the deadline for turning in his paper approached, he had not written much. So I arranged for a group of us to go to the offices at Botwinik Brothers, my family's factory four miles from campus. Working from the evening into the morning hours, Celeste finished a draft of his essay by dictating chapters that his friends typed up.

As a child, like millions of other American boys, Celeste had visions of Tarzan in Africa, "an impression of something with the romantic appeal of excitement and mystery." More immediately several things sparked his interest. In his junior year he took Harry R. Rudin's course on African history and then encountered an activist from Africa at a Methodist student gathering in New York. Brimming with optimism stemming from historical circumstances, his political commitments, and his own ebullience, Celeste wrote his 160-page paper on the Pan-African Movement then emerging on the continent. In the Cold War context, he argued, Pan-Africanism leapt to prominence as part of a larger effort to solidify the power of the nations that had gathered in 1955 at the Bandung Conference, a meeting of non-aligned Asian and African nations.[2]

Celeste was unusual for a white scholar in his reliance on African and African American sources and in his advocacy of a Pan-Africanism associated with Kwame Nkrumah, the leader of Ghana and the influential advocate for Pan-Africanism. Drawing on E. David Cronon's work on Marcus Garvey, the writings of W. E. B. Du Bois and St. Claire Drake, and contemporary African sources, Celeste traced the history of Pan-Africanism. At a 1958 meeting in Accra, he noted, African leaders committed themselves to "the realization of 'Africa for Africans' and to the assertion of an 'African Personality.'" Minimizing the power of divisions based on religion and what contemporary observers called tribalism, but acknowledging the problems posed by colonialism, nationalism, regionalism, and race, Celeste looked forward to a time when

Pan-Africanism assumed a "real significance for the mass of Africans." He believed that as it did so through an "all-African Commonwealth," the continent would far surpass what Du Bois and others "dared to imagine." In the process, it would reject both "white racialism" and "black chauvinism." He stated that what made the movement significant was the "growing number of politically and socially self-conscious individuals throughout" the continent who were coming "to identify themselves as Africans with a set of common African values and a common African vision."[3]

A humorous anecdote seals the experience of this powerful and hopeful essay in my memory. At the last minute, Celeste realized that his notes revealed the title and content but not the name of the author of two articles. So for one, he put down Kenneth Gary Magee (the names of three compatriots helping him) and for another L. Botwinik (the name of my cousin who worked in the family firm). In the oral defense, Celeste grew nervous when one professor asked him about the Botwinik article; Celeste turned from panic to relief when he realized that the questioner was interested in the author's argument, not the alleged author's identity.[4]

What Faculty Wrote on Africa

In the late 1950s only three Yale professors gave more than minimal attention to the continent in their scholarship, and the university offered only two courses on Africa, one for undergraduates and one for graduate students. Although beginning in fall 1957 a program in African studies had emerged on paper, not until the late 1960s did the field actually become one. Yale was hardly unique in its relative inattention to Africa. For decades most of those who wrote about the continent were African Americans at historically black institutions. More widely, the turning point came with the 1958 founding of the African Studies Association and the 1960 launching of the *Journal of African History*. At a few American universities, notably Northwestern under the leadership of Melville J. Herskovits, African studies had developed in more extensive and less backward-looking ways by the late 1950s. At Yale in the late 1950s the world that mattered in the curriculum began in the United States and extended across the Atlantic to western Europe and the USSR, and across the Pacific to China and Japan.[5]

The Yale professors who wrote more than minimally on Africa—Harry R. Rudin, Leonard Doob, and George ("Pete") Murdock—did so in ways that pointed more to an imperial past than the postcolonial present. Unlike Celeste, they offered a paternalistic and Eurocentric vision that highlighted how Europe brought civilization to Africa. Each of them came to Yale along a different path but all spent most of their careers there. Doob was the outsider, not having been at Yale before he joined the faculty in 1934. Rudin, who grew up in a working-class, Swedish American family in Vermont, came to Yale from a public high school and except for years in the military and in China, and a short stint teaching at Hotchkiss, remained in New Haven. Even more so than Rudin, his college classmate Murdock was at home at Yale, having been born into a family from which generations of men had matriculated and having come to Yale from Andover. After Franz Boas told Murdock he was a dilettante and discouraged him from applying to Columbia, which housed the most important anthropology department in the nation, Murdock continued his education at Yale. Thus he remained there almost without interruption from 1915 when he entered as an undergraduate until forty-five years later when mandatory retirement forced him to leave.[6]

Rudin, the sole professor for whom Africa was central and the Africanist faculty member who influenced so many of us even though his scholarship was dated, was part of the generation of historians that focused on the continent as an extension of European diplomatic history. In *Germans in the Cameroons, 1884–1914: A Case Study in Modern Imperialism* (1938), he examined documents in European archives but did not rely on local sources. He saw native Africans as highly intelligent people who in some instances had developed impressive systems of governing, and he acknowledged the brutality and violence of the colonists. Yet he concluded that "Germany's colonial accomplishments in thirty short years constitute a record of unusual achievement" entitling the nation "to a very high rank as a successful colonial power." He emphasized the benevolence and efficiency of German colonialism, praising "the throbbing and omnipresent energy" that infused its efforts. Although he carried out some of his research in the archives in Berlin during the year Hitler came to power, he did not connect the racism evident during his time there with the motives that played some role in driving Germany's imperial ventures.

Beginning in the early 1950s, Rudin expressed his grave concern that anti-colonialism, by eroding a stable and peaceful world order, would undermine Westerners' sense of security, intensify nationalism, and replace universal brotherhood with barbarism. In the fight against the USSR, he asserted, the United States should support the struggle of African nations for self-government because it needed the continent's inexpensive labor, ample land for Western nations' excess population, abundant raw materials, and strategically placed military bases. John Bing, the author of the senior thesis on racial integration in Deerfield, Illinois, reported from Africa in July 1961 that Rudin, while on a trip there, asserted that "political independence now is not the way to solve technical problems and that independence will not be real until 2000.[7]

Doob focused on the continent as only one of many of his scholarly interests, and he did so to test social science hypotheses rather than to understand the region. He looked at Africa through Western lenses that privileged a Eurocentric interpretation of historical change. He saw colonial settlers as people who conferred civilization's benefits on natives. He knew the path forward from colonial rule was far from smooth: as the settlers proved unwilling to distribute the "gifts" of civilization "more widely or swiftly," the locals grew more resentful. In turn the colonizers were surprised by the lack of gratitude. Doob nonetheless maintained the hope that "uncivilized" Africans would become "civilized" and embrace rationality, tolerance, and self-awareness.[8]

Even more than Rudin and Doob, Murdock could not shed his cultural blinders. He never carried out fieldwork in Africa and was there for a total of less than four weeks. He did not emphasize the historical particularism and cultural relativism developed by Boas and his students such as Ruth Benedict and Hershkovits. Instead, Murdock stressed the amassing of data on hundreds of cultures worldwide in order to test hypotheses within a framework of evolutionary change. In his 1959 book on Africa he presented photographs reminiscent of *National Geographic* coverage in the period: scantily clothed men and women who displayed ritual markers on their bodies. When talking of the past, he used the present tense to describe traditional customs, giving the strong impression of how backward black Africans remained. Thus, just when African nations were rebelling against colonial rule and achieving independence, he advanced an old-fashioned picture of the continent.[9]

"A strange aboriginal past and luxurious but bloody future."

During my junior year, my mother and father offered me an option: they would buy me a car or support my travel during the following summer. Given how important travel was in my family, my choice was easy. Three factors shaped the specific plans. First was the trip my Botwinik grandmother had recently made to Africa. Second was my friendship with my Johannesburg cousin Ivor Schwartzman; a half dozen or so years my senior, in the late 1950s he had come to New Haven several times, as he agonized over whether to switch from being a barrister in South Africa to a lawyer in the United States. Third were the preferences of my classmate and traveling companion John Gordon Haverly. He had arrived at Yale from the Thatcher School in Ojai, California. He lived above me in Trumbull College, we participated in the same underground senior society, and he was a member of the conservative campus political organization the Calliopean Society. Our fourteen-week trip during the summer of 1959 began in Europe and ended in Africa at a critical point in the continent's history.[10]

In letters I wrote home, I thought about the meaning of race in Africa and America, what it meant for me to be an American, and my nation's role in a changing world. Mixing naïveté and insight, my letters revealed the distance I had come on issues of racial politics since I had written the paper on Reconstruction eighteen months before.

I pondered the meaning of race even before I arrived in Africa. While in London in early June, I described a "'racial' stabbing" in Notting Hill that I saw more through the lens of America than as a turning point in British race relations. "It is with great adroitness and alacrity that Parliament and the press cover it up," I remarked. Then from Rome two weeks later, I told my grandmother, who had little formal education but was always eager to hear of books she might learn from, that I was reading *The Price of Diamonds* (1958) by the South African novelist Dan Jacobson. It was, I wrote her with regret, a book that "touches on the color problem lightly." On the eve of my arrival in Africa I wrote home that soon I would go "into what must be a strange aboriginal past and luxurious but bloody future—Africa." In a letter from Kenya's Amboselli Park on my first night on the continent, I told my parents that there were two Africas. One, the "primitive, still in a kind of anachronistic splendor, is a thing of grace and of color." In contrast stood "the Africa in transition." One image caught my attention: "the tall, clay-colored shepherd at the side of the road" as "a symbol of the country" who waved "to every passing automobile. Only those not yet initiated into the laws of life in Africa think of waving back."

I made this remark because I was drawing a comparison between myself as the innocent American and the third-generation white African who, serving as our guide and driver, continually did things both "symbolic and small . . . to remind the natives of their position." He boasted of his role in brutally putting down the Mau Mau insurgency earlier in the 1950s. He criticized Nkrumah for turning away from a two-party system. He talked about "taking no cheek from a native." He insisted that he and his peers had to continue to lead and that most black Africans were "gracious, courteous, but quiet and oppressively humble." Carried away by what I must have thought was my ability to elicit rich material in interviews, I wrote my parents asking them to inquire at Yale University Press if they could imagine the publication of "a book on Apartheid in So. Africa patterned after Robert Penn Warren's *Segregation*."[11]

The next day I wrote a letter in which I explored the contrasts between race in Africa and America. I criticized the arrogance of our guide's "white superiority." Trying to figure out the situation of black Africans, I divided them into three groups: "the largest and happiest" who were "still living a primitive life"; those who were "superficially Westernized"; and a small group of "European educated intellectuals" who were alienated from the masses. If white "liberals" had so excessively patted black Africans on the back that they had wrongfully concluded "that self-government can come immediately," I believed that self-government in east Africa was scores of decades in the future. In contrast and in my naïveté, what struck me was how successfully America had incorporated African Americans into society, one instance of many during this trip when my experiences with colonial racism impelled me to defend the situation back home. "The American negro was able to rise en masse [triple underlined] so quickly" for several reasons: "lack of a language barrier"; a "social order . . . not that different from that of the whites"; the absence of specific affiliations that made democracy more difficult to achieve; the fact that most of them were Christians; and the availability of industrial jobs for which they could obtain the necessary skills.[12]

At the end of July I began a month-long stay in South Africa. The period around our visit was especially fraught in the nation's history. The Afrikaner National Party, which had begun to rule in 1948, was consolidating both its own power and the system of apartheid it imposed. Shortly before my arrival in Johannesburg, the government had passed an act that intensified the efforts to move black Africans into supposedly self-governing rural areas organized on what officials saw as a tribal basis. In 1959 in the world of English-speaking whites, the Progressive Party split off from the more conservative United Party, and among black Africans, the Pan Africanist Congress (PAC) from the African National Congress (ANC). Not long after I left South Africa, the government banned the ANC and the PAC and in March 1960 put down protests in Sharpeville.

Before I went to South Africa I had learned of apartheid from extensive conversations with Ivor and from my classmate Jim Walker's November 1957 article "South Africa's Approach to Race Relations," published in the Yale Political Union's *Rostrum*. Walker was one of two classmates from Africa, both of them white. Race relations in his country, he remarked, had recently "become acute," with "the increasing urbanization and education of the African and the dissolution of the tribal system." The National Party's apartheid policy, he asserted, was the "only concrete solution to the racial problem to be proposed by a major political party." It was "the most practical solution," allowing black Africans "to rise to positions of the highest responsibility within their own areas, until eventually they will control themselves," even as he admitted that this was economically problematic and avoided the moral issues apartheid raised.[13]

I now faced South Africa's oppressive system from the protected space of the Schwartzmans' world, once again within my family's orbit. When in the 1890s some members of my mother's family left eastern Europe, they scattered, some to Palestine, most to the United States, and one couple, Ivor's parents, Isaac and Pauline Schwartzman, to South Africa. The Schwartzmans prospered: Isaac owned a store near the city's downtown, where he sold dry goods to black Africans. In 1959 Ivor, Isaac, Pauline, and my contemporary Margot lived in a wealthy suburb of Johannesburg where Haverly and I stayed in the family's large house, staffed by six black African servants. Several in my Johannesburg family, including Ivor, had prominent roles fighting apartheid. They were among those relatively few Jews who opposed apartheid, in their case as liberals who did so from within the legal and political system in contrast to the Jewish radicals who joined the Communist Party. Just before I arrived Ivor had secured the acquittal of fifteen black Africans accused of murder. He was "serving the most vital function possible for a liberal in this society," I wrote home, to "preserve what rule of law is still preservable." For white liberals caught "between the two extremes of white supremacy and African Nationalism, there seems to be no mediating point which will ever be possible here."[14]

Through her friendship with Francie Suzman, Margot Schwartzman arranged for me to spend time at the home of Francie's mother, Helen Suzman, the only member of the all-white national parliament who opposed apartheid. With others she was in the process of forming the Progressive Party.[15] When I was in Johannesburg she was hosting Al Lowenstein, who was there on a secret and dangerous mission. He was about to travel to South-West Africa, then governed by the Republic of South Africa under a UN mandate and now the Republic of Namibia, to smuggle out material that would reveal how repressively South Africa governed the territory. Successful, Lowenstein, who was on the verge on becoming a major figure in the civil rights movement and progressive politics, flew back to America to present damning evidence to a committee of the UN, which in turn launched an appeal to the International Court of Justice challenging South Africa's rule of the territory.[16]

The racial situation under apartheid commanded my attention. The Schwartzmans, especially Ivor and Margot, made sure that my education was thorough. They arranged for me to go to the treason trial, which had among its thirty defendants members of the African National Congress, Nelson Mandela included. One day, during a recess in the trial I talked to one of the black African defendants, who told me his life story. The trial took place in what was once a synagogue, which I noted was "quite metaphorical since it points to the breakdown of religion as a provider of morally positive force in the community," a remark that neglected the role of religious leaders in opposing apartheid. The trial, I wrote home, "somehow recalls" the one that ended in the execution of the Rosenbergs. The Schwartzman's library contained a copy of *The Death House Letters of Ethel and Julius Rosenberg* (1953), and reading them, I wrote, "leaves one with a very sad and distasteful feeling. The question of guilt aside," I insisted, as I used "one" to distance myself, "it is a page in Americana one wishes to skip."[17]

The Schwartzmans continued my education by making sure that I encountered the Afrikaner viewpoint. They took me to the Voortrekker Monument in Pretoria "used to incite racialist feelings," I wrote home, built by Afrikaners to commemorate their ancestors who on their march from Cape Town to the Transvaal wiped out "African tribes." They arranged for me to go to a farm where I listened to a wealthy Afrikaner justify apartheid. They set up a situation where, while visiting Alexandra township, I vigorously debated a defender of apartheid who contended that it was the only way of dealing with black Africans, who were "gentlemen" as long as they remained in their "native reserves" provided by the government. I responded by pointing out that most of the land the government granted black Africans was "unsuitable for anything better than subsistence." I argued that "paternalism" was not "a very noble attitude" and expressed a preference for giving black Africans "their own chance."[18]

The Schwartzmans insisted I read about South Africa, pointing me to Alan Paton's *Cry, the Beloved Country* (1948), to Father Trevor Huddleston's *Naught for Your Comfort* (1956), and to Arthur M. Keppel Jones's *When Smuts Goes* (1947), the speculative dystopian history of South Africa that predicted the rise of the National Party and a repressive order at least as harsh as what emerged under apartheid. They arranged for me to see organized "tribal" dances and visit a mine where the black Africans worked under grueling conditions for little pay, separated into tribes to divide and conquer. Margot, Ivor, a niece of Helen Suzman, John Haverly, and I traveled to Swaziland, the independent British protectorate. There my South African companions enjoyed "the presence of an unstrained and almost unconscious series of relationships" with black Africans who, unaffected by apartheid, "were neither afraid of our presence nor felt restrained by it." My hosts arranged for me to go to a rally for free speech and against apartheid on my second day in the country, after which the anti-apartheid *Rand Daily Mail* ran a picture of the event (with me a barely visible member of the audience). The caption said that the president of the student body at University of Witwatersrand called on his peers in the mixed-race audience "'to step down into the wider arena of political conflict' and to align themselves with the liberatory forces against apartheid."[19]

The omnipresence of apartheid presented me with what I saw as insoluble dilemmas. "The race question is ever-present on one's mental horizon," I remarked to my grandmother, adding that it was a "frightening, complicated, all pervading issue." Divisiveness seemed almost universal. "Perhaps the most pitiful thing across which one runs here is *hate*." I lamented how one of the mixed-race men I met referred to "the African as a Kafir," a derogatory term used for black Africans. The pervasiveness of hatred had "even affected me so that whenever I hear Afrikaans spoken I mutter under my breath, you damn Dutchman!" Yet I also found that black "Africans seem to be the only group that does not hate every other group." Given all this, resistance to apartheid seemed nearly impossible. "One can oppose by force which at the present time is senseless; or by symbolic protests which, practically speaking, are useless."[20]

Again and again, I made clear that the racial situation in South Africa prompted me to think about how what my South African relatives experienced resembled and differed from what I knew in America. I offered conflicting responses when I compared the situation in the two countries. On the one hand, what I witnessed in South Africa deepened my understanding of the situation back home. "The enormity of evil" of the situation in South Africa helped me "realize how much bad both in race relations and in the government's intervention into the lives of the people does exist in America." The other impulse—defending America as better—was more prominent. When I wrote of a conversation with a black African woman I met in a township, I reported telling her that African Americans lived in my neighborhood and that whites and blacks could go to movie theaters together, but I did not make clear that this was not true in the South. "Bad though things might be in America," I insisted, the picture was "ever improving," unlike what was true in South Africa. Similarly, I innocently explained that in America "it was not the government that blocked progress but private prejudice." Stories of the American situation reported in the Johannesburg publication *Drum,* I remarked, lamentably provide "a much more well-known impression of America" than that conveyed by news of the successful integration of schools in Louisville, Kentucky, or the life of Ralph Bunche, a UN official who won the Nobel Peace Prize in 1950, or George Crawford, the prominent African American lawyer in New Haven.

My Yale professor Cushing Strout wrote me that my response to what I saw in South Africa reminded him of the theme Louis Hartz "pushed—the American discovers the mildness of his own social conflicts when he ventures abroad into a much more dramatic kind of warfare." Indeed my visit to Sophiatown drove home to me how black Africans admired some of what America stood for. This was a township that the government was bulldozing because it represented all that they wished to destroy: a vital multiracial community home to black African political leaders as well as those who created distinctive music based on American jazz and blues. While there, I visited a shebeen, an illegal beer and music hall, run, I noted, by an African who had "unconsciously cultivated an American accent."[21]

I also pondered the future of South Africa, reflecting the concerns that the Schwartzmans expressed. Some mixed-race young men talked to me of the likelihood of a violent revolution, and I told my family back home that my Johannesburg hosts frequently talked of a "blood bath" supported by arms smuggled into the country. I considered the possibility that the ruling National Party might triumph but rejected this as "impossible in light of African leadership and eventual external forces." I naively hoped that the English-speaking opposition party might "be driven farther and farther left due to the vindictiveness, speed, and viciousness with which the government is proceeding on its road to totalitarianism." Without explicitly emphasizing the role of black Africans in such endeavors, I wondered whether boycotts and strikes might succeed in pressuring the government to change. Either black Africans would acquiesce to the current situation, I concluded, or there would be "a disastrous revolution," two "dim alternatives" avoidable only by "intervention, probably non-violent, from the outside" such as boycotts led by America and Britain.[22]

Haverly and I left South Africa in late August and made our way home via Victoria Falls in what was then Southern Rhodesia, Brazzaville in French Equatorial Africa across the river from Leopoldville in the Belgian Congo, and then onward with stops in Accra, Ghana, and Dakar, Senegal. At the Pan Am office in Leopoldville I asked whether my hometown street name, Colony Road, was a dirty word. "No, not yet," was the answer. "Tension and hate are quite absent here," I remarked of a country where, I noted, the ratio of blacks to whites was 3,000 to 1. In early September I reported on a conversation in Leopoldville with a black African who (accurately) predicted that "there would be a revolution here within 6 months," as his countrymen rejected the compromise plans that came too late from the royal Belgian family who for decades had ruled the country as a private corporation. "This belief in imminent revolution," I remarked, once again naively, "is somewhat hard to be convinced of" since I saw "a great deal of" racial mixing in public spaces. "I'm sure there is plenty of rigidity in the relationships—whites usually have the homes, cars, and best jobs," I concluded in the last sentence I wrote from Africa. Here I grossly underestimated the extremity of the situation. In 1960 there were fewer than forty black African university graduates in the Belgian Congo and of five thousand management positions in the nation's civil service, black Africans held only three. My visit came soon after riots and nationalist organizing, some of them under the leadership of Patrice Lumumba, had broken the surface calm of Belgian rule. Ten months after my visit the Congolese achieved independence. Within months of Lumumba's coming to power by a democratic election in June 1960, the Congo's president had dismissed him and America's National Security Council approved his assassination, which occurred in January 1961.[23]

Among the many things that strike me as I read over these letters five decades later knowing the future that actually came about is how much I missed or misinterpreted. I was very much an innocent abroad. Like many Westerners I had no grasp of the speed with which independence was coming. I hardly understood what drove black Africans to risk and achieve so much. Nor did I fully understand what was at stake for the United States in decolonialization and independence. I understood the situation in South Africa much more clearly, because of both the brutality of apartheid and the commitment of the Schwartzmans to educate me. Even here, though, I was less than fully aware of the forces at work, especially those that would bring the ANC to power decades later. Yet I have to be careful not to judge myself too harshly. Although I used the word "primitive," elsewhere I undercut the common claim that native Africans disliked people taking their pictures because that meant stealing something precious from them.[24] In the 1950s Rudin, who had studied Africa for decades, misunderstood much more than I did six years later. He praised the Belgian royal family for its benevolence. In 1959 George Murdock, who spent less time in Africa in his lifetime than I did in the summer of 1959 but who for decades had dedicated himself to understanding traditional societies, had less of a historical sense and a less realistic picture than I had. Then again, who could have foreseen in 1959 that in 1990 the National Party and the ANC would participate in talks that would lead to the formation of a multiracial democracy, let alone that in 1994 South Africa would elect Mandela as its president and that he in turn would appoint as his deputy F. W. de Klerk, formerly the head of the National Party and the president of South Africa.

After I returned to New Haven I gave talks on apartheid at local high schools. While still at Yale, I worked to call the attention of my peers to what I had learned. On May 4, 1960, I moderated a discussion by English- and Afrikaner-speaking students at Yale on "apartheid, South-west Africa, and the Cape Negroes." Although the headline said the panelists condemned apartheid, they seemed more intent on criticizing it as unrealistic than as immoral, and an Afrikaner undergraduate focused on how descendants of Dutch settlers had nowhere else to go. "Giving the vote to the Negro," he asserted, "would likely result in the white losing his country."[25] At the same time, I arranged for the *Yale Daily News* to reprint a long letter from Ivor Schwartzman to my mother, one that offered a vastly different picture of the situation than did the panelists.

The letter began with "Dear Miriam" but ended unsigned because, as an editor noted, it could not be printed in the "supposedly free country" of South Africa. Correcting the South African government's distorted rendering of what happened at Sharpeville, Schwartzman offered a dire picture—characterized by "violence and repression" carried out with "Teutonic ruthlessness" of a "police state." He reported that the government, "in typical Nazi fashion," arrested his friends in early morning raids. However, "in a revolutionary situation where two forces of nationalism are opposed to each other" and with civil liberties suspended, as a "White Liberal" there was little for him to do. He could not bring his legal skills to bear except in criminal cases, although he could help black Africans by giving material aid. Yet, he insisted, "one cannot really contribute to the African's struggle because it is the struggle that the African must undertake more or less on his own." The only hope he held out was that British and American boycotts of goods from South Africa, as well as the refusal of dock workers to handle exports, might convince the Afrikaner government to change its mind.[26]

My trip to Africa, especially to South Africa, had a profound effect on me, helping as it did to shape my views of race at home and abroad. My parents had afforded me an opportunity, unusual for even the most privileged of my classmates, to travel somewhere dramatically different. What connected my life in New Haven and abroad was the importance of family, travel, and cosmopolitanism, as well as fresh perspectives on the lives of Jews in the diaspora. Although I often resisted, the extended trip provided me with key building blocks for a fresh understanding of the continent and the world, not available in the formal curriculum or professorial writing at Yale. Apartheid, Celeste's paper, the struggles for national independence, the Rosenberg letters, the confrontation with both evil and new forms of political action challenged how I saw liberalism, race, and America's relationship to the world. Sometimes I clung to a Cold War vision that all was good with America; sometimes experience moved me to new perspectives. Caught between naïveté and openness to thinking in new ways placed me right on the cusp.

Classmates Encounter Africa after Graduation

I can identify thirteen classmates whose engagement with Africa loomed large through residencies there that began in the early 1960s.[27] Although this is a small percentage of the class, their experiences nonetheless illuminate the dynamics that shaped many people in my generation. In the years right after graduation Africa was the lodestar shaping our lives in ways that were direct, nuanced, and unexpected—and in which William Sloane Coffin Jr. played a major role. Like other college graduates who in the early 1960s would go abroad in the Peace Corps and similar programs, my classmates went to Africa for varied reasons. Some acted on altruistic, idealistic, and existential impulses, while others hoped for adventure that would extend their horizons beyond the provincial confines of their upbringing. Some were trying to explore engagement in the world with purposes larger than anticommunism. What my peers found in Africa varied, but the experience of clashes between naïve expectations and reality shaped their futures. Although no one fits perfectly into any one category, I group my discussion into three categories: academics and civil servants who later focused their professional lives on the continent; classmates for whom Africa transformed their religious, spiritual, artistic, and political outlooks; and sons from elite families whose lives testify to how the 1960s transformed the dynamics of social class.

Africa and the Reshaping of American Professions

"Much of my life has been involved with Africa," remarked John Dwyer in our twenty-fifth reunion book, and the same can be said for the other four classmates whose time in Africa in the early to mid-1960s profoundly shaped them personally and professionally.[28] Dwyer taught in Uganda and then after graduate school was a professor of African history at Pomona College. Lowenstein's talk at Yale on South-West Africa, more than Rudin's course, inspired Harvey Feinberg to study Africa and then to teach African history at Southern Connecticut State University. Feinberg cherished his journey to South Africa in 1994 as an official observer of South Africa's first democratic election. In their PhD theses, both Dwyer and Feinberg deployed an approach that broke from Rudin's imperial and administrative perspectives.[29] John Bing has acknowledged that his time in Africa led him to earn a PhD in African politics and later to teach on that subject at Heidelberg College. More so than Dwyer or Feinberg, Bing combined his interest in African politics with issues of race and social justice at home, inflected by his pre-Yale encounters with Social Gospel Protestantism.[30] After teaching in Ethiopia, Owen Cylke spent twenty-five years in the Foreign Service, and then worked for the Agency for International Development and for the World Wildlife Fund, where he focused mainly on Africa. In retirement he has helped run a microfinance program in Uganda.[31]

The fifth of these professional Africanists, Ed Elmendorf, was the only one who was politically active at Yale. He was a member of several organizations on the left, including the George Orwell Forum, through which he became friendly with Robert Bone, author of *The Negro Novel in America*. With Bone, Elmendorf went on the April 18, 1959, Youth March for Integrated Schools in Washington, where he listened to speeches by Martin Luther King Jr., A. Philip Randolph, Bayard Rustin, Roy Wilkins, and the Kenyan Tom Mboya. What caught Elmendorf's eye as graduation approached was Yale Men Abroad, a program Coffin had developed, which placed him in a job teaching English at a secondary school in Ghana. There he found his optimistic hopes challenged by harsh realities. Returning to America, in 1963 he began a career in international affairs, working at the United Nations for six years as the assistant to American ambassadors, taking a position at the World Bank with a focus on Africa, and serving in 2010–11 as president and CEO of United Nations Association of the United States. Almost fifty years after he had marched on Washington, he and his wife Sue joined more than a million others "deeply affected to witness the inauguration of the first black President of the USA."[32]

The lives of these five share several characteristics. They all came from middle- to upper-middle-class suburban families that were, as far as can be determined, liberal in their politics. Elmendorf grew up in an internationally oriented house and after his sophomore year spent a year in Germany, but the others had more provincial young adulthoods. At Yale, none of them participated in the activities—fraternities, senior societies, varsity athletics, singing groups—that would have marked them as prototypical Yale men. Much more than the curriculum, it was Coffin and speakers who came to campus who influenced their lives. With JFK's election, several of them felt a desire to do something for their country and, more generally, a restlessness that impelled them to seek experiences that would expand their lives beyond their relatively protected upbringing. Going to Africa pointed them forward to careers as teachers of African history and politics and as government and NGO officials.

Transformative Voyages

For five different classmates the years in Africa provided experiences that, while affecting them professionally, were more powerfully transformative in religious, spiritual, and political terms. I begin with Dick Peace, whose way of life growing up and then at Yale was atypical both for classmates in general and, more specifically, for those who encountered Africa. He came to Yale from a Detroit household whose southern background and working-class life shaped his parents' disapproval of his high school friendships with the

African Americans he met through participation in a Christian fellowship group. Peace majored in electrical engineering, not in the humanities or social sciences, the choice of all others venturing to Africa soon after graduation. His undergraduate focus reminds us how irrelevant our majors were for many of us in determining our careers. A number of extracurricular experiences framed his years at Yale in ways deeply connected to his calling to Christian work. First was his involvement with religious organizations, especially the evangelical Inter-Varsity Christian Fellowship. Second was hearing Martin Luther King Jr. speak, an event arranged by another evangelical classmate. Finally, Coffin's suggestion that he focus on Africa after graduation reverberated with his awareness of independence movements and with his long-standing desire to do missionary work abroad.[33]

Soon after graduating, Peace enrolled at Fuller Theological School, there continuing his political and spiritual transformation. Over time he became a Democrat, and he moved from the Baptist church to the United Church of Christ, a denomination that was inclining toward theological and political liberalism in the 1960s. After returning from his first trip to Africa in 1962, while at Fuller he met and married Judy Boppell, and they decided to do missionary work in Africa. From 1964 to 1971 they helped establish interdenominational evangelical churches serving black Africans, mostly in South Africa. The time in South Africa helped foster a politics he had lacked on graduating from Yale. There he and his wife learned how Christian love made respect possible across racial lines; how to work to repair the harshness, racism, and evil of apartheid; and how to develop commitments to treat all people as equals and with dignity. There they also became aware of the ways a nationalistic, militaristic, and fearful America lent its support to a repressive regime because it wanted to protect its own economic interests.[34]

Peace continued his theological education in Africa, eventually earning his PhD in biblical studies from the University of Natal. In the early 1970s he returned with Judy to the United States and worked on media projects that promoted the evangelical ministry and helped secular organizations. In 1976 he began more than three decades as a professor of theology, first at Gordon-Conwell Theological Seminary and then at Fuller, writing or editing more than eighty religious books. After Africa opened him up to "the world beyond America," he remarked, he "could never be provincial again."[35]

For Rod Marriott, going to Africa involved a different kind of journey, one shaped by the quest for intense experiences that fed his artistic sensibilities. At Yale he belonged to the literati, an identity represented especially by his activity in student theater organizations. In addition, his joining the United World Federalists and the UN Committee made clear his commitment to internationalism. Soon after graduation he spent time in a "small Nigerian Village where there was grammar in the morning and James Joyce at night." After he returned from Nigeria, he taught at Exeter for a dozen years. During vacations he leapt "into a Land Rover with other seekers" and sailed "across the vast Sahara to leopard masks and dance rites and Kilimanjaro, to the ever more exotic" until a charging elephant taught him "that each present moment is a precious gift." Then in the late 1970s he fulfilled his lifelong dream by moving to New York to direct plays. Marriott died in 1990. "Africa seemed to energize him in a profound way," wrote his friend Peter Parsons, it "seemed to inspire the best in him as well as provide him a ground for his natural exotic extravagances."[36]

Karl Robinson's time in Africa helped launch him on a countercultural quest.[37] In his final two years at Yale, several events underscored the nature of his emerging commitment to embark on a venturesome path. He protested DKE's rejection of Raleigh Davenport as a member. His close contact with Coffin provided him with a model of engagement. He developed a friendship with Rudin after taking his course on African history. An internship in the office of Mayor Richard C. Lee led him to interview leaders of the local African American community, an experience he called "transformative" because until then he had lived a sheltered life. Thinking of how he and like-minded peers might draw on public service abroad to benefit the nation, in early 1959 he composed a letter, which the *Christian Science Monitor* published, proposing the kind of effort that two years later would emerge as the Peace Corps. Writing at a time when most male undergraduates had to shape their futures in light of compulsory military service, he advocated work abroad and the drafting of "intelligent and highly qualified college student into a civil corps" as an alternative to "the colossal waste" of military service.[38]

Soon after graduation, Robinson followed his own suggestion and headed for Africa. There he taught school and lived among expatriates whose narrowness and separation from the local Africans, he later recalled, "drove him crazy." During the summer between his two years in Nigeria he traveled to Europe where he met followers of Gurdjieff, a Russian spiritualist who taught people how to transcend the "waking sleep" of purposeless lives and achieve a higher state of consciousness. In 1966 Robinson returned to Africa as a freelance reporter, where a motorcycle accident landed him in the Albert Schweitzer Hospital in French Equatorial Africa. While recuperating, he learned of how Schweitzer blended music, theology, philosophy, and medicine with criticism of colonialism. This led him to his life's work, which combines medicine and spiritualism. He earned his MD and over time embraced homeopathy. In his practice he has followed Schweitzer's interest in Asian Indian approaches, embracing an emphasis on healing the mind-body dichotomy through higher consciousness.[39]

Al Lee's experiences in Africa combined creative writing and radical politics in a heady mixture. Early on at Yale, he articulated an adversarial politics. In a letter to the editor of the *Yale Daily News* he wrote in our first year, he critiqued the way prominent Yalies such as William F. Buckley Jr. and the conservative political scientist Wilmoore Kendall kept alive the fires of McCarthyism after the death of Senator McCarthy. Then responding to the battle over integration at Central High School in Little Rock in the fall of our sophomore year, he drew on John Dollard's *Caste and Class in a Southern Town* to criticize the self-righteousness of northern whites who failed to see patterns of segregation in the North and the way southern elites joined with "mobs of riffraff" to block racial integration as they hid under the banner of states' rights.[40] After graduation, Lee began to "drift . . . leftward" as he pursued an MFA at the University of Iowa. He then joined the Peace Corps both to avoid the draft and to find excitement abroad. From 1962 to 1964, he taught at a Muslim secondary school in Kumasi, Ghana, the center of opposition to Nkrumah. By the time of his stay, the situation had changed since Celeste wrote his paper on Pan-Africanism. Experiencing both the government of Ghana and the Peace Corps as morally problematic, Lee turned even more radical. He asserted that the frequently heard judgment of people in host countries that Peace Corps Volunteers were spies "had an indirect truth to it." What the volunteers reported to their supervisors ended up being conveyed to the CIA and other federal agencies, "the whole octopus, of which we were the longest, most sensitive, and most innocent-looking tentacle[s]." He and his peers in the Peace Corps were, Lee came to realize, wrapped in "a blanket thrown around the world to keep American hearts warm."[41]

Lee made clear how powerfully transformative his Peace Corps experience was when he wrote soon after that "being outside America is today like being born anew." His years in Africa intensified his race consciousness and made him aware of the limits of his liberalism. With wit and sharpness he criticized Nkrumah's regime for its venality and repressive authoritarianism. Ghana was a "never-never land," an embodiment of Black Power that "rivaled the Tammany Tiger in its corruption" and was hypocritical in claiming its commitment to socialism. His encounters with Africans taught him that most of them believed "Mau Mau was as worthy a cause as Loyalist Spain, that the CIA is more menacing than the K. G. B., and that South Africa is more distasteful to a lorry driver in the West African bush than Cuba is to a United Fruit shareholder in Miami Beach." Leaving Ghana, Lee lived the life of a writer on Paris's Left Bank for a year, moved to New York, married, in 1968 began teaching at what became New Jersey Institute of Technology, and continued to write poetry and prose. He died in his mid-fifties.[42]

Jamie Kunz was another classmate whose time in Africa profoundly affected his life and his politics. Growing up in a middle-class suburb of Chicago, he was sensitized to racial prejudice early, learning from his parents of the Daughters of the American Revolution's refusal to let Marian Anderson sing at Constitution Hall in 1939, and watching Jackie Robinson break through baseball's color line in 1947. A combination of guilt and sense of responsibility prompted him to question the privilege of his birthright at a young age as he realized that good fortune in life came through chance, not merit. In his senior year at Yale, he heard Coffin speak skeptically about Charles Van Doren's attempt to explain away his complicity in the quiz show scandal. When shortly after we graduated he read of Coffin's organizing Yale undergraduates to join him on the Freedom Rides, Kunz later recalled that "it had never occurred to me that that sort of world-grappling was possible." After Yale, Kunz drifted for several years, a graduate student more interested in exploring Beat culture than in scholarship. JFK's assassination in November 1963 ended his aimlessness and prompted him to join the Peace Corps. He ended up spending four and a half years teaching in Malawi, a British protectorate that gained its independence just before he arrived in July 1964.[43]

During his first year in Malawi, Kunz shared living quarters with Paul Theroux, who was beginning to collect material for his novels and travel writing. His friendship with Theroux was important in his political transformation. The American ambassador in Malawi summoned Kunz after Theroux wrote an editorial in an in-house Peace Corps newspaper denouncing LBJ as a murderer in Vietnam. Theroux drew Kunz into involvement in what the ruling dictator Hastings Blanda construed as an attempt to assassinate him and overthrow the government. Theroux, ejected from the Peace Corps, left Malawi; Kunz remained, continuing to teach as a government employee after his Peace Corps stint ended.[44]

Nothing in his experience abroad, however, prepared Kunz for what he found soon after his return to enter University of Chicago Law School in the summer of 1969: the intensification of the war in Vietnam, the documentary film *Medium Cool*, which highlighted the violence in Chicago in the summer of 1968, the 1969–70 conspiracy trial of the Chicago Seven, and the murder in early December 1969 of Black Panther Party leader Fred Hampton by law enforcement officials who entered his apartment while he slept. All this, plus his encounters in Malawi with American and African officialdom, impelled

Kunz toward his career as a public defender, especially in death penalty cases. Decades in that role, he later remarked, involved "redistributing the wealth of my class to where I thought it belonged."[45]

These five classmates embarked on transformative voyages when they went to Africa, journeys that broke them out of the provincialism of their years growing up and at Yale. Coffin, their own restlessness, JFK, encounters with American racism, and a desire to combine mind-awakening experiences with service impelled them forward. Evangelical Protestant, experience-seeking artist, pursurer of alternative medicine and Eastern religions, radicalized writer, and defense attorney for death row inmates—their paths were compellingly different. Their backgrounds ranged from blue collar (Peace and Lee) to upper middle class (Robinson), but for all of them Africa shaped their careers and impelled them leftward.

Africa and the Transformation of American Elites

Three members of the Yale class of 1960 who experienced Africa after graduation came from highly privileged backgrounds. Their experiences reveal the transformation of American elites in the years after 1960—parallel to yet different from the better-known experiences of their elders such as William Sloane Coffin Jr. and Kingman Brewster.

Sam Bowles, named after a famous mid-nineteenth century antislavery publisher, came from the most storied background in the group of Africanists. His engagement with the African continent seems like a liberal interlude between leftist activism as an undergraduate and a radicalism that emerged only after the mid-1960s, when he shifted his attention from abroad to home. His interest in Africa stemmed from several sources, especially his father, Chester Bowles, who had a distinguished lineage, a notable four years at Yale, and a remarkable career in business and public affairs. His success in advertising made it possible for him to retire from business in 1941 and launch an outstanding career in politics and diplomacy. The senior Bowles was a forceful advocate of antidiscrimination policies in college admissions, the extension of New Deal social programs, civil rights for African Americans, and support for those in the Third World who struggled responsibly for independence. He opposed military responses to the USSR and emphasized positive foreign relations.[46]

Soon after he graduated from Yale, Sam Bowles married Nancy Lamont, a Smith College student and a granddaughter of Thomas W. Lamont, who had chaired the board of J. P. Morgan. Late in the summer of 1960 they began a two-year stint as schoolteachers in Nigeria. Nigeria achieved independence a few weeks before their arrival, and in the early 1960s was a model of successful development and a foil against Nkrumah's radicalism, authoritarianism, and alliance with the USSR. Early in their stay they were enthusiastic and, like me, both naïve about what they witnessed and on occasion prone to racial stereotyping, seeing Africans as happy-go-lucky. Over time, however, their doubts about Nigeria deepened. They feared that the clash of cultures would thwart modernization and in letters home acknowledged how problematic it was to expect newly independent African nations to embrace Western traditions of free speech and democracy. Like others, they came to believe that, as the first new nation, America had much to teach emerging countries about how to govern themselves. Yet they were also sympathetic to African radicalism, even if it meant an alliance with the USSR, and to the way Africans were melding socialism, democracy, autocracy, communism, and African ideals. They believed that education might foster Nigeria's modernization, a process aided by teachers who came from the United States in programs similar to what Karl Robinson had earlier recommended.[47]

Sam and Nancy Bowles also emphasized the connections between foreign policy and race. They minimized the racial bitterness and color consciousness of Africans and believed that their own extensive contact with black Africans would eventually make them color blind. Consistent with their elitism, they were confident that more interaction between black Africans and highly educated Americans would ease cross-cultural tensions. Countermanding this notion in their minds, however, was the way racial discrimination in America was impeding improvement of diplomatic relations between Nigeria and the United States. They shared Chester Bowles's concern that American foreign policy relied too heavily on Cold War assumptions and strategies. Nonetheless, a 1961 feature in *Look* magazine described Sam and Nancy Bowles as "busy, happy emissaries to the new Africa."[48]

The couple moved to Cambridge in 1962 so Nancy could finish her undergraduate education at Radcliffe and Sam could begin graduate study in economics at Harvard. He finished his dissertation on education in Nigeria at a critical point in that nation's history. In 1966 Nigerians had begun to grow increasingly dissatisfied with American aid, and Americans had become disillusioned with the corruption and the slow pace of economic development in the new nation. That year a coup installed a military government; deadly factional violence and a bloody civil war ensued. In *Planning Educational Systems for Economic Growth* (1969), the book that grew out of his thesis, Bowles focused on how nations might plan the efficient allocation of educational resources. Almost lost in the highly technical discussions in his book, however, was his expression of regret that, focusing so much on efficiency, he had not adequately addressed the issue of equity.

By the time Bowles published his book, he had already shifted his attention from Nigeria to the United States and from efficiency to equity in education, prompted by several factors. By the mid-1960s black Africans were beginning to perceive the work of American researchers as a version of neocolonialism. Events in Nigeria undermined Bowles's faith in the continent's future. The war in Vietnam, the rise of Black Power, and the increasing awareness of the connection between education and poverty in America refocused his concerns. His increasingly tenuous position in the economics department at Harvard, discussed in a later chapter, along with events of the late 1960s, drove him to the left and transformed his politics and his life. Bowles was both amplifying his father's commitments and turning in a more radical direction.[49]

Compared with Bowles's, John Ostheimer's elite background had more to do with wealth and conventional politics. He grew up on an estate on the Main Line outside Philadelphia in a Republican household with parents who were more busy than attentive. Two events in his childhood deeply affected him and over time enabled him to take a different path from that of his successful businessman father. In 1946 he was taken to see *The Yearling* by the two African American servants he later called his "surrogate parents." They sat in the balcony of the theater because African Americans had to sit there. It is not hard to imagine how the film may have reverberated in him: it was about a young boy struggling to achieve independence from his parents for whom expressing their love for him was a strain. Then in the summer of 1955 Ostheimer traveled around the world with his family, a trip that opened his eyes to poverty, helped him realize that he did not want to follow his father into business, and shaped his resolve to study Africa and to use his skills to improve people's lives.[50]

Key experiences at Yale involved race and Africa. At the fall 1958 meeting of DKE during which Raleigh Davenport was considered for membership, what some southerners said in opposition shocked Ostheimer. Normally quiet, he spoke up in support of admitting Davenport. After the meeting was over, he left the fraternity house and never returned. Increasingly he turned his attention to his studies, and Rudin's course in his senior year strengthened his resolve to focus on Africa. After graduation, he went there for the first time, spending five months in a series of African countries on a museum expedition to collect shells, a project family members had long pursued. He returned to Yale in 1961 for graduate work and went back to Africa to research his dissertation while teaching at the University of East Africa in Dar es Salaam. In 1967 he earned his PhD in international relations with a thesis Doob supervised, one in which, following his mentor, Ostheimer tested a social science hypothesis with material drawn from Africa. In the ensuing years,

Ostheimer published widely, initially on African topics and eventually with a focus on environmental issues.[51] After teaching American and African politics at Northern Arizona University from 1957 to 1985, he became a university administrator before retiring in 2001. In entries to reunion books he made clear his commitment to environmental issues, his opposition to the ways greed ravaged the earth, and how money in politics caused Americans to lose a sense of the public good. His encounters with African America and Africa thus profoundly shaped his career and his politics, even as it widened the gap between his elite, Republican origins and his liberal perspective.[52]

Tom Miller's story is one of an elite background, conventionally prestigious experiences at Yale, and a powerful political transformation in which his years in Africa played a role. His life demonstrates that what it meant to be a Yale man was changing. His father was a lawyer who helped corporations fight the power of labor unions. His mother, a Norman Thomas socialist and like her husband from a socially prominent family, took the lead in sending their young son to the Farm School in exurban Chicago, which combined a traditional curriculum with farmwork, and to its summer camp in Vermont. His commitment to fight social injustice, Miller later wrote, drew inspiration from the two women (lesbians, he later realized) who led the Farm School and by example taught the mostly Jewish and Quaker students and campers the values of toleration and fairness, which they exemplified by bringing African American school children from the inner city to the school.

Miller attended the highly regarded New Trier Township High School, and then headed to Yale, where for generations dozens of relatives had preceded him. He expressed a preference for an African American roommate and ended up living with Raleigh Davenport for all four years. Miller participated in three conventionally prestigious extracurricular activities: DKE (where with others he protested the blackballing of Davenport), the senior society Scroll and Key, and the varsity wrestling team, which he captained, earning him a major "Y." Although not deeply committed to Christianity, he was active in mainstream undergraduate religious organizations. Like so many others who became interested in Africa, Miller was inspired by Coffin, with whom he worked to establish Yale Men Abroad. Coffin led him to Lowenstein, who in turn, completing the circle that began with Tom's mother, introduced him to the socialist Norman Thomas. During two summers at Yale, he later reported, he "prospected for gold in Alaska, worked for logging camps in California and Oregon, and served as a Frontier College 'laborer-teacher' on railway gangs in Western Canada."[53]

His early experiences, together with an awareness of independence movements in Africa, propelled Miller to go to Ghana, where he taught from 1960 to 1962. What he witnessed there intensified his awareness of race in America. Although he was conscious of what were then seen as Ghana's tribal conflicts, he believed that racial prejudice played less of a role in Ghana than in America. Home in the summer of 1961 and listening to the interview of James Baldwin by Studs Terkel, he empathized with African Americans. The experience in Africa, plus a connection to Sargent Shriver (through Sam's sister Sally Bowles, who worked for Shriver in Washington), led Miller to help train the first groups of Peace Corps Volunteers in efforts directed by St. Clair Drake, an African American sociologist who focused on race relations, and David Apter, a political scientist who studied development of nations in Africa. "I feel I am part of something new," he wrote in the *Chicago Tribune* soon after graduation, as he referred to not only to "the New Africa but [also to] the new generation of Americans" who had come to Africa "with a love of human dignity and a quiet willingness to help."[54] Entering Stanford Law School in 1962, Miller developed an interest in international law. That led him in the summer of 1964 to work in the Office of the Legal Adviser at the State Department, where, during the naval confrontation between the United States and North Vietnam, he helped research and compose a document that led to the Gulf of Tonkin Resolution, only later realizing that the underlying "facts" were fabricated. He pursued the establishment career that so many of our classmates followed, especially those with his Yale man profile. Yet his experiences at the Farm School and in Africa would impel him to move beyond the 1950s complacency, a shift that the war in Vietnam would intensify. His trajectory underscores how the 1960s helped transform some of the Yale men born into America's elite and groomed for it in college.

The Lives of a Baker's Dozen

Each of our paths intersected with the promise of Africa's future at different times and different places and we each had a distinctive experience. Yet some generalizations are possible. Demographically those headed for Africa were not dramatically different from their classmates. Most of them, Miller notably excepted, did not fully fit the mainstream image of Yale man—which perhaps calls into question whether there was at Yale in our years as dominant a mainstream as many of us assumed to have existed. The social origins of the thirteen ranged widely, from the blue collar to the higher reaches of the nation's elite. They tended to come from small towns and suburbs. Two went to prestigious prep schools, one to a private day school, and the rest to public high schools, including highly ranked ones. Four of them were legacies—five if we count Cylke as the son of a Yale employee—and at least three were on scholarship. Two of them had major athletic careers at Yale. Four joined fraternities, and two were members of aboveground senior societies. All were white, but given the composition of the class that is hardly surprising. Two were Scholars of the House, and only Peace earned a place in an organization whose membership was based on academic achievement. The lives of three reveal how change from the 1950s to the 1960s emerged from within America's elite and elite institutions, just as the lives of Kingman Brewster and William Sloane Coffin Jr. point in the same direction for an older generation. Moreover, thinking about the lives of several of them calls to my mind "The Moral Equivalent of War," William James's 1906 essay in which he wondered how young men from America's elite could find ways of engaging the world that built on the manly virtues without actually fighting in battle.

What impelled us forward was a combination of our religious and family backgrounds, news from Africa, the impact of Coffin, and the desire to break out of the confines imposed by protected upbringings—all of which thrust us into new, unfamiliar, and daunting environments. Leaving Yale, we were innocents going abroad to gain an education that neither I nor most of my thirteen classmates who spent time in Africa had gotten in the classroom. By and large, our time in Africa made us more sensitive to key aspects of American life. Celeste's high hopes generated from New Haven in our junior year contrasted sharply with the more sober lessons we learned when actually on the continent. In most cases our times in Africa awakened or sharpened our awareness of America's racial situation, something that often built on childhood incidents or events at Yale.

Writing about this group of peers, I was struck with the extent to which we lived in very different, often separate worlds. At the time I knew only three: Feinberg because we went to the same high school, Bing through our major, and Bowles because, as the two of us did on campus activities, our fathers worked together in Connecticut politics. In the ensuing years, I came to know Dwyer well when we both taught at the Claremont Colleges. The nine others I met only as I researched this book. What also impresses me is how often what happened after graduation was unpredictable. Moreover, the power of a liberal arts education helps us understand how an engineering major became a theologian, an English major a homeopathic doctor, a philosophy major an activist who focused his efforts on Vietnam, and an American studies major a professor of political science interested in Africa. Among us there was a wide range of religious engagements which affected our decisions. In addition, Coffin, Rudin, JFK, and Lowenstein worked their magic, as did rebellion against provincialism and news of the emergence of newly independent nations in Africa.

Africa and Global Consciousness

In some important respects, what we now think of as the 1960s was not yet on the horizon. Yet in our engagement with Africa, we were on the cusp of a new era—especially in our interest in the world beyond our provincial, Cold War, and nation-centered perspectives. Compared with Rudin, Doob, and Murdock, we shied away from the language of civilization and the imperatives of imperialism, trying instead to see Africa in more complicated ways. Few of the thirteen reveal direct and powerful connections between their time at Yale at the end of the 1950s, their years in Africa, and the turmoil of the 1960s. Yet over time their experiences abroad shaped their politics in profound ways, often playing a role in the way many of us moved to the left. In no case as far as I can determine did political awakening in Africa propel a movement rightward.[55] Indeed, time in Africa did what other experiences accomplished for many classmates who did not go to Africa: pushed my classmates to the left, complicated their views of race, and made them question their assumptions about the continent, their vision of the inevitability of a quick path to democracy and modernization, and their Cold War belief in a bipolar world of the USSR versus the West.

Finally, we can grasp how things changed in our four years at Yale by tracking coverage of international events in the *Yale Daily News*. In our freshman and sophomore years, aside from the crisis in Suez during our first semester, American-Soviet relations dominated the news. Dozens of articles and editorials covered the Soviet invasion of Hungary in our first semester. The *News* highlighted debates over who was winning the Cold War, calls for a tough stance against Moscow, questions about the legitimacy of nonaligned nations, issues about how Yale should respond to advances in Soviet science and technology, and worries about the expansion of communism abroad.

Although concern about the USSR persisted throughout our years at Yale, by junior year Africa commanded increasing attention. Soon after he arrived on campus in September 1958, Coffin began to host chapel talks about Africa, including apartheid in South Africa. In May 1959, calling on Christians to open their hearts to the world, he announced that during the summer Gerry Studds, class of 1959 and later a congressman from Massachusetts, would travel to the continent to help plan the launch of a major effort to connect Yale students with Africa.[56] In our senior year coverage of Africa was becoming at least as frequent as that of the USSR. Coffin, Rudin, and several student organizations hosted speakers from and about Africa. Coffin brought to campus Reverend James Robinson, founder of Operation Crossroads Africa, and announced that several classmates would travel there after graduation under its auspices. At the same time, attention to South African apartheid intensi-fied. I hosted the panel on the subject and arranged to have *Yale Daily News* publish Ivor Schwartzman's letter to my mother about conditions in South Africa. Lowenstein spoke about the massacre on March 21 at Sharpeville. Especially convincing of change from the 1950s to the 1960s were efforts in the spring of 1960 to move from listening to acting. In late April and early May, Murray Last, a Clare fellow who would return to Britain and become a professor specializing in African anthropology, led an effort to raise money to help victims of apartheid and to develop support on campus for a boycott of South African goods.[57] In our last two years attention to Africa, often linked to a focus on race relations in America, intensified significantly.

CHAPTER FIVE
Becoming an Academic Man

Every hour was taken up with the effort of mastering his lessons, which he then regarded, in common with the majority of his class, as a laborious task, a sort of necessary evil, the price to be paid for the privilege of passing four years in pleasant places with congenial companions.

OWEN JOHNSON, *Stover at Yale* (1912)

My freshman counselor, a Yale College graduate and a student at Yale Law School who lived in my dormitory, periodically wrote reports on how I was faring in my first year, reports I read only when researching this book. What concerned him most was that I did not show signs of becoming a well-rounded Yale man by developing what he thought was my latent talent for leadership which I could best express through participation in extracurricular activities. There seem to be "few really salient features about his personality which have commanded my attention," he wrote in the fall of 1956. He described me as "rather short and slightly built" and having no "really noticeable strong or weak points" to my personality. An observer, he wrote, might incorrectly believe I was "a meek or innocuous sort of person." Several months later he continued in the same vein, remarking that I was studious but had not shown "much energy or enthusiasm in any other respects. His personality seems to me rather uncolorful . . . yet despite this and the impression of lack of general enthusiasm I get about him, he does not seem flaccid or listless." In his final report, made as the academic year ended, he remarked that he was having "difficulty elaborating Dan's personality" because I exhibited "little that might be called eccentricity or personal color." Then he returned to his major concern, that I was not drawing on my latent leadership abilities. Had he read an essay by John Knowles, class of 1949, he might have noted the danger that I would become one of the scholars who "cogitate in little cells, sometimes creeping out like ants to nibble a crumb from the great loaf and bear it back to their holes."[1]

My counselor could hardly fathom what could transform me from someone who might seem colorless, bland, and listless into someone with intense, sustained intellectual and political interests. What he mistook for a "lack of general enthusiasm" was in fact a cautious, thoughtful approach I instinctively adopted as I positioned myself within a college community that for centuries had done its best to exclude or marginalize people like me. He had no idea of how frightening it was for a Jewish townie freshman to make the transition from a protected life in New Haven to a more exposed one at Yale. Nor could he imagine that a Yale education involved not learning how to fit in socially but how to stand out intellectually. Finally, he could not predict that when I became engaged in extracurricular activities I would do so in ways that challenged, albeit cautiously, the institution's and the nation's complacency. As a Jew and someone near the left end of the contemporary Yale political spectrum, I had my own version of "For God, For Country, and For Yale," an invocation that the humorist James Thurber in 1951 called "the outstanding single anti-climax in the English language."

In the late 1950s Yale College was not an especially intellectual location—at least in my imagination, if not in reality—compared with Harvard in the same years and with Yale as it would soon become. In terms of students, change happened in good measure as a result of shifts in admissions policies during the mid-1960s. With faculty in American fields who arrived in the years surrounding my graduation, the continuing transformation from gentlemen-scholars to professional scholars was dramatic. Until the late 1950s approximately half the faculty had earned a Yale degree and no woman had yet achieved tenure in a major department. Joining prominent Americanists already there were Edmund Morgan in 1955, John Morton Blum in 1957, R. W. B. Lewis in 1959, and C. Vann Woodward in 1961. None of these newer Americanists had studied at Yale; except for Woodward, they all had degrees from Harvard. Geoffrey Hartman and Harold Bloom both joined the English department as assistant professors in 1955, heralding a future marked by dramatic increases in the number of Jews on the Yale College faculty who were openly proud of their identity. While I was an undergraduate, Yale made its first hires of tenure-bound women in major fields in the arts and sciences. All these changes were part of a broader transformation of a faculty known for its maleness, Yaleness, and WASPishness. A look at American studies reveals the complexities of change in the field I chose as a major, in what my professors wrote and taught, in my peers, and in me.

American Studies in the American Century

I majored in American studies because I wanted to figure out my relationship to my homeland, a process that involved coming to terms with the tension between my parents—my father's full embrace of the society, both despite and because of his deeply felt commitment to Judaism, and my mother's sense of herself as a dissenter from hosannas to America, despite or perhaps because of the fact that she came from a more assimilated family than my father did. Some of my curiosity also had to do with figuring out my relationship as a Jew to Yale and to the wider world.

Nationally and at Yale, American studies originated in the 1930s when some professors of history and English had grown weary of the narrow and elitist nature of their disciplines. At Yale the 1950s marked a major turning point: William Robertson Coe gave the university $500,000 to support the field; when he died in 1955 he left an additional $1,240,000 for the department—in 2014 terms, approximately $10 million adjusted for inflation, $32 million adjusted for stock market value. Coe, who had emigrated from England and then made his fortune in insurance and railroads and by marrying a Standard Oil heiress, had assurances that American studies at Yale would, as one administrator wrote, draw "on the conviction that the best safeguards against totalitarian developments in our economy are an understanding of our cultural heritage and an affirmative belief in the validity of our institutions of free enterprise and individual liberty."[2]

Yale administrators wrestled with Coe and among themselves over the terms of the gift. They insisted on the importance of academic freedom, of not turning the curriculum into a political weapon, while Coe wanted commitments, expressed in the course catalog, that American studies would play an important role in the fight against communism and for free enterprise. If Coe lost the battle, Yale tried to convince him that he had won the war. As A. Whitney Griswold wrote him in November 1951, soon after he had taken over the presidency, "It is not what is on the label, but what is in the bottle that counts." Coe would have had reason to be pleased had he seen what administrators said privately. For example, Dean William C. DeVane wrote President Charles Seymour in May 1949 that "the superb English stock which first settled and consolidated our Eastern Seaboard" paved the way for "our most native university" to build a program that "as a weapon in the 'cold war'" would promote "the merits of our way of thinking and living in America" so that "we shall be able to convince the wavering peoples of the world that we have something infinitely better than communism to offer them." Less than three years later the *New York Times* used Cold War language in a story fea-

focusing on what he saw as the fallacies of communist ideology, underscoring the incompatibility of communism with American conditions and beliefs.[8] McCoubrey's path-breaking *American Tradition in Painting* (1963) amplified key aspects of the consensus, especially the restlessness and loneliness of a people living in a vast virgin land whose New World wildness stood in opposition to the Old World's civilization.[9] Stone's *The Innocent Eye: Childhood in Mark Twain's Imagination* (1961) focused on boyhood and not girlhood, avoided how Leslie Fiedler in 1948 had used Twain to explore the connections between race and homosexuality, and shied away from discussing how the novelist's work illuminated the challenges that scholars faced when dealing with popular culture. Only Strout wrote directly and more than minimally about contemporary politics—and he did so in a way that generally followed the lines of contemporary liberalism.[10] Influenced by Louis Hartz and Arthur M. Schlesinger Jr., he focused on how progressive intellectuals relied too heavily on an excessive and tender-minded faith that they hoped would usher in a utopian future. Instead, Strout asserted that "a genuinely hard-headed feeling for morality must be nurtured . . . with its awareness of the stubborn variety of human life, and its changing, concrete responsibilities so impervious to the demands of hedonists and reformers alike."[11]

Chisolm's scholarship most fully pointed toward the transformation of the field in the later 1960s and beyond. His *Fenollosa: The Far East and American Culture* (1963) pioneered a transnational approach that American studies did not really begin to incorporate until very late in the twentieth century. He explored the contribution of this American collector and cultural interpreter of Japanese art who helped lead the way toward an "existential modernism." He celebrated his subject for avoiding "intellectual ethnocentrism." In an implicit critique of 1950s America, he remarked that Fenollosa "would never conform timidly to narrow rules of living and the deadening 'pressure of the average.'" Reading Chisolm's book now, it is hard for me to separate his picture of his subject from my sense of my teacher: a "cosmopolitan intellectual" who, embracing change, individuality, and diversity, opposed the "static absolutes of every variety," including "the narrow complacencies of racism."[12]

"In Junior Year We Take Our Ease / We Smoke Our Pipes and Sing Our Glees"

Despite their iconic popularity at Yale, neither this quote from "Bright College Years" nor Dink Stover's view of his studies as a "necessary evil" capture the impact my education in American studies had on me beginning in my junior year. Let me start with a largely conventional seminar that Stone taught on American literature to 1900. The catalog announced that the course would concentrate on works "whose aesthetic value has given them lasting stature."[13] The reading list followed suit with a full range of the era's canonical texts, from poems by Puritans to a novel by Frank Norris. In almost all respects this course offered the conventional wisdom and relied on New Criticism more than American studies. Stone emphasized the relationship between form and content, paid little attention to the historical forces that shaped prose and poetry, eschewed the myth and symbol approach, and focused minimally on distinctively American traditions that texts might reveal. Instead, he generally explored the richness of literary texts, with an emphasis more on their creativity than anything they might have revealed about American culture.[14]

There were other missed opportunities to break through the confines of the field.[15] With one exception, we focused on texts written by white, male authors, even though Stone could have assigned what his colleague Robert A. Bone recovered in *The Negro Novel in America.* When Stone discussed Mark Twain's *Adventures of Huckleberry Finn,* he did not use Jim's relationship to Huck to talk about race.[16] He balked at using the study of popular culture or the lives of ordinary people to understand America.[17] In his discussion of Emily Dickinson's life, other than that her relationships with men were troubled, the fact that she was a woman seemed unworthy of note. When the class turned to Whitman's poetry, although sexuality was discussed, Stone treated it in a conventional manner. In his class notes, John Bing recorded Stone using the term "autoerotic rather than homosexual." In treating a key passage in "Song of Myself," Stone remarked that Whitman developed "affection for men together," thus providing "potential object for earlier homo experiences."[18] By desexualizing masturbation and using the word "affection" rather than a stronger one such as passion, Stone undercut the power of homosexual experiences.[19]

Strout's double-credit course on intellectual history had the greatest impact on me. From seventeenth-century Puritanism to "New Conservatism" of the postwar period, we read extensively in primary sources, supplemented by scholarly material. Because they offered views of the human condition that balanced tragedy with a sense of possibility, Strout's favorite authors were Jonathan Edwards, William James, and Reinhold Niebuhr.[20] Bing's notes on the course confirm my memory of several aspects. Striking is how serious, precise, and uncompromising Strout was in conveying to us how thinkers had pondered compelling questions. Moreover, and this is true of all the courses, it appears that even in so small a class, Strout mostly lectured and we listened. Although at the outset he said we would focus on ideas in context, pay attention to literature and the arts, discuss how ordinary people received ideas generated by intellectuals, treat the consequences of ideas and consider their distinctively American characteristics, there is almost no evidence of such considerations.[21] Instead, Strout taught us how careful readings of canonical texts introduced us to the ways their authors had wrestled with major issues.

Louis Hartz's 1955 *The Liberal Tradition in America* shaped much of the course, serving as the biblical, or perhaps more appropriately, the Talmudic, commentary.[22] Strout followed Hartz in emphasizing the lack of class consciousness in America; the absence of native-born and genuinely radical or conservative traditions; the hold of a pragmatism that assumed no fundamental conflict; the danger that liberalism rested on the "hidden absolutism" that consensus fostered; and the consequence that there was often a "conservative liberal mix up." Because of a compressed social system that stemmed from the lack of an aristocracy and a peasantry, the liberal tradition, so characteristically the focus of the time, dominated. And those inside it and those outside it on the left and right often failed to recognize how much they had in common with each other.[23]

The final assignment, Strout's 1955 essay from *Partisan Review,* "Liberalism, Conservatism, and the Babel of Tongues," reveals his politics. He hailed "liberal programs for limited welfare-state measures, collective security in foreign affairs, and equal rights for Negroes," yet he insisted that the utopian paths liberals and fellow travelers took in the 1930s had caused them to lose "the philosophical initiative to conservatism." Still, he found contemporary conservatism problematic, taking special aim at Russell Kirk for "brandishing his Burke with the fervor of a radical appealing to the holy writ of Marxism."[24] Similarly, Bing's notes reveal how Strout lamented the way conservative aspects of the current religious revival promoted "self-righteousness" and made "secular criticism difficult." More generally, Strout was critical of contemporary conservatives for not understanding democracy and civil liberties at the same time that he acknowledged that America was the "chief bastion of conservatism in the world." Drawing on William H. Whyte Jr.'s *The Organization Man* (1956) and on books by C. Wright Mills, Strout enumerated what threatened liberal, constitutional democracy: the power of demagogues, a "closed society in South," the "nuclear arms race," the "military as influence in U.S. life," and the "spread of large scale organizations and group-centered man." Despite these dangers, Strout ended the semester on a positive note, telling us that "liberal traditions still have vitality" because of "Negro support" and the way "the Supreme Court defends civil liberties."[25]

In many ways, what Strout taught followed conventional 1950s imperatives. Not at all surprising is the lack of attention to class, gender, and sexuality. My most specific memory of the course, confirmed by Bing's notes, underscores how centrist his vision was. He maintained that the birth of both Thomas Paine and Alexander Hamilton outside the United States proved Hartz's insistence on a compressed spectrum in American political ideology. This memory reminds me that I sensed even then that something was wrong with the course's perspective. Strout focused much more on a complicated and often conflicted liberalism and on a problematic conservatism than he did on radicalism. *Commentary* and *Partisan Review* were his favorites, not *Dissent* or *Liberation,* both founded in the mid-1950s. Characteristically, he used writings of Granville Hicks and Sidney Hook, after they were no longer sympathetic to communism and the Soviet Union, to suggest why the communist god had failed, rather than why some had once found this alternative compelling. In contrast, again and again he impressed upon us the importance of a tragic and anti-utopian vision rather than calling attention to new stirrings represented by Martin Luther King Jr. and Herbert Marcuse.

Yet Strout offered something that propelled me forward: a model of what it meant to be a professor engaged in a sustained, disciplined, and exciting exploration of ideas. He provided me with an example of a person with a calling in which wrestling with ideas was more important than making money. Years later Lewis Lapham, class of 1956, remarked that a Yale diploma was "the ticket of admission to Wall Street." However, my education and my reaction to my father's life helped impel me in a different direction. "Pecuniary success is meaningless to my own future though I will always want enough money to buy my loved ones anything they expect," I wrote Helen in early June 1960, before going on to say that I was "convinced that to TEACH, almost regardless of where, is going to be grand." At the same time, I articulated how important intellectual creativity was. I remembered that when "I made an original discovery" while writing a paper and listening to the last movement of Beethoven's Ninth Symphony, I wrote Helen, I "forgot all questions of the validity of the idea" as I "paced up and down the room working off the energy and happiness generated." Strout was responsive to my engagement. When I insisted that the Constitution called for a strict separation of church and state, he brought me material that supported my position. At one point, I offered him a prize if he actually read my footnotes—which he did, though he refused to accept the reward.[26]

Strout's impact on me was transformative. I might have become a U.S. historian anyway but he offered me a model and a path. As he wrote me in the fall of 1964, I was among the small group of his "first academic sons." However, there were downsides to his approach. Strout's super-seriousness intensified the way that by my sophomore year I had begun to elevate intellect over emotion. Equally important, although to this I was somewhat more resistant, Strout opposed utopian impulses and emphasized instead how human nature—fallen man in the Protestant sense—shaped and constrained human action. Yet these are minor issues compared with the fact that he taught me what it meant to be an intellectual historian.[27] As Bart Giamatti remarked when he was Yale's president, the teacher should encourage "the student in imitation and then in repetition . . . so that the student may turn himself not into you but into himself."[28]

Interlude: Letters Home, Summer 1959

Strout's influence was so strong that in the summer of 1959 I was trying out my wings as I worked to configure what it meant to be a kind of Yale man different from what my freshman counselor expected and the dominant undergraduate cultures reinforced. The letters I wrote home as I traveled to Europe, Israel, and Africa reveal how, halfway through my undergraduate education in American studies, I was attempting to explore what it meant to be intellectually engaged, to figure out my politics, and to become a scholar who applied what I learned in the classroom to new situations. Early in my stay in London, thinking ahead to my senior thesis on U.S. government sponsorship of the arts, I went to a government office to obtain information on British policies. I reported to my parents that "I naturally gained a great deal of satisfaction from being accepted as a scholar and treated as one." The next day, I wrote my sister and brother-in-law that at Yale there were two "incompatible" worlds: "the College (dances, athletics, chumminess) and the University (Griswold's community of scholars)." A few days later I continued in this vein, suggesting that Yale could not reconcile the two realms unless it "thoroughly" changed its undergraduate admissions policies (whose biases I sensed but did not yet fully understand) and made the curriculum "much more difficult." I doubted then that either of these changes would ever happen.[29]

Again and again during my travels, I was trying out this newly discovered sense of myself as someone developing analytical tools to understand the world. Looking at the trajectory of my trip that moved me from the United States to London, Vienna, Rome, Athens, Istanbul, Israel, and Africa, I used archaic language to talk of "reversing the path which civilization has taken." I played with the terms and people that Strout had introduced me to. "My observations are sociological," I noted, "though by traveling from country to country my sociology gains a historic or developmental sense." As an example I observed that "London, on my 17th century Puritan yardstick, is much more sinful than New York. The women are more conscious of their womanhood and want everyone else to be so." Approached by a prostitute in Rome who asked me if I wanted to make love, I noted that this was "an absurdly ambiguous question." I went on to remark, priggishly, that "I refused to insult her persistent 'why' with the righteous truth" of myself as "temperamental inheritor of the tradition of John Winthrop and John Cotton." In a somewhat different vein that nonetheless invoked other figures from Strout's course, I responded to my mother's statement that it was unreasonable for me to expect my friends to get along with one another by suggesting that she read about the relationship between Henry Adams and Clarence King which revealed how to combine male friendship with intellectual engagement.[30]

Strout also sharpened my sense of my future. He had offered me, I wrote home, a valuable way of "looking at a job," a perspective which combined "a discipline and an organization in the realm of which this discipline is to be exercised." What Strout impressed upon me in my junior year, though I rarely followed his advice, was to be loyal to a disciplinary field but keep my distance from institutional claims. And so on this trip as I met strangers I looked at how "other people's perceptions are affected by their disciplines and how their lives are governed by their organizational allegiances."[31]

My most extensive application of what I was learning came when I compared what I witnessed in Israel with what I absorbed from American studies. Among the factors that intensified my reaction was my recognition of how important to my parents, my father especially, the belief was that Israel and America were two Zions worthy of my embrace. Thus I wrote how life in the State of Israel, less than a dozen years after the creation of the new nation, evoked the spirit of the frontier and Manifest Destiny. Innocent of what it had taken to establish America in the West and Israel in Palestine, I underscored a whole range of commonalities: "pioneer, frontier importance, love and attachment to the land." I saw each nation becoming "a classless, democratic society of immigrants built by people who felt a strange parallel between themselves and the Bible . . . as God's Chosen People." Using phrases that had probably jumped out at me from the pages of Daniel J. Boorstin's *The Americans: The Colonial Experience* (1958), I talked of the shared "subordination of first principles to the *facts* of the situation."[32]

My letters home also revealed that my education at Yale, both in and outside the classroom, was giving me ways of thinking about politics and society, albeit ones that at times were conflicted and ambiguous. After a tour of social welfare agencies in Copenhagen, I incorrectly remarked that "I really don't think they are ahead of us in all respects." At one point, I drew on what John Kenneth Galbraith had called conventional wisdom to lament that "Democracy and Capitalism are too united." Remembering William Burdick and Eugene Lederer's 1958 immensely influential *The Ugly American* (1958),

FAMILY

Dan and Judy, with their parents William and Miriam Horowitz, c. 1950.
Author family photo.

Freshman Commons, where all first-year students ate their meals. *1957 Class Book,* 12.
Copyright © 1957 Yale Banner Publications. Reprinted by permission.

A gentleman's club, Linonia and Brothers Reading Room. Sterling Memorial Library Photographs, Manuscripts and Archives, Yale University Library.

Skull and Bones, a senior society. *1960 Class Book,* 88. Copyright © 1960 Yale Banner Publications. Reprinted by permission.

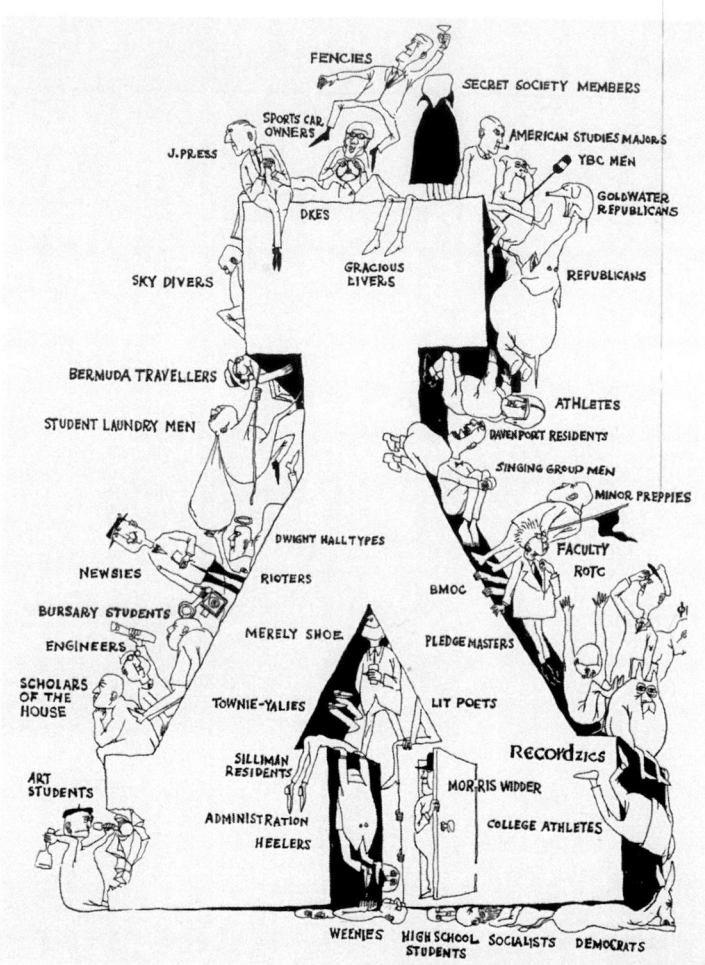

Inverted "Y," illustrating the Yale status hierarchy: at the top, members of Fence Club and secret societies, sports car owners, J. Press; at the bottom, weenies (later known as nerds), high school students, socialists, and Democrats. *YDN*, May 9, 1959, 1. Copyright Yale Daily News Publishing Company, Inc. All rights reserved. Reprinted with permission.

Growing up provincial, learning how to "dress British." A Yalie would quickly learn to wear a J. Press shirt and tie, if he could afford them. *1957 Class Book,* 11. Copyright © 1957 Yale Banner Publications. Reprinted by permission.

RITUALS

Yale–Vassar Beer 'n' Bike Race. Jim Sale, pushed by Dave Frohman, begins the first lap; after a lap, the rider chugged beer and passed the bike to the next contestant. *1960 Class Book,* 23. Copyright © 1960 Yale Banner Publications. Reprinted by permission.

Tang Cup competition, Timothy Dwight College, 1962, with the award going to the residential college whose students could guzzle the most beer the fastest. Student Life at Yale Photographs, circa 1779–1988, Manuscripts and Archives, Yale University Library.

Ivy League protest, 1950s style. Yale students protest visit of Adlai Stevenson in 1956. "Going My Way Tigers?" refers to Yale's athletic victories over Stevenson's Princeton. *1957 Class Book,* 35. Copyright © 1957 Yale Banner Publications. Reprinted by permission.

The executive board of Undergraduate Lecture Committee advertises the upcoming speech by Henry Ford. They illustrate that some of the initial stirring against student apathy came from traditional Yale men. From left to right: David G. Ball, Ambler H. Moss Jr. (driving), Charles O. Wood III, and Thomas E. Currier. *YDN,* Feb. 17, 1959, 1. Copyright Yale Daily News Publishing Company, Inc. All rights reserved. Reprinted with permission.

Eight Yale Students Picket Downtown Woolworth Store; Five of Group Apprehended by City Police Officers

by Gideon Gordon

Eight Yale students picketed the downtown New Haven store of the F.W. Woolworth Co. Friday afternoon protesting the discriminatory policies of some of the chain's southern stores.

The incident, which was reported by both the Associated Press and the United Press International wire services, received national publicity. During a midnight post mortem meeting which the group held at George and Harry's Restaurant on Wall Street, a Bridgeport radio station, WICC, tape-recorded a telephone interview with John Barber, 1961L, and Sam Bowles, 1960, the group's spokesman. WICC used the interview extensively on its new broadcasts Saturday.

The picketing began at 2:15 Friday afternoon when the group, carrying signs reading "Oppose Segregation, Support the Constitution," and "We Support Southern Student Protest," began marching in an orderly single-file line in front of Woolworth's. One of the picketers carried a small American flag.

Two other members of the group stood near the two entrances of the store and distributed a mimeographed flyer describing the group's goals in question and answer form. The flyer stated that the picketing was "demonstration of support for southern students who are protest-

Eight Yale students picket the downtown New Haven store of the F.W. Woolworth Co., protesting against discriminatory policies in some of the chain's southern stores. L. EIDEN, (center) the manager of the store, asks who organized the demonstration.

ing racial discrimination. We are attempting to communicate the fact that Woolworth's branches in Greensboro, Raleigh, Fayetteville, and Durham, N.C., treat their Negro customers undemocratically and deny to them the same seated meal service provided to white people," it said.

The flyer added that the demonstration was being conducted as "Jesus or Gandhi would have wanted us to: Non-violently with respect for everybody's rights. . ."

Pedestrians were exhorted to "write to the managers of the Wool-

(Continued on Page 4)

Ivy League protest, 1960s style. In response to how Woolworth stores in the South refused to serve African Americans, Yale students picketed the Woolworth's in New Haven. The *Yale Daily News* tried to hide the identity of the protestors. This action was the first civil rights protest by Yale undergraduates. *YDN*, Feb. 22, 1960, 1. Copyright Yale Daily News Publishing Company, Inc. All rights reserved. Reprinted with permission.

Yale men keep their eyes on two women. "Woman is man's ruin" is the translation of the caption "Mulier hominis confusion," from Geoffrey Chaucer's *Canterbury Tales*. *1957 Class Book*, 21. Copyright © 1957 Yale Banner Publications. Reprinted by permission.

Toga Party or Roman Orgy, held annually in Jonathan Edwards College. *1957 Class Book*, 132. Copyright © 1957 Yale Banner Publications. Reprinted by permission.

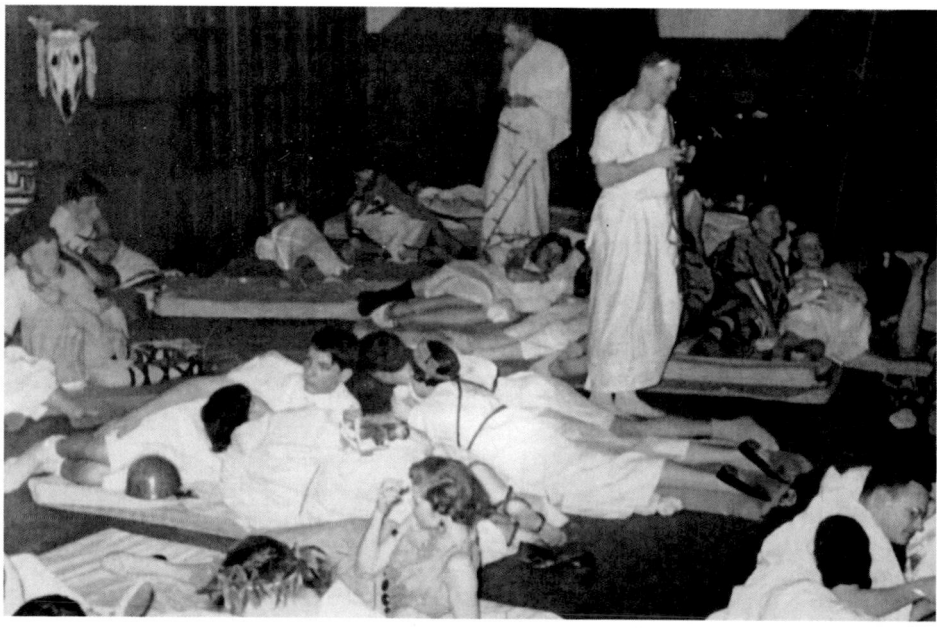

Students and a faculty member gather in the dining room at Trumbull College. *Left to right:* Leslie Epstein, Henry Townsend, Charles Blitzer (back to camera), Jonny Weiss (in distance at another table), and Conrad Cafritz. The residential colleges offered the most important alternative to fraternities. *1960 Class Book,* 171. Copyright © 1960 Yale Banner Publications. Reprinted by permission.

Dan and Helen L. Horowitz, c. 1965. Author family photo.

Captains of varsity teams. *Upper left:* Tom Miller, captain of the wrestling team who went to Africa after graduation, his life later transformed by the Vietnam War. *1960 Class Book,* 250. Copyright © 1960 Yale Banner Publications. Reprinted by permission.

Undergraduate Deacons, students who served at Battell Chapel, Church of Christ in Yale University. *Back row, left to right:* Stuart H. Clement (treasurer, Church of Christ), Winston W. Davidson, Carter Doran, Edwin J. Allen Jr., William Sloane Coffin Jr. Middle row: Bruce L. Krag, John H. Bing, Lawrence B. Gibbs, Leo T. Chylack Jr., George R. Munson. *Front row:* Karl E. Robinson Jr., George D. McClain, Talmage G. Rogers Jr., Raleigh L. Davenport. *1960 Class Book,* 328. Copyright © 1960 Yale Banner Publications. Reprinted by permission.

Whiffenpoofs of 1960, the premier a cappella singing group. Pictured at the eating club Mory's, with the cup from which patrons drank a famous brew and with pictures of Yale athletic teams behind them. *Back row, from left:* Ernest S. Harris Jr., Norman Klopp, Allison B. Durfee, David W. P. Elliott, Hawley Rogers, Peter R. Wells. *Front row:* Barney Stewart III, Gilbert H. Marquardt Jr., William Weber, Robert Lindgren. Stewart H. Cole, Harold B. Finn III. *1960 Class Book,* 312. Copyright © 1960 Yale Banner Publications. Reprinted by permission of Yale Banner Publications.

Yale Daily News staff. Monroe Price ("Men Working" sign); Brian Jensen (dark glasses, left arm raised), Jim Ottaway (pointing épée), Jack Herrera (in clerical collar), Gordon Chamberlain (tooting horn), Henri Fraise (below two men in trench coats, head cocked), William Borders (in bathrobe), John Pepper (with cowboy hat), Albert Pergam (reading newspaper), Jonathan Seagle (pointing pistol). *On the ground:* Neil Herring (smoking hookah), William Martin (lying down). *1960 Class Book,* 283. Copyright © 1960 Yale Banner Publications. Reprinted by permission.

Trumbull College 1959 Marble Team, a protest by outsiders. *Top row, from left:* John Dollard, Ken Baer (partial view), Robert A. Dentan, Leslie Epstein, Steve Lefkowitz, Dan Popp, Monroe Price, John Haverly. *Kneeling below:* Pete Magee and Dan Horowitz. *1959 Class Book,* 13. Copyright © 1959 Yale Banner Publications. Reprinted by permission.

Pundits of Yale 1960. Satirical group portrait in nineteenth-century style. *Front row, from left:* Joe Mathewson, Ralph Hirshorn, Professor Norman Holmes Pearson, Peter Parsons. *Middle row:* Leslie Epstein, Bart Giamatti, Jim Ottaway, Gordon Chamberlain, Bill ("Jamie") Kunz. *Top row:* John Davies and Peter Knipe. *1960 Class Book,* 324. Copyright © 1960 Yale Banner Publications. Reprinted by permission.

Contrasting views of Dan Horowitz in Africa, August 1959: attending a rally against apartheid (circled in upper left) and being pulled on a rickshaw by a black African dressed in a tribal outfit. *Rand Daily Mail* (Johannesburg), August 1, 1959; author family photo.

Rev. William Sloane Coffin Jr. ending his performance with a folk song that celebrated the African American folk hero John Henry. *YDN*, Nov. 2, 1959, 1. Copyright Yale Daily News Publishing Company, Inc. All rights reserved. Reprinted with permission.

Nancy and Sam Bowles as teachers in Nigeria, 1961, with Nigerian student between them. "U.S. Teachers in Africa . . . BUSY COUPLE," *Look,* March 28, 1961, 51. Douglas Jones, staff photographer. LOOK Magazine Photograph Collection, Library of Congress, Prints & Photographs Division, LC-L9-60-9111-TT, #37.

David and Mai Elliott greeting Mai's relatives at their wedding reception in Saigon, March 4, 1964. Reproduced with permission of David and Duong Van Mai Elliott.

"Otium Cum Dignitate" ("Leisure with Dignity"), drawing of four classmates at fiftieth reunion of class of 1960, by classmate Steve Johnson. *Class of Its Own*, 1. Reproduced with permission of Steve Johnson.

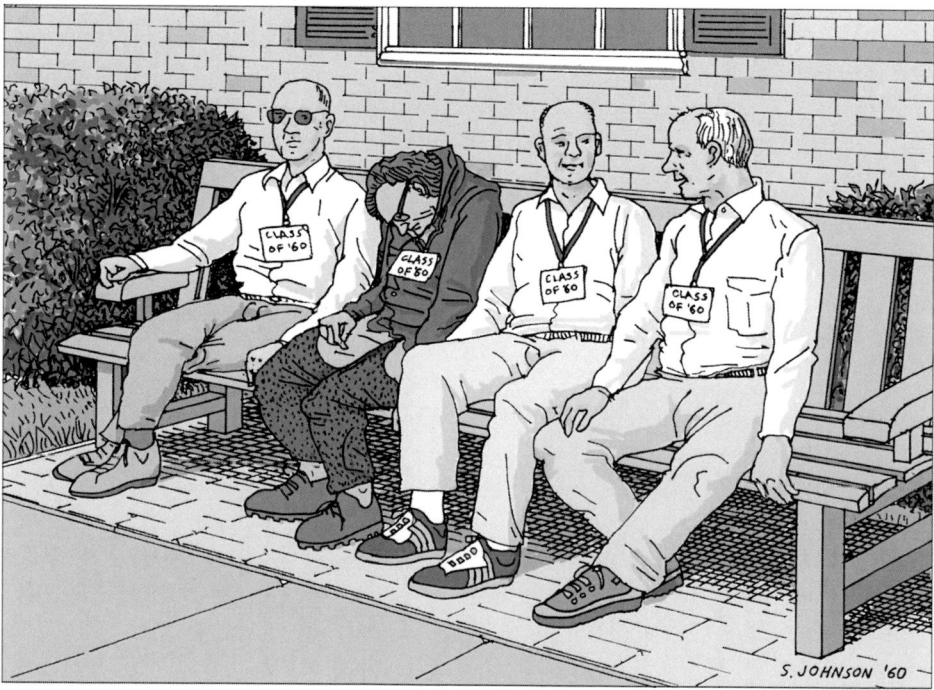

I offered a sense of how I distanced myself from that stereotyped picture. "Americans are living as non-conquering colonials," I wrote from Athens soon after I had sat uncomfortably near boisterous Americans at an outdoor café. I criticized the "way they are naturally disassociated from most of the native life."[33]

Encountering poverty more serious than what I knew in New Haven also commanded my attention. From Athens I observed that "poverty always strikes one differently—depending on whether it is viewed as quaint local color or a lesson in man's brutality and unkindness," even as I made clear that the latter was usually my approach. Seeing how poor people lived in Istanbul struck me even more forcefully. "It would be too callous a statement to feel that it is quaint or interesting," I wrote my parents, "too impossible in terms of psychological well-being to take their burden on my sentiment's back." I am learning, I continued, how what "I am able to feel, think, try, and do (both mentally and physically) is conditioned by the fact that I live in America." Playing on the title of a Jonathan Edwards sermon, I concluded by saying, "Images and shadows of unsublime things."[34]

"In Senior Year We Act Our Parts / In Making Love and Winning Hearts"

Although in my senior year I did follow some version of what this passage from "Bright College Years" described, the seriousness of my education in American studies continued. I took a seminar on American literature that was largely conventional in its content, even though as a professor Pearson was unconventional. During World War II, he ran the London-based American counterintelligence and clandestine operations. While his formal association with OSS and its successor, the CIA, ended in 1946, Pearson's involvement in the world of spies continued. Not surprisingly, in the classroom he was mysterious and compelling. Bent over, he walked with a decided limp that resulted from a childhood illness and that made him look like a hunchback. In the course I took from him, he dropped hints of what he had done: parachuting behind enemy lines, being the first American officer to enter Norway after the defeat of Germany, and going on top secret missions to Portugal. Along with Strout, Pearson helped inoculate me against ideological certainty. "I guess I would emphasize his sense of irony and paradox," I wrote Stone about Pearson decades later.[35]

Pearson's course on American literature in the twentieth century, like Stone's that preceded it, was largely conventional. Although he was well versed in women's poetry, Edith Wharton's *House of Mirth* was the only work by a woman he included. Nor did he ask us to read anything by African American writers, even though he had recently supervised Bone's dissertation. Bing's notes reveal how much Pearson tried to evade or smooth over an author's politics, especially if they were controversially reactionary. Ezra Pound's "errors in judgment," Bing wrote, relying on what Pearson said in class, "are done out of love and loyalty."

In some respects, Pearson pursued traditional themes: the development of character and plot; the relationship between form and content; a focus on humanistic questions such as the relationship between freedom and fate; and the impact one author had on another. Yet in other ways, much more than was true of Stone, Pearson was breaking with traditional approaches. He paid considerable attention to how social class shaped literary themes. On occasion, he explored distinctly American themes or suggestively hinted at connections we might make across a long span of time, such as what it might mean to think of *Sister Carrie* and *Catcher in the Rye* as novels about coming of age in America. He also paid some attention to historical and biographical contexts, as well as to how editors, critics, and publishers shaped what we read. As New Historicists of the 1980s would do, at key moments he suggested that we could learn about literary texts by looking at nonliterary ones, for example, juxtaposing writings by the sexologist Havelock Ellis with *Light in August* and *The Lonely Crowd*.[36]

Chisolm and Wheeler fully challenged both 1950s consensus and the myth and symbol approach in the course they taught in my senior year, American Character and Institutions. Wheeler's knowledge of the New York literary scene and American radicalism, along with Chisolm's intellectual double-jointedness, enabled them to experiment suggestively in ways that pointed to the other side of the cusp. If the courses by Stone, Strout, and Pearson were discipline-based, this one was inter- or multidisciplinary. Chisolm and Wheeler drew on the perspectives of the social sciences and transnationalism. For categories of identity, they focused extensively on region, religion, class, and ethnicity. The readings on race were exceptionally extensive: not only sociological studies of segregation and discrimination in postwar America and the role of African Americans in the development of jazz, but also works by Gunnar Myrdal, Ralph Ellison, C. Vann Woodward, Lorraine Hansberry, and James Baldwin. In addition, we covered the relationships between the individual and American institutions, especially corporations, labor unions, the legal and educational systems, "Social Structure," religious organizations, and cities. We spent a good deal of time on what are now classics of 1940s and 1950s social and cultural criticism, books by John Kouwenhoven, August Hollingshead, David Potter, David Riesman, William H. Whyte Jr., John Kenneth Galbraith, and C. Wright Mills. All of these affected me powerfully with their emphasis on critical assessments of contemporary America.[37]

The most intriguing part of the course came with the section titled "The Individual." They divided coverage into four topics: Love, Aggression, Creativity, and History, through which they were providing us with a brilliant rendering of contemporary American society. We examined the tensions that the isolated nuclear family experienced.[38] Readings by Sigmund Freud, Talcott Parsons, and Eric Hoffer explored how personal, social, and political aggression operated in contemporary society. The implications of socially sanctioned aggression became clear in the two selections from the writings of Clarence Darrow. In one on the death penalty Darrow remarked, "We teach people to kill, and the State is the one that teaches them." With the Sweet case of 1926, he successfully defended members of a highly educated African American family who killed one white person and wounded another as they protected themselves from a white mob attempting to drive them out of the house they owned in a white neighborhood in Detroit. The African Americans, Bing interpreted Darrow as saying, were "good law upstanding people like us, not like a mob." Chisolm and Wheeler were breaking through the consensus by emphasizing aggression and the contradictions in American life.[39]

Several things strike me powerfully as I look back at my undergraduate education in American studies. Those of us in the honors program represented a fairly typical cross section of the class of 1960. Four of the eight were legacies, two came to Yale from boarding schools and two from private day schools. At Yale none of us participated in varsity athletics in a major way, though three joined aboveground senior societies. The major difference from the norm was what the future held: two of us went into law; one was an expat businessman in France; while five had careers in universities—Charlie Newman as a teacher of creative writing, Joel Jones eventually as president of Fort Lewis College, and the other three (Bing, Church, and me) principally as professors.

Reading over the syllabi and tracking the class discussion has impressed upon me how much my professors expected of us. The extensive and demanding reading lists, including references to current scholarship, conveyed how seriously they took our education. Although I am struck by how much they talked and we listened, and how rarely if ever they relied on the interactive pedagogical strategies I later learned, what they said in class involved profound, sustained instruction. Then there were the extraordinary resources we benefited from thanks to the financial support Coe had bequeathed just eighteen months before we enrolled: an independent study each year; two seminars a year with a small group of highly committed students; teaching by regular, engaged, and talented members of the faculty; almost no exams for two years; and encouragement to audit courses. Many changes swept American studies in the ensuing half century, making the field more inclusive. But future generations have missed the deep and chronologically extensive grounding in American literature, ideas, and institutions that I gained at Yale.

The Gap between What Our Professors Taught and What We Wrote

As someone who has directed more than a hundred senior theses in history and American studies over forty years, what has fascinated me has been the gap between what my colleagues and I taught and what our students learned. So too with the senior theses my peers and I wrote in 1959–60, seven of which I could gain access to. Gus Weidlich wrote on the impact of Thomas Nast's cartoons in bringing down New York's Boss Tweed by providing images that even uneducated voters could understand. Balanced in its judgments, it was a solid work, influenced by the concerns of contemporary American studies through its careful reading of visual materials and exploration of the impact they had on popular consciousness. Joel Jones wove together material from interviews, novels, magazine articles, and social science studies in "The Economic Status of the Faculty Members of American Institutions of Higher Learning." Throughout most of American history, he revealed, the nation was "more interested in railroads than rhetoric, in construction rather than Cicero, and 'living' instead of Livy," which resulted in professorial salaries lagging significantly behind those of professionals whose training was equally demanding. Bob Church wrote a sophisticated, scholarly essay informed by current issues in American studies, including the myth and symbol approach. Focusing on the mid-nineteenth-century novelist John William DeForest, he explored how fiction illuminated American culture, as he emphasized the dynamic tensions produced when a European-oriented author wrote for an American audience and tried to mediate between literary traditions and popular culture.[40]

My honors thesis was on American art at international fairs in Europe between 1851 and 1900. Influenced by McCoubrey's course, by Strout's interest in the relationship between Europeans and Americans, and by my own curiosity about how the U.S. government had supported the arts, I discussed how the lack of government money and leadership undermined what American artists could display and Europeans could encounter. More so than was true of the work of some of my peers, my essay revealed how fully I had absorbed the issues then animating American studies at Yale. European juries and critics, I argued, almost consistently preferred Americans, usually expatriates, who provided pale imitations of European academic art, never selecting "the works of the most American and vigorously native and individual artists" such as Winslow Homer or Thomas Eakins. Had they recognized uniquely American characteristics, I insisted (as I problematically evoked contemporary nationalist boasts), they would have recognized that "America's unphilosophical stance; the freedom of choice of subject matter; the absence of traditional subject matter and institutions; the isolated individualism of the artist, . . . were interrelated factors" to be valued despite what "cultivated" critics thought.[41]

All of our theses were interdisciplinary—in the sense that we used the material, though rarely the approaches, of two or more fields to illuminate a topic. In most of what my peers wrote there were very few nods to the myth and symbol school or notions of American exceptionalism that observers have assumed American studies in the late 1950s promoted. Not surprisingly, most of us went our own way, picking topics that compelled us personally. We saw this earlier in how Bing and John Train placed race in a position far more central than had any of our teachers; in Weidlich's exploration of the impact of popular culture on political behavior; in how Jones combined statistical analysis, policy considerations, and novels to examine an issue of immense concern to those of us thinking about academic careers; in Church's exploration of the tension between popular and literary cultures; and in my interest in government sponsorship of the arts. We will later see how Newman wrote about himself when he focused on Hutchins Hapgood. Generally speaking, our theses were well written, without the aid of responses to multiple drafts from peers, tutors, and professors on which later generations would rely.[42]

Becoming a New Haven Jewish Intellectual/Historian

During my last two years at Yale, I struggled to develop a sense of myself as a scholar, Jew, and intellectual to stand in contrast to the models my father and some Yale professors provided. The clearest, albeit hard-won, gains came in my academic work. What I wrote for Pearson made clear that literary analysis was not my forte.[43] In contrast, my work for Chisolm and Wheeler reveals how significantly I was learning to think as a cultural analyst, and focusing on issues that would engage me for the rest of my professional life, such as the conflicts between levels of taste and the relationship of abundance to national character. Above all, it was Strout's teaching that enabled me to find my voice as an apprentice intellectual historian. The difference in quality between what I wrote for Martin Duberman on Reconstruction in the middle of my sophomore year and for Strout as a junior marks a sea change. In papers composed with real verve and even playfulness, I revealed that Strout had helped me carry off ambitious projects that drew on a synthesis of what he and Louis Hartz argued. Historical struggles, I insisted, in ways that showed at times that I was adopting a consensus view of American history, were "never between capital and labor but between capitalists and expectant capitalists." All this, I concluded, underscored "the strength of American liberalism" and "the plight of American conservatism."[44]

In my courses I also pondered what it meant to be an American Jew. From the 1930s through the late 1950s and long after, a close connection existed in the United States between being a Jew, an academic, and an intellectual. Nonetheless, all of those who taught me in American studies were Protestants. I took courses outside American studies with a variety of Jews: the closeted Leonard Doob; the convert to Christianity Hans Frei; and Martin Duberman, for whom, the historian Paul Robinson suggests, there was some "connection between his repressed ethnicity and the paralyzing trouble he experienced with his sexuality." In my first year, Richard Bernstein taught me in an intro-ductory philosophy course, although I was then too young to appreciate fully how he stood as an example of an engaged Jewish intellectual. Outside the classroom, I came to know two Jewish assistant professors who lived in Trum-bull College, the philosopher Irwin C. ("Chet") Lieb and the political scientist Charles Blitzer. These six men provided contrasting models of what it meant to be a Jew in an American academic world.[45]

In these contexts I was becoming even more of a secular Jew, similar to my mother in her skepticism about the value of religion and different from my father in his commitments to Zionism, formal affiliations, and leadership in the community but similar to him in pride about the people and culture that formed an essential part of my identity. This change did not come out of nowhere, for if in my early adolescence my classmates in religious school used to call me "the little rabbi," not long after my bar mitzvah I had rebelled against my formal religious education and commitments.[46] The question of whether God existed has never interested me. I have always been proud of being a Jew, one who loved the round of ritual celebrations, who felt a strong sense of connection to a historic people, and who drew the connection between being a Jew and being an outsider. During my four years at Yale, I belonged to Hillel, although I typically celebrated holidays at home and in my family's synagogue.

In what I wrote in my last three years at Yale, I explored the tension between Judaism as a set of religious, textually based beliefs and practices, on the one hand, and Jewishness as a set of cultural expressions, on the other. I made clear that what so strongly appealed to me was the emphasis on the links between tradition and ritual which I saw as sustaining the Judaism/Jewishness' connection.[47] I distanced myself from my father's Zionism, expressing doubt that the new nation could serve as what I characterized "a unifying symbol for Judaism as a people-religion."[48] My experience at the Simchat Torah service at the Lubavicher shul in Williamsburg early in my senior year reinforced my interest in rituals even as it underscored how assimilated I was, experiencing traditional Judaism principally through my father's connections. "The accul-turated Jew," I wrote in December 1959, "is apt to look at Williamsburg with both appreciation and sadness: the tradition is no longer available to one who is primarily American."[49] I hammered out my own identity as a Jew when I wrote papers on Nathan Glazer's *American Judaism* (1957) and Will Herberg's *Protestant, Catholic, Jew: An Essay in American Religious Sociology* (1955), both typical of how Jewish intellectuals in the 1950s worked to explain America to itself and Jews to themselves. Pulled as I was between my father's intense but often unspoken loyalties and my mother's secular vision, between my sense of exclusion at Yale as a Jew and my exploration through American studies of what it meant to be an American, I was struggling to achieve independence from my parents even as, like them, I wove together Jewish and American identities.[50]

I was thinking of becoming a professor when New York Jewish intellectu-als of an earlier generation, such as Alfred Kazin, were coming to positions of prominence as academics and public intellectuals. My life was different from theirs. I was from a leafy suburban neighborhood within the city of New Haven, not a borough of New York. When, as a child, I went to Manhattan, I did so not on a subway but in my father's shiny new Lincoln or Cadillac, and we stayed overnight in an expense-account suite in the Waldorf-Astoria. I had not grown up in an eastern European Orthodox Jewish family but with a secular mother and an observant father who had gone to Yale and not City College or Brooklyn College. What shaped my political consciousness was the distinctive, albeit liberal, anti-Stalinist politics of my parents—as well as the differences between the two of them.

As a Jew and aspiring academic, I was grateful not only for the cultural, social, and economic capital I carried with me but also for how those who came before me had broken the barriers that had long kept Jews out of the professoriate. In 1946 there was only one Jewish full professor at Yale College, but change was in the air, and by the time I got my PhD in 1967, roughly 17 percent of the tenured and tenure-track faculty at the nation's leading univer-sities were Jews.[51] Yet prejudices still existed in the halls of academe. Nowhere was this clearer than in the 1962 presidential address to the American Histori-cal Association by Carl Bridenbaugh, who had recently moved from Berkeley to Brown, just in time to miss the transformation of Cal's history department by the arrival of professors such as Larry Levine and Leon Litwack. "Many of the younger practitioners of our craft, and those who are still apprentices," Bridenbaugh asserted, "are products of lower middle-class or foreign origins, and their emotions not infrequently get in the way of historical reconstructions"—unlike what he presumed to be true of himself. "They find themselves in a very real sense outsiders on our past and feel themselves shut out." Bridenbaugh's remarks stung me and many members of my generation just then entering the historical profession. Yet he was right about me in one sense. I knew on some level that I had a better feel for American history that began in the 1890s than the one that ended in the 1790s. The late nineteenth century had long marked the earliest point of my serious interest in history of the United States, not coincidentally about the time my grandparents had arrived from eastern Europe.[52]

My sense of myself as someone whose outsider status was shaped by being a Jew and an intellectual drew inspiration from the Norwegian American Thorstein Veblen's 1919 essay "The Intellectual Pre-eminence of the Jews in Modern Europe," which I first read as an undergraduate. The renegade economist and acerbic social critic noted appreciatively the disproportionately significant contributions Jews had made to intellectual life. Yet he worried about how the Jew "becomes a disturber of the intellectual peace, but only at the cost of becoming an intellectual wayfaring man, a wanderer in the intellectual no-man's-land, seeking another place to rest, farther along the road, somewhere over the horizon." If Veblen's thesis helped reinforce my sense of myself as an outsider at Yale, I have to acknowledge the importance in my life of what he missed: economic privilege, growing up in a household and community that honored books and scholarship, and the importance of the sustaining communities, shaped by Jews and gentiles alike, that transformed me from what my freshman counselor misperceived as an unenthusiastic and colorless eighteen-year old into who I became.[53]

Learning to Balance Intellect and Emotions

There was a cost to my intellectual intensity at Yale. Coming there as a townie from a high school that did not adequately prepare me to study, think, and learn, I was working against a strong sense of insecurity. As I wrote to Helen somewhat later, "If only you knew what physical and mental agony I have gone through these last two years because of a lack of confidence in my ability." Things had come to a head in January of my junior year. While trying to write a paper, I remarked soon after to Helen, "Everything exploded. All that had been building up in me for two years burst into the open: my rebellion against my former high school self, my sensitivity to new areas of perception and feeling, everything that made me feel restless inside. I broke into hysterics," "thrashed, cried. . . . Shaking all over and unable to control my limbs."[54]

I calmed down enough to seek help. With my parents out of town, I went to see one of my professors, Hans Frei, whom I described with some exaggeration as "the *only* person with whom I had ever been able to talk in a meaningful way." As I talked to him I "discovered for myself" that what was involved was "a question of a conflict, tension . . . between several SELVES, one emerging, one dying, and one waiting in the distance for the obvious outcome of the battle." Frei responded appropriately: before arranging for me to see a psychiatrist at Yale's health services, he told me he could not give me the answers, but that, he, my parents, and my friends would be "standing at the end line of the battling selves, . . . confident that after the storm had cleared there would emerge something beautiful."[55]

Ironically, it was from Frei that I had taken a course on American religion in my sophomore year in which I wrote a paper on American Judaism. I say ironically because Frei, though born a Jew in Germany, at a young age had converted to Christianity and then in his maturity become a major scholar of the New Testament. Yet his consciousness of what had happened to Jews in Germany after he left in 1935 was never far from his mind. In 1959–60 he spent a year at University of Göttingen, feeling more like an American professor than a German in exile. As he was about to leave New Haven I wrote him to express my concern that he might hide his past. He answered saying that when Germans realized by listening to him speak that he was born there and asked him why he left, "after a slight, barely perceptible awkward pause the conversation continues."[56]

The crisis that turned me to Frei was part of my struggle during my final eighteen months at Yale to resolve what I was coming to think of as a series of powerful tensions between commitments to sharpen my mind and, at the same time, to foster the emotional side of my life. Friendships with male and female contemporaries were crucial in this effort. Also important was what I was reading, especially in my junior year. *The Education of Henry Adams* helped me think about what it meant to be a person out of sync with his times. Reading the Transcendentalists and debating their virtues with Charlie Newman helped awaken me to what it meant to think and feel simultaneously. As I remarked toward the end of my senior year in a way that reflected a certain youthful arrogance, "Like Emerson, I think I came to a Romantic stance as a reaction against the sterility of the extended Enlightenment."[57]

Mitigating this emotional turmoil was the dramatic improvement in my academic record. My best year was my junior one, when my grades placed me in the upper 1–2 percent of my class. I ended up graduating with an academic record that placed me in a position more elevated than Yale predicted when considering whether to admit me.

Transformations

My education in American studies illuminates a field, an institution, and me as an individual on the cusp of enormous changes. What my teachers published offers some evidence of the hold of the Cold War consensus, along with signs that pointed to the future. Similarly, my experience and that of my peers in the honors program resonates with the 1950s even as it points forward to what was to come. What I wrote for my courses reveals all the contradictions I was struggling to reconcile. Key elements of my education in American studies gave me (as aspects of their education gave many others) ways of looking at the world that helped position me on the cusp and even break through, however unevenly, toward new understandings. For many of my classmates, their informal education at Yale gained them access to the corporate world. For me and some of my peers, Yale offered a formal curriculum that provided entry into the world of ideas and a professional future. For the class of 1960 there was more than one way to be a Yale man.

CHAPTER SIX

Recasting Gender in a Masculine World

When the sons of Eli
Break through the line
That is the sign we hail
Bulldog! Bulldog!
Bow, wow, wow
Our team can never fail!

Words and music by
COLE PORTER, Yale class of 1913

After every touchdown at football games, Yalies sang this song. Porter, who we later learned was gay, had the perfect profile of a Yale man. He arrived in New Haven from a very wealthy Indiana family via a New England prep school. As an undergraduate he was a member of DKE and Scroll and Key, as well as president of the Glee Club. In his Yale anthem he conveyed not only the inarticulateness of the sons of Eli but also their determination never to fail. Much of what we experienced at Yale, Porter's song included, drew on and expressed a seemingly confident and all-pervasive masculinity.

Experiencing Gender in a Man's World

I intentionally titled the previous chapter "Becoming an Academic Man" because masculinity was so central to our experiences at Yale. The military academies excepted, Jerome Karabel has noted, "perhaps no American college was more assertively 'male' in its reputation and self-image than Yale," with its "identity . . . inextricably joined to the notion of the 'Yale man'—that gentlemanly, athletic, intelligent (but not intellectual), competitive, and good-looking young man who gave the college its distinctive character." One of the

major changes wrought in the 1960s was the transformation of gender relations. All this was most vividly revealed in my family's history, especially in
the differences between my parents' marriage and mine, in the impact that the
women's movement would have on my mother, and in what it meant for me to
be a man. At some point in the 1960s I emerged as a partner in an egalitarian,
companionate marriage and, for a man of my generation, as someone with
strong commitments to women's issues and women's education. The roots of
that change lay in my experience growing up and at college, where I struggled
to reconfigure what it meant to be a man different from my father.[1]

My parents provided a clear sense of "proper" roles. My father was a career
man who brought in almost all the family's income and controlled outgo
by putting my mother on a generous allowance for household and personal
expenses. Away from the house most of the day and many evenings as well,
he worked tirelessly at making a living and at making his mark as a community stalwart. Although like many men of his generation and background he
was better when it came to carrying out decisions than in acknowledging and
expressing emotions, his demeanor was sweet. He was not the 1950s father
and husband stereotypically pictured in *I Love Lucy, Ozzie and Harriet, Rebel
without a Cause, The Organization Man,* or retrospectively, *Mad Men.* He
was neither domineering nor henpecked, did not work in a large, impersonal
bureaucracy, or spend his weekends on a golf course, at a backyard grill, or at
cocktail parties. Although in the 1950s my mother was an elected city official,
by and large she stayed home, ran the household, and worked as a community
volunteer. She was one of several women who played a significant role in my
youth—the list also included my sister, the live-in maid who cooked meals
and kept the house clean, my New Haven grandmother, the female teachers
who taught me from kindergarten through high school, and, once I reached
adolescence, the girls who were my friends or dates or sometimes both.

If girls and women filled my world before and during in high school, Yale
College in the late 1950s was a man's world. The Yale Corporation and the
administration were all male. Late in my undergraduate years, two women
joined the faculty with regular appointments in major departments. Their
presence did nothing to change the fact that after I graduated from high
school, no woman had a role in my formal education. There were female students in the graduate and professional schools but most of my classmates had
nothing to do with them. The admission of women as undergraduates did not
take place until almost a decade after my time at Yale. Women, mostly from
nearby women's colleges, arrived on campus on many weekends, and we traveled to see them on their home turf. The rituals we participated in, the clothes
we wore, the physical environments we inhabited, the multiple groups that

claimed our allegiance, our relationships to dates, our attitudes toward homosexuality, and what we read about and listened to in the courses we took—all these reminded us daily that we inhabited a man's world. Undergraduate culture at Yale was masculine in its emphasis on toughness, male bonding, and aspirations to marry the right women.

If all this is true, how did many of us get from such a masculine world to where we ended up? Although I can only speculate about the experience of others, in my case the answer lies in the nature of my relationship with my parents, dissatisfaction with the dating scene at Yale, the contrast between deep and significant relationships with male peers and more sporadic, less satisfying ones with most females; disquiet with the hyper-masculine world of Yale, which some of us experienced as elitist and socially offensive; and the fact that I, as did many of my classmates, moved with the times. A major issue of our lives involved thinking about what it meant to be Yale men, a process central to the story of what it meant to be on the cusp. We were living in a very male world, although the fact that women were absent struck many of us as part of a natural, unchangeable order.

Initiation into a Masculine World

While at Yale, I knew of but did not participate in a number of collegiate rituals of masculinity: trips to a house of prostitution in Bridgeport inhabited by African American women, alcoholic binges, enactments of Roman orgies, fraternity rushes, athletic competitions, Tap Day for aboveground senior societies, and a cappella singing. Yet in my first week as a freshman I engaged in a ritual intended to transform me into an athletic Yale man. Like all entering students I had to show up at Payne Whitney Gymnasium during orientation week. Seeing how slight I was, the person who recorded my height and weight urged me to try out for the position of coxswain on the crew, something I did not even think of considering. Next came the photographing of my almost-nude body, with stickers attached at various places in order to determine whether my posture was correct. I passed that test, principally because Len Katz, a member of the class of 1957 and my future brother-in-law, had given me a lesson in how to ace it. The practice originated in eugenics decades earlier, but by the time I entered Yale, it had more to do with measuring and creating the physically perfect Yale man. In addition to being subjected to the taking of these infamous posture pictures, I had to pass another more rigorous trial, which if I was among the 8 percent who succeeded in this and the posture test, would exempt me from a year-long regimen of physical training. I could not possibly do the requisite fifty sit-ups and so, loosely monitored, I counted by dozens—one / twelve / twenty-four / thirty-six / forty-eight. When I reached "forty-eight," Yale's legendary swimming coach, Bob Kiphuth, came by and, seeing me exhausted, remarked that I could pass without doing the final two. I then went to the swimming pool and completed the requisite laps, but when I got out I upchucked. Only rarely did I return to the gym, and when I did it was as a spectator. I had passed the first ritual of masculinity at Yale, but as an outsider who was also what David Riesman called an inside dopester, and one engaged in subterfuge.

Sites of Masculinity

That test in my first week at Yale took place in one of many campus sites of masculinity. Payne Whitney was the quintessential Yale man, arriving there from Groton and joining DKE and Skull and Bones and captaining the rowing team before he graduated in 1898. When he died in 1927 he left money for the gym that bears his name. A 1953 essay in *Holiday* titled "The Yale Man" described the gym as a place for students who spent little of their time studying and instead took advantage of the university's unmatched athletic facilities, "elaborate sets" for their "rehearsal" for "future roles as leaders." Nine stories high and Gothic in style, it contained the world's largest suspended swimming pool, used only for practice; a second pool where 3,400 spectators could watch meets; an artificial river where crew members could practice; and squash and basketball courts. Yale men could also benefit from facilities farther from campus, an eighteen-hole golf course, forty-three tennis courts, a huge indoor track facility, and eleven football fields, including the 1914 Yale Bowl.[2]

These athletic facilities were not Yale's only masculinized spaces. The residential colleges had been funded by Edward S. Harkness in 1933 (a philanthropy made possible by his inheritance from a father who was an early partner with John D. Rockefeller). Harkness had come to Yale from St. Paul's School and as a member of the class of 1897 joined Wolf's Head. In his class book, it was said of him that his "blood is pure Scotch," a phrase with double meanings.[3] Inspired by Oxford and Cambridge, the residential colleges, such as Trumbull, where I lived for my last three years, prepared us for a world of clubs—the common rooms had their wood paneling, elaborate fireplaces, oriental rugs, and comfortable leather chairs. Similarly outfitted nonresidential fraternities competed as sites for the performance of masculinity.

No space was more masculine that the Linonia and Brothers (known as L and B) Reading Room in Sterling Memorial Library, funded by a gift from John William Sterling, a member of Skull and Bones from the class of 1864.

In 1939 an observer noted that the reading room, a place where men could smoke cigars and women readers could not enter, "was designed to stimulate leisurely browsing and reading for pleasure in an atmosphere of informal comfort." Nine years later, at a time when half of the library staff was female, L and B remained "a 'stag' room" closed to women. Another observer described its décor as similar to that of a "gentlemen's club"—"leather divans, ottomans, thick rugs, and smoking stands." Only in 1963, in response to protests from female graduate students, was L and B opened to women.[4]

Mory's, a private club that occupied a central place on campus, was another masculine space. Over time it had become what a writer in 1999 called "a self-conscious monument to Yale life." It accepted as a member any upperclass-man who could ante up the modest lifetime fee and get an existing member to sponsor him. Not until 1972, threatened by protesters (including my mother) who staged sit-ins, did it admit undergraduate women as members. Still, it remained a masculine place. "The presence of women notwithstanding," the reporter continued, "Mory's still has the air of a 19th-century ale house," with drawings of Yale memorabilia on its menu, the Whiffenpoofs singing "To the Tables Down at Mory's," its atmosphere steeped in cigar smoke, its men dressed in the requisite coats and ties, and its "set of rooms decorated with Yale team pictures and oars hanging from the ceiling." Laden with history, its discreet entry door with an equally discreet sign that read simply "Mory's," windows with curtains that prevented the curious from looking in, and a membership policy that required a sponsor surely made many an uncertain, shy, poor, or provincial upperclassman hesitate before thinking about trying to enter or join.[5]

What reinforced this aura of masculine exclusivity was what the former Yale faculty member and anthropologist Sidney Mintz, referring to mysterious buildings and their opaque procedures for entry, told me many were "doors you could not get through," a sense that "permeated the campus like a perfume." The residential colleges presented themselves to the street and to visitors with points of entry that were generally neither clear nor inviting. Above all, there was the presence on campus of the formidable tomblike buildings of above-ground senior societies, many on central campus, not its periphery. In 1953 John Knowles described them as "enormous icebergs glimpsed through the fog, and pondered over because of their immense Unknowable." Their build-ings were "forbidding, windowless sepulchers."[6] Skull and Bones sat between the Yale University art gallery and Jonathan Edwards College, with the Old Campus across the street. It faced the street with a dark, recessed doorway and window frames with no real windows. What surrounded Scroll and Key were Woodbridge Hall, the building that housed the office of the university's president; Woolsey Hall, the main performance space; the music school; and Silliman College. Its Moorish-style architecture reeked of mystery and inaccessibility, with a forbidding entry door, two columns on each side, and three windowless windows above. At Yale secrecy and exclusivity were linked to a masculinity that was preparing us for a future in an elite, manly world.

Quite different in style and masculine in its own way was the Elizabethan Club, located in a historic house on campus. Founded in 1911, with its membership open by invitation to a limited number of undergraduates, it offered a precious version of masculine exclusivity, one with a British feel different from the more assertive residential colleges. Men across generations talked of literature as they sipped tea and delicately ate cucumber sandwiches. On occasion of the 400th anniversary of the crowning of Elizabeth I in 1959, a *New Yorker* writer described the club as "a place where undergraduates with literary interests could meet in comfort and a certain amount of grandeur," in an earlier day being "served by a dignified Negro steward . . . who was widely believed to converse easily only with his opposite number at Skull & Bones." Just before I graduated, of its 1,500 members, only one was a woman, a bibliographer of Shakespeare's works and Shakespearian scholarship.[7]

Rituals of Masculinity

Among the arenas for playing out the dramas of masculinity were the locations of tryouts for many organizations, including a cappella singing groups. In my years at Yale there were nine, including four with names that evoked their maleness—Alley Cats, Bachelors, The Duke's Men, and Orpheus and Bacchus. At the top of the heap stood the Whiffenpoofs. I never gave it a moment's thought that I might compete for a coveted spot in any of them, principally because I lacked musical talent. Other obstacles as well made it difficult for someone like me, and many other classmates, to join any of these groups. The rigorous and time-consuming schedule kept away almost anyone who wanted to devote his time to academics or athletics. The proportion of men who had gone to private high schools was way above the class norm. As far as I can determine, John Levin was the only Jew among the approximately eighty-five of my classmates in any of these singing groups, which had in their ranks no person of color. Rituals bound their members together. With the Whiffenpoofs these began in the spring of our junior year with member selection, followed by a night of alcohol-infused revelry. During the summer before senior year the group spent two weeks at an inn overlooking Lake Placid, where they practiced for the upcoming year, drank, engaged in high jinks, and learned to call one another by special names such as Pitchpipe,

Sasper, Two Car G's, and Linger Longer. During the academic year they gave a series of concerts—on campus at fraternities, residential colleges, Mory's, and Woolsey Hall; off campus at colleges in the Northeast, in the homes of parents and alums, at private clubs in major cities, at gatherings sponsored by corporations, and then in Bermuda for nine days of spring vacation.[8]

A discussion of the Alley Cats makes clear just how extensively gender inflected the experiences of singing groups with their opportunities for male bonding and female seduction. A somewhat tongue-in-cheek essay on the group in the class book described the scene at one Alley Cats concert: "sultry coeds sat with glazed eyes" and listened to one of the group's members "croon" a song which ended with "So love me tonight" because "Tomorrow may never come." Then at the Bedford Junior League Ball in upper Westchester County, "the female members of the crunchy gravel set fought to tear the clothes off of another member of the group as he sang *Love Me Tender*." Back at Yale, while performing at DKE, "a vivacious creature removed her date's hand from her knee and dreamily whispered the three little words" the Alley Cats loved to hear, "Aren't they adorable."[9]

"Man, Man Is for the Woman Made and the Woman Is Made for Man"

This Caribbean tune, like so much popular music sung by the a cappella groups in the 1950s, was characteristically redolent of strongly masculine visions of life. The groups drew on African American spirituals, vaudeville, Broadway shows, Calypso, minstrels, and barbershop quartets. One old American folk tune in the Whiffenpoofs' 1960 repertoire, "Tear It Down," played on the common theme of infidelity but with racially inflected lyrics: a man comes home in the afternoon to find "another black sheep within my stall." On many a weekend, Yale men went to railroad station to pick up their dates singing "My Cutey's Due at Two-to-Two Today." I whistled this tune while preparing to greet Helen on our first date as I evoked this experience of anticipation and longing.[10] "Button Up Your Overcoat," written in 1928, with its call on a woman to "take good care of yourself" because "you belong to me" reverberated with both care for a partner's well-being and assertion of male possessiveness.[11] "Aphrodite" called on the wife to "put on her nightie to keep those married men home," away from the new temptress performing in a theater in town. From a 1926 musical by Rogers and Hart came "Blue Room," in which a woman pictured a "small room . . . Where you can smoke your pipe away. With my wee head upon your knee, we will thrive on," the song continued, "keep alive on. Just nothing but kisses. With mister and missus."

If these lyrics were about heterosexual relationships, two Cole Porter songs in the repertoire involved intense expressions of love that few of us suspected could be about the passion between two men. "It's Delovely," from the 1934 musical *Anything Goes,* can be heard as involving a same-sex relationship. "You can tell at a glance what a swell night this is for romance," the Whiffs crooned in their soothing tones. "You can hear dear Mother Nature murmuring low, 'Let yourself go!'" Porter's "You'd Be So Nice to Come Home To" from the 1943 film *Something to Shout About,* describes what can be interpreted as impossible love: "You'd be all that I could desire . . . You'd be so nice, you'd be paradise to come home to and love."[12]

Male-Male Friendships

Most of us at Yale yearned for deep friendships with other men. In high school I began to realize my hopes for close male friends when I cast my lot with a group we called our "United Nations" because of its ethnic and racial diversity.[13] Once at Yale, however, I was not especially close to the two men I chose to live with when I moved to Trumbull: Don Isenberg, a high school classmate, and Fritz Steele, one of my two freshmen roommates. I soon rebelled against them because of what I saw as their conformity and what I later called my "intellectual snobbery." My rebellion was focused on music: because of their attraction to popular music, I listened to classical symphonies, folk music, and jazz. In my sophomore year I began to form meaningful friendships with men in my classes. Then in my junior and senior years participation in my major and in extracurricular organizations connected me with new friends. At last I had found men who offered me what in late May 1960 I called "that combination of seriousness and self-spoofing seriousness."[14]

Especially important were the opportunities for close male friendships afforded by membership in an underground senior society. The formal invitation from the group I joined had cautioned that its "existence, name, and membership are secret."[15] Being an underground meant that our existence as a group was not publicly acknowledged, that we had a vastly less prestigious and continuous history than the well-known aboveground senior societies, and that we met not in a large, historic "tomb" but in a rented apartment on the top floor of a modest building not far from campus. We dressed, as the invitation to join the society stated, in "dark suit, white shirt, black tie, and dark shoes." Like other societies, we met twice weekly on Sunday and Thursday evenings, with, in our case, meals once a week prepared and served by a chef in training from the local Culinary Institute of America, then located in New Haven.[16]

In some ways our composition was not unlike the larger class of 1960: we had among us one who had a major career as an athlete, one fraternity member, and a usual percentage of legacies and graduates of prestigious prep and day schools. On the other hand, we had one African American member and a higher percentage than usual of those who achieved academically. Joining the group enabled me to get to know well people outside the usual range of types I had been comfortable with. The group was unusual for its internationalism, containing as it did two men who had grown up in Europe and one in Asia and at least three others who already had serious commitments to pursue international careers. With one engineering major and three serious Protestants among us, the society introduced me to classmates with academic and religious interests I rarely encountered otherwise.

I remember remarkably little of what went on in my year, but several moments stand out. I recall a not very spooky initiation in the spring. At our meetings we talked about our lives and about our academic work, and three stories have stayed in my memory One member spoke of how he came to commit himself as a devout Christian: he sat on the banks of a lake and said to himself that if a fish jumped out of the water soon, that would be a sign that God had called him. A fish did jump and my colleague did answer the call, at least for the time being. Then David Caplin, a Clare fellow from Britain, told of the impact the 1956 Suez crisis had had on him, raising his political consciousness and strengthening his commitment to socialism and anticolonialism. This was the first time I had ever heard such clear, well-considered political commitments. Another member mentioned that he and his wife fought over little things, like whether to squeeze the toothpaste tube from the middle or the end. In addition, in the group I met two peers—Peter Parsons and Michael Dobbins—whose lyrical, playful selves provided a counter to my intense intellectuality and self-seriousness. As I wrote Helen, participation in the society "taught me tolerance of people" who were unlike me and was "one of the factors leading to the deintellectualization of danny and the rise of romanticism and the irrational."[17]

Critiques of Yale Men

"The Trumbull Marble Team requests the pleasure of your company for its Annual Banquet," complete with "Sherry and Black Tie," announced an invitation for an event in our senior year. Helen's *Campus Life* ran a picture of the 1959 team with the caption, "By the end of the 1950s some undergraduate rebels publicly mocked the presumptions of college men." There are ten of us parodying Yale life, as we stood in the men's bathroom of Trumbull College, in various poses. We were five juniors, Dan Popp, Monroe Price, Leslie Epstein, John Haverly, and I; four seniors, Steve Lefkowitz, Pete Magee, Ken Baer, and John Dollard (son of the Yale professor); and a recent graduate, Robert A. Dentan. A disproportionate percentage of us were Jews; high achievers academically; not athletes, fraternity or aboveground senior society members, except for Elihu; not that different from classmates in terms of legacies and attendance at private schools. Most of us were headed to careers as professors; the exceptions were Haverly, who became a psychiatrist, and Lefkowitz, the son of New York State's attorney general, who became a real estate lawyer in Manhattan, although even he occasionally served as a professor of law. I had the honored but meaningless position of historian of the Trumbull Marble Team (a position I believe André Schriffin held before me—though in his year the group may have played the game of tiddlywinks).[18]

We were parodying the pretentiousness of banquets of athletic teams and more broadly of formal Yale rituals. Many markers of an adversarial culture were there: dark glasses, our ironic location in a bathroom, reading or holding serious materials, cigarettes hanging, formal ties over T-shirts and jeans, one of us dressed like James Dean, Popp playing the recorder. Price held Gus, a stuffed bird that served as the team's mascot. The *Yale Daily News* played along with an article (likely by Price) announcing the victory of our team over Berkeley College's "New Jello Institute" and describing our celebration dinner. Dentan's "stirring speech on the character-building virtues of marble playing," the reporter continued, "brought members to their feet and tears to their eyes." The team mascot Gus, the story continued, sat quietly at dinner "soberly reflecting on the good old days of Trumbull College, when marble teams were really marble teams, before football made its rude intrusion on the American scene." When as editor of the class yearbook Price assembled pictures for the section on Trumbull, at the top of one page were pictures of Emery Olcott, captain of Trumbull's touch football team, and David Sellers, captain of the softball and tennis teams, both of them in poses imitating the captains of varsity teams—sitting on a Yale fence, super-serious, a large "T" emblazoned on their white sweaters. Below on the same page was a picture of the invitation to the marble team banquet.[19]

The publication in November 1958 of an underground newspaper by several marble team members further illuminates the nature of our protests against traditional college life. This one-time issue of the *Trumbullian,* which at the time was rumored to have sparked an FBI investigation, offered a caustic critique of life in Trumbull College and by extension at Yale College. Earlier, when writing for the more official *Trumbull Times* in the fall of 1957, Magee had protested that the house master had tried to "to bolster the Yale student's natural desire to be part of the crowd" by issuing an "edict" requiring Trumbull students to wear a coat and tie to all meals and to purchase a "social season ticket." These policies, he noted, "neglect the basic point that enforced uniformity is something which has no place in a University whose function is to strengthen individuals, not press them into prefabricated molds."[20]

The *Trumbullian* began with an article titled "The Natural Order," which argued that since Trumbull had such a poor record in intramural athletics, it should simply end its participation in such activities. Next came an essay whose title and message now seems highly problematic. "Princeton Weekend Ape-Rape Highlights College Social Season" told of how Master John Nicholas, having seen how unattractive were the dates brought to New Haven for the Dartmouth weekend, was arranging for Trumbull men to have apes as dates. Among the patrons was "United Shoe Shine Boys' Association, Les Aspin, local 802," a reference to my friends' feelings about how the master's chief student aide (and future secretary of defense) did the bidding of his boss. A not-so-oblique criticism of students who worked for the master said they "Must be: obsequious groveling shoe. Only W.A.S.P.S. need apply." Then came an editorial that critiqued how the *Trumbull Times,* the official college organ, insisted we participate in college life in any way possible, "just as long as we are active as little beavers." Perhaps, the essay continued, "we prefer to remain unadjusted and unidentified with the I.B.M. machine's homogenous unit."

Other essays continued in the same vein, offering critiques of the social world of Yale undergraduates. With "In Laud of Lust," a writer poked fun at what he saw as the sexual gymnastics that contemporary mores dictated. At dances, "great care is taken to keep the young gentleman's and young lady's bodies from touching as you conform to the gay and sparkling patterns of polite ballroom gestures." What followed was "a good nite kiss in which the female lips are delicately brushed by your own," which led the student to return to his room and masturbate. Collegians thus engaged in "an unnatural restraint of lust and of the Sex Act . . . subjecting you to frustration and anxiety." This contrasted with the author's view that outsiders like he and his friends were more manly than insiders because of knowing "how to use our bodies and those of our female friends." Their first date ended with a "warm French kiss"; the second, with "a tentative exploration of the various delightful aspects of the female form." On the third came "a spell of passionate petting; and, glorious climax." This meant that the writer "enjoyed what should be the inalienable right of every young American male, the rights of free love, mutual gratification, and blissful afterglow." Then came the call for undergraduates of the world to "rise erect: you have nothing to lose but your virginity!"

Finally, there was the attack on restrictive parietal hours, violation of which could result in a student's having to leave Yale. In the spring of our senior year women were allowed in the rooms of upperclassmen from noon until seven p.m. on Sunday, Friday from noon until eight-thirty p.m., and Saturday from eleven a.m. until midnight. "Is it necessary," wrote a *Trumbullian* contributor, "to state that the orgasm must be achieved before 8:30 on Fridays and midnights on Saturday?"

In other ways as well, the *Trumbullian* poked fun at campus rituals. There was "The Trumbull College Blues," sung to "Cotton Mill Blues," another reminder of the role of folk music in 1950s adversarial culture: "Go to tea at masters / Put a teacup in my hand / So I can get recommended to the promised land." Finally there were several suggestions of how conventional students, unlike those in my peer group, had such awkward relationships with faculty fellows, including this fake ad from the "FELLOWS' SELF-PRESERVATION COMMITTEE" that read "Please Don't Pester The Fellows."[21]

In an essay about Trumbull College which I composed in fall 1959 at the invitation of Monroe Price but was not published, I expressed my dissent from prevailing norms of undergraduate life. I wrote of the "boisterous vigor" of social events to which "status seekers flocked." Trumbullians mastered "various forms of diversion" like, I noted, "master-bating," a double entendre with both an obvious meaning and reference to attacking Master Nicholas. The most "thorough of triumphs" was "the ascendency of the Trumbull Television Team," which "having secured its second world championship, added the final crippling blow to the disappearance of the *Trumbullian,* a short lived protest newspaper." In contrast to these "successes in areas with pretensions of seriousness" were values and experiences I admired. I noted the importance of student-faculty relations "for those for whom a college meant more than participation on a dance floor or a football field." I applauded "a persistent spirit of rebellion" that appeared "in spite of Master Nicholas' drive for the success of college athletic functions and his attempt to impose a new order of well-roundedness of Trumbullians." I lamented how with official life in Trumbull "this mysterious college spirit . . . finds fulfillment of those areas most distantly removed from the realm of serious academic endeavor." I criticized how the college spirit was "antithetical to the primary purpose of a university." Those who developed it, I concluded, supported "Yale's somewhat imaginary well-rounded men." In contrast, I proposed that the residential colleges "embark on a program of bold experimentation . . . that would develop new forms for participation in the college on a seriously academic level."[22]

In writing this, I had two models in mind. One was the economics seminar in Trumbull in my sophomore year. The other, more compelling one was the frequent and long lunches in Trumbull, the locus of our true education in literature, philosophy, art, and politics. Most of the conversationalists turned out to be Jews: among students Ken Baer, Conrad Cafritz, Leslie Epstein, Steve Lefkowitz, and me, and from the faculty two residential fellows, Charles Blitzer and Chet Lieb.[23]

My essay, like the Marble Team Banquet and the *Trumbullian,* offered a contrast between well-rounded college men and intellectually engaged members of a community. Within our playful high jinks was something more: evidence of an adversarial stance, using parodies to protest what we saw as the problematic pretension of the dominant undergraduate culture at Yale, along with hints of influence of the Beat Generation but with little sense of any underlying political ideology. This was a classic rebellion of outsiders which Helen explored in *Campus Life* and what a later generation might have called revenge of the nerds. We were offering a version of masculinity different from that participated in by most members of Skull and Bones, the Whiffenpoofs, DKE, major varsity athletic teams, and even by most of those who played on intramural teams in Trumbull. A moment in my junior year demonstrated how college authorities perceived this. Yale had recently required coats and ties at all meals and Master Nicholas had told me that because I was coming to the dining room wearing a striped tie on a plaid shirt, my "dress at meals had become increasingly sloppy . . . in excess of what I feel is common decency." I risked losing my meal privileges, he warned, unless I started dressing properly.[24]

"To me, your emphasis on friendships and your valuing of them is sharply sensitive (if that's not incongruous)," a girlfriend wrote me in the fall of my senior year. Undergraduate friendships with male peers provided me with emotional support, intellectual exchanges, and political education. As I wrote in the fall of 1959 referring to male friendships, the ability to create and nurture "personal relationships of the most close and significant sort has been a source of continuing happiness. Friendship has remained," I insisted, "an area where imagination, intuitions, and irrationalities have had full reign." By example and in some cases by advice, my friends taught me how to be someone who not only studied and gained a growing commitment to the world of ideas, but also a person who could lead an emotionally rich life. Above all, in different ways they placed me on the cusp, helping me become a man different from my father, who lacked close friends, and from what I saw as the blackslapping and superficial models of masculinity the wider world at Yale provided.[25]

Gay Men in a Heterosexual World

In the late 1980s, Yale College began to develop a reputation as the Gay Ivy. In the late 1950s, we lived in a very different world, one where hetero normativity suffused our lives. It is likely that in my class there were several score of men who were homosexuals at one time or another and in one sense or another, yet decades after we graduated only three came out to classmates in reunion books: John Bing, Gerald Busby, and Joe Mathewson. Busby did so on our thirty-fifth reunion, telling us he "had wonderful times, especially making love to my best friend." Mathewson was more political: the reunion question-naire, he remarked, assumed that no form of "human relationship" other than marriage "is possible (or perhaps, worthy of mention)" before going on to say that for twenty years he had "been living under the same roof and on pretty good terms with a man." Several classmates took their own lives well after we graduated, in part as the result of struggles over their sexuality. Oth-ers hid behind seemingly conventional marriages and public expressions of homophobia.[26]

As an undergraduate I had no inkling that any of my classmates or profes-sors were homosexual. I met Bing often as American studies honors majors and in our work on *Criterion,* but because he was in the closet, his homosexu-ality had no impact on me. By reputation and guess, I was sure that some fac-ulty members were homosexuals, but I never paused to think or wonder what that meant, aside from what I took as stylized affectations. We discussed Walt Whitman's poetry in my junior year, but Al Stone assured us Whitman was describing autoeroticism. We also read biographies that the Smith College professor Newton Arvin wrote, but graduated before we could read in early September 1960 that the Massachusetts State Police had entered his apartment in Northampton and taken away evidence of his homosexual activity, which involved a network of gay men at colleges and universities on the East Coast. A 1958 Yale study of undergraduates discussed homosexuality only in terms of "homosexual panic." It located the source of these "uncontrollable perverse sexual cravings" in "ego weakness" due to "growing up in an atmosphere of parental discord."[27]

As a historian, one of the pieces of the puzzle that compels me is how gay men of the late 1950s could not speak of their sexuality but could publicly identify themselves with others' struggles to achieve justice and recognition. Bing provides us with a moving example. Responding to *The Grapes of Wrath* and to hearing peers talk about "homos" or "fairies" in high school, he wrote a poem titled "Okie," in which he expressed his pain through that of migrants from Oklahoma.

This name burns a jagged line
Reaching at my heart.
Every letter a burning nail
Driving me apart.

I fight back and win some ground
Then lose near all I gain.
They spray [strain?] my very soul with pain.
God smite this hell-sent rain.

Be merciful, oh help me Lord;
Swab out the stabs of men!
Cool off the devil tongues that sear
And let me live again.[28]

Poignant and painful: Bing conveyed how homophobia tore at his heart. The way he publicly used hateful expressions levied against one group to speak covertly about those directed against another reminds us of how a closeted homosexual could powerfully project his feelings. In our fortieth reunion book Bing came out when he announced to classmates his partnership with Edward Goshe.[29]

This way of speaking out involved advocating recognition for others when it was difficult and dangerous to do so for oneself. Martin Duberman played an important role in my education but neither I nor any of my friends knew about his sexuality. We have already seen how Duberman talked of his own struggles when he wrote first about upper-class white men and then soon after about African Americans. We have also seen how Bing wrote about the fight for racial integration in Deerfield, Illinois, when he could not write about his desire for acceptance into American society. Then there is Sherwin Goldman, whom we will meet in the next chapter as the author of a *Criterion* essay on liberalism. He grew up in Fort Worth as a Jewish boy who knew he was gay. In his mid-teens, with a friend he tried to break up KKK rallies, got tossed out of high school, and entered Yale a year early. Like others, he could speak of difference by identifying with African Americans—something he did years later when he produced "Porgy and Bess" for the Houston Grand Opera.[30]

We are fortunate to have writers who have offered astute observations of gay life at Yale in the late 1950s. In *Remembering Denny*, Calvin Trillin pondered the meaning of the life of his classmate, a golden boy he and his friends thought was headed for greatness when he left Yale, his life later cut short by a suicide related to his struggles with his sexuality. Trillin notes Denny Hansen's misfortune in graduating from Yale when he did—years after members of a generation could remain in the closet as married men or bachelors and before the time when gays themselves and others in cosmopolitan cities accepted homosexuality without undue attention and with little concern. Even though Trillin took it for granted that before coming to Yale he "had never run across an actual live homosexual," he had already learned to use words "homo," "fairy," and "queer"; once in New Haven, he added "faggot" to his lexicon. If anyone had asked him during his Yale years what gay men were like, Trillin "would have taken it for granted that these theoretical creatures were effeminate or odd."[31]

Another perspective on gay life at Yale comes from George Chauncey, who had earned his degrees from Yale and later joined the faculty after the publication of his award-winning *Gay New York: Gender, Urban Culture, and the Making of the Gay Male World, 1890–1940* (1994). His essay "Gay at Yale: How Things Changed" was the focus of a summer 2009 issue of the *Yale Alumni Magazine* (*YAM*), in which he revealed Yale's rich and complicated history with homosexuality. Until the turn to the twentieth century, he showed, many Yale undergraduates participated in acts, like sleeping in a bed together, that were intensely emotional and intimate. Such male bonding could involve overtly sexual behavior but did not necessarily do so. It did not cross a divide between heterosexual and homosexual, in part because that was a divide that experts had not yet invented. Then around 1900, at Yale as throughout the nation, there emerged a binary that created borders that had to be policed and signs of homosexuality that had to be suppressed. Before homosexuality was widely named, male culture at Yale allowed a continuum of intimacy, including sexual. Once homosexuality became pathologized during and after World War II, it was easier to name but actually harder to express. Chauncey goes on to note that it was not until after the Stonewall demonstrations in New York City in the summer of 1969 that gays and lesbians at Yale began to come out of the closet.

Chauncey also tells the story of Larry Kramer, Trillin's classmate and someone with whom I went to summer camp in the late 1940s. Kramer's long-term relationship with Yale is historically emblematic. While at Yale, anguished about his sexual identity, Kramer tried to kill himself. A psychiatrist at the health services attempted to persuade him to end his homosexual activity and associations; he refused and soon after had his first requited love affair, with a Yale professor. After Yale, he went on to a distinguished career as a playwright and a gay rights and HIV/AIDS activist. In 1997, he offered to write into his will a provision for a professorship in gay studies. Yale turned down the offer, claiming it was too narrowly conceived, but six years later his brother, a Yale graduate and a highly successful corporate lawyer, gave the university a million dollars for the Larry Kramer Initiative for Lesbian and Gay Studies.

In his essay, Chauncey ingeniously analyzed photographs of Yale athletes from 1902 and 1968. He noted that for the earlier year "the most striking thing to our eyes is the degree of physical intimacy between the men, who drape their arms over each other and put their hands on one another's shoulders, knees, and hearts." In contrast, in the late 1960s athletes in such pictures kept their hands and arms to themselves. What Chauncey observed was entirely true for our class. In almost all pictures—of individuals and of athletic, fraternal, literary, religious, and musical groups—there we sit, usually dressed in dark suits, our hair short, our faces unsmilingly serious, and our hands to ourselves. There were a few exceptions: photos of those involved with the *Yale Banner,* the Augmented Seven, and the *Yale Literary Magazine* in antic poses, though not touching; and the men involved with the Yale Film Society, all wearing 3-D glasses and most of them in humorous poses. There is one great exception, or sort of. A picture of the Pundits, a group of classmates engaged in clever talk, shows nine students and one professor (Norman Holmes Pearson) with their faces pasted onto the bodies of men from what appears to be a late nineteenth-century yearbook picture. That allows one student to have his elbow on the shoulder of another. Another, Leslie Epstein (the future Rhodes Scholar and novelist) has his hand resting of the shoulder of Bart Giamatti (the future Yale president).[32]

The responses to the *YAM* issue were varied, but two from my classmates deserve special note. Richard Webster had come to Yale from a public high school in Kansas City, Missouri. As an undergraduate he focused on his major in economics and on his participation in singing groups, and then went on to work for General Motors for thirty years. On the occasion of our fiftieth reunion, he remarked that Yale had taught him "how to have a heart for others."[33] Yet at about the same time that he wrote those words for our classmates, in a letter to the editor of *YAM* he offered a very different response. When he first saw the magazine, he was "horrified and embarrassed. To even realize that my postal deliverer had seen the cover was in itself a shock!" Insisting that sexual preference was "a personal matter in the secular world," he went on to say it is "not suitable for thrusting it on another, and worse, to vilify a reader, such as me, who does not subscribe to that culture. In the Judeo-Christian world, and as expressed in our Bible, man-man and woman-woman sexual relationships are unhealthy, un-natural and non-procreative." Though he appreciated much of what Chauncey had done, Webster found "the presentation, headline, and some of the content to be offensive, abhorrent, repugnant, nauseating, and violative of certain mores, values, and standards that have influenced my life."

In response to the issue came a short letter from Steve Baruch, who said what I would have said. He was in many ways like me: a Jew from a high school like mine, with a strong record of academic achievement at Yale, and without evidence of major participation in the activities that would have marked him as a well-rounded Yale man. He congratulated *YAM* for its work and stated that as a married heterosexual with children and grandchildren he assumed to be straight, he would "be even more proud and comfortable to be at Yale now" than he was from 1956 to 1960.[34]

Invisible and Problematic Women

Gender can reign even though women are hidden or of questionable social location. Yale's curriculum in the late 1950s highlighted men and largely ignored women. Attention came principally in a sociology course on the family, with the catalog announcing that it focused on "modern domestic institutions and their historical backgrounds; courtship practices; domestic relationships; the role of the child; family disorganization; divorce." Women did make some appearances in the books by Robert Penn Warren, Rollin G. Osterweis, John Dollard, Leonard Doob, and Robert Bone: as wives, schoolteachers, objects of sexual aggression, part of a subculture of southern romanticism, reformers, writers, and figures in novels—and as dedicatees, typists, secretaries, and wives who made work on these books possible. What Dollard wrote in *Caste and Class in a Southern Town* is especially instructive. The overwhelming impression the book gave was that men were sexually aggressive and women, their victims, had no agency. The one exception lay in the myths behind lynching. In the fantasies of white men, the African American woman was "a seducing, accessible person dominated by sexual feeling." In contrast were pure and innocent white women, brought down from their pedestals by rapaciously sexual African American men.[35]

In my sophomore year survey of American history, the only mention of women in what we read was in the textbook. In the first volume, Harry J. Carman and Harold G. Syrett devoted two paragraphs to the entry of women into the work force and a somewhat longer section to them as teachers, students, and reformers. "Despite the agitation of the feminists," they wrote, "the movement for the liberation of women from civil and political restraints made relatively little progress" before 1860, with "feminists . . . regarded by some as cranks and by others as dangerous fanatics." In the second volume, the authors devoted only two paragraphs to women, one on their entry into the work force between 1865 and 1914 and the other on the successful campaign for suffrage. Unlike what was true for the antebellum period, for the later period they supplied no narrative arc. If my education and that of my peers was about the relative absence of African Americans in a white world, even more striking was the absence of women in a man's world.[36]

To be sure, during my years as an undergraduate, prominent women came to speak, including Hannah Arendt, Pearl Buck, Mary McCarthy, Margaret Mead, and Iris Murdock. Yet women on the faculty were scarce. Marie Boroff, a poet and scholar in the English department, and Mary Wright, a historian of China, were the first women to earn tenure at Yale College, Wright in 1959–60 and Boroff the following year.[37] Yet neither appointment constituted a break-through toward a new order; that would have to wait for at least a decade. The hiring of Mary Wright illustrates one dimension of contemporary gender dynamics in university life. Wright, who had impeccable credentials, came to Yale from her position as a librarian at the Hoover Institute because Yale wanted to hire her husband, Arthur Wright. A tenured member of Stanford's history department, he insisted that she have a faculty appointment as well. In the academic world at major universities, the Wrights were exceptional as a married couple who both held full-time positions. To their credit, the editors of our yearbook featured Mary Wright as one of twenty-one faculty members highlighted. "The Wrights deny any significance to the fact that their campus offices are in separate buildings and their home offices on different floors," the article noted, before adding that "they always read and help polish one another's articles." More common for my generation in male and coeducational colleges and universities were male professors with their wives who modeled traditional gender roles for us.[38]

In other ways women at Yale in the late 1950s occupied positions that were less than prominent and even invisible. In *Yards and Gates: Gender in Harvard and Radcliffe History,* the historian Laurel Thatcher Ulrich and the contributors to the volume she edited explore how generations assumed Harvard was a womanless world and then how historians revealed to us the varied roles they played in its history. She reminds us that *"gender is present even when women are not."*[39] The histories of Harvard and Yale are different, yet what the scholars discovered for Cambridge applies to New Haven: from early on women donated money; served as wives and helpmates to presidents, faculty, and administrators; cleaned rooms; cooked and served meals; did research and prepared its results for publication; selected, cataloged, and made books available; and counseled community members.

We already know a lot about Yale, but more knowledge will undermine the vision of the university's past as womanless and make invisible women visible, albeit mostly in supporting roles.[40] To take some important examples: women were admitted to the schools of art and music from the beginning, in 1869 and 1894 respectively, but initially were not allowed to pursue degrees. In the

1880s, a woman applied to the law school using her gender unspecific initials instead of her first name, Alice. The law school accepted her and when they discovered what had happened, they allowed her to enter and complete the degree. Not until 1918 did Yale Law School admit women on a regular basis. In 1892 Yale let women into the graduate school: twenty enrolled; seven of them earned their doctorates. Two went on to distinguished careers on the Vassar faculty, two at Smith, and one at Wellesley. One stayed at Yale, returning to her prior position as a research assistant at the Yale Observatory. The career of the other remains lost to history.[41]

Dating and Mating

"Love and Self-Knowledge"
The tower for directing airplanes home,
At times seen dimly through the foggy night,
Suggested a lonely lighthouse in the foam
A beacon so informing after a flight.
The grasping spire, attaining truth above;
Half giving and half asking those in prayer
To seek beyond the clouds for right and love
To search together for something rarely there.
The lovers near the sea—by distant banks
Once touched, once blessed, now two are one
To unite always—intent to offer thanks
For knowledge gained before all else was done.
A flyer, tower, spire, two united minds
All searching, struggling to what one once finds.

This is a poem I turned in on April 8, 1957, for my first-year English class. "Some of your lines are marvelously loaded with meaning," my professor responded. "And the connection between the single, rare tower + the two lovers (also love, self-knowledge making one) forming into one is daring + works." Then and now I consider myself among the least poetic of people, but aside from walking into class to see my poem on the blackboard as an example to be admired, what I remember most is my professor's question: "do you really believe one only once finds love?"[42] Although it is tempting to give it a Freudian reading, with the erect tower helping an airplane find home, other things strike me: the emphasis on finding true love only once and on two "united minds" struggling and searching together for knowledge of each other and themselves.

In my senior year an event occurred that highlighted a very different kind of relationship with women: a sexual scandal that erupted at Yale and gained national attention. In mid-January Yale officials and local police found out that "Susie," a local fourteen-year-old girl, had provided oral sex to as many as forty Yale students. Some of them withdrew from Yale before legal action began; the courts brought others to trial, where they were convicted and given small fines and suspended from Yale for a year. In juvenile court, "Susie" was charged with delinquency. I was aware of the situation but at the time had little idea of what a blow job was. This story illustrates how some of the social class and sexual dimensions of town-gown relations played out.[43]

Some Yale men chose this and other exploitative ways of relating with women at a time when most other options such as long-distance dating or short weekend encounters were problematic in different ways. Thus, in the fall of 1957, the administration squashed a campaign, titled "She Is Coming," which involved seven students offering three women all-expense paid trips to the Yale-Harvard game. Two entries from the campus humor magazine, the *Yale Record*, highlight the exploitative sexism of many of my peers. In the fall of my first year, an author advised us to "put a tie on the knob outside your door when you are ruining young ladies within." Then a year later the cover of the same magazine promised posture pictures of women from the Seven Sisters colleges; among the images inside was those of elephants seen from the rear with a caption underneath that read, "Two hapless Smith girls are assigned to the jungle-gym as a corrective measure."[44]

Yale did not admit women as undergraduates until 1969.[45] In the late nineteenth century Yale had considered following Harvard's lead by opening an annex like Radcliffe College for undergraduate women, but nothing came of that idea. Twice in my years at Yale, discussions of coeducation came to the fore. In fall 1956, the director of admissions floated the idea of Yale's admitting female undergraduates, which President A. Whitney Griswold quickly squashed. In my junior year a handful of students from prominent women's colleges spent their senior years at Yale earning a teaching degree, without sullying the college's purity by taking regular courses, being allowed in the gym during the week, or receiving Yale degrees.

The discussion of the possibility of coeducation in the *Yale Daily News* reveals just how horrible an idea many of my peers considered the prospect.[46] Under the title "Oh Save Us!" an editorial written by Calvin Trillin, both of whose daughters would later go to Yale and whose wife later taught at Hofstra, breathed a comic sigh of relief that Griswold had wisely prevented Mory's from being the "scene of chattering bridge parties" and of our "having

to spend our 25th reunion drinking with overweight matrons and their hus-
bands who went to Hofstra." Yet some contemporaries displayed no humor
in their opposition. One of them claimed that Yale had to protect Western
civilization and its own traditions by denying admission to the "brainy female
automatons" from Radcliffe who spoiled Harvard. And two of my classmates
decried, I now assume without being intentionally funny, the "creeping feminism" represented by the actions of women students visiting Yale. "Can you
imagine Mory's decorated with knitting needles in place of the" rowing oars
that hung from their ceilings "or women in the Whiffs." Yet at least two Yalies
greeted the prospect with pleasure, both of them lefties, New Yorkers, and
Jews. Gerald Jonas wrote that having a college for men without women was
like wearing a tweed jacket without gray flannel pants. The "ova-envy" of most
Yale men, he asserted, "cloaked their jealousy of the opposite sex in the azure
robes of academic snobbery." Jesse Lemisch, who would later marry Naomi
Weisstein, the noted feminist psychologist, emphasized how "brutalizing"
and "superficial" male-female relationships were among his contemporaries.
At Yale, he insisted, "we speak of women as things, not as individuals," thus
revealing the deleterious effect of "separating classes of people."[47]

Although the late 1950s at times seems innocent compared with early
twenty-first-century practices of "friends with benefits" and "hookups," for
Yalies of my generation dating and mating posed a number of challenges.
There were women from local high schools, from nearby Albertus Magnus
College, and from the ranks of those attending Yale's professional and graduate schools, but few of us took advantage of opportunities to meet them, in
part because each group was generally frowned upon. More common were a
series of rites that involved the importing of college women and the exporting
of ourselves, mostly to women's colleges in the region. To identify potential
dates, we explored networks of classmates and family and sometimes lavished
our attention on picture books published by women's colleges. Regularly
scheduled mixers brought women by bus to New Haven, especially from
women's colleges such as Smith, Mount Holyoke, Vassar, and Connecticut
College for Women. Several hundred of us would meet several hundred of
them in a large room and then awkwardly sort things out in something like a
stand-up version of speed dating. We also imported women for special weekends that centered on football games in the fall and parties in fraternities and
residential colleges year-round. As one classmate later commented, women
arrived "dressed, brushed, curried, made-up, perfumed, and manicured—
probably nothing like their real selves back on their home campuses and very
little like our movie dates back home." The lack of privacy and of birth control
pills, to say nothing of our own qualms and awkwardness, meant many a date

featured "a hand-holding tour of the campus by night, and a chaste return" of our visitors to the hotel rooms where we housed them.

Or we left New Haven on weekends, traveling to meet young women, often for the first time in person. Sometimes as the weekend approached, we would call a girl we had known in high school or someone whose name we secured from a classmate and asked her to find dates for three or four friends with whom we were coming to Northampton, South Hadley, Poughkeepsie, or New London. Although many Yale-Smith or Yale-Vassar marriages resulted, these routines were romantically awkward, dangerous for those of us who drove back to Yale in the early morning, and expensive for those with limited financial resources. Restrictive visiting hours necessitated awkward good-nights performed as house mothers watched the clock and us. All these conditions, along with often uneasy romantic and sexual norms of the day, made dating problematic.[48]

Faced with these challenges, I had some advantages. I dated girls from Hillhouse High School who were one or two years behind me. However, out of the insecurity of a townie dating a townie, once or twice I listed my date in a published dance program as someone coming not from Hillhouse but from Potrzebie High School, a nonsense name derived from a word of Polish origin and Yiddish inflection then used by writers for *Mad Magazine*. When importing dates, I could have them stay in the room in my parents' home that my sister had vacated when she went off to Sarah Lawrence College in 1954. Whether importing girls or exporting myself, I benefited from free gas from Botwinik Brothers to fuel either my mother's snazzy 1955 turquoise-and-white Chevrolet convertible or my father's impressive but inappropriate black Cadillac sedan of more recent vintage. What really shaped my dating patterns, however, was the deep and varied network that helped me identify eligible Jewish women. The one non-Jew I dated during college was a Smith student that a New Haven friend at Smith fixed me up with. After a few dates, she wrote to say that her mother, a "very staunch Episcopalian" and her father, a corporate executive and a church elder, both wanted her to date only Episcopalians, a commitment with which she said she agreed.[49] My usual dates were those arranged by my sister at Sarah Lawrence or by female friends from New Haven at their women's colleges and those drawn from the long lists of collegiate women provided by relatives and friends of the family. The extensive world of upper-middle-class Jews—Jewish geography we called it then—was out to protect and perpetuate itself.

Despite these advantages, as college friendships with men grew more sustained, those with women by and large remained only potentially so. My guess is that in the course of four years I dated in excess of fifty young women, kissed many of them, went not much further with few of them, and remained a virgin until several years after graduation. In a dozen or so instances I sustained a relationship for several months but not for longer. To put it mildly, I was sexually naïve and unaggressive, and, unlike many of my peers, I did not believe in the double standard. I rarely if ever exploited what power my social location and maleness might have given me. Inexperience, contemporary mores, the awkwardness of distance, ignorance about contraception, and perhaps normal late adolescence issues with intimacy all stood in the way of something more than relatively chaste serial dating.

At the time I was dissatisfied with the sorts of relationships with female peers my situation at Yale made possible. In high school, I benefited from the wide range of experiences with girls a coed environment afforded me—casual and sustained, friendly and romantic relationships. Given that prior experience, being at Yale was a shock, intensified by the inability to meet girls on campus by accident or design, in formal and informal situations. I was not alone in my dissatisfaction with these limitations. For example, in the spring of our junior year, five classmates from Beta Theta Pi, having not been tapped by a senior society but understanding that societies offered something useful, formed their own distinctive version. They wanted to develop meaningful relationships with women outside the limits that dating imposed. Twice a week during our senior year, they met with five Vassar women, calling their group YAVA when it met in New Haven and VAYA when it met in Poughkeepsie.[50]

Later I made my views known to my father—in 1967 when the Yale Corporation was considering coeducation. "Thirty years ago," I suggested, "the type of social style among faculty at Yale had a great deal of gentility, one of whose elements was keeping women seen and not heard." Now, I continued, with faculty "recruited from a greater variety of social types," increasing numbers felt that women belonged in the classroom. Similarly with students, I insisted, decades ago "the psycho-sexual development" of late adolescents "was such as to recommend keeping women away from young men during some of the week." With youths maturing earlier, I said, "more young men are interested in having women easily around in the college years." Having women at Yale College would enable "undergraduates to lead more normal lives, which, it seems to me, is essential to their development into men." Recalling my years at Yale, I remarked that my social life there "was essentially very strained" because women were not around. I then explained what I meant: "Driving 80–110 miles for a four hour date (blind) and then returning to New Haven, having women down only on 'special' occasions, and not being able to easily meet young college women on an informal basis seemed, to me, to promote the worst in undergraduates. Decisions had to be made swiftly, pressure was always on, and, in all, dating had an unnatural sense to it. The week and the weekend were artificially separated and often left a bad taste. Any ordinary strains in young college relations became intensified."[51]

The Quest for Authenticity

In these worlds of male and female friendships, we pursued what the historian Babette Faehmel has called "a preoccupation with questions of authenticity," a quest late adolescents typically embarked on but one that had specific cultural meanings in the late 1950s.[52] As a teacher at Smith College in the early twenty-first century, I often surprised my students when I told them that when I was in college I thought that I could discover my authentic self and connect with the authentic selves of male and female friends. For them this stood in dramatic and informative contrast to their own sense that, lacking stable, self-constituted, and authentic selves, they instead experienced only the performative selves that theorists like Judith Butler described for them.

If in the late 1950s at Yale and elsewhere paradox and irony were in the political air, authenticity was in the relational air. Kahlil Gibran's *The Prophet* was a book I never read, but his ideas seemed to be everywhere, more prominently among women than men. J. D. Salinger's *Catcher in the Rye* (1951) taught me and millions of other adolescents to try to avoid phoniness and hypocrisy. As an undergraduate I read Allen Ginsberg's "Howl" (1956) to dates I hoped to transform from being "nice" or insipid to being profound, perhaps in the process convincing them that I was worthy of their affection, even though I remained unaware of the poem's homosexual implications. I also read and talked about Martin Buber's *I and Thou* (1923). A girlfriend who was studying Buber in class at Sarah Lawrence wrote me, "This man has the answer! It is the key to our relationship"—though she did not go on to explain what she meant.[53] The copy of Buber's book I still have is unmarked, but I thought what it told me was that the authentic "I" could connect to the authentic "Thou." As I read it over now, I am not sure I then understood its poetic sense, its underlying philosophy, or its religious implications. I think I can now comprehend what Buber was calling for, that we lighten our commitments to things and intensify our relationships to people and to God.[54]

I also read Erich Fromm's *The Art of Loving* (1956) and William Barrett's *Irrational Man: A Study in Existential Philosophy* (1958), the latter recommended by Charlie Newman.[55] Several passages I marked up in Barrett's book deserve notice—the "divorce of mind from life," "the individual human personality itself struggling for self-realization," "the fractured being of modern man," and "the West's fateful encounter with Nothingness."[56] Other passages spoke to what I was going through in 1960. Barrett's mention of "man's alienation from his own self" because he becomes so over-identified with "his own particular social function" surely reverberated with my sense of the limitations of my father's life and the possibilities of my own. His discussion of existentialism's "struggle to awaken in the individual the possibilities of an authentic and genuine life" helped me understand what I aspired to. Finally, when Barrett remarked how strong in the writings of Jean-Paul Sartre was "the element of masculine protest," I wondered about the relationship between being a man and being authentic in my own life. Soon after I graduated, I referred to several of these passages in a letter I wrote to Helen. Thinking about my own struggles to reconcile heart and mind, but also about how this dichotomy played out in our relationship, I pointed to a passage where Barrett commented how "the intimacy and concreteness of personal feeling taught" about "the incompleteness of all philosophies that deal in purely intellectual abstractions."[57]

The scores of letters from women I was dating strikingly reveal the dynamics of our relationships. They show how seriously we took ourselves. For example, I often conveyed to them how especially important to me was my encounter during my junior year with Henry Adams's *The Education of Henry Adams,* whose life he saw, as I saw my own, as that of a man out of place in his world. Yet despite the intellectuality that I had developed in my sophomore year, I am struck by the emphasis in the letters on playfulness and spontaneity. Reading the letters now gives me a sense of how I was wandering the worlds of women's colleges, dating and writing, as I engaged myself and them in trials of intimacy and exploration. I was trying to find someone who would both accept me for who I was but also try to help me to become a person who could manage competing claims of mind, emotion, family, career, commitment, and independence. We all seemed involved in often tumultuous and always intense, emotionally charged struggles to define who we were, as individuals and in relationships to one another. We were intimate strangers to each other as we pondered issues of dependence, independence, and identity formation. Attraction was strongest with young women who combined spontaneity and intellectual playfulness in an effort to avoid hypocrisy and conformity.[58]

It is tempting, but mistaken, to overemphasize the dynamics of these letters, and the relationships they reveal, as mainly sexual. During my college years I was able develop a number of relationships that were either non-romantic from the start or became so over time. It did not strike me then and does not now that sexuality was the principal terrain of identity formation, as it is—along with race, class, and gender—for many students early in the twenty-first century. In the late 1950s, for me and for many peers religious and political issues were of considerable importance. Rarely in the letters were there even hints at the sexual dimension of our relationships, and on the rare occasions when there was, young women couched issues in terms of the propriety their parents would expect. From what I can remember, it seems that the women I dated trusted me not to be sexually aggressive and take advantage of them. To be sure, there were seductive dimensions to my approach to courtship: the gifts I sent; the intellectual, cultural, and emotional engagement I offered; the combination of neediness and command I conveyed; the impression my going to Yale helped create; and the way that over time I brought my dates into the circle of compelling friends and an encompassing family. In a world where white, upper-middle-class guys dated white upper-middle-class girls, I was respectable, reasonably good looking, honorable, smart—and as a man more sensitive to women's needs than much of the competition.

Sure, sex was on our minds, but if it was my intention to conquer my dates sexually, I was surely a failure. Lots of kissing, caressing, hand holding, bodies moving against each other—but no touching of genitals, oral sex, or nakedness. Something different was involved, something characteristic of collegiate dating for me at that time and in that social place. My dates and I were involved in a process of self-discovery through encounters with someone else. Whatever my girlfriends gained from me, I gained considerably from them. Re-reading their letters more than half a century later and having such wisdom as age and historical acuity bring, I realize what a vitally important role girlfriends played in my emotional development. The advice and encouragement they offered helped me mature as a person and to find the right balance between past experiences and present possibilities. Women, in offering advice and frequently working against my intellectuality and in some cases my sense of intellectual superiority, gave me advice that was crucial to my development. Written at the time, the words of a Yale psychiatrist captured what I was going through. "Highly intellectualizing individuals," he asserted, "use intellectualization both as a defense mechanism and an adaptive process."[59]

With friends, male and female alike, I was weaving a complex tapestry in a charged emotional world. I am struck now by how interlocking my worlds were. Watching Monroe Price's relationship with Jean Rosen, a girlfriend from Walnut Hills High School, or with Ruth Osterweis. Driving Charlie Newman's girlfriend, Carol Brightman, to Poughkeepsie. Writing back and forth between Dick Munich and Jacky Gutman, the Wellesley student who later fixed me up with Helen. Going into New York to see my sister and brother-in-law while on a date with a Sarah Lawrence woman. Making sure my parents met my favorite professors. Introducing male and female friends to my parents. Writing letters was important; more important was how embedded I was in a world of friends and family.

"Two united minds / All searching, struggling to what one once finds"

While at Yale, most of my classmates dated women, and most of us who married did so within the first five or six years after graduation. To be sure a few ("Bucky" Bush, Jim Ottaway, Peter Parsons, and Dick West among them) married before we graduated. In many respects, my own story was not atypical: I met my future wife in my senior year and married her a few years later. What is probably unusual is that we saved the courtship letters we wrote to each other in the spring and summer of 1960. Now our letters provide a rare window into not only our thoughts and feelings but also the times.

Helen Lefkowitz and I met in a way many couples did before speed dating, JDate, and the bar scene flourished. In late summer 1959, Jacky Gutman told me that when she arrived at Wellesley College in September, she would find my wife. She came home for Thanksgiving and told me of a first-year student she had met in gym class to whom she would eventually introduce me. Three months later she gave me Helen's name and address. For my brief, initial encounter with Helen, I traveled to Wellesley on February 28, 1960, between Helen's eighteenth birthday and my twenty-second. Helen came to New Haven in early May for our first real date. The rest is history. However, how history worked its magic was richly complicated, something illuminated by the letters we exchanged, the only case in which I have those both to and from me. Helen and I rarely talked on the telephone, which then cost the 2014 equivalent of almost $4.00 a minute. Our letters were expressively emotional, mine more playful than hers and hers better written than mine. We offered each other advice about how to deal with the emotional ups and downs each of us was going through. We worked together to deepen our relationship and our commitment to each other. Very early on we each made clear how significant and quickly growing was our mutual interest in something lasting.

From the start we focused on communication and commitment. The day after we first met, I wrote her that "I was sort of overcome by your ability to sit down and, in a most quiet manner, talk intelligently for an extended period of time." A week later, I remarked that I had worried that her "gentility" as a "Southern girl" from Louisiana might have prevented her being honest about herself. I was wrong, I continued, because right away she had revealed "the greatness to be honest, to take off the mask before I even dared to do so." For a relationship to work, I insisted, an individual had to have the "daring to put

himself in a stance where empathy, gentleness, and sensitivity are of importance." Right after the first weekend we spent together, I told her that "if I can
hold a mirror up to you so that you can begin to see yourself more clearly,
I will be overjoyed." At the same time she was holding a mirror up to me,
one that enabled me to see myself more clearly. Hearing her talk of her own
insecurities, I remarked, helped me "return to subjectivity, youth, romanticism," which I had submerged when early at Yale I had hidden emotions in
the name of intellectualization. "Communication," I insisted, was "the basic
level on which our future will blossom or wither. . . . I don't want to be writing
at you or to you—but talking *with* you." Talking with her about the pain I
was feeling, pain both emotional in nature and physical from gastrointestinal
problems, I told Helen she was "the first person I have ever articulated all this
to," and it was important "that you see all this in me and still accept me."[60]

Helen responded in kind. In April, between our brief first meeting and our
first date, she remarked that "real friendship is possible only when one is oneself," a process in which open communication was essential. Soon after our
first date, she wrote to tell me that she was trying to learn "to give of myself to
establish 'closeness,'" and that for the first time in her life people were becoming people, not objects. Soon after she told me how important to her was my
acceptance of who she was, a process central to her search for her "true self"
and truth about who I was. "The degree to which you shared a part of yourself
with me," she remarked, "overwhelmed me" and "still makes me glow." To be
sure, she continued, she could not know the future, but "I do know that now,
here, you have come to have great meaning in my life. To me, that is enough."
In later letters, she continued in this vein. Toward the end of May she quoted
Albert Camus, who had written that "friendship is more than the responsibility of loving; it is the responsibility of being loved." Again, reciprocity of
knowledge and self-knowledge stood at the center of our relationship. When
in my last weeks at Yale I wrote her that not having done well in my final
exams meant that I might not become an academic, she responded reassuringly: "I do know from what you have given me, that if Danny Horowitz wants
to teach, he can, and he will teach. . . . You are much more than what you produce on an examination." Finally, she wrote in the late summer of the beauty
of "sharing your consciousness and your sharing mine."[61]

In addition to the role of communication, four other specific issues shaped
our relationship: the world of books we shared, our common interest in
America's racial situation, hints of a feminist consciousness, and what was
for then and for me a relative openness about sex. To begin with, important
to us was what we read in common and then discussed. Immediately after
we met, Helen readily accepted my invitation to enter into the intellectual

universe I was exploring, a world of books and essays by Ralph Waldo Emerson, Henry David Thoreau, William James, Arthur Koestler, William Barrett,
and John Kenneth Galbraith. Race was also very much on our minds. When
I learned that an African American man, facing multiple difficulties, had
threatened my aunt Marjorie Botwinik, I told Helen I wished that my uncle
Norman "would make a leap of faith," not press charges, and "treat him as
if he were a person." Instead, I continued, the man "will probably end up in
jail and the vicious cycle of economic and social pressures will return him to
society unreconstructed." Then during the summer of 1960, I wrote Helen
that I had begun to notice "a change that has come over either my knowledge
or America in the last year." When I was in South Africa the summer before
I had told my relatives "that, although things might be bad in the U.S., the
difference between So. Africa and the U.S. was that in the latter things were
getting better and government was at least neutral. Now I do not know what I
would say." In July 1960, when visiting my friend Dick Munich in Lexington,
Kentucky, I wrote Helen that when I refused to patronize a Woolworth's his
cousin had said, "I love Negroes, but not that much." I then went on to note
that Munich was working for CORE, "a group a bit left of NAACP—younger
and more impatient—and has been participating in Sit-ins." In reaction his
increasingly angry father had told him, "It will jeopardize your future position in the community."[62]

As a southerner who grew up in a household headed by a rabbi who spoke
of justice for African Americans only in abstract terms, Helen felt race as an
issue more keenly than I. Indeed, I wrote the letter about the change in my
views of South Africa in response not only to the series of lunch counter sit-
ins in Greensboro, North Carolina, but also to a letter Helen wrote me that
included a discussion of how concerned she was about the dynamics of race
in her family. The situation she found in Shreveport when she returned home
after her first year at Wellesley disturbed her "very deeply, mainly because no
one is *doing* anything. My family has very lofty ideals," she wrote at a time
when southern rabbis like her father were in a dangerous situation, "but the
desire to maintain the security of our house stifles any action—or even words
outside the house." She told me that she wanted to do something positive but
that the color of her skin would make her unwelcome in the African American community. "It's so easy when all one does is to carry a sign in front of
Woolworth's or to give money" to an organization. "But when one tries to
strike more deeply than the outside shell there the difficulty sets in." A week
later I wrote about Murray Last, a Clare fellow at Yale who had organized the
protests against apartheid a few months before, as someone who had "spent

most of the summer travelling through the South, sleeping in the street and eating in grocery stores since he refused to patronize any segregated facility."[63]

There were even hints of feminist consciousness in our correspondence. In June 1960, I wrote what a "revelation to me" it had been when I realized that my mother had "'Mrs. Miriam B. Horowitz' on some of her stationary— 'Mrs. William Horowitz'" on some other. Stronger and more explicit was her experience. When her mother, a rebbetzin and housewife, criticized Helen for being "unwilling to accept the 'woman's role,'" Helen told me she responded by trying "to explain that she was correct in assuming that I am not planning as my primary goal to be an efficient homemaker but that I hope I could achieve this position as one aspect of a full life. . . . Mother," she continued, "thinks I am a confirmed feminist, wondering 'Where did I fail?' . . . So last night I read to her the 'different drummer' passage in *Walden*— without success."[64]

Moreover, our letters reveal what was exceedingly rare for me in my relationships with girlfriends—any explicit mention of physical intimacy. Just after our first date, I told her that when as I was driving she held my hand, there was so "much softness and tenderness in you for me." Her "affection" for me, I told her soon after, "caught me completely off guard and has overwhelmed me." Then not long after our first date, she wrote me about the barriers that her sexual restraint posed for us and how much she wanted not to feel this way so that there could be a greater sense of connectedness. "How do you stop feeling what you have been taught to feel but no longer want to feel?" she asked. "How do you transcend self and reach beyond?" In response I wrote that "I hope you are not maligning my intensions. I have no thought of taking anything sacred from you." It disturbed me greatly, I told her, that her wrestling with issues of intimacy in our relationship was so painful, "for the only sense in which all this disturbs me is that your being trapped makes sex too explicit a problem in a relationship."[65]

Although we would not marry until August 18, 1963, with surprising rapidity we were moving to express our commitment to each other. Very soon after she left New Haven following her first visit, I wrote her that I had "unconditionally accepted her. . . . This means" that "regardless of what you say, write, or do, I will accept you as a person who has meaning in my life." Within weeks after that first date in early May, I wrote her that "for the first time in my life, I have actually thought of making a serious proposal to a girl," but backed off because I did not have sufficient knowledge and I did sense what I called "the *fin de siècle* pressure on me at this moment in my youth." Then I went on to "wonder why you attract me—initially it is certainly your looks. . . . What holds me next is your affection for me and what seems to keep me lingering near you is you—your youth and the growth you must be experiencing—excitement—a quick mind—and a wandering one." Helen's response was clear. "Don't you know that what you wrote didn't have to be written; that, whether you asked me to or not, the thought of marrying you has been a source of happiness to me for many weeks. And this is the only answer that I can give to you now. And too much is unknown to me now. You. Me. Us (yes, the implicitness is overwhelming). And there is the feeling that this can only become known as I am with you."[66]

In one letter she brought together a range of issues that we were coming to talk with each other about. I had written about marriage as "freedom-giving, rather than freedom-taking," which evoked from her the statement that she "now had the freedom to hope for what I had wanted to hope for, for far too long." Yet she talked of her "own haunting feeling of unpreparedness and . . . inability to grasp what marriage and marriage to you would be." She mentioned "the natural depression caused by my menstrual cycle," the first time any girlfriend had written to me of this aspect of the mind-body relationship. She talked of how she had benefited from reading what William James had to say about learning from experience and Henry Adams about education in the "Vis Inertia" chapter in *The Education*. She went on to emphasize the closeness she felt when thinking about holding my hand and the affection she experienced. "I feel when I read something that you have read—and its meaning suddenly helps me to know Danny better."[67]

Transformative Relationships

Looking back, I can understand how over time relationships with women transformed many Yale men of my generation. We see this in a number of instances. Tom Miller's Debsian socialist mother had laid the ground for his turn to the left in the mid-1960s, which his marriage to Tran Tuong Nhu also influenced. In a similar but less dramatic way, David Elliott's marriage to Duong Van Mai shaped both his interest in Vietnam and his politics. And the situation with Kirke Wilson is even subtler, involving as it did the way his border-crossing Mexican American mother may have influenced his interest in improving the lot of less privileged Mexican Americans in California's Central Valley. More generally, reunion books make clear that the rise of feminism shaped our marriages and partnerships.

In ways I did not understand then but do now, the combination of all my experiences as a child and an undergraduate enabled me to reconfigure gender, shape my identity, become an academic man, and develop into a loving and effective husband. In high school I inhabited a world of male and female teachers, male and female peers, which opened up for me a range of relationships with boys but especially with girls. Growing up in my parents' household I experienced a gender order shaped by a powerful father who worked outside the home and a less visibly powerful mother who stayed home, organized housework, and did unpaid volunteer work that often took her outside the domestic sphere. As treasurer of the city of New Haven she had a public position that, although she occupied it to a considerable extent as a representative of my father, nonetheless marked a major change in her life and in the role of women in local politics. As a child and adolescent I sensed my mother's disquiet as she struggled quietly and privately to configure a life independent of a powerful mother and husband. These dynamics spurred my belief that I could help my mother, and over a long period of time other women, fulfill their aspirations. I never sensed that these rescue impulses were problematic. Reading Erik Erikson in the 1960s, I came to see what I was engaged in as generative and productive, for me and for those women I tried to help—girlfriends in the late 1950s, the woman I married in 1963, the several thousand women I taught over a career of almost fifty years, and dozens of younger colleagues, male and female, whom I mentored. As someone who throughout my career taught in a series of women's colleges, I spent the rest of my life helping to liberate women (and myself) and to develop ways of being a man, husband, father, teacher, and colleague for which I had virtually no models.

As I left Yale, I struggled mightily about my future in terms shaped by my gendered experiences. I wrote Helen in late August of 1960 that "I sort of got drunk with the idea of remaining in New Haven and entering" politics. I bragged that I was confident I could be a city alderman by twenty-six and mayor or congressman by thirty-two. Then reality came crashing: when I went to the country club and actually encountered the kind of people I would have to persuade to vote for me, I realized how lost I would be in that world and how "anonymous I often feel I must remain in the country club." I applied to Yale Law School (which admitted me) because I thought I might remain in New Haven and follow a career in business, politics, and public service not unlike my father's. On the other hand, I applied to universities in both Cambridges, and in Berkeley and in Madison, Wisconsin, because I wanted to generate ideas and scholarship, not votes and income. My father and I never fought. I respected him but did not want to live a life like the one he led, one with a sharp division between family and career, ideas and profession. I knew, profoundly, that I wanted something more. Helen and I talked about our desire for careers and family life that were more integrated and emotionally meaningful than our parents'.[68]

Experiences at Yale helped push me to the other side of the cusp that separated the 1950s from the 1960s. In my sophomore year I had rebelled against friends I saw as excessively conformist and in reaction had become overly intellectualized; over time, through friendships with men and women, I learned how to integrate the intellectual and the emotional. My dissatisfaction with the dating scene played some role in this process. Also influential was my unhappiness with what I experienced then but could only put into words later—the versions of masculinity that Yale offered, ones that seemed shallow, exploitative, boisterous, elitist, and just plain offensive. An alternative version of manliness and relationships with collegiate women was visible in my role as the historian of the marble team, familiarity with those who wrote the *Trumbullian,* my taking studies seriously and thinking of myself as an intellectual. In the late 1950s, as a hyper-masculine all-men's college Yale was hardly on the cusp in the transformation of gender relations even though I, and surely some of my classmates, struggled to reconfigure what being a man meant. My letters, experiences, and memories help counter the image of a totally buttoned-down 1950s. In important ways, writing this book, a combination of an emotional memoir, an intellectual history, and social analysis, brings together heart and mind. By means implicit and explicit Yale trained us to be a certain kind of man. More in defiance and in spite of the models and signals it offered, I and some of my peers recast masculinity and gender relations in ways that pointed more toward the future than they drew on the past.

CHAPTER SEVEN

Political Engagement in an Apolitical World

"A Series of Lessons in Political Systems"
DANIEL HOROWITZ, "To the members of the
Rhodes Scholarship Committee," fall 1959

Most classmates, uninterested in politics, vaguely identified as run-of-the-mill Eisenhower Republicans or Stevenson Democrats. A spring 1960 poll of Yale upperclassmen reveals that 41 percent considered themselves Republicans, 42 percent independents, and 17 percent Democrats.[1] It was not cool to be politically engaged; after all, most of our elders preferred informed but casual spectatorship. Indeed, as I researched this chapter I was struck by what someone recently characterized as a predominant male attribute of "being simultaneously with-it and disengaged, in control but nonchalant, knowing but ironically self-aware, and above all inscrutably undemonstrative." I will touch hardly at all on the aspiring politicos active in the Yale Political Union, according to our class book "the largest undergraduate organization at Yale." After all, what marked the 1960s was not the familiar presence of consensus views organized around allegiance to the two major parties but the emergence of more wide-ranging alternatives. This involved a shift from equating being an informed citizen with one who voted once a year to more oppositional and sustained efforts.[2]

Some readers will find in what I write, especially given the small numbers of those on the organized left and right, further evidence of 1950s consensus. Others will recognize that change was beginning to occur. Although I organize some of the story by going from right to left, those of us who from a variety of political positions were dissatisfied with politics-as-usual saw attacking apathy as important as the advancement of a specific political agenda.[3] As a consequence, we worked to create new public spaces, venues for discussion and even action beyond the well-established ones such as the *Yale Daily News* and the Political Union. "The transformation of public into mass is of particular concern to us," C. Wright Mills wrote in *The Power Elite* (1956).[4] Some of us had read this book, but even if we had not, we were nonetheless determined to develop genuine public arenas on campus that countered anomie and informed a more adversarial politics.

Most of those who dissented from politics-as-usual were not typical undergraduates. Some who came from elite backgrounds by choice or family heritage did not fit the norm of the college man. To the extent that the focus of this chapter is more on the left at Yale in the late 1950s than on the right, it is because no conservative organization had as vigorous a public presence, speaker series, or impact as the left-leaning ones

Yale Daily News on Politics

In its news coverage the undergraduate newspaper appeared to be even-handed, covering with reasonable objectivity the full range of stories on campus and off. Yet, by and large, the editorials and opinion pieces were closer to the center and right than the left. When he took over the chairmanship of the *News* in February 1957, Scott Sullivan, class of 1958, focused on the rights of labor unions when he declared that "of the myriad injustices staring the American people in the face today, perhaps the most flagrant is the existence of the so-called 'closed shops.' "[5] His successor, Robert Semple Jr., attacked the most radical campus organization, and in turn his successor, James Ottaway Jr., according to the chaplain William Sloane Coffin Jr., paid too little attention to civil rights protests. The three most prominent political commentators during my years at Yale ranged in their politics from a centrist Democrat (Robert Rifkind, class of 1958), to a Stevenson Democrat deeply influenced by Edmund Burke (Jonathan Seagle, class of 1960), to a libertarian conservative (Michael Uhlmann, class of 1962).[6] Further evidence of the middle-of-the-road orientation of the *Yale Daily News* comes from the reporting of Neil Herring Although one of the most radical of my classmates, he even-handedly covered people with the widest possible range of perspectives. And when he wrote about those on the left, he tended to downplay adversarial elements of their politics.[7]

Conservative Organizations

When the conservative writer M. Stanton Evans returned to campus in February 1960, he found to his "astonishment" that campus conservatism had "become a full-blooded and purposeful movement" unheard of when he graduated in 1955. In my years at Yale there were several undergraduate conservative groups. The Society of King Charles the Martyr took its name from an early seventeenth-century English king who was beheaded because he refused to abandon the Church of England. At Yale in the late 1950s the society was Anglo-Catholic in nature.[8] The class book listed three members, two of whom (Jared Lobdell and Doug Wagner) appear on other lists of members of conservative organizations. The society's private, unpublicized gatherings focused less on politics than on a combination of undergraduate antics, serious religious discussions, and prayer.[9]

If the somewhat moribund and centrist Conservative Party did not have much of a presence, two other groups with overlapping membership—the Party of the Right and the Calliopean Society—drew their inspiration from the *National Review* and its editor, outspoken Yale alumnus William F. Buckley Jr. Among my classmates there were only two members I can identify as associated with the Party of the Right—Lobdell and Jim Hinish.[10] There were seven members of the Calliopean Society, including David Stuhr, who along with Hinish was a founding member of Young Americans for Freedom (YAF), launched nationally soon after we graduated.[11] The Calliopean Society, increasingly active in my years and operating outside the traditional strictures of the Political Union, focused mainly on defending free enterprise and opposing Communism, labor unions, and an intrusive federal government. It sponsored talks by the chronicler of American conservatism Russell Kirk; the founder of the John Birch Society Robert Welch; and the novelist Ayn Rand. Like those on the left, conservatives could identify only a few like-minded faculty members, Cleanth Brooks, Wilmoore Kendall, David Rowe, and H. Bradford Westerfield among them. Indeed, Lobdell told me that most Yale faculty, if at all "politically interested were marginally left of center—centrist enough for my lefty friends to call them conservative, left enough for my conservative friends to call them liberals or worse."[12]

Compared with those on the left, fewer of the conservatives came from prestigious private schools and had legacies of any significance. They had a lower level of academic achievement than those on the left. If Christians on the left came from Social Gospel traditions, the Christianity of those on the right originated elsewhere—in Roman Catholicism and more conservative Protestant traditions. One marked similarity between those active on the left and on the right was that they were both outsiders to the principal avenues of prestige at Yale. Among the conservatives, as among the lefties, there were no members of an a cappella group; none in an aboveground senior society, except for Lobdell, who was in Manuscript, which like Elihu had many

members with serious artistic ambitions; no athletes who earned a major "Y";
no fraternity members. Several among them worked on the *Yale Lit* but none
on the *Yale Daily News.*

Varieties of Conservative Experience

Writing in the *National Review* in 1969, Lobdell explained the difference
between "libertarians and traditionalists." The first group emphasized "the
freedom to play John Galt," the hero of *Atlas Shrugged,* and the other stressed
"the perfect freedom of service to God."[13] Robert M. Schuchman's "Libertarian Reflection on the Failure of Democracy," which appeared in a February
1960 student publication, represents the first strand. His parents were great
admirers of FDR, and he graduated from Bronx High School of Science and
Queens College in New York. Born a Jew but a convert to Episcopalianism
in the late 1950s, he wrote the piece as he was completing his first year at Yale
Law School and was about to serve as first national chairman of YAF. Schuchman argued that democracy had failed because Americans turned their back
on liberty, which he considered the first among "eternal verities, discernible
from the very nature of man and society." He insisted that "the doctrine which
teaches that we must penalize the successful in order to uplift the unsuccessful, currently called 'liberalism,' calls for the same type of mind as the belief
that the Negro must toil so the Southern white may escape menial labor." If
other ideologies focused on the "collective whole," for libertarians the individual was supreme and the purpose of both state and society was "the fulfillment of one's identity." Only with "an unfettered industrial enterprise" and
"self-realization . . . unrestrained" "can the free society be achieved, and only
then will democracy become a desirable and an attainable goal."[14]

Lobdell offered a very different version of conservatism. He grew up in Ho-
Ho-Kus, New Jersey, in what he called an "old line Republican" family, one
with a distinguished Republican lineage identified with Abraham Lincoln and
Emancipation. His was an Anglophilic, Episcopal household. The religious
services he attended, he later noted, revealed a "ceremonial, hierarchical, and
sacramental church." At age thirteen he read *Out of the Silent Planet* and *That
Hideous Strength* by C. S. Lewis and put J. R. R. Tolkien's *The Fellowship of
the Ring* on his Christmas list. Important to the books he read as a child, he
later recalled, "was their Englishness," fostering an awareness "of England as a
separate realm—this *other* Eden, demi-Paradise."[15]

A Taft Republican, he came to Yale from Wooster, an Episcopal prep school
in Connecticut with a strong commitment to self-help. At Yale, although he
was affiliated with conservative organizations, he moved outside that silo

through close friendships with Yalies on the left: Richard Posner from the class of 1959, and not yet the conservative jurist and writer he would later become, and Jonny Weiss, among my classmates a key figure on the left. As an undergraduate, Lobdell achieved academically, was a member of Manuscript, and published poems in the *Yale Literary Magazine* in which he focused on Christian religious themes. Christ "Whose joy it was to dance upon the cross / For our redemption," he wrote in mid-1959. Like many of the most talented of my classmates, Lobdell was a Scholar of the House, but illness intervened and he never finished his project, composing sonnets on Holy Communion.[16]

In "The Wisdom to Know the Difference," an essay he wrote in February 1960, Lobdell offered his distinctive version of conservatism, one strikingly different from Schuchman's libertarianism. He asserted that as a Royalist, antiquarian, and Anglophile, he embraced alternatives to living here and now in America. No "political question, or any question at all, can be considered without considering God," he insisted, specifically a Christian God. He supported a "righteous war." He advocated limited government because the state was "only an instrument of fallen man." Because the government could minimize evil but not "legislate good," he found problematic the Supreme Court's decision in *Brown v. Board of Education*. His view of sinful man and problematic government also meant he preferred that people be loyal to and rely on the institutions closest to them: the family rather than the town, the town rather than the country, the country rather than the world. With charity beginning at home, "any N.A.A.C.P. and civil-rights or anti-nationalist group" was "devoted to an absurdity." His "next-door neighbor" was thus more real to him than "a thousand starving Chinese." With democracy impossible, "each person should govern himself" in accordance with God's will. "Social awareness and the pursuit of civil liberties" were "praiseworthy precisely insofar as they lead the individual soul to salvation."[17]

Criterion

The articles by Schuchman and Lobdell appeared in the undergraduate periodical *Criterion* published under the auspices of Dwight Hall, the principal campus Protestant organization. In October 1959, as a new editorial board was taking over, Monroe Price noted how the problems with established undergraduate publications had opened the way for one that took a fresh approach. In the spring of my senior year observers remarked that *Criterion* existed in reaction to the undergraduate emphasis on joining organizations to enhance personal prestige, especially as a stepping stone to membership in an aboveground senior society. With an editorial process that involved spirited discussions, *Criterion* offered poems, fiction, and essays, including the article on segregation in the North by Raleigh Davenport. In my senior year I was on its board, the most sustained and intense extracurricular activity of my Yale years, and one my freshman counselor could neither have anticipated nor likely would have approved. The other board members were like me: academic achievers who were not typically varsity athletes, members of a singing group, fraternity or, except for Elihu, an aboveground senior society. Because *Criterion* welcomed statements that ranged across the political spectrum, it provides the fullest window into the political ideology of politically engaged Yale students of my generation. Moreover, it offers a view into the kind of public space that politically oriented Yalies outside the mainstream created.[18]

Charlie Newman, encountered earlier as an American studies honors major and as my partner-in-crime in the protest against the holding of our senior prom at an exclusive club, was *Criterion*'s driving force in our senior year. He grew up in an upper-middle-class family on Chicago's North Shore, where he went to a private day school. Although he had the choice of becoming a professional baseball player, he came to Yale. As an undergraduate, he combined academic achievement with a range of extracurricular activities: varsity baseball early on and later membership in a variety of organizations, including the Elizabethan Club and Elihu. Years later, not long after Newman died at age sixty-seven, David Brooks hailed an essay by Robert Boyers for his portrait of Newman as someone whose beauty "inspired intensities of admiration and interest." Yet my own sense is that it was less his beauty than his intellectual flair that inspired his peers. As I wrote in a memorial for our fiftieth reunion, he was "a passionate, brilliant, blustery young man. He energized the classroom and small gatherings of students with his biting wit and penetrating questions." If Cushing Strout was the faculty member who served me as a model of engaged intelligence, Newman was the counterpart among my friends. Newman was among the small number of very close non-Jewish friends I have ever had in my life.[19]

Newman's senior thesis on the early twentieth-century writer and critic Hutchins Hapgood makes clear how much he shared with his subject: they were both baseball-playing sons of the Middle West who went east to an Ivy League university; anarchists because they found socialism, as Newman put it, "too structured"; and men who tried to make it big on the national literary scene. Rereading the thesis, I find it hard to tell the difference between Newman and Hapgood. He saw his subject as a romantic who "wishes to change reality not escape it," who assumed man "is an infinite reservoir of possibilities, and if one can rearrange society by the destruction of an oppressive order, then these possibilities will have an opportunity for fulfillment, and progress will ensue." Romanticism propelled Hapgood, as it did Newman, to engage in a "Faustian search and struggle," in which "alienation becomes the price as well as the foundation of awareness." Newman insisted that his subject's life revealed how "defiance" staved off defeat. The problem was "one of weighing" one's "personal insignificance with the monumental ideas and events of which he is a part." Eerily, not only did Newman use Hapgood to describe his own life until 1960, but it turned out that he was writing as if he knew his subject's trajectory prefigured the rest of his own, filled as they both were with early promise followed by turmoil.[20]

It is impossible for me to write about Newman without talking about his girlfriend from Vassar, Carol Brightman, who, as beautiful as Newman was handsome, equaled him in brilliance. In the spring and summer of 1960 I wrote Helen that "Charlie and I semi-dreamed about the future." We would "take Carol's inheritance money and her farm in Virginia," I wrote, "get our Ph.D's and go to the farm and WRITE and teach. Hundreds of our own children." Then several months later I continued in a similar vein. "The new decision is this," I announced to Helen, "Buy a 60 foot yacht on which we will live and write—sailing back and forth to Europe, according to the Seasons." Newman would be captain (of course) with Brightman as first mate, Helen as second mate, and me as Bo-swain. "Also," I continued "we decided I would marry Carol and Charlie will marry you so that we can all commit adultery, get divorces, etc. Sometimes I fear Charlie is serious," I remarked ruefully.[21]

In my junior and senior years *Criterion* featured student reflections on Yale, many of which expressed a great deal of dissatisfaction with the collegiate experience. Most of these statements were more angry than constructive or focused. A notable exception was by Posner, whose Old Left mother had left her imprint on her son. He offered a well-argued radical critique of Yale similar to those that would emerge in the 1960s. Posner blamed the college's weakness on the influence of wealthy alumni. As a result, what dominated Yale were "social hierarchy and distinctions, exclusiveness, clubbiness." Extracurricular activities, such as student agencies and publications, acted like "model corporations." Fraternities, senior societies, and honor societies, by emphasizing "meticulous preoccupation with minute social distinctions," prepared Yale men for lives in corporations and country clubs. Admissions policies discriminated against high school graduates and Jews in the name of "cosmopolitanism," in the process lowering academic standards and preserving "the traditional Christian and conservative nature of the student body." The Jewish quota persisted even though half of the Junior Phi Beta Kappas of the class of 1959, including him, were Jews. The administration had to "tailor

an education" to the "tastes and interests" of the sons of the rich, and of the
not so privileged who aped their "dress, manners, and attitudes." The college
thus provided a significant number of "escape-hatches for the intellectually
indolent," including a plethora of gut courses. Posner was pessimistic about
whether change would come in a situation that often made the "bright student" feel "himself isolated by the hostility of a mass of mediocre minds." The
only hope he held out, with a partial accuracy he could not anticipate, was
the rising cost of higher education would force Yale to rely on government
funding which in turn would counter alumni influence. Then Yale would
"maintain its greatness and integrity" and supply the nation with "leadership
of trained intellects."[22]

Criterion's fullest consideration of politics came in the "Ideological Issue"
of February 1960. Influenced by Strout's emphasis on the importance of
contemporary conservatism, Newman included the essays by Lobdell and
Schuchman. As editor, Newman stated that he hoped the issue would redress
the problem of America's consensus ideology and avoidance of philosophy,
thereby overcoming the fact that "American thoughtlessness harbors as much
destructive potential as Communist maliciousness."[23]

The opening essay, "Perspective from Abroad," a stinging critique of American politics, was written by David Caplin, an English socialist and aspiring
physicist. I had come to know him through participation in an underground
senior society, and well remember how central America's racial situation was
to his consciousness. In his essay Caplin mentioned hearing that in the South
"dilapidated Anglo-Saxon aristocrats" called "Negroes by another unpleasant
name." He found U.S. politics dangerous, believing as he did that the nation
was filled with "cunning bandits in the form of political fanatics of all colours
and -isms, confident that she will arrive at her goal with virtue intact and
uncompromised." This "political adolescence" meant that Americans invoked
free enterprise when what they actually objected to was communism as "free
love," socialism as "free medicine," and capitalism as "free subsidies." Drawing on John Kenneth Galbraith's The Affluent Society (1958), he went on to
criticize Americans for tolerating poverty, ugliness, and poor health, which
he believed could only be eliminated by "public enterprise." Countering the
critique of socialism as materialistic, he insisted that it was in fact a system
that enabled people to have abundance and good health care as rights and
thus allow them to fulfill themselves by making full use of freedom of thought
and expression. The Western world will fail with America if the country could
not "cope with the problems of a free, democratic and materially abundant
society."[24]

This issue of *Criterion* contained a second essay by a socialist, Peter Paul Bergman, a member of the class of 1961, who had come to Yale on a scholarship from Ohio's Shaker Heights High School. He offered a robust statement of how dissatisfied he was with America, a country he saw governed by a "powerful owning class" that stood in opposition to the realization of "true economic democracy," ran an economy based on profit as opposed to "service and need," fostered a class system, and relied on exploiting fear to promote armaments, including nuclear ones. He called for a "radical third party to serve as a political gadfly, constantly pecking at the hides of our two political goliaths." He envisioned a society that embraced both "political and economic democracy," that offered "opportunity according to ability and not to class," and that was "dedicated to man and not to money."[25]

More toward the center, "Liberalism: A Prologue," by Sherwin Goldman, who came to Yale from a public high school in Fort Worth, argued that liberals tended to rely on truisms, on "an attitude, a tone, a goal." Goldman emphasized equal opportunity more than equality, because of "the moral worth, the absolute value, and the essential dignity of the human personality." He hailed the promotion of a "genuine aristocracy" that did not deny privilege to anyone based on "birth, wealth, race, creed or sex," ensured by government under "just laws" that would make it possible "for every individual to develop his fullest potentialities." Yet having celebrated liberty much as a conservative might on first glance do, Goldman made it clear that he embraced the New Deal's liberal welfare state—the right to a decent job, home and education, as well as protection against "the economic fears of old age, sickness, accidents and unemployment *for every individual.*"[26]

What are we to make of the authors and these essays as statements by students precisely at the turn from the 1950s to the 1960s? All of those on the left—Posner, Caplin, Bergman, and Goldman—were Jews, as was Schuchman on the right. Interestingly, race figures more significantly in the contributions from the right than from the left, with Schuchman and Loddell marking their distance from the civil rights movement. All assumed America was an affluent society; believed American politics were moribund at best; and except for Lobdell invoked freedom, individualism, human potential, democracy, and liberty, however differently they interpreted them. When Trumbull College's resident faculty member Charles Blitzer reviewed the issue he noted how all except Caplin and Lobdell shared commitments to "liberal individualism." Nonetheless, *Criterion* had provided what C. Wright Mills might have considered a public space for Yale students to articulate and exchange their contending perspectives.[27]

George Orwell Forum (GOF)

This was the farthest left group at Yale.[28] Those involved gave it that name to distinguish it from the Communist Party while making it clear they were on the left.[29] Two faculty members, Robert Bone and the art historian Robert Herbert, were active in the GOF, along with four students, including Charlie Newman and A. J. Leddy (also now deceased). Neil Herring, one of the two surviving members, grew up in Brookline, Massachusetts, in a comfortable and conventionally liberal household. Before he came to Yale, reading the works of Marx and Lenin along with those of French existentialists began to awaken his political consciousness. At Yale, he joined Air Force ROTC because of the financial aid it afforded. In ways that reflected the isolation of radicals, he believed he was the only socialist in our midst. He was, in fact, the only classmate who listed in the class book his involvement in a full range of left-liberal organizations. For the GOF he organized the visits of union and civil rights activists, *Dissent*'s editor Irving Howe, democratic socialists Michael Harrington and Norman Thomas, and the renegade Marxist Raya Dunayevskaya. In and outside the classroom, Herring's education continued: he read Bone's book on the Negro novel and C. Wright Mills's *The Power Elite*. Inspired by Robert Herbert's suggestion that he explore the connections between politics and the arts, he wrote his senior honors paper on French communist existentialist writers.[30]

Kirke Wilson, the fourth member, came to Yale as a Protestant with a Yale grandfather in his background and as what he later called "an unreflective Republican of inherited beliefs." His mother, Margarita Canales, had grown up in a Spanish-speaking family that moved back and forth across the Texas-Mexico border, before settling in the early 1930s in San Francisco, where she met his father. This made Wilson, as far as I can determine, the only classmate a later generation might consider a Latino. He was initially raised speaking Spanish and English, but this changed after his mother died and his father in 1948 married an Anglo woman. Wilson attended Berkeley High School and began to move to the left only when he got to Yale. We can track his political trajectory as an undergraduate by looking at his memberships: from the Young Republicans as a freshman, to Dwight Hall in his first two years, to GOF in his junior year, and as a senior to Challenge (an organization discussed in the following chapter). Experiences that occurred during his sophomore year intensified his feeling, as he remarked later, that at Yale he was living in an "exclusively male, an overwhelmingly white and comfortably privileged" community, one "isolated from the grim realities of the surrounding city." When walking back to campus through an African American neighborhood after visiting a girlfriend from Berkeley who was living in New Haven, he struck up conversations with African Americans. Then he wondered about the relationship between what he had experienced on the street and the more abstract knowledge being imparted in his economics class.[31]

In his junior year, Wilson accompanied Bone to New York and Philadelphia to hear him deliver political speeches. Wilson participated in a number of protests: he marched across Connecticut for peace and against testing of nuclear bombs in the Pacific, something that led to his being kicked out of ROTC. He went into Hartford schools with Jackie Robinson to recruit students for an April 1959 Youth March for Integrated Schools in the nation's capital and later participated in the march itself. Yet like others committed to breaking through the silences of the 1950s, whether through liberal or conservative activity, he was determined to keep undergraduate organizations politically diverse, an impulse that also stemmed from his friendship with Schuchman. Nonetheless, his experiences in left politics at Yale, he acknowledged on the occasion of our fiftieth reunion, "propelled" him "into a career of social change and social justice."[32]

In November of 1958 some members of GOF wrote a remarkable letter to the *Yale Daily News.* They were responding to the controversy that resulted when the USSR told Boris Pasternak that if he went to Stockholm to receive the Nobel Prize for Literature, he would not be allowed to return. Posner joined GOF members Leddy and Newman in trying to extend the discussion from its comfortable anticommunist assumptions by calling on peers to defend "intellectual freedom and nonconformity *everywhere,*" in America *and* the Soviet Union. Why, they asked, did students say they were in favor of ending racial segregation or nuclear testing, but were unwilling to march or sign petitions. This reluctance was a holdover from the McCarthy period, "when the oppression of nonconformist opinion differed only in degree from" what Pasternak faced in the USSR. Only when Yale students could embrace controversial stands without fear of reprisal and Yale hired a professor who was "competent professionally and a Communist politically" could Yale men speak out against the USSR "with compelling moral authority." In response, an editorial, presumably written by *News* chairman Robert Semple Jr., denounced the naïveté and "sheer absurdity" of the letter, based on the impossibility of a professor's being both politically accomplished and a Communist. The relativism of the letter writers "would debilitate any effective action on the part of the free world against the Communist conspiracy."[33]

Given GOF's existence out on a left limb, it is not surprising that the FBI monitored its activities during my junior and senior years, albeit without turning up any evidence of a serious threat. Following our graduation, deans at Yale grew concerned about the speakers GOF brought to campus. In spring 1961 the director of campus security, formerly a special agent for the FBI, relied on the report of a "confidential but reliable source" when he wrote to the dean of undergraduate affairs that a New Haven man who was a member of the Socialist Workers Party and of the local branch of the Fair Play for Cuba Committee was using GOF to hold meetings at Yale that supposedly were of more interest to townspeople than to Yale students. The administration, he recommended, should consider making a "discreet check" to prevent "this type of meeting from being held again." This occurred after GOF announced a lecture by Robert F. Williams, the head of a North Carolina chapter of the NAACP who advocated that African Americans use force against those who attacked them.[34]

SLIDing into SDS

With its small membership, GOF paled in comparison with the John Dewey Society (JDS), the Yale chapter of the Student League for Industrial Democracy (SLID). Founded nationally in 1905, just after I graduated SLID changed its name to Students for a Democratic Society (SDS), becoming the most important radical student political organization of the 1960s. André Schiffrin created JDS soon after he arrived at Yale in fall 1953. He had come to the United States with his parents in 1940 when the Nazi occupation of Paris made it dangerous for Jews to remain. "Ironically," he notes in his memoir, "the old-boy network had gotten" him there through the intervention of a friend of his father, Mary Mellon, wife of Paul Mellon. In Paris his father was an important publisher. Soon after graduating from college in 1957, Schiffrin became a prominent publisher of left wing books, first at Pantheon and later at the nonprofit New Press.[35] SLID in the late 1950s and early 1960s was but one piece of evidence of student activism struggling for daylight, with organizations forming elsewhere, including SLATE at Berkeley, Toscin at Harvard, and YAF nationally.[36]

Schiffrin worked to build as broad and large a membership as possible, and in the process created both a new sense of what was politically possible and public space in which those who came after him could explore a wide range of issues. In an effort that was emblematic of our generation's attempts to create a big tent in order to fight apathy, he told prospective members they would "meet other students who call themselves liberals or socialists, independents or progressive moderates." Of the forty or so student members in the mid-1950s, about half were Jews, many of them from New York City and some from émigré families. In 1956–57, the one year my classmates were at Yale with Schiffrin, the only member of the class of 1960 who joined was Jonny Weiss, the son of the philosophy professor Paul Weiss.[37] "If we were nonconformists, we were far from being extremists," Schiffrin remarked later, as he pointed to JDS's support for NATO and its preference for criticizing the foreign policies of the USSR at least as forcefully as those of the United States.[38] Determined to build membership and to avoid criticism from anticommunists, Schiffrin, using quintessentially Cold War language, remarked that JDS would be "a strictly nonpartisan educational organization open to anyone who does not advocate totalitarian ideals." He chose to avoid calling the Yale branch SLID because it "sounds pretty communistic" or even "blatantly socialistic."[39]

Schiffrin patiently built JDS into an organization that by the fall of 1954 had a major public presence on campus. Under his leadership JDS addressed a broad spectrum of issues. Close to home he criticized senior societies and Yale's anti-Semitic admissions policies. In addition, JDS sponsored talks on national health insurance, conscientious objection to military service, defense of victims of the Smith Act, college students in the silent generation, the purposes of a university, America's religious revival, existentialism, disarmament, the impact of mass communication on American youth, the dangers of big government and big corporations, the challenges of an affluent society, the problem of income inequality, the promise of anti-colonialism, American foreign policy in an age of uncommitted nations, and programs for enhancing democracy in the United States locally and nationally. Several programs Schiffrin arranged are especially striking. In May 1954, just before the defeat of the French at Dien Bien Phu, JDS sponsored a colloquium on Indochina.[40] Because Schiffrin wanted to demonstrate that a member of the Communist Party could speak at Yale, he invited Herbert Aptheker to talk in May 1956 about whether developing countries would choose democracy. Ironically all his efforts in building JDS led to an offer (which he turned down) to join Skull and Bones. As the perfect bookend to his career at Yale, he won a two-year fellowship to study at Clare College, Cambridge, an award funded by Paul Mellon. His career at Yale, like that of his classmate Calvin Trillin, revealed that an outsider could become an insider.[41]

The 1960 class book listed twelve members of JDS, but there were other classmates, including me, who were active in the group. The percentage of legacies and graduates of private schools was similar to the Yale norm, but the six Jews constituted a disproportionate number. All twelve were academic achievers, none joined a fraternity or earned a major "Y," and one was a member of an aboveground senior society (albeit Elihu). Several of them hailed from families that were at least left-liberal, not only Sam Bowles, Jonny Weiss, and Jeremy Nahum but also Dick Beals, who was one of the very few, if not the only, classmate whose father was a factory worker. A number

of the members had become involved in protests against segregation: Gary
Gelber began such a project in high school in Atlanta and continued at Yale;
Neil Herring joined the NAACP. Beat poetry and jazz shaped the outlook of
several members at least as much as politics. Again indicative of how many
of us crossed lines, the conservative Paul Blanshard joined JDS because of
friendship and curiosity.[42]

Jonny Weiss was one of the co-organizers of JDS during my junior and
senior years, when JDS remained active but not with the presence it had had
during Schiffrin's time. Weiss came to Yale from the Loomis School, and
the college assigned him Bill Moses, an African American, as his first-year
roommate, most likely because of the commitment of the Weiss family to
civil rights. At Yale Weiss had a strong academic record, was on the varsity
wrestling team, and, in addition to the JDS, participated in various organizations, including the Elizabethan Club. The other co-organizer was Eric Walther, who grew up in a non-religious and conservative Republican household,
headed by a father who published a trade journal for heating and plumbing
contractors. He prepared for Yale as a day student at Blair Academy and at
Yale rebelled against his father's politics, in part because of the influence of
Weiss, his roommate for their last three years. Like Weiss, Walther declared
himself a conscientious objector on philosophical grounds. As an alternative, he studied intentional communities and nonviolent resistance. He went
with classmates on a trip to Baltimore to protest segregation, joined Fair Play
for Cuba, read *Liberation* magazine, and, like me, had dinner with socialists
Norman Thomas and Michael Harrington. He served on the *Criterion* board,
played in the football and concert bands, and ran on the varsity cross-country
and track teams.[43]

Edmund Leites was another important JDS member. He grew up in Manhattan, the son of Nathan Leites, an émigré who wrote influential works on
movies and on Stalin. The senior Leites was a visiting professor at Yale when
his son applied for admission. After the divorce of Edmund's parents, his
mother married the émigré physicist Hyman Goldsmith, one of the founders
of the *Bulletin of Atomic Scientists*. Leites lived on Manhattan's Upper West
Side and graduated from the High School of Music and Art. Before coming to
Yale, the *Yale Daily News* reported in our first year, Edmund Leites had "some
years experiencing bohemian parties and intellectual discussions."[44]

Growing up in a world of émigrés from Weimar Germany and knowing
the New York writers Paul Goodman, Dwight Macdonald, and Harold Rosenberg, before college, he experienced a shock on arriving at Yale. It struck him
as an anachronism from another era. He had not realized, he later recalled,

that Protestants ran the nation and that Yale was a Protestant institution. Feeling terribly isolated as a cosmopolitan New York Jew, he completed his degree a year early, yet he paused long enough at Yale to bring some of Manhattan to New Haven.[45] Operating under the umbrella of highly personal and evanescent organizations, he hosted readings by Paul Goodman as well as by Beat poets Kenneth Patchen, Gregory Corso, and Allen Ginsberg. He scheduled Ginsberg's performance for a small seminar room; when almost three hundred showed up, many of them not the usual literary types who came to poetry readings, he moved the event to a large lecture hall. When he went to American studies professor Norman Holmes Pearson in search of money to support these readings, Pearson told him "You want the University to give you gin, Leites, but all the University wants to give you is milk"—and then provided the funds.[46]

Along with Weiss and Walther, Leites was a classmate who played key roles in SLID as it transformed into SDS. As SLID's education vice president in 1958, he reported in September—in a way that reflects the hesitation among students on the left in the late 1950s—that "there is almost universal awareness that" major issues such as big government and disarmament "give rise to a great deal of concern, and even apprehension when their implications are explored, but that they are extraordinarily complex, often interrelated and defy easy solution."[47] At the first convention of SDS, held in mid June 1960, the largest contingent came from the University of Michigan, but three Yalies were present: Weiss, Walther, and Jesse Lemisch, who after graduating in 1957 remained at Yale as a graduate student in history.[48] In September 1960, just after the transition from SLID into SDS was complete, two of its four national officers were classmates: Weiss as vice president and Walther as international vice president. That month's issue of SDS's publication *Venture* reprinted David Caplin's essay from *Criterion*.[49] Indeed, material in the SLID archives makes clear that in the late 1950s the chapter at Yale was the nation's most significant one.[50]

The fact that Leites, Walther, and Weiss were philosophy majors underscores how central the field was to the history of the left at Yale in the late 1950s.[51] In an effort to prevent analytic philosophy from triumphing, more than almost any department at Yale it opened itself up earlier to a greater diversity of people and approaches, committed to bringing to the university what Leites later called "strong, even idiosyncratic" views.[52] The central figures were Charles Hendel and Brand Blanshard, themselves influenced by John Dewey and who as chairs of the department from 1940 until 1961 played key roles in hiring other scholars affected by him. This included Richard

Bernstein, who helped develop and teach a course on Marxism, though its catalog description reassured potential critics that it was a "critical" treatment of its subject as "a description and a philosophy." Parodying Yale's reigning political ideology, the campus humor magazine remarked that students in the course had to "prepare a fifty thousand word term paper on the glories of capitalism, strike-breaking, starvation wages, imperialism, and the American Way of Life."[53]

If philosophy opened classmates to a wide range of possibilities, it also reinforced the contemporary emphasis on debate rather than action, even though Dewey and many of his followers had connected the two. In retrospect, Leites, Walther, and Weiss do not regard JDS as especially political, although their own political activity and the speakers they invited were on the left, including Dorothy Day, David Dellinger, Dwight Macdonald, and Mark Starr. This emphasis on outside speakers to inform and spark discussion, common across the Yale undergraduate political spectrum, underscores the difference between the 1950s, when education was a focus, and the Sixties, when education led to activism.[54]

Thus JDS did and did not point forward to 1960s radicalism. Beginning with Schiffrin's work and up to 1960, JDS paid no attention to issues concerning the environment, gender, or sexuality. It focused less on labor unions than an earlier generation did and less on civil rights than a later one. Yet I find much to admire in the ways the organization that Schiffrin started and my classmates continued bridged the two decades. They created chinks in the wall of 1950s consensus. Following Schiffrin's lead, his successors put forward a wide range of issues. JDS worked to break down barriers that divided people; sustained a commitment to critiquing powerful institutions including the military; were concerned with civil rights, poverty, and inequality; questioned whether universities were as open and democratic as they could be; and longed for a world that would ameliorate alienation. Members of my class built on Schiffrin's commitment to working through nonhierarchical organizations and his capacious definition of politics to educate a generation. In the process we helped break through the sleepiness of the 1950s by creating at Yale new venues for engaged, serious discussion of political issues. The silent generation had cleared its throat and was finding its voice.

Cultural Politics

In addition to political organizations and discussions, there were unmistakable but often elusive cultural influences that shaped many peers, both those identified with the left and those without known or explicit political commitments. There was some discussion of existentialism among incipient intellectuals, the religiously inclined, and collegiate rebels. One day in fall 1956, Leites, who had promoted the wearing of "I Like Ludwig" buttons featuring a picture of Beethoven, approached our classmate Tim Light in the library. Overhearing their conversation, another student who was sitting across the table stood up and leaned way over to Light and said, "We don't have to put up with those Existentialists, you know."[55]

More prominent than readers of existentialism were those who watched avant-garde movies and listened to folk music and jazz. In inventive and antic ways my classmate Ralph Hirshorn made Yalies aware of cinema's ability to shock, disorient, and please. He and a group of friends made a short film, "The End of Summer," which Grove Press distributed and the Screen Producers Guild honored with the Jesse L. Lasky Gold Medallion for the best film by a college student. In reviews in the *Yale Daily News* and in screenings sponsored by the Yale Film Society and the local art house, he taught us about European and art cinema classics like *Black Orpheus, The 400 Blows, Diabolique, The Bicycle Thief, Wild Strawberries,* and *On the Bowery.*[56] Jazz in all its varieties as an expression of alternative values commanded the passionate attention of a small cohort of my contemporaries; as entertainment, it appealed to a multitude. Similarly, folk music made its appearance on campus. Two classmates, John Burgis and Bill Arnold, organized the Indian Neck Festival, which brought performers such as Pete Seeger, the Weavers, Oscar Brand, and Odetta, who offered the genuine "song created by the people."[57]

News of Beat culture became increasingly prominent. In December 1958, Norman Mailer assessed the Beats in a talk titled "The White Negro," easily filling a large auditorium. Steve Lefkowitz, my Trumbull marble teammate and someone who alternated his dress between Ivy League and bohemian, wrote several reviews of Beat prose and poetry. He conveyed what the lives of Beats were like and found their poetry compelling: though it did not offer remedies to the problems it identified, he asserted, it provided humorous and ironic attacks on the superficiality and materialism of contemporary American life. Leslie Epstein, another Trumbull marble teammate, found the poetry of Gregory Corso "vital" but like others worried that Madison Avenue would kill the movement. R. W. B. Lewis, a specialist in American literature recently tenured at Yale, made clear that he admired New Criticism but recognized that it was now on the defensive; indeed he remarked that he found Beat poetry represented "the eruption of instinct, feeling, and spontaneity against a cultural situation that seems hard and dry." That Mailer and Ginsberg, among others, commanded so much interest from so many undergraduates suggests something was stirring among us.[58]

"A Series of Lessons in Political Systems"

The formation of my own political consciousness went hand in hand with political and cultural developments at Yale. Compared with my more conventional peers, I found Beat poetry compelling and at times dressed in a more bohemian, less Ivy style. In my senior year, my grandmother called my mother in horror when she heard I was wearing sandals while walking in front of the J. Press store on a warm spring day. Wearing sandals was one thing, however, and having a clear political vision on which I acted, another. Although my own ideological position was hardly consistent or fully developed, I had absorbed enough of my mother's democratic socialism to believe that the government ought to provide all citizens with the basics of food, clothing, and shelter. I recall fondly my participation in the world of *Criterion*, something centrally connected to my friendship with Newman, although I fear the raucous fun at its annual banquet is more vivid in my memory than any editorial discussions.

What I wrote at the time reveals more clearly what I was thinking. In a draft of my application for a Rhodes, I talked of how my trip to South Africa produced "a series of lessons in political systems. I was emotionally overcome by a sense of involvement in and understanding of a system of repulsive ugliness. . . . I was intellectually challenged to redefine America's and my own commitment to aspects of a liberal society." There and in other applications, I wrote of how important extracurricular activities had become. In my first two years at Yale I had not participated in many because of "the stress on commercial values, and the generally impersonal tone of their approaches." All that changed in my junior year. I joined the editorial board of *Criterion* "out of a sense of responsibility" to friends and Yale and then responded "favorably" to its "fluid organizational framework." As I now read over what I wrote, I am tempted to ascribe my vagueness to my naïveté about what such applications demanded and to my reluctance in this forum to be specific about my political commitments and ideas, out of the political caution instilled by McCarthyism. Indeed, Leites and I recently agreed that McCarthyism had cast an invisible pall over intellectual life at Yale, shaping whom the university hired and our sense of what we could discuss.[59]

My letters home during the summer of 1959 and to Helen somewhat later are clearer and more explicit. I stood against America's Cold War ideology, including claims about the glories of free enterprise, because I recognized, in good Galbraithian fashion, the importance of the federal government's role in the economy especially when it came to military contracts. Feeling I was operating against the grain of conventional politics, I opposed militarism and was fascinated by socialism. I understood how powerfully my experience growing up in America shaped my view of the poverty I encountered abroad. I pondered the meaning of racial prejudice, as I thought about both South African apartheid and American segregation.[60]

In one letter I told my parents that I did not hate Russia and "found communism (ideally) not at all attractive but quite interesting and significant in terms of an analysis of the modern world. Yet," I continued, "I by no means harbor any ugly sentiments concerning communists." What also bothered me was the impact of the Cold War on American thought, in which, I asserted, "Democracy and Capitalism are too united." My dissent from American anti-communism came out when I took exception to how Connecticut senator Thomas Dodd criticized President Eisenhower's invitation to Khrushchev to visit the United States. Though his position would "have popularity with Eastern Catholics and Western *ignorami*," I assumed he would not object to visits by "Franco the gangster of Guernica, and Verwoerd (P.M. of South Africa) the slaughterer of Sophiatown."[61]

My politics also came through clearly in my letters to Helen. In mid-February of 1960, just before we first met, I offered to pay her train fare to New Haven "since capitalists (my father) should be punished," a statement that gives some sense of how my gentle rebellion against my father played out politically. I also said that "back in my days of radicalism . . . I was quite active in several political organizations. Although I have somewhat cut the ties since," a statement I assume refers to some unarticulated disenchantment I was beginning to feel with JDS and Challenge. Then on February 29, 1960, the day after our first meeting, I ironically referred to myself as "a visionary radical (my sometimes garb)." I went on to say that I told one of my professors "that I would rather give aid to Fidel Castro than to Trujillo because the former has a beard." Following a discussion with a neighbor who was member of my local draft board, I remarked with elitist arrogance that "I cannot see myself able to subject myself to authoritarianism other than one based on intellectual superiority." On a summer 1960 trip across the country with David Caplin, the Clare fellow from Britain, and the Trumbull College resident fellow Charles Blitzer, heading for the Democratic convention in Los Angeles, I wrote of the three of us as "politically left, deracinated/dereligious Jews (to varying extents)."[62]

In the spring and summer of 1960, race relations and civil rights were very much on my mind. Writing to Helen in early June, soon after she had left Wellesley and once again confronted segregation in her hometown of Shreveport, I remarked that I was rethinking what I had felt the summer before about the comparison of apartheid in South Africa with race relations in the

United States. In response to a letter Helen had written about how painful it was for her to face segregation, I said that I was learning "the long and hard way" that segregation and Apartheid were not poles apart.[63]

The Left at Yale in the Late 1950s

So, what can we say of the undergraduate left at Yale in the late 1950s—of who we were, of the politics we envisioned, and of the public spheres we created? We were from white, affluent, and disproportionately Jewish backgrounds, although Protestant students also played important roles. Many of us came from liberal families, but a few if any of us had familial connections with the 1930s Old Left. Some were athletes, a few were active in Christian organizations, and none of us participated in a cappella groups, fraternities, or, with the exception of Elihu, aboveground senior societies. Although for many of us our politics were influenced by our backgrounds, at Yale friendships played a key role in shaping our political consciousness. Almost all of us achieved academically in the humanities and social sciences. Intensifying interest in race and in political protest, folk music and jazz played a transformative role in the lives of a handful of my classmates.[64] Yet most of us were better heralds of the political 1960s than of its countercultural strand. For example, I could uncover very little evidence that recreational drugs played any role in our lives in the 1950s, although one classmate alerted me to a small underworld of bikers and marijuana smokers.[65] An adversarial culture is visible in Leites's passing out essays by Goodman and in the role that Beat poetry played in his life, Gelber's, and my own. The Trumbull Marble Team and the *Trumbullian* provided antic, culturally infused protest as well. As Jesse Lemisch later remarked, "We did obscene pre-political things, ridiculing the 'shoe' culture of the day." Those of us who dissented from collegiate politics as usual were attempting to overcome our sense of isolation and alienation by creating public spaces that involved more adventuresome and adversarial political choices than those readily available. Dick Celeste, the author of the 1959 paper on Pan-Africanism, recently remarked that at Yale, feeling alienated from the mainstream of undergraduate life, he wanted to break through its apathetic veneer.[66] This was true for those of us, on both left and right, who were determined to create new kinds of public discussions.

CHAPTER EIGHT

It All Comes Together

If you hear soft noises of rebellion on the college campus, it is not likely to be the protest of freshmen confined to their quarters after a "panty raid." Nor is it the explosive revolt of political radicals or of idealistic reformers. The voices are not violent. They are only impatient. They seek escape, not from the social order, but merely from the protective, peaceful ivory tower.

FRED M. HECHINGER, "All Too Quiet on the Campus Front:
Some Students Seek a Challenge," *New York Times*, February 7, 1960

In our senior year, and especially in the first five months of 1960, political engagement on campus intensified. Challenge, a political forum created by a group of us on the left, held two major conferences that attracted widespread attention both locally and nationally. The spring conference, "The Challenge of Democracy," took place as many of us were confronting how problematic race relations were in America. Simultaneously, in response to lunch counter sit-ins in the South and the Sharpeville massacre in South Africa, a handful of my peers moved from discussion to action.

Challenge

"'The Silent Generation' has gotten its voice back. Not entirely, perhaps," wrote Benjamin Fine in March 1960. The former education editor of the *New York Times* pointed to activity on more than a dozen campuses, yet what commanded his greatest attention was Yale's Challenge.[1]

While *Criterion* brought undergraduates together through intense and private discussions in a little magazine, Challenge created a much broader public arena. It originated in our sophomore year when Sam Bowles (who, as discussed in chapter 3, would later teach in Nigeria) thought about ways to stir things up politically. It was then that he and a handful of classmates representing divergent politics launched the first Yale Model United Nations conference, an effort to stimulate formal debate on international issues that began nationally in the early 1950s and eventually spread throughout much of the world. To break through the boundaries that circumscribed participation in other political organizations, Yale's Model UN sponsored programs in a local high school that focused attention of international issues. In our junior year, Bowles and the conservative Dale Collinson, along with other Democrats and Republicans from the class of 1960, formed the Franklin Society, a current affairs discussion group.[2]

The weakness of other political organizations eased the way for Challenge to emerge. In February 1958, an editorial in the *Yale Daily News* announced that the university's student government organization was "long the repository of little ambition and little issues."[3] The Political Union was encumbered by parliamentary procedures and the maneuvering of campus political parties. On the right, the Society of King Charles the Martyr always met in private, and even the Calliopean Society sometimes had closed meetings. On the left, the George Orwell Forum had a committed but limited following, and after André Schiffrin graduated in 1957 the John Dewey Society did not provide the capacious programs offered under his direction. The origin of the Undergraduate Lecture Committee offered Challenge the precedent of relying on student leadership, but that some of its meetings were held at the elite fraternity Fence Club made clear the limitations of its reach and inventiveness.[4]

New Kinds of Organization Men

This context gave Challenge room to flourish, but the more immediate catalyst was Sam Bowles's seeing a billboard in spring 1959 that proclaimed, "Sleep Well. Your National Guard Is Awake." He told Dick Celeste and Ralph Bryant, which sparked their talking about how they could burst the bubble college students were living in. The three invited others to join them, and several carloads of us drove to Bowles's parents' home in Essex. There, listening to folk music and union songs, we planned events for the academic year 1959–60. As seed money we used the proceeds of a peace prize essay contest Celeste won at Yale, which brought in $1,000 (about $7,500 in 2014 dollars), promptly deposited in the General Industrial Bank headed by my father. A spirit of "happy anarchy," Celeste later recalled, characterized the running of what turned out to be a major enterprise. A group without officers, Challenge nonetheless needed a treasurer to manage the bank account—a role for which I was the obvious candidate. Bowles and Celeste also asked me to take on the task of finding lodging in the homes of New Haveners for visiting students—something that my parents' wide friendship networks and my own organizational skills made possible. Political activity before Challenge typically involved lectures by faculty and talks by visitors; Challenge required serious organizing by a small group of students.[5]

Many of the students involved in Challenge were legacies, Jews, public school graduates, and academic achievers—outsiders like me engaged in Yale life but in different ways from the conventional Yalie. In contrast to us were the insiders on Challenge's alumni committee. On that list were seven Yale graduates, including three who were fathers of classmates: Congressman Chester Bowles, Senator Prescott Bush, and Henry J. Heinz II, president of the corporation that carried his family's name. A sponsors committee of more than two dozen included prominent members of the Yale faculty and administration, along with leading figures from local and regional religious, political, civic, and business communities. We successfully sought financial help from foundations, including the New Haven Foundation, aided by the presence of both of my parents on its board. The budget for 1959–60 was $20,000 ($161,000 in 2014 dollars).[6]

Not surprisingly, Coffin helped considerably, lending moral and administrative support. Harry Rudin, Yale's leading African specialist, was the key faculty member involved. The most important Yale official was Reuben ("Ben") Holden IV, secretary of the Yale Corporation and chief of staff to President A. Whitney Griswold. Holden bridged old and new Yale from a secure position. A member of the class of 1940, as an undergraduate he had a notable career: Phi Beta Kappa, Skull and Bones, chair of the Class Council, and managing editor of the *Yale Daily News*. He was what Malcolm Gladwell has called a connector, someone who knew how to work the bureaucratic, public relations, alumni, and New Haven networks. He connected us with Frank Altschul, a loyal alumnus, wealthy investment banker, and civic leader who made good on his commitment to support student political engagement.[7]

The author of the Scholar of the House paper on Pan-Africanism, Celeste was no newcomer to social action. He grew up in Lakewood, a suburb west of Cleveland. When he was twelve, his parents converted from Roman Catholicism to Methodism and brought their children along. His political education began with his father's involvement in the local Democratic Party and continued with his own participation in the Methodist student movement. At Methodist summer camp, he worked with African American students. Then, at a gathering of young Methodist leaders in spring 1958 in New York, he encountered Eduardo Mondlane, an American-educated anthropologist who would serve as head of the Mozambique Liberation Front from 1962 until his assassination in 1969. Celeste's election to the presidency of the national Methodist youth movement in fall 1958 provided him with a sense of how to build audiences by mixing politics with politically inflected entertainment. A critical moment helped launch Challenge. In the spring of 1958 Celeste testified before Congress on behalf of the Methodist student movement in opposition to the military draft. After he spoke, Dorothy Stebbins Bowles, Sam's mother, came up to him and said he had to meet her son.[8]

The grounding of Sam Bowles in liberal Democratic Party politics was even deeper than Celeste's or mine. Although our fathers knew each other through their involvement in Connecticut politics, Bowles and I met during our first week at Yale while standing in line waiting to see our academic adviser. A member of the Yale Political Union in his freshman year, involved in the Model UN conference as a sophomore, a major leader in Challenge in our junior and senior years, and a member of John Dewey Society in his senior year, his leftward trajectory was clear.

Bryant I discussed as one of my classmates who, like Celeste, headed to Oxford on a Rhodes after graduation. On his mother's side, he descended from a prominent Philadelphia Quaker family. His paternal grandfather taught at Yale's School of Forestry for thirty-three years beginning in 1906, and his father had two degrees from Yale. Just as Bryant was beginning adolescence, the family moved from Ouray, Colorado, to Raleigh, North Carolina, so his father could continue his education in forestry. Bryant spent his last two high school years at Exeter, and during the summer before he arrived at Yale, the dean's office wrote to ask if he would accept an African American roommate. Imbued with Quaker values, he said yes and roomed with Greg Tignor during his freshman year. As an undergraduate Bryant was active in Dwight Hall and was elected to Phi Beta Kappa as a junior. Until his involvement in Challenge, his major political activity centered on issues of nuclear disarmament, which he approached as the head of Yale's National Student Council for a SANE Nuclear Policy. His antinuclear activity spurred two undergraduates to write letters to the editor of the *Yale Daily News* attacking him for being a resident of the island of "Eleanorroosevelt" who was unaware of the threat of atheistic communism. Bryant responded trenchantly and with humor. "By McCarthy's ghost," he wrote in March 1959, "someone ought to investigate those junior espionage agents in the George Orwell Forum" as well as "all students who sign petitions on" nuclear disarmament and segregation.[9]

For our class book, Bryant composed fictional letters that offered a witty, acerbic view of Yale men. He parodied back-slapping students who saw themselves as rebels but hid behind "the pious façade of fatuity and foppish self-satisfaction." He critiqued Yalies who had "a real fighting good time!" when they threw snowballs at policemen during the St. Patrick's Day Riot in 1959, as well as those who used what they learned in art history and English courses to impress dates. He poked fun at senior societies by inventing names for them like "Sighs and Groans." He decried those who celebrated free enterprise that was "free for those who are free to practice it." He criticized classmates who were seeking security in bomb shelters or by "marching off to Suburbia" where they would linger in "fashionable, posh" living rooms complete with coffee tables on which lay "pseudo-liberal magazines." Rather than pursue rigorous careers, they were heading "for a nice home, green lawn, sweet wife, and the commuting train." Finally, he scoffed at apathetic classmates who saw Challenge as representing "creeping awareism."[10]

Certain patterns emerge when we look at the paths to Challenge taken by these three. Two of them came to college with significant Yale legacies. Unlike Celeste's more modest social background, Bowles and Bryant hailed from elite families with storied pasts. Not outsiders by the usual yardsticks, they chose to cast themselves in opposition. Each of the three represents a major tradition in American liberalism: Celeste, Protestant student activism; Bowles, New England, upper-class left-liberal commitments; and Bryant, Quakerism. Academic achievement marked their undergraduate careers, and none of them pursued traditional avenues to campus fame, although Celeste earned a major "Y" in fencing. Bowles and Bryant turned down offers to join prestigious aboveground senior societies out of principle and so they could concentrate on Challenge. Celeste was a member of an underground society.

Celeste recently remarked that at Yale his politics were those of a "conventional liberal Democrat." Perhaps a true characterization of Bowles and Bryant also in the late 1950s, but qualifications are in order. All three had long-standing commitments to racial justice and peaceful resolution of international conflicts. Above all, what marks them as different from more conventional students, even liberal ones, was their determination to create public forums that would enable students to break through the common apathetic inattention to public issues.[11]

Challenge Innovatively Creates Public Space

On its stationery, brochures, and posters, an asterisk after "Challenge" led to the cautious statement that this was "A Student Program at Yale University to Confront with Realistic Concern and Responsible Action the Critical Issues of Today's World."[12] The organizers stayed clear of linking Challenge to specific policies and instead emphasized a combination of urgency, thoughtfulness, inclusiveness, and responsibility.[13] In December 1959 Challenge announced that its organizers were determined to awaken "students from the indifference and self-centered apathy produced by their sense of estrangement and isolation."[14] With America having become "a symbol to most of the world," it was time to focus on "whether we can give to that symbol the vitality and dynamism which will continue to make it meaningful."[15] Challenge sought to break down barriers between students and faculty, town and gown, speakers and students, and Yale and other colleges and universities.

The program both resembled and differed from teach-ins that developed in the mid-1960s to protest American involvement in the war in Vietnam. Both emphasized the special obligation that college students had to wrestle with urgent issues; offered large lectures, panel presentations, and small discussion groups; and relied on having what one observer remarked of Challenge as a "lack of formal organization or hierarchy." They differed because those involved in Challenge took many steps to avoid identifying with one ideology and offered only vague promises of turning talk into action. At least in public, breaking through student apathy seemed more important than commitment to a point of view or moving beyond listening.[16]

The focus in fall 1959 was "The Challenge of the Nuclear Age." Throughout the semester, events pointed forward to the three-day colloquium held in December. Early on, a debate between conservative William F. Buckley Jr. and democratic socialist Norman Thomas attracted an audience of two thousand, which suggested that a good number of students were ready to break through their apathy. Then came Jerome Frank's talk, "A Psychiatrist Looks at the Arms Race," followed by opposing perspectives on American foreign policy—James P. Warburg calling for universal disarmament supervised by world law versus Walter Berns warning that world government threatened the nation's democracy.[17] At the December colloquium, Senator Hubert Humphrey offered a program to regulate nuclear arms and urged students not to give up their "idealistic goals for an expedient and unguided 'realism.'" Carlos Romulo, former president of the United National General Assembly and at the time the Philippine ambassador to the United States, gave a talk titled "The Non-Nuclear Nations in a Bi-Polar World." Retired army general James Gavin, who believed that the emphasis on nuclear war was edging aside the importance of conventional warfare, asked "Is War Obsolete in the Nuclear Age?" And the geneticist James Crow, whose work revealed the effects of radiation on humans, spoke on "The Challenging Problems of Nuclear Energy." On Saturday night students listened to a performance by the folk music group the Weavers.[18]

Ayn Rand kicked off Challenge's second semester with a talk attacking socialism and defending libertarianism and atheism. Then came the extensive

March 1960 forum, "The Challenge of American Democracy." Senator Barry Goldwater, whose *Conscience of a Conservative* would appear later in the year, gave a talk titled "Toward a Freer Free Enterprise." The commitments of the other major speakers dovetailed more closely with those of the Challenge's principal leaders. The recently retired president of Sarah Lawrence College, Harold Taylor, who had spoken out against McCarthyism and for racial integration, gave the lecture "Crisis in Liberal Democracy." There were addresses by two prominent African Americans: Thurgood Marshall of the NAACP, "Segregation in the North," and the union leader A. Philip Randolph, "Minority Groups in Labor and Politics." In addition, Challenge sponsored the seminars "Racial Discrimination in the North," "The Bill of Rights in Crisis," "American Labor Movement," "The Responsibility of Mass Media and Education," and "United States Economy and Socialism." On Saturday evening we listened to a concert by Pete Seeger and Odetta. Afterward, a large group gathered to hear to Seeger and collect money to support those arrested at sit-ins in the South.[19]

In planning Challenge, Bowles, Bryant, and Celeste realized that if they invited women, principally from nearby women's colleges, they might make the participation of Yale men more likely.[20] Challenge also involved the leadership of a group of women in capacities outside the typical restricted ones. As far as I can reconstruct, several played key roles, including Bowles's sister Sally, a student government leader from Smith College. The most influential woman involved in Challenge was Coralie ("Corky") Marcus, a 1959 Barnard graduate who came to New Haven to attend Yale Law School. Soon after arriving, she met Bowles, who in turn introduced her to Bryant. Marcus and Bryant fell in love and stayed in town for the summer in 1959, when they planned the events of the coming academic year with Celeste.

Assessing the importance and impact of Challenge reveals the obstacles it faced and the promises it offered. At the time I said simply that Challenge had enabled me to confront "some contemporary political problems, such as foreign policy and economic orientation in a changing world."[21] By contrast, I know of at least one classmate whom Challenge impelled forward to a career in international relations. Chuck Schmitz told me recently that the program had "bombarded" him "with spirited goads by eminent people," who were trying to persuade Yalies "to get out there and do something for the country and the world." Steve Kass, who with others assumed leadership of Challenge for the year after our graduation, recently remarked that Challenge was "the beginning, I think, of Yale's political awakening." His insertion of "I think" should caution us against concluding that Challenge represented a decisive turn to the 1960s.[22]

An article in the *Wellesley College News* about the December 1959 program helps evaluate the program's impact. The organizers were "rebelling against the epithet" of the silent generation, Virginia Tansey reported, in their attempt to "counteract apathy" among American students who were seeking an elusive "security through resignation or indifference." She noted that thirteen hundred students came from elsewhere, including Antioch, Chatham, Harvard, Radcliffe, Smith, Sarah Lawrence, Douglass, Princeton, and West Point, while she claimed that only two hundred from Yale participated. Yalies who stayed away, she commented, did so because they believed the program was "socialistic" or "too idealistic."[23] As a classmate remarked in spring 1960, students may have "poured in from other colleges," but "many of us in a Hegelian fashion took up the antithesis to Challenge . . . apathy."[24]

Challenge was not without its critics. Some conservatives saw through the claims that it transcended political divisions. At the time of the fall colloquium, a satirical advertisement appeared in the *Yale Daily News* sponsored by the fictitious National Committee for Unconditional Surrender, whose supporters included Evangeline Goodfriend and Alfred R. Youngturk.[25] However, the main critique centered on the issue of apathy and its proposed solution, commitment. Throughout my years at Yale, discussions of whether we represented an apathetic silent generation had prevailed, and this was the language that supporters and critics used when evaluating Challenge.[26] Sympathetic observers congratulated the organizers and participants for having helped to dispel the characterization. In contrast, the sharpest criticism came from Richard B. Stewart, class of 1961. Try as he might, he wrote, as he spoofed the notion of challenge itself, he could not think of anything "to be challenged about: our bar bill and J. Press account were paid up, we had a tremendous date coming down this weekend, and we hadn't flunked an hour test in two weeks." "As much as the fear of being shallow and valueless" nagged his consciousness, committing his soul to the Challenge organizers "sounded too easy, like one of these cake mixes; pay a dollar, expose well, and you'll be perfectly baked to a crunchy liberalism."[27]

The Wellesley reporter Virginia Tansey had asserted, with only some exaggeration, that although some of its leaders were "outspoken socialists," others ranged "from the fringes of socialism to conservative republicanism."[28] The programs, with their inclusion of Walter Berns, Ayn Rand, and Barry Goldwater, make clear that to some extent Challenge's leaders placed a higher priority on countering political apathy than on simply promoting their own ideological agenda. Indeed, those involved in Challenge were diverse—from socialists to those who would soon go on to play a key role in the founding

of the conservative YAF. Even among Challenge's core group there was ideological diversity, although the principal organizers were internationalist in
outlook and to the left of America's vital center.[29]

Within limits, the programs emphasized diversity of opinion. The fall
program, however, featured no one with a conservative position—unless
you include Gavin because he wanted to shift the balance in military planning from nuclear to traditional warfare. The others emphasized policies
geared more to peace than defense or war, to dangers of nuclear destruction
than to embracing its possibilities. Without Henry Kissinger, whose *Nuclear
Weapons and Foreign Policy* came out in 1957, or Herman Kahn, whose *On
Thermonuclear War* appeared later in 1960, there was no one on the program
ready to defend America's nuclear policies. The March 1960 session was more
balanced, as it included a talk by Barry Goldwater. In contrast, the presence
of Marshall, Randolph, and Taylor placed civil rights in a central position.
Finally, musical performances underscored the importance of the connection
between folk music and left-of-center politics. When my classmates and I
sang songs recorded by the Kingston Trio or Harry Belafonte, we may have
been only vaguely aware of the political implications of the music. Nonetheless, featuring folk music at Challenge weekends was political statement
enough. Folk music, an alternative to soothing Hit Parade songs, conveyed a
kind of musical populism with ties to older left wing traditions. Pete Seeger,
Odetta, and the Weavers encouraged us to sing along, to transcend the barrier
between performer and audience. It is important to recognize, however, that
in the late 1950s folk music meant different things to different people, ranging
from those on the left who saw it as the expression of a genuine "folk" who
helped promote a political vision to others who experienced it as an extension
of apolitical a cappella singing.[30]

Challenge created new approaches to politics at Yale. It provided a big tent
that welcomed all, even as its program made clear its commitment to liberal
perspectives. In the days surrounding the fall and especially the spring col-
loquia, news of Challenge dominated the pages of the *Yale Daily News*. It
built significant audiences—for the March meeting those from seventy-five
colleges.[31] Our success placed campus conservative groups in a difficult position. They cooperated with Challenge, to the extent of sponsoring their own
meetings that featured speakers with whom they agreed. Yet they also tried
to compete with Challenge's liberal orientation to advance their own agenda.
Reports circulated that dozens if not scores of other colleges would launch
their own programs based on the Challenge model.[32]

From Talk to Action

"The promised programs for action were not handed out," the *Yale Daily News* reported after the December colloquium. Nor is there any evidence that the organizers of the March session proposed that attendees do anything with what they learned. However, in our last semester, Challenge, combined with events beyond New Haven, prompted some of us who were politically engaged to act on our beliefs. The lunch counter sit-ins in Greensboro and other cities in February and the massacre of South African blacks at Sharpeville on March 21 were what the sociologist Richard Flacks in 1970 called "triggering experiences," turning some of us from outsiders into rebels. "The Sharpeville massacre," writes the historian Ruth Feldstein, "marked a turning point in Americans' awareness of South African apartheid." If the *Yale Daily News* is an accurate barometer, the same can be said of the closely connected lunch counter sit-ins.[33]

There was evidence during senior year of the shift from discussion to action. "Strange as it may seem," wrote Monroe Price, "there are times when the Yale undergraduate, tired from raising his glass on high and unable to play another hand of bridge, decided to abandon the normal schedule to do 'some good' in the community of New Haven." Price was referring to the result of fall 1959 town-gown meetings. Hillel rabbi Richard Israel and school principal Isadore Wexler helped launch "semi-academic after-school clubs" that brought together eighteen undergraduates and students at an elementary school on Dixwell Avenue, located in an African American neighborhood not far from the Yale campus.[34]

Then on February 19, eight Yale students marched in front of the local Woolworth's, located a few blocks away, to protest discrimination at the corporation's stores in the South. They carried an American flag and invoked the power of the nation's Constitution as well as the spirit of Gandhi and Jesus. Among undergraduates, Sam Bowles and Peter Paul Bergman, who wrote the essay on socialism in *Criterion,* emerged as spokesmen. Bowles and JDS member Eric Walther were among the five arrested, but they were released when Mayor Richard C. Lee intervened. According to the *Yale Daily News,* this was a rare instance where Yale led and Harvard followed, although the Cambridge contingent, led by graduate student Michael Walzer, was several times larger than Yale's.[35]

Soon after the Challenge colloquium ended, Bowles and Bryant, along with GOF member A. J. Leddy, announced the formation of the Freedom Fund for Southern Students to raise money at Yale for scholarships and legal aid for those African American students recently expelled from Alabama State College. This effort, suggested by Al Lowenstein, drew support from Coffin and several prominent professors. On March 23 several hundred students from the School of Medicine and Divinity School marched to the New Haven Green to protest racial discrimination in New Haven and the South. Finally, in early May, on the sixth anniversary of the Supreme Court's *Brown v. Board of Education* decision, Bergman and Bowles led an effort to have students submit letters to their hometown newspapers calling on citizens to take action against racial discrimination in housing, hotels, restaurants, and employment.[36]

At the same time, and closely related to these activities, a Yale chapter of the NAACP was formed, an effort led by two members of the class of 1961: Barry Loncke, an African American, and Charles Keil, a white, two activists with distinctive backgrounds. Loncke attended the same junior high as I did, but between then and his entry into Yale at age fifteen he went to Hotchkiss, a far cry from the modest circumstances he had grown up in in New Haven. Finding Yale "unforgiving" and himself subject to racism in both subtle and not so subtle ways, he helped found the campus NAACP as a way of expressing his commitments publicly. In addition to Raleigh Davenport, Loncke was one of the few African American undergraduates of my era who spoke out publicly on race issues. After serving in the air force for five years after graduation, Loncke went to Cornell Law School, where in 1969 he played a key role in mediating the conflict between African American students and the university's administration to protect interracial cooperation.[37]

In 1991 Keil described himself as "an Aryan from Darien, Connecticut (no blacks or Jews allowed), who served time at Yale (a few of each allowed) and could afford to choose a deep identification with Afro-Americans values and aspirations." A third-generation Yale man, Keil grew up influenced by a mother who early on took up jazz as a drummer. Keil himself had begun his engagement with jazz at age thirteen, in Westport, Connecticut, where he learned from and played alongside African American musicians. In his junior year, he remembered, he tried "to blacken myself in thought, feeling, and action." At Yale he was an American studies major, learning everything he could about Africa and Africans in the diaspora from classes and from meetings with Malcolm X and jazz musicians, as well as novelists James Baldwin and Ralph Ellison. In the summer of 1960 he participated in Operation Crossroads Africa, a forerunner of the Peace Corps founded by the African American minister James H. Robinson. In spring 1961, he brought Malcolm X to speak at Yale.

After Yale, Keil's engagement with African America continued. Soon after graduation, he wrote essays for *Muhammad Speaks,* the official publication of the Nation of Islam. He went to the University of Chicago, where he earned a

PhD in anthropology. He turned his dissertation into the path-breaking book *Urban Blues* (1966), which he dedicated to the memory of Malcolm X, in gratitude for "our frequent discussions during my senior year in college" which "had a profound effect upon my understanding of the American malady." Lawrence Chisolm, who had taught the innovative American studies seminar in my senior year, recruited Keil to SUNY-Buffalo, where they built an American studies program notable for its anthropological focus and recruitment of African American students.[38]

Loncke and Keil focused their NAACP efforts on persuading more African American high school students to apply to Yale. In doing so they recognized what they were up against: the belief that Harvard's more liberal reputation would enable it to best its competitors, the widely held perception at Yale and elsewhere that there were very few African Americans who had the qualifications to gain admission to elite private universities, and the entrenched system of recruitment that relied on an alumni network of often narrowly focused Yale men. They cooperated with JDS, GOF, and Challenge in signing petitions, bringing speakers to campus, and picketing at Woolworth's. Yet they also knew that they had to be more inventive. Loncke was aware of the special efforts taken to place him on the path from a public junior high school to Hotchkiss and to Yale. Committed generally to erasing "discrimination on the basis of skin color from American life," he and Keil reached far back to students in the sixth grade. Working with the admissions office, they also enlisted Yale undergraduates to spend time during their spring vacations going into communities across the country and even in the West Indies and encourage African American students to apply, well before the admissions office embarked more systematically on such efforts.[39]

Opposition to South African apartheid was another focus of attention in the spring of 1960. I moderated a panel on apartheid and arranged for the publication of my cousin Ivor Schwartzman's letter to my mother. Leadership in the protests against apartheid came from familiar sources, not only Bowles, but also Murray Last, the Clare fellow from England who, as I mentioned earlier, refused to sleep in segregated accommodations when he was traveling in the South. The group Last formed at Yale, associated with a nationwide Emergency Relief Fund, was among the first at an American university to raise money for the legal defense of black Africans jailed in Sharpeville and to circulate a petition urging a boycott of goods from South Africa.[40]

The pushback against all these protests was considerable, revealing both how much they threatened life as usual at Yale and how little the opposition understood the dynamics of social movements, even fledgling ones. Editorials, letters, and commentators criticized protestors for threatening racial progress by weakening the power of white southern moderates and thereby making compromise less possible. They saw those picketing Woolworth's in New Haven or protesting apartheid as seeking to be martyrs while not achieving anything constructive; tilting against windmills as they paraded their emotionalism under the pretense of idealism; and insincere and immature students who were screaming instead of thinking and in the process insulting those not marching. Northern whites, critics asserted, were not really helping African Americans in the South.[41]

Responses to these criticisms came from several quarters. The libertarian Robert Schuchman joined with the head of Law School Democrats to protest the way an editorial in the *Yale Daily News* dismissed the efforts of those demonstrating at New Haven's Woolworth's. Protestors, they argued, were making it clear to African American students in the South that they were not alone. They did not impede efforts in the South, because extremists were sweeping aside white moderates regardless of what northerners did. John Maguire, a Divinity School student, asked, "Are world-weary, so wise editorials as yours commended as contributions to the concrete, tough-minded unpublicized action which your cynical little heart longs for?"[42]

An especially powerful response came from Loncke, Keil, and two others active in Yale's NAACP. They took on an editorial that criticized Yale's NAACP chapter for launching a "propaganda campaign." Education, not propaganda, was the NAACP's goal, they replied, attempting to help educate Yale undergraduates by putting them in more frequent contact with African American students. The NAACP leaders took issue with the implication of another editorial that stated it was best to avoid controversy on sensitive topics. They responded to the charge that the NAACP was un-American because it was pointing out the discriminatory nature of Yale's "sacred institutions" of fraternities and senior societies, in the process emphasizing the differences rather than the commonalities among Yalies. "Unfortunately," they insisted, "big differences between the black and white races do exist, differences in educational opportunities, voting rights, employment, housing, and lunch counter services provided in department stores."[43]

In early April, a columnist for the *Yale Daily News* looked back at the year's events and found plenty of evidence of campus protests that undermined the notion that ours was an apathetic generation.[44] Political engagement in my last semester was qualitatively different from what had gone before. Nowhere is this clearer than by looking at what the campus newspaper published on March 23, 1960, my twenty-second birthday. On that day the British historian Marcus Cunliffe gave a talk in which he declared that stories of the power elite and men in gray flannel suits were weakening the image of America abroad.

In contrast, the front page carried the reports of George Akerlof and Monroe Price from Montgomery, Alabama, and of protests by freshmen against Yale's requirement of compulsory work by bursary students. It also highlighted talks sponsored by the Freedom Fund for Southern Students and of students from graduate and professional schools marching to protest racial discrimination in the South and New Haven.[45]

Bill Arnold is the classmate whose life most fully represents how in spring 1960 all the strands of the story came together. He grew up in a cosmopolitan, internationalist household, headed by his father, a Yale graduate, who from 1935 to 1952 worked in the administrations of FDR and Truman before moving to the Ford Foundation. Bill experienced a constant stream of international visitors in his parents' home. He came to Yale from Deerfield, eager upon arrival in New Haven to break out of the traditional prep school mold. He built on the internationalism of his upbringing by majoring in Chinese area studies and singing in the Russian Chorus. He developed his commitment to progressive causes by traveling in the summer of 1957 to Africa, visiting in Johannesburg with Helen Suzman and staying for a week with Quentin White of the Institute of Race Relations. In spring 1960 he joined a sit-in and picketed at Woolworth's. Where Arnold made his distinctive contribution, however, was in bringing folk music to Yale. He more than anyone else injected politics into music. As a freshman he developed a folk music program on the college radio station. He went to New York to hear folk music and worked with the folk music manager Manny Greenhill to bring established and emerging singers to campus. He showcased Miriam Makeba, Judy Collins, Doc Watson, Oscar Brand, Joan Baez, and Bob Dylan. In our senior year, he organized the concert by Odetta and Pete Seeger for the March 1960 Challenge colloquium. For Arnold, everything was connected.[46]

Present Near the Creation

Protests at Yale did not come out of nowhere, and that somewhere preceded Challenge. Coffin and Bone, along with a handful of undergraduates, played especially crucial roles, as did events on campus, in the city, and throughout the nation. Nonetheless, 1960 marked an important awakening of interest in doing something about issues such as segregation in America and apartheid in South Africa.[47] Yale produced the norms against which we rebelled even as it provided, often unintentionally, the wherewithal for our critiques to develop. The political silence of the majority of Yale men, palpable if hard to see, was the sound of consensus that McCarthyism and elite culture helped produce. The speakers we brought from a wider world to campus—from Ayn

Rand to Raya Dunayevskaya—were co-conspirators in the effort of those of us on the right and left to insist that political commitment mattered. The alienation of many of us from mainstream collegiate culture generally and the ideal of a well-rounded Yale man specifically spurred us on to take adversarial stances.

To those who take the mid- to late sixties as the yardstick, the ventures of some of my contemporaries into political debate and action might seem mostly calm and often politically unformed. Few issues animated the entire campus, and when they did they were apolitical/pre-political (the St. Patrick's Day Riot or the hostile reception of Adlai Stevenson's candidacy) or mostly Cold War–infused (the anticommunism of the protest against the Soviet invasion of Hungary). In general, most of my classmates spent more time singing, making money, playing, socializing, and drinking than they did concerning themselves with political issues. With Challenge, JDS, and GOF, the left wisely broke from the confines of the Political Union and created significant public forums. In contrast, the individualism and privatism of conservatives militated against organizing to create robust public discussions. Indeed, the Party of the Right had an intense debate over whether it should join the broader conservative movement or let members go their own way.[48] As we were beginning our senior year, Rosa Parks, Martin Luther King Jr., and John Fitzgerald Kennedy (or for that matter Ayn Rand or William F. Buckley Jr.) had compelled few of us to act. Some of us were no longer members of the silent generation, but for most of us organizing a speaker series was more possible than organizing a sit-in or boycott. After we graduated most of the organizations we created waned or disappeared.[49]

However, taking a long view, we can see that the spring of 1960 marked an important turning point. We had a peer group culture, friendships, and a sense of being outsiders that helped create the space, both emotional and public, to begin to challenge 1950s complacency, the hold of the silent generation. To do so we had to do two things. First, we had to bypass the usual campus organizations and create innovative forums for public discussion of urgent and wide-ranging issues. Second, those on the right and the left had to cooperate in fostering political debate and engagement. We see abundant evidence of this: when Calliopean Society member John Haverly and I traveled together in summer 1959; when Lobdell and Posner were roommates; when conservatives participated in the activities of JDS and Challenge; when Charlie Newman made sure to solicit essays from conservatives; when Challenge sponsored talks by conservatives. Tactical considerations and capacious commitments dictated inclusiveness; to many of us a big tent was more important than a small room housing like-minded members of an ideological cadre.

When we entered college, the *Yale Daily News* featured well-worn stories of conflicts between labor and management and of the threat of communism at home and abroad.[50] In contrast, in the spring of 1960 stories of protests against racial segregation and discrimination in America and apartheid in South Africa filled its pages. Attention had shifted from the evils of labor unions to the evils of racial segregation; from the threat of communism in the USSR and United States to the danger of South African apartheid. Through our improvised organizations classmates on the left and the right had created public space in which we could challenge apathy and foster a more genuinely unsilent generation.

On campus in spring 1960 it was all coming together, for many of us. During February in my American studies seminar, I read of members of a respectable African American family forcefully defending themselves against whites trying to drive them out of their home in a racially integrated neighborhood. In late March I read news by Akerlof and Price of whites segregating and African Americans resisting. In April four classmates (three of whom I knew well) were completing their honors theses on the struggles for racial justice. Throughout the spring and early summer, in our letters Helen and I discussed our concerns about America's denial of opportunity to African Americans. Coffin persisted in his efforts to oppose racism in America and South Africa. Challenge's March program highlighted the limits of democracy in America. Events in Greensboro and Sharpeville moved some of us from talk to action. The Sixties had not arrived, but the 1950s were in retreat.

CHAPTER NINE

Postpartum Politics

In after years should trouble rise
To cloud the blue of sunny skies
How bright will seem through mem'ry's haze
Those happy golden bygone days
O let us strive that ever we
May let these words our watch cry be
Where e'er upon life's sea we sail:
"For God, for country, and for Yale!"

"Bright College Years," words by
H. S. DURAND, class of 1881

Under the June 5, 1960, headline "The Class of '60: No Heroes, No Causes, No Crusades," two Associated Press reporters talked about what they found when they visited Yale that eventful spring. They relied on every possible cliché about this generation of students at elite universities. Dressed "in their rich tweed jackets and plebian chino pants," they reported, my classmates were "concerned but not committed," "skeptical of panaceas," "more interested in abstract truth than concrete crusades." Since the typical student was "more concerned about the state of his psyche than the state of the nation," he was "vaguely cynical, an unromantic rebel—yet with an undefined sense of mission." So it was not surprising that Jim Ottaway, editor of the *Yale Daily News*, remarked that he was skeptical about Challenge, the political forums held in our senior year, because commitment was a "substitute for thoughtful discussion." Many classmates agreed. One asserted that it was "impossible to associate with" activists "who are convinced they are on God's side on every issue." As we faced the future, the reporters observed, we had the "luxury of choice," but knew we did not want to follow those who went before us into the rat race of organization men and status seekers. With conformity as "his great bogeyman," the average classmate nonetheless seemed to be a conformist. Having said all that, they nevertheless concluded, "Before the century runs out, we will hear from them."[1]

Tracking what happened with us politically after graduation illuminates not only the power of chance but also the dynamics of privilege and leadership in America. It helps us understand the continuities and discontinuities in the political trajectories of a generation. For most of us, the troubles that arose after June 1960 may have made our undergraduate years seem like "happy bygone golden days." More likely, what we were to experience in the public world after 1960 did indeed "cloud the blue of sunny skies."

After commencement, we witnessed and participated in dramatic and tumultuous events at home and abroad. Reading through reunion books of the class of 1960 made me realize how important the war in Vietnam was to my peers. U.S. intervention there was for many of us the event that most powerfully shaped our politics and our views of America's role in the world. The experiences of two classmates who flew hundreds of missions over Vietnam, along with the experiences of two others shaped by their marriages to Vietnamese women, reveal important dimensions of the war's impact. Radical antiwar protests and what some of my peers saw as threats to American patriotism turned them to the right, while the same events impelled many of us leftward.

Persistence and change mark the trajectories of prominent classmates on both the left and the right. The career of Sam Bowles, who was among the most politically active on the left and after graduation spent two years in Africa, reveals that, like many of his like-minded peers, he lived his postgraduate future in ways that both grew out of and diverged from his undergraduate past. In contrast, the conservatives in the class of 1960 were generally not as successful in turning their college political concerns into publicly visible, life-long commitments, something that the life of Jared Lobdell, while at Yale the most articulate religious conservative in the class, suggests. Moreover, there was little in the undergraduate political experiences of Lew Lehrman that would have predicted the future of our most influential conservative public intellectual. Interestingly, the classmates who achieved the greatest national prominence in politics after we graduated—Secretary of Defense Les Aspin, Director of the Central Intelligence Agency Porter Goss, Senator Jack Heinz, and Director of National Intelligence John Negroponte—evidenced little involvement in politics as undergraduates.

Anecdotal evidence, gathered mainly from reunion books and interviews with well over one hundred peers, offers a window into the political trajectories of a larger number of classmates. In the late 1950s, the ethos at Yale and in the nation, as well as the formal curriculum, may not have fostered political engagement; but over the longer term many of us became leaders, primed by our backgrounds and the college's informal curriculum.

Vietnam

Vietnam is more than five thousand miles from Africa, the site of our international hopes in 1960. For many of my classmates of all political persuasions, if Africa in 1960 prompted optimism, American intervention in Vietnam, which began in 1955 and escalated under Kennedy and Johnson, shattered dreams. In the long run, the war in Vietnam transformed how we viewed international relations more than independence movements in Africa. As undergraduates few of us knew anything about Vietnam and Southeast Asia. Only once in my four years did the *Yale Daily News* offer a substantive story, a 1956 piece on the trip to Vietnam by Professor James Fesler, a political scientist who had no scholarly expertise in the region. With its location among communist-dominated states, Fesler remarked, "Free Vietnam" under the leadership of Premier Ngo Dinh Diem was steadily making progress against both communist subversion and the legacy of French rule. In the late 1950s Yale had on its faculty one of the most knowledgeable scholars of Vietnam living in America, Professor Paul Mus. His *Viêt-Nam, sociologie d'une guerre* (1952), not available in English, made clear his opposition to French colonialism and his support for Vietnamese nationalism. Few if any of us took advantage of Mus's presence.[2]

Age, privilege, fatherhood, and enrollment in graduate and professional schools kept almost all of us out of military service in Southeast Asia. But two classmates stand out as exceptions. Mike Dickerson, mentioned in the preface, came to Yale from a family of modest circumstances and from a high school where, captain of his football team and president of the student body, he was the first graduate to go to an Ivy League college. As an academically underprepared small fish in a large pond at Yale, he experienced his first year as a "form of living hell." His participation in the navy ROTC program and in the singing group Augmented Seven helped him navigate what initially seemed forbidding territory. After graduation, he joined the Marine Corps and beginning in 1965 flew four-hundred missions and earned twenty-four Air Medals. His service, he wrote for our fiftieth reunion book, "provided life-defining experiences and purpose," whose importance he underscored by providing a picture of himself from 1969 surrounded by six squadron patches. An economics major at Yale, he became a Goldwater Republican in the early

1960s. After completing military service Dickerson had a career in investment management. His experience in Vietnam strengthened not only his sense of patriotism but also his belief that what justified his activity as an attack pilot was that, as he said to me, "Freedom is so unique and powerful in the history of man, that my life was worth risking if I could give one man one day of freedom."[3]

For our fiftieth reunion Rob Hanke sent in a picture of himself on a Marine Corps recruiting poster widely circulated during the Vietnam War. Born in Britain but adopted by a wealthy American family during World War II, he more fully fit the mold of the Yale man than Dickerson. Coming to Yale from Andover, he joined DKE, was on three varsity teams, and earned a major "Y" in skiing. Heroism, physical prowess, achievement, and bravery marked his service to the nation. Graduating first in his class at naval flight school, during the Cuban missile crisis he flew 50 missions, then 126 in Vietnam, where he was shot down, seriously injured, and dramatically rescued. Later on, Hanke became a jack-of-all-trades: an organizer for Republican candidates and office holders, a Wall Street investment analyst and counselor, an executive vice president of the Asia Society, as well as a philanthropist, actor, director, and producer. Like Dickerson, Hanke felt that people in the military did their jobs successfully, while politicians failed to support them.[4]

Other classmates experienced the war in Vietnam from a distance but in ways that nonetheless transformed them. At least three who became college professors—Matt Gardner, Dick Minear, and Pete Karsten—describe how opposition to the war shaped their scholarship and teaching. For our twenty-fifth reunion, Gardner, whom the navy sent to Vietnam, wrote that the "tragic episode" in Vietnam led him to a career teaching international relations with a focus on Asia. Minear, a Japanese historian, related that the war in Vietnam challenged the "objectivity" that our education had instilled in him. In spring 1969 he developed a course on Vietnam, remarking soon after that the war turned his "scholarship in a political direction" at odds with the lack of activism of our college years and the "timidity" of his graduate education.[5] Karsten served in the military after graduation and then earned his PhD at University of Wisconsin–Madison, where he studied with the radical historian William Appleman Williams. As early as 1965 Karsten opposed the war in Vietnam and with fellow graduate students went into local high schools to give anti-war talks. In response to the My Lai Massacre and to the debate on American campuses about ROTC, in 1971 he published the results of a survey, in which he showed that since students at service academies were "consistently more aggressive and absolutistic" than their ROTC peers, eliminating ROTC programs would keep out of the military citizen-officers who were more likely to refuse "to obey immoral orders." In the ensuing decades he played a major role in developing the "new" military history, which involved shifting the focus from battles, leaders, and strategies to the experiences of ordinary soldiers and more generally the relationships between the military and society.[6]

A Classmate Marries a Vietnamese Woman:
Part I, Tom Miller and Tran Tuong Nhu

Tom Miller's life provides a compelling reminder of the connection between Africa and Vietnam, as well as how the war in Vietnam propelled some of us to the left. I introduced him in chapter 4 as a classmate who went to Africa in the early 1960s, having juggled embrace of and challenges to privilege before and during his years at Yale. It was the war in Vietnam and his marriage to a Vietnamese woman, however, that helped give him an unexpected but transformative sense of direction. In an earlier draft of this book, I had confined references to Vietnam to a note. But in 2013, when Helen and I had dinner with Tom and his wife Nhu in Berkeley, Nhu, having listened to me talk of the importance of Africa to classmates, wisely urged me to write about the impact of Vietnam.

"Vietnam," Tom Miller wrote in 1995, "was the crucible that formed the rest of my life." The key moment came in 1966 when he read articles by Martha Gellhorn on how American forces were killing and maiming Vietnamese citizens. Senior partners at the Manhattan law firm where he was working connected him with Dr. Arthur Barsky, a plastic surgeon who had helped heal the wounds of children injured by the atomic bombs Americans dropped on Hiroshima and Nagasaki. After traveling to Vietnam for the first time in 1966, Miller teamed with Barsky to found the Children's Medical Relief International and then the Center for Plastic and Reconstructive Surgery, which treated thousands of children, including Kim Phuoc, the subject of the iconic photograph as she fled, naked and terrified, from the explosion of a napalm bomb.[7]

Over the years, Miller sustained his interest in Vietnam, something intensified by his marriage in 1973 to Tran Tuong Nhu, who had grown up in Vietnam and graduated from the University of California at Berkeley—and whom Tom met through his work in her homeland. From the 1970s on they worked together for the release of political prisoners, the lifting of the American embargo of Vietnam, the return to Vietnam of children falsely classified as orphans, the establishment of the first American legal office in Vietnam, and the production of an award-winning documentary *Daughter from Danang*. When classmates write for reunions, relatively rarely do they speak forcefully of their politics. Miller is a notable exception, especially on the left. On the occasion of our twenty-fifth reunion he pointed to "the bumper sticker of my mind: 'I'd rather be fighting imperialism'" and then continued by emphasizing how the presidency of Ronald Reagan revealed the "economic imbalance in the Third World and elsewhere—shocking extremes of wealth and poverty . . . My current goal is to continue to participate in this struggle as effectively as possible—with humor and humanity."[8]

A Classmate Marries a Vietnamese Woman: Part II, David Elliott and Duong Van Mai

In the summer of 1973, after the January cease-fire in Vietnam, the Millers traveled in Vietnam with David and Duong Van Mai Elliott. Martha Gellhorn, whose articles had compelled Tom Miller's attention in 1966, in that year also reported on Mai Elliott, "a beautiful young Vietnamese woman, educated in Washington, DC, and married to an American, [who] acted generously as my hostess and interpreter." The Elliotts together provide compelling ways of understanding Vietnam, especially how the Vietnamese experienced the war, as opposed to how it looked from the perspective of Americans in military jets flying above, in Washington, and at the Pentagon.[9] The experiences of the Elliotts in Vietnam paralleled what classmates had earlier found in Africa, the drama of decolonialization that countered the emphasis on Moscow, in the case of Africa, and in here, Beijing.

David Elliott has written extensively in Vietnam, but his magnum opus is *The Vietnamese War: Revolution and Social Change in the Mekong Delta, 1930–1975* (2003). Jonathan Mirsky in the *New York Review of Books* called it "the most comprehensive and enlightening book on that war" since the publication of *The Pentagon Papers* in 1971.[10] David's father was William Yandell Elliott, a Harvard political scientist, prominent presidential adviser from the 1930s until the 1970s, and influential Cold Warrior. His father, David writes movingly, "made a genuine effort to understand why his son, on the other side of the Vietnam generational divide, had moved away from Cold War orthodoxy and how the Vietnam experience led to this."[11]

In many ways David Elliott carried the markings of the classic Yale man. After coming to Yale from Deerfield, he was blasé about his studies, focusing instead on social life and extracurricular activities, including the Whiffenpoofs. After Yale, he went to University of Virginia to earn a PhD with a focus on Latin American politics. Leaving graduate school, he volunteered for the army in 1963. Sent to the Defense Language Institute in Monterey, California, he was assigned to learn Vietnamese. He was in Vietnam from 1963 to

1967, initially with the army and then with the Rand Corporation, where he managed a government-commissioned study of insurgency in Dinh Tuong, a rice-producing area in the Mekong Delta, southwest of Saigon. After Elliott left Vietnam in late 1967, he spent time in Taiwan to learn Chinese and then switched to Cornell for his doctoral study. He returned to Vietnam in 1971 for several months to work on his dissertation. Initially setting out to influence the American war effort by advocating better-informed counterinsurgency strategies, in which he failed, he shifted to scholarly issues surrounding what Mai Elliott, in her commanding book on the history of RAND's role in Vietnam, called "the larger social and political context of the Viet Cong movement itself."[12]

David Elliott initially supported American involvement in Vietnam, but his experiences eventually undermined this position. He emphasized the deep roots of the nationalist insurgency in which communists played roles that varied considerably over time. He explored the waxing and waning of the intensely local nature of the struggles of Vietnamese revolutionaries and insurgents (terms he preferred to the derogatory Viet Cong), thus contradicting those who insisted on seeing events from the perspective of Moscow, Beijing, or Washington. He revealed that despite differences between southern and northern insurgencies, the revolutionaries in the south wanted independence and national unification.

Interviewing the insurgents, he remarked, was a transformative experience. Struck by their "political sophistication and analytic skills" he "agonized over the hard hand dealt them by fate and force of circumstances and admired what for many had been genuine idealism and real accomplishment, whether or not one agreed with the ends toward which it was directed." Elliott made clear how his findings profoundly contradicted the goals not only of American foreign policy but also of Ho Chi Minh's efforts to extend his revolution from north to south. Among the unintended consequences of American intervention "was the emergence of a rural middle class" in the Mekong Delta that after 1975 "proved stubbornly resistant to collectivization." It "brought socialist transformation in South Vietnam to a halt" and along with other forces led to the adoption in a unified Vietnam of "a sweeping program of market reforms." This was hardly a victory for American capitalism since the shift to a market-oriented economy did not come as the result of American policies and was "too late to salvage American political and strategic interests in Vietnam." "The final irony," he remarked, "is that it was the United States, perhaps the war itself, that produced the greatest revolution in Vietnam, building on a process started by the revolutionaries but taking it in a different direction" with the "the painful but impersonal dislocations of war" ending up as "a stronger revolutionary force than the rational but harshly authoritarian social engineering of the communist revolutionaries."[13]

The compelling stories in Mai Elliott's *The Sacred Willow: Four Generations in the Life of a Vietnamese Family* (1999) confirm her husband's analysis while adding emotional intensity and historical depth.[14] She focuses on four generations of her family that, like a willow tree, bent but did not break. It begins with her great-grandfather's becoming a mandarin and ends with the scattering of her and her siblings across the globe after the end of the American war in Vietnam. Her narrative reveals the traumatic events that generations of her family experienced as they had to negotiate between the French, Japanese, and American invaders, on the one hand, and competing versions of nationalism sponsored by natives and foreign interlopers on the other. Some family members ambivalently cast their lot with the French or the Americans, while others, strategically or passionately, with the communists. She illuminates the changing tides of Vietnamese history through dramatic stories of shifts in her family's social and geographical situation. "Until 1954," with her family residing in a commodious villa and taken care of by many servants, "our cocoon-like existence enveloped me and my siblings in a false sense of security." Soon she was living with her parents and six siblings in a two-room house, her father now an ordinary Saigon bureaucrat in a divided Vietnam. What dominates the book's second half are narratives of diasporic redemption and reconciliation of family and nation. Writing *The Sacred Willow* enabled Mai Elliott to fulfill a long-held dream to convey the richness of her family's history.[15]

Mai also recounts how she came to the United States and met David. As a teen she began to dream of America as an affluent nation, enlivened by Hollywood movies and pop music and with large, convenience-filled homes. In 1960 at age nineteen she left Vietnam to attend Georgetown University on a scholarship. Popular culture continued to serve as a bridge between herself, "a martian in the middle of earthlings," and the American girls who lived in her dorm. She met David in late 1961 at a party in Washington to which Vietnamese colleagues from the University of Virginia had invited him, suggesting he bring along his guitar and sing American folk songs. "His obvious interest and attention flattered me," she wrote of their meeting, "coming as I did from a culture that admired men of good breeding and learning." She quickly learned how true this was, as she realized that he was "as WASP as they came" and his father was "the model scholar-statesman" that men in her family aspired to be. They married in Saigon in 1964, soon after she had earned her undergraduate degree, and Mai served as an interviewer, transcriber, and translator on

David's project before developing her own career, first in the corporate world in Los Angeles and then as a writer.[16]

As happened with David Elliott, working on the interviews helped change her mind about events in Vietnam. Like many other South Vietnamese with similar backgrounds, until 1964 she was an anticommunist hardliner. The material she translated and pored over revealed to her that the communists had not only organization, discipline, and leadership but more important, a cause and ideology that compelled them. By 1968 she was participating in national antiwar protests in Washington, finally breaking free, like her husband, of the grip of her family's heritage as she pondered what was good for her homeland in a larger sense and over the longer term.[17]

On the Left from 1960 to the Present

Tom Miller and David Elliott were transformed into opponents of the war in Vietnam. For Sam Bowles and many of us on the left as undergraduates, the years after 1960 provide evidence of a move further leftward. By the late 1960s Bowles emerged as one of the nation's most important radical economists. This involved a shift away from his father's left liberalism within the establishment.

Bowles and I entered Harvard graduate school in the early 1960s, and from then until around 1967, Helen and I sustained close friendships with him and his wife Nancy. Gradually, we began to drift apart, both personally and politically. By 1965 Bowles was emerging at Harvard as an activist while I focused more on my teaching, scholarly work, and marriage; though still on the left, I remained more a spectator than an activist. When in 1965 Harvard hired Bowles as an assistant professor, he refused to sign a loyalty oath. He won an important victory when the Supreme Judicial Court of Massachusetts declared the oath unconstitutional. Speaking to a reporter for the *Harvard Alumni Magazine* in 1967, he said he found "dissent very disruptive of his academic work." Then he concluded by remarking that "in view of the way things turned out, I'm going to shut up and be happy." Shut up he did not. Rather, he played a leading role in forming the Union for Radical Political Economics in 1968. National and international events, along with his participation in a radical curriculum in the Department of Social Relations and his resistance to the political economy offered by most senior economists at Harvard, intensified his radicalization.

Reflecting on his work in education in Nigeria, Bowles regretted that he had focused on efficiency and neglected equity. By the late 1960s, he made a number of significant shifts: from Africa to America; from efficiency to equity; from neoclassical to radical, Marxist economics; from highly technical, specialized economics to accessible writing in political economy; and from carefully hedged left liberalism to robust radicalism.[18]

The eventual result was the 1976 groundbreaking *Schooling in Capitalist America: Educational Reform and the Contradictions of Economic Life* written with Herb Gintis. They asserted that liberal efforts to reform schools had failed because they did not undermine "the basic structure of property and power in economic life." Exploring the way the capitalist system shaped the internal organization of schools, they examined how schools socialized young people to the rhythms and demands of modern production, replicating the pressures and conditions of the workplace. They demonstrated how the economic benefits of privilege blocked equality of opportunity. Relying on "an egalitarian and humanistic socialism," they called for "a revolutionary transformation of social life" achieved through "a prolonged struggle based on hope and a total vision of a qualitatively new society." As they wrote in the book's final paragraph, "the moribund capitalist order" needed an undertaker not a doctor. To bring that about, they called for "a mass based party able to aid in the daily struggles of working people . . . committed to a revolutionary transformation of the U.S. economy."[19]

Bowles's turn to radicalism reshaped his career. When Harvard did not grant him tenure in the early 1970s, he denounced his department for purging radicals. The decision, he asserted, "reflects a commitment shared by all but a small minority of senior faculty to defend the structure of power and privilege, both within the Economics Department and in the larger capitalist society." In contrast, it was his task "to develop an economic analysis which can contribute to the elimination of the structure of power which characterizes the social, political and economic institutions of the capitalist system." Bowles joined the economics department at the University of Massachusetts Amherst, one that included several radical economists. From the late 1960s on, he published books that made him one of the most widely read radical economists in the nation, even as over time he moved away from a reductionist Marxism. His latest book, also written with Gintis, is *A Cooperative Species: Human Reciprocity and Its Evolution,* in which they show that, despite the claims of most economists and evolutionary biologists, altruism has shaped human behavior.[20]

Most of my peers who were visibly on the left as undergraduates ended up as professors, public interest lawyers, and in the helping professions, many of them in ways that fulfilled political commitments evident at Yale and that Yale often played some role in nurturing. This is true of those who with Bowles led Challenge. Ralph Bryant married Corky Marcus in summer 1961 and over the ensuing decades both had distinguished careers that focused, respectively, on the economics of monetary policy and international relationships and development of third world nations. Dick Celeste, one of the trio who led Challenge, developed a career in public service, fighting for progressive causes as a member of the House of Representatives, lieutenant governor and governor of Ohio, director of the Peace Corps, ambassador to India, and president of Colorado College. The trajectory of others involved in the John Dewey Society offers similar if less spectacular stories, with most of those who were liberals in the late 1950s remaining on the left. For more than thirty-five years Jonny Weiss, the head of the JDS in our senior year, directed Legal Services for the Elderly, a small nonprofit advocacy group in Manhattan. The two surviving members of the George Orwell Forum had careers fully consistent with the commitments they developed at Yale. Neil Herring spent most of his career as a lawyer in California fighting for justice for workers and in our fortieth reunion book remarked "Down with imperialism, racism, and patriarchy." Kirke Wilson dedicated himself to improving the lives of California's rural poor, working people, and immigrants.[21]

Most of those who wrote left-of-center essays for *Criterion* followed paths consistent with their undergraduate positions. Sherwin Goldman, who authored the defense of liberalism, is a major cultural impresario who won a Tony award in 1977 as the producer of the Houston Grand Opera's "Porgy and Bess."[22] Peter Paul Bergman, author of the defense of socialism, became a major figure in the counterculture when he developed the Firesign Theater, a project that underscores the intertwined histories of left politics and the counterculture in the 1960s. David Caplin, the British socialist who wrote "Perspective from Abroad," returned home to a career as a physicist at Imperial College London, focusing his political efforts on anti–nuclear arms issues. The story of Charlie Newman, editor of *Criterion* and member of GOF, is more complicated. By the mid-1960s he had developed a spectacular career as an editor and novelist.[23] He was someone whose passion and intellectual power were clearer than his political commitments, which with hindsight seem those of an anarchist. By the time he died 2006, he had grown bitterly angry about what he saw as the impact of multiculturalism on academic standards. In contrast, his Vassar girlfriend in the late 1950s, Carol Brightman, went on to a career as an antiwar activist and editor, as well as an award-winning writer whose work focused on American radicalism, women, and popular music.[24] Sally Bowles, Sam's sister, another woman involved in Challenge, ranged from working on formation of the Peace Corps in the 1960s to the anti-apartheid struggles in the 1980s.

On the Right from 1960 to the Present

The story of what happened in the postgraduate lives of conservatives is complicated. Lew Lehrman, the most prominent conservative member of the class of 1960, was a college man and hardly a political activist at Yale. More generally, in contrast to their counterparts on the left, many of the conservatives in the class apparently did not emerge as significant, visible, or leading forces. Admittedly, the fact that the sample is small leaves unresolved the question of what these patterns signify.

The two conservatives who contributed to *Criterion* are a case in point. Early death ended the career of Robert Schuchman, who had written a libertarian essay for *Criterion* and then went on to serve as the first head of Young Americans for Freedom.[25] After Yale, Jared Lobdell, who in *Criterion* offered a religious conservatism, earned his PhD and MBA and went on to teach at more than a dozen colleges and universities and to work at the American Enterprise Institute. From 1961 to 1969, he wrote witty, learned, and philosophical articles for a conservative magazine at University of Wisconsin–Madison. Here he remained true to his early commitments: to sustain a role for tradition and religion in public life and in opposition to the excesses of democracy and late 1960s radicalism. Yet he was skeptical of American involvement in Vietnam; critical of conservatives who did not support civil rights in the movement's more moderate phase; and concerned about what he saw as the tendency of conservatives to become more bureaucratic.[26] Between 1969 and 1972 he wrote for the *National Review,* attacking "the incessant 'gimme' of the welfare state" and insisting that late 1960s American radicalism was "the direct outgrowth of the liberalism of the Roosevelt-Truman era." He minimized the differences between traditionalist and libertarian conservatives, with both groups providing "our best defense against the ravages of liberalism, against the ill fare of the welfare state, against the anomie which by barrio and barricade is taking America into itself." And making clear the continuity with his position at Yale, in 1969 Lobdell celebrated King Charles the Martyr for saving the monarchy and "the liberties of his people."[27]

From the mid-1970s on, Lobdell wrote books on C. S. Lewis and J. R. R. Tolkien, whose visions had undergirded his undergraduate worldview.[28] By and large his work on these writers existed on a separate track from the political conservatism he expressed in what he published elsewhere. Nonetheless, from his Yale years on, Lobdell remained what he later called "a traditionalist libertarian" or "Christian conservative anarchist," but increasingly moved to the "sidelines watching" local and national politics.[29]

Most of those who were active as conservatives at Yale remained on the right for the rest of their lives. They were more likely to enter the corporate world than their peers on the left, and when they practiced law it was corporate, not public interest; still, there were plenty of doctors and some professors in both groups. Some of my conservative contemporaries at Yale played key roles on the state and national level in the early history of the conservative YAF. A Taft Republican in high school, Dave Stuhr, a member of the Calliopean Society, has sustained an involvement with the conservative Philadelphia Society. For more than two decades beginning in the early 1970s, Jim Hinish, head of the Party of the Right in 1959, worked in the federal government for conservative Republicans.[30] The most influential conservative of the class of 1959 was Richard Posner. Having offered a Marxist critique as a Yale undergraduate, his politics soon after shifted from left to right

Lew Lehrman became the most influential conservative from our class. He grew up in an upper-middle-class assimilated Jewish household near Harrisburg, Pennsylvania. He arrived at Yale from the Hill School and as an undergraduate had a career that combined academic achievement, membership in the fraternity Fence Club and the senior society Wolf's Head, and service as the undergraduate director of the Yale Summer Camp for Underprivileged Children. When Malcolm X came to speak, Lehrman stood up to ask a question, and afterwards, he went to the front of the auditorium to continue the conversation. Initially bodyguards stopped him, but Malcolm X told them to let him come forward. What Lehrman said to Malcolm was that emancipation and not slavery was the great story of African American history.[31]

After graduation, Lehrman was headed toward a career as a professor of history. He earned his masters degree at Harvard, where in 1962–63 he and I shared an apartment with two other history graduate students. I remember him with considerable admiration and affection: not only as a loyal friend but also as a compelling person who possessed a fierce and brilliant intelligence. In spring of 1963, he left for Princeton to study with Martin Duberman, having written to him as "a most respected and revered teacher and Mentor, friend and sometime patron, who, moreover, shall not perish from the earth." Lehrman and I corresponded for a while into the 1970s and then went our separate ways, only to reconnect as I worked on this book.[32]

Lehrman left Harvard thinking he could juggle graduate school and the family business, but before long, after a stint in the army, he went on to help transform his family's firm into Rite Aid Corporation, which he headed from 1968 until 1977. In these years it grew from 69 to 648 stores. In the meantime he had married Louise Stillman, whose father was an executive at Time, Inc., and whose ancestors included members of the Stanford and Stillman families, both having made fortunes in railroads and the latter with the National City Bank of New York as well.

When he left Harvard in the spring of 1963, Lehrman told me that he planned to make enough money so he could devote himself to history and public affairs. Lots of people have such dreams, but few fulfill them so abundantly. His rise to political prominence began in 1978 when he chaired New York state's Republican Party platform committee and challenged the dominance of Nelson Rockefeller and liberal Republicanism. Appealing to the kind of family-oriented, often Catholic men he hired to manage Rite Aid stores, Lehrman connected social conservatism with free market capitalism. Two years later he secured the nomination for governor of New York on the Republican and Conservative Party tickets and then ran against Mario Cuomo. Relying on what an astute observer called "a mixture of personal magnetism and ideological purity," he overcame great odds and came very close to capturing the prize. In 1985 Lehrman, raised as a Jew and married to an Episcopalian, converted to Catholicism. Having encountered early church writings at Yale, he sought, in the writer Samuel Freedman's words, "in religion a truth unavailable in the secular world."[33]

Since the mid-1970s, Lehrman has devoted himself to investment banking—and to history and conservative causes. At various times, he has been a trustee of prominent conservative and cultural organizations. He created a series of institutions that support the study and teaching of American history at Yale and nationally, most notably the immensely influential Gilder Lehrman Institute of American History. Consistent with his values, he has served on the board of the NAACP Legal Defense Fund.

As a writer and activist, his views in many ways resembled those of most conservatives, advocating as he did dismantling communist governments in order to expand freedom, defending free market capitalism, and opposing abortion.[34] His most distinctive contributions came with his advocacy of the gold standard and the grounding of his politics in the writings of Abraham Lincoln. What unites Lehrman's commitment to Catholicism, the gold standard, and Lincoln is a belief in absolute, enduring values. Consistent with what he said to Malcolm X when we were at Yale, he honors the study of slavery *and* emancipation, Abraham Lincoln *and* Frederick Douglass.[35]

When I recently asked Lehrman about his conservatism, he responded that the advocacy of the gold standard was "not only an economic issue; it is a metaphor for the history of the collapse of all objective cultural standards during the past century in the so-called advanced, developed countries."[36] He first developed an interest in the restoration of the gold standard while he was an undergraduate, although not until much later did it become such a prominent issue for him.[37] He has argued that if historic adherence to the gold standard produced economic growth and stable prices, its abandonment has had disastrous economic results. Its reinstatement would end cycles of inflation and deflation, stop the Federal Reserve's power to print paper money endlessly, foster savings instead of speculation, reduce inequality, terminate the nation's path to "*soft indulgence,*" stabilize currencies, provide an alternative to Keynesian economics, end the ability of the nation to incur debt and deficits, restore the nation's competitiveness, foster production and savings instead of consumption, reduce speculation, and end politically driven federal intervention into the economy.[38]

As I wrote the initial draft of this section, I puzzled over why for more than half a century Lehrman has advocated restoration of the gold standard despite what I see as an uphill and, I assume, losing battle. Then when I was preparing to write about his *Lincoln at Peoria: The Turning Point: Getting Right with the Declaration of Independence* (2008), I encountered what he said of the Great Emancipator's antislavery stance: Lincoln was "relentless in moving public sentiment toward his position." Although most observers have assumed that those advocating single, moral issues "cannot prevail in presidential contests, Lincoln thought otherwise."[39]

Where Does Political Prominence Come From?

Four members of the class of 1960 became major political figures after 1960, and in most cases their formal education and undergraduate political involvement offered few hints as to how they would later emerge.[40] For Porter Goss, family history combined with his Yale years in shaping his career. He grew up in Waterbury, Connecticut, where beginning in the 1860s members of his family had helped run the Scovill Manufacturing Company. As the historian Ferdinando Fasce had written in his award-winning history of Scovill, during World War I under the leadership of members of the Goss family the corporation developed "a formidable spying machine" that was "able to exercise a function of social control, build up relationships of psychological subjugation, and enter the privacy of individual workers and their families."[41] Of the more than one hundred classmates I interviewed for this book, Goss was the only one who lamented the passage of the old Yale. He believed a new order began during our years with the administration's attempt to reorient undergraduate life away from fraternities and toward the residential colleges. His entry in our class book lists his having come to Yale from Hotchkiss but little else—not even that he was a third-generation Yalie, a member of Fence Club and Book and Snake; a hockey player; in ROTC; and a magna cum laude graduate. H. Bradford Westerfield, a conservative political scientist who taught a course known as "Lies and Spies," had a powerful impact on his future. Goss came to him through their common association with Book and Snake. Yale led seamlessly to his career—from ROTC to army intelligence after college, to clandestine work for the CIA for much of the 1960s, to the House of Representatives from 1989 to 2004 with a focus on national intelligence, and eventually to heading the CIA for sixteen months in 2004–6.[42]

Both Goss and John Negroponte were members of Fence Club, along with William H. T. ("Bucky") Bush (brother of one president and uncle of another), David George Ball (who had invited Martin Luther King Jr. to Yale), and Lew Lehrman. Born in London and raised on Manhattan's Upper East Side in a family of Greek origin involved in international shipping, Negroponte grew up in a home of Stevensonian Democrats, with his parents seeing the Republican Party of the 1950s as insufficiently internationalist. He came to Yale from Exeter and majored in political science, spending his junior year in Paris at his father's alma mater, the legendary Sciences Po. His main extracurricular activity at Yale was playing poker—something, he told me, that trained him in negotiating skills.[43]

From an early age Negroponte set his heart on a career as a diplomat and entered the Foreign Service in the fall of 1960. He then went on to a long, distinguished, and at times controversial career. Skeptical about negotiations, he worked with and dissented from Henry Kissinger in the discussions to end the war in Vietnam. As ambassador to Honduras from 1981 to 1985, he often turned a blind eye to the government's human rights abuses in order to support intensified covert efforts against the Sandinistas in Nicaragua. He and his wife, an Englishwoman with an aristocratic lineage whom he had met in Vietnam in 1968, adopted five Nicaraguan children. As assistant secretary of state (1985–89) he helped negotiate the Montreal Protocol on Ozone and then as ambassador to Mexico (1989–93) played a significant role in negotiating NAFTA. In 2001, after four years in the private sector, he served as ambassador to the United Nations, where, despite his reservations about the second Iraq War, he eased the way for the passage of Security Council resolutions demanding that Saddam Hussein comply with the mandates of the international organization. After serving as ambassador to Iraq (2004–5), Negroponte was the first director of National Intelligence, a cabinet-level position charged with coordinating all of the nation's intelligence efforts, and then served as second in command of the Department of State (2007–9). After Negroponte was victorious over Goss in turf disputes with the CIA, Goss left his position as the agency's head. Fraternal ties go only so far. Negroponte retired for a second time from government service in 2009 to join a consulting firm and to return to Yale through an association with the Jackson Institute for Global Affairs.[44]

H. J. ("Jack") Heinz III, the great-grandson and namesake of the founder of his family's business, was another politically prominent classmate. His father, who went to Yale and was a member of Skull and Bones, was CEO of the family business from 1941 to 1966 and then chair of its board until he died in 1987. Entering Yale from Exeter, his son was active in Chi Psi (one of the few fraternities that had a relatively diverse membership), the senior society Manuscript, the varsity ski team, and Dwight Hall. After Yale he earned his MBA from Harvard and joined the Air Force Reserve. In the mid- to late 1960s, he experimented with several career options: politics, working for Senator Hugh Scott; business, employed in the family company; and academics, teaching at Carnegie-Mellon University.

Soon political opportunities opened up, and Heinz was among the last of a disappearing breed of moderate Republicans, serving in the House of Representatives from 1971 to 1977 and then in the Senate until his death in 1991, as the result of an airplane crash. He compiled a solid record in Washington, working across the aisle and making his mark on issues concerning the environment, the elderly, and international commerce. Had he lived longer and had he been able to navigate the changes in the Republican Party or shifted to the Democrats, he might have become president of the United States, a frequent speculation among those around him. Ted Stebbins, who knew Heinz at Exeter, Yale, Manuscript, Harvard, and after, captured him effectively: "movie-star handsome, wealthy, intelligent, athletic, having a wide range of interests and holding a Senate seat that was his for life."[45] In 1966 Heinz married Teresa Thierstein Simões-Ferreira; after his death she married Senator John Kerry.

Of my four classmates who later emerged as major public officials, Les Aspin was the only one I knew at Yale (though not very well), the only one with a strong record of achievement as an undergraduate, and the only Democrat.[46] He grew up in an upper-middle-class home in suburban Milwaukee, where his liberal Republican parents rarely talked about politics. He came to Yale from a public high school in Milwaukee after spending his junior year at Magdalen College School in Oxford. As an undergraduate he was an award-winning member of Army ROTC, as well as a member of Phi Beta Kappa, Linonia, Zeta Psi, Torch, and along with Goss, Book and Snake. After a fellowship to Oxford, Aspin earned his PhD at MIT in 1966. Following a stint as an analyst in the Pentagon under Robert S. McNamara, he returned to Milwaukee to join the economics department at Marquette University. He ran the senatorial campaign of William Proxmire in 1964 and was unsuccessful in his initial venture in local electoral politics.

Then in 1970 Aspin successfully ran for Congress as an anti-war candidate. Serving in the House of Representatives from 1971 to 1993, he turned increasingly interventionist. As secretary of defense for a year beginning in January 1993, he ran into trouble in September when, having turned down Chairman of the Joint Chiefs of Staff Colin Powell's request for more firepower in Somalia, rebels killed eighteen Americans, wounded seventy-five, and shot down two helicopters—all this dramatically captured in the 2001 film *Black Hawk Down*. Aspin resigned and went to a think tank in the capital. After a long struggle with heart disease, he died at age fifty-six in 1995. As his classmate and fellow spook Clint Brooks said on the occasion of our fiftieth reunion, Aspin's ability "to seek a middle ground on contentious issues, trying to facilitate understanding and drawing back from hardened positions," visible when he was at Yale and helpful in most of his career, became a liability in the wake of the disaster in Somalia when "grilled by a congressional committee . . . he came across as weak," a factor contributing to his resignation.[47]

A number of characteristics mark the careers of these four politically prominent classmates. Aspin excepted, they came from families whose wealth, social prominence, and noblesse oblige reached back, even well into the nineteenth century. Although Aspin was probably a member of the John Dewey Society, for none of them is there any indication of significant political engagement as undergraduates. Two came to Yale with legacies, and all of them had prepared at private institutions All were members of fraternities and, except for Negroponte, aboveground senior societies; none of them achieved significant recognition as an athlete. Two were in ROTC, and three served in the military early in the 1960s. Aspin was the only one whose formal achievements at Yale, both academic and extracurricular, provided any indication of what he would accomplish later on; for the other three, the advantages they brought with them when they came to Yale, as well as participation in the informal curriculum, prepared them for their futures. Of the four, Goss grew up more insulated from the global world and Negroponte's background was the most cosmopolitan. The three who came to Yale from American prep schools were Republicans, although Negroponte started out identified as a Democrat. Aspin, the only graduate of a public high school, was a lifelong Democrat. With the exception of Heinz, they made their mark in foreign more than domestic issues.

What Yale Meant for Our Futures

The causal connections between collegiate experiences and futures is often elusive. Yet by looking back, we can explore very different origins and outcomes, as well as the often unpredictable nature of political trajectories. The career of George McClain, who wrote his thesis on integration in the Methodist church and went on to dedicate his life to the fight for civil rights, suggests the transformative power of a Yale education. The stories of Tom Miller and others highlight the relative political quiescence of the Yale years for classmates, the complications of history, and the impact of external events, the war in Vietnam especially. With the benefit of hindsight we see the pattern of what happened to the joiners of the late 1950s. On the left was Bowles, active politically as an undergraduate and someone who sustained his politics as a writer. On the right was one classmate, Lehrman, who revealed little of himself politically in the late 1950s but did so amply later on.

When I had lunch in Manhattan in December 2012 with Edmund Leites, active at Yale through various adversarial political and cultural commitments, he pressed me on whether our classmates had fulfilled the call to leadership that A. Whitney Griswold made to our class at commencement. He might also have invoked Bart Giamatti's hope as we left Yale that his classmates would gradually develop "a noble and creative way of life." Pointing to the likes of Negroponte and Goss, Leites concluded that by Griswold's standard we had failed. In my often nonconfrontational way I responded that it all depended on what leadership means, on whether you focused on the famous and national or on those of us working out of the limelight.[48]

As I wrote this chapter, I returned again and again to the question Leites had posed. How does one weigh the impact on the world of a Goss, Aspin, Heinz, or Negroponte? And with what does one compare it? In this context, I think of my dear friend Stuart Stoddard, who entered Yale as a member of the class of 1960 but took time out and graduated in 1962. Stoddard, whom I did not meet until the mid-1970s, has as good a Yale and New England pedigree as anyone. Among his ancestors were not only generations of Yalies but also the first librarian of Harvard College, the first governor of Massachusetts Bay Colony, John Winthrop, and the great eighteenth-century minister Jonathan Edwards. Stoddard's father would have been my father's classmate, but his mother insisted he take a round-the-world trip before entering Yale. I do wonder how to evaluate Negroponte's impact compared with what Stoddard accomplished as a primary school teacher in a modest California suburb. Where does one place Goss's achievements in relation to those of Tom Miller or George McClain? Or the contributions that dozens of other teachers have made compared with those of the scores of bankers and corporate lawyers in the class of 1960?

And what is the relation between college experience and future political engagement? Shaped first by family and then by the formal and informal curricula and off-campus events, after graduation the class of 1960 encountered civil rights, the war in Vietnam, the women's and gay liberation movements, and the changing domestic and international landscape. All of these intensified and clarified our politics. What we became, nonetheless, is hard to see from what we were. As these many biographical sketches of classmates demonstrate, political trajectories are easier to understand retrospectively than to predict.[49]

CONCLUSION
Looking Backward

The class of 1960 was an 'in-between' generation—not really representative of the 1950s and the 'silent generation' and not yet culturally or politically reflective of the great impending changes that occurred during the decade ushered in by our year of graduation. . . . [T]he gray flannel suit conformism that became a stereotypical image of the 1950s was a thin veneer covering the emerging movements of change in civil rights, political orientation, and cultural attitudes that are now associated primarily with the decade of the 1960s. We were on the cusp of that decade, but had to learn lessons that required much more mental adjustment and reevaluation of assumptions than was the case for those who graduated only a few years later.

DAVID ELLIOTT, class of 1960, *Class of Its Own* (2010)

A college class is a community that is simultaneously experienced, imagined, and ignored. Through monthly columns in the alumni magazine and reunions held every five years, Yale, like its peer institutions, fosters a sense of cohesion that is useful in raising money and sustaining for each class a sense of itself as group. A reunion book, James Atlas wrote in 2012 as he pondered the one published forty years after his graduation from Harvard, is a "trance-inducing volume, a facebook that came before Facebook." When the self-selected classmates who actually write in a reunion book in more than minimal ways, they cull the truth from what they want to tell their peers. These books contain, Atlas notes, "a sometimes ghastly mix of covert self-congratulation, awkward confession and wry philosophizing undercut by heavy-handed irony." Though often "an exercise in confessional self-concealment," they also present "the truth inadvertently revealed," something "that makes these thick volumes so horribly fascinating."[1] Reunion books reveal how a group as ephemeral as a college class constructs and reconstructs its memory.

The reunion books for Yale's class of 1960 yield an abundant sense of how my class defines itself even as classmates indulge in "confessional self-concealment." Of course, caution is in order. For our fiftieth reunion, only half the class responded; presumably what motivated those who did not was some combination of illness, disinterest, alienation, protection of privacy, pressure of other commitments, and dissent from an often boastful genre. The essays submitted, ranging from a few words to thousands, are problematic but rich sources. We learn about the lives of the famous among us. We see what it means for a cohort to move through life and encounter history. We notice how personal, generational, and national experiences intersect.

An exploration of what happened to the class, individually and collectively, does several things. It enables us to understand the intersection of individual lives, a Yale education, and historical change. It contributes to discussions about American higher education by exploring how the liberal arts did and did not prepare us for our futures; how an elite education influenced patterns of social mobility; and whether four years in college broadened our horizons. Finally, a look at the lives of members of the class of 1960 reinforces what it has meant for us to begin on the cusp and then experience dramatically changing worlds. In those stories, memory, dreams, and experiences—painful, joyful, and ordinary—intersect.

A. Bartlett Giamatti and Class Consciousness

Recognition of those who have achieved mightily plays a key role in fostering how the class thinks about itself. In that respect, no one is more important than Bart Giamatti. The two events that most powerfully shaped class loyalty were his ascendency to the Yale presidency in 1978 at age forty and then his death on September 1, 1989, at age fifty-one. If the first made us feel a collective pride, the second stirred among us a sense of our mortality and of loss of a classmate who represented and exceeded our own aspirations. The respect Giamatti earned from classmates by the time he spoke to us as class orator when we graduated paled in comparison to what he garnered later in his all-too-short life. Except for a few years at Princeton (1964–66), he was at Yale for almost three decades—marrying a Yale drama student, Toni Smith, in 1960, earning his PhD, joining the faculty and moving up in its ranks, serving as master of Ezra Stiles College, heading the humanities division, and becoming president. He left Yale in 1986 to take the position of president of the National League and then in 1989 became commissioner of Major League Baseball. In professional sports as in university administration, his tenure was not without controversy. A cultural conservative who defended tradition, at Yale he took tough and principled stands during a bitter strike of technical and clerical workers and then did the same in response to protests against the university's investments in South Africa. As baseball commissioner, he engineered the permanent suspension of Pete Rose from the game. Giamatti died of a massive heart attack eight days later. Smoking, the strike at Yale, his lack of a thick skin, his aversion to conflict, and his administrative style took a tremendous toll on him.

Writing soon after in the *Yale Daily News,* a reporter noted that, "almost all" of those he interviewed "cited his personal qualities as a more lasting gift to the community than his administrative achievements." Bart was known, he continued, for his "integrity, strength of character, warmth and his courage to make decisions."[2] At Yale, he soothed the ruffled feathers of disaffected alums, healed the wounds of town-gown relations, balanced budgets, and raised money. "Call me Bart the Refurbisher," he remarked as his Yale presidency neared its end. "If my name goes on anything, it will be the Giamatti Memorial Wiring System."[3] Actually, his name did go on something—a bench on the Old Campus designed by our classmate David Sellers on which is inscribed one of Giamatti's more compelling statements: "A liberal education is at the heart of a civil society, and at the heart of a liberal education is the art of teaching."[4] Giamatti understood that leadership of Yale was, as he put it in 1987, "an essentially moral act" which involved "the moral courage to assert a vision of the institution in the future and the intellectual energy to persuade the community or the culture of the wisdom and validity of the vision."[5]

Classmates and others admiringly remember his personal qualities and eloquence. The sports writer Roger Angell captured what Giamatti looked like in a 1988 *New Yorker* essay: "He was solid and shaggy, with a noble beard, a seafaring complexion, a Homeric brow, a lidded but burning outward-inward bound gaze, a rumbling laugh, and a smile by turns gentle and razory."[6] Soon after Giamatti died, our classmate Bill Borders talked of his "lifelong battle against everything bogus and shoddy. He always made us proud. So we *knew* that in a world full of compromise and corner-cutting, Bart's position would be uncompromising and correct." Moreover, he continued, Giamatti was "so marvelously self-mocking, both in private and public, taking his job seriously, but not himself."[7] Those I interviewed confirmed and amplified such judgments, speaking of his democratic sensibility, his biting humor, his integrity, his brilliant storytelling, his warmth, his gregariousness, and his ability to relate sympathetically to the widest range of people.[8]

"Bart Giamatti's distinction as a Spenserian Scholar may have had little to do with his becoming Commissioner of Major League Baseball," wrote Paul Alpers, someone more distinguished than Giamatti as a scholar of the pastoral and just about his equal as a Red Sox fan. "But," he continued in a 1997 essay, "his views of baseball and of *The Faerie Queene* have remarkable similarities." He went on to point out Giamatti's emphasis on civility, his preference for "A Free and Ordered Space," the title of one of Giamatti's books, and his realization of, in Giamatti's words, "the evanescence of vision, the failure of harmony, the vulnerability of ideal revelations to the pressures of the world." Alpers insisted that "Bart's intense scholarly focus on ideal gardens and green spaces recapitulates and, I think, derives from the experience of the young boy entering Fenway Park."[9]

On May 31, 1985, Giamatti charmed and captivated us with his address at our twenty-fifth reunion banquet. He began this way: "Being a President of a university is no way for an adult to make a living. . . . It is to hold a mid-nineteenth century ecclesiastical position on top of a late twentieth century corporation." He then turned to develop an imaginative narrative of what he had done. A few months before he took office, "crouched . . . between the lawnmower and the snow tires" in his garage, he composed a memo that he issued on his first day in office. Drawing on Milton's poetry, he announced that henceforth at Yale "evil will be abolished and Paradise is restored."[10] The response to the memo was swift. From every constituency came warnings and criticism.

The reaction of the Standing Committee on Special Interests—formed to "pursue a special interest if there is no pre-existent special interest group empowered to pursue that special interest"—typified what he faced. He agreed to meet them in the room where the Yale Corporation met, but they hesitated, saying they were not sure that room was large enough to accommodate them. He asked them to send delegates, but "they said they did not trust each other enough to delegate any of their number." So he suggested they meet in Woolsey Hall, which could seat 2,650. They agreed, but at the appointed hour only seven of them showed up. They told him that no one with authority at Yale was "paying any attention to the most pressing problem of our time. The problem of evil and the restoration of Paradise." When he reminded them he had done exactly that on the first day of his presidency, they informed him that they had not been at Yale then. Giamatti, having used humor to articulate to his classmates what a president faced, celebrated conversations at Yale—"the sound of all those voices, over centuries, overlapping, giving and taking, that is finally the music of civilization." Then he concluded by noting, "That may be as close to paradise for a moment as any one of us ever comes."[11]

If the twenty-fifth reunion was, as Borders said, "a wonderfully jubilant, unique celebration of Bart" during his presidency, the mood of our thirtieth, held some nine months after his death, was somber.[12] Many classmates wrote that they lamented Giamatti's dying too young but found solace in his writings. Tom Miller, fresh from the memorial service on campus, told us, "He was the nearest to poet/king in our generation" and hoped his grandchildren will, "in their own way, carry on the battle Bart fought with words and pen to slay ignorance, and bring us together as we travel to our common destiny."[13] Twenty years later, on the occasion of our fiftieth, Lew Lehrman remarked that "Fenway was his Elysian way" and teaching "his true vocation." Giamatti was "an unselfconscious unapologetic patriot. But in him there was no screaming eagle. His ironic sensibility—his sense of proportion, his mastery of the rise and fall of ancient empires—regulated his passions. His historical perspective endowed his patriotism with understanding of the limitations of his country-men and of their history. . . . He understood his destiny was to share his great gifts with family, with friends, with students, with baseball players."[14]

Whatever Happened to the Class of 1960?

In addition to Giamatti, we have certainly had our full share of prominent peers. In politics and public service classmates have served on school boards, in state and national legislatures, in government bureaucracies, as ambassa-dors, and on the benches of a full range of judicial courts. In the corporate world, John Pepper was CEO and then chairman of the board of Procter and Gamble and later of Walt Disney Corporation. Among academics Peter Dia-mond stands out as a winner of the Nobel Prize in Economics, Leslie Epstein as a novelist, Monroe Price as an expert in international media law, David Elliott as a political scientist, Ralph Bryant and Sam Bowles as economists. Among the eminent scientists in the class are Carl Akerlof in physics, Dick Beals in mathematics, Bob Coates in chemistry, Steve Easter in neuroscience, Walt Eckhart in molecular biology, David Krantz in psychology, and Dale Purves in neurobiology.

As prolific and influential as some of us are as writers, in sheer numbers it is hard to match Russ Munson, who made the photographs for *Jonathan Livingston Seagull,* a book that sold 30 million copies; Pete Palmer, author of a series of sports books, including the one hundredth edition of *Who's Who in Baseball;* or Dick Peace, who has authored, co-authored, or edited more than eighty religious books. Then there are pioneers in distinctive areas. Don Dell helped create the field of sports management, as Don Catlin did for drug testing for athletes. Sidney Baker did path-breaking work in alternative medicine with an emphasis on chronic health problems. As an entrepreneur, Emery Olcott created and led a financially successful high tech company that was one of the nation's first employee-owned firms. David Sellers focused on disaster relief and ecological architecture. Rob Northrup helped develop an oral rehydration solution for cholera patients that has saved the lives of millions of children.

As our twenty-fifth reunion approached, we occupied a patterned range of occupations. More than 40 percent of us were in education, law, medicine, or science. Some returned to their hometowns and took over the modest businesses their fathers and even grandfathers had developed. Others started their own companies. Scores and scores of classmates headed businesses that bore some version of their or their family's names; some of these firms had a significant impact on the regional, national, and international level, while others were one- or two-person local operations. Many members of the class of 1960 gravitated to major firms, with IBM and General Motors among the most frequently mentioned. Despite *Mad Men*'s reputation, remarkably few worked on Madison Avenue; the reunion book for our twenty-fifth listed only five classmates in advertising and only one of those in Manhattan. Some had jobs in industries like steel that were in decline, while scores ended up in working with new technologies, computers especially.

Some of us had modest achievements, while others stumbled, cautioning us against assuming that all Yale graduates were tremendously successful. In law, classmates ranged from partners in major firms serving global corporations to Alan Caplan, a single practitioner who defended outcasts, including members of the Italian Mafia and Hell's Angels. In medicine, some were professors in major universities, others, single practitioners in rural areas. In education, we have high-level administrators at a range of institutions; professors at major universities and at small liberal arts and community colleges; and teachers in high schools and grade schools. In government, the range was from a U.S. senator to one who had a career delivering mail for the Post Office. In the corporate world, among our ranks were CEOs of companies large and small (finance, banking, and investment management the most commonly mentioned), a union member who worked as a lineman, and someone who bagged groceries at a supermarket. In between were scores of mid-level managers, heads of divisions and local offices, and vice presidents.

As reunions approached, classmates recalled events that shaped their lives. We went to graduate and professional schools, got married and divorced, hired and fired; had children and grandchildren. Although it was rarely mentioned, surely a high percentage of us benefited from psychotherapy. We bought second and even third homes and went in and out of and back into retirement. We devoted a remarkable amount of time and effort to philanthropic and nonprofit work—at every level from volunteering for local charities, to working to improve the lives of Native Americans, to serving on or chairing the boards of major institutions such as the Metropolitan Museum of

Art, Andover, Yale University, the World Press Freedom Committee, and the Anti-Defamation League. Over time, in reunion books and at reunions, the tone of our conversations shifted from boastful to reflective and even tragic.

Events discussed in reunion books remind us of the limits of what we could achieve or control: the deaths of children, spouses and partners, friends, and parents; illnesses that struck us and ones we loved. Some of us made and lost fortunes and then, sometimes, recovered; still others remarked that joining Alcoholics Anonymous saved their lives. Then there were the complicated ways in which we experienced events that connected the public and the private. There are only a few references to the women's movement in the more than two thousand pages of six reunion books, but reading lines and between lines makes clear the impact of changing gender relations, most notably in the pride expressed in the achievements of our wives (often described as best friends) and daughters and the painful lessons learned from divorces and remarriages.[15] Only three classmates have revealed to their peers that they are gay; some memorial essays discuss struggles others had with their sexuality, and some fathers tell us about gay sons (but none that I saw noted lesbian daughters), but no one mentions the struggle for gay rights as a social movement. Even more surprising is how few members of the class of 1960 mention the civil rights or environmental movements, though there is evidence, especially in the latter case, of their participation. The most frequently discussed public events were the assassinations of JFK and MLK, but especially the war in Vietnam. The final note, of course, is the inexorable march of classmates toward poor health and death.

Yale 1960 and American Higher Education

The experiences of my classmates shed light on many of the issues that today animate discussions of higher education.[16] Now faced with tremendous pressure to ensure links between college and careers, some critics find the humanities and soft social sciences irrelevant when compared to STEM—science, technology, engineering, and math. With few exceptions (the theologian Dick Peace majored in electrical engineering), the members of the engineering honor society Tau Beta Pi ended up drawing on their undergraduate education when they became lawyers, engineers, computer scientists, or corporate executives. Chris Argyris, an industrial administration professor, inspired several classmates to enter into business and utilize his management theories. While the backgrounds of engineering majors reveal no clear pattern, the same is not true for math majors: only three of twenty-eight came from boarding schools and six from private day schools; only four had relatives who preceded them to Yale—percentages well below the class average. Almost all of them ended up in fields where they could draw on their undergraduate major. In contrast and not surprisingly, for most of those who focused on the humanities and social sciences there was a relatively weak correlation between majors and careers. Yale's exceptionally well regarded English department produced no major figure in literary studies. In contrast, a significant number of classmates ended up as professors of history, and Howard Lamar inspired Bill MacKinnon to write prolifically as a historian of the American West, even while he rose through the corporate ranks to become a vice president of General Motors.

Like scores on my classmates who headed toward careers in teaching, for me there a direct connection between what I studied at Yale and my future as a teacher and scholar. During my senior year, I talked with several faculty members about pursuing a PhD. They advised me to apply to programs in history rather than American studies because they believed there were plenty of jobs in the first field but few in the second. In fall 1961 I entered Harvard's doctoral program in history. Ironically, in virtually every job I held during my teaching career, American studies remained the focus of my administrative commitments and my most imaginative teaching. At Skidmore, Scripps, and Smith, I was in an ideal position to witness and participate in the changes that transformed the field. About the time I assumed my first tenure-track position in fall 1970, the war in Vietnam, along with the powerful social movements led by people of color, women, and gay men and lesbians, posed fundamental challenges to the approaches American studies had consolidated by the mid-1950s. Over the course of my career I embraced or tried on new paradigms that emerged—including the emphasis on border crossing and transnationalism that was so prominent as I approached retirement in 2012. Now the people involved in American studies—African Americans, Asian Americans, women, Jews, lesbians and gay men, and Latinos, as well as representatives of fields beyond history, art history, and literature—are quite different from those who taught me at Yale.

We can look at the relationship between college major and professional future in other ways. Yale's storied art history department did not produce Ted Stebbins or Dennis Longwell, among the most distinguished art historians in the class; the former majored in political science and then set out for law school while the latter was in philosophy. Our most important art dealers—Brooke Alexander and Peter Tatistcheff—majored in Greek and English. The most important art collectors—Sam Heyman, Jim Ross, Oscar Tang, and Norman Dolph—majored in American studies, English, mechanical engineering, and electrical engineering. Almost half of the seventeen who majored in art history came to Yale with legacies and from prep schools. Only one of them, my high school classmate Gene Santomasso, became an art historian, but he died too young to realize his full potential. The rest, although their majors may have enriched their lives, pursued careers, mostly as doctors and businessmen, in apparently unrelated fields.

If the careers of many of us suggest a weak to nonexistent link between a liberal arts education and career, what are other justifications for a broad-gauged approach to an undergraduate education? Although many of my classmates stressed that friends were more important than professors, scores reported in reunion books that classes at Yale had taught them how to think critically. There is abundant evidence in the trajectory of our careers that, inventing and reinventing ourselves, we successfully navigated the shifting tides that we faced in job markets and life, even though it is impossible to determine the role that formal undergraduate education played in such adaptability. Then there is the question of the relationship between education and leadership, now highlighted by undergraduate programs in leadership education. Classmates accomplished what they did without such formal, curriculum-based training. At least three who focused on American history and American studies went on to head major corporations: Sam Heyman at GAF Material, John Pepper at Procter and Gamble, and Lew Lehrman at Rite Aid. Perhaps in their corporate roles they drew on what they learned when studying the past. More likely, however, is the impact of his undergraduate education on John Pepper's work as CEO of the National Underground Railroad Freedom Center and Lew Lehrman's as a writer and philanthropist in American history. Peter Workman founded Workman Publishing, where he achieved a stunning record of having one-third of his titles sell at least one hundred thousand copies, but the wisdom of bringing *The Official Preppie Handbook* into print had less to do with taking English courses on campus than buying clothes off-campus at J. Press. As Yale's president, Bart Giamatti's eloquence derived in good measure from his command of Renaissance literature, though surely his chairing the Yale Charities Drive in our senior year bore a more direct relationship to his skill as a fund-raiser.

The question, then, is if few or none of us learned about leadership in the classroom, how did so many of us become leaders? We brought to our futures abundant kinds of capital—economic, which had its origin in family financial resources; social, provided by connections and skills we developed before we came to Yale and when we were there; and cultural, which enabled us to maneuver successfully at work and play. Regardless of our backgrounds, our Yale degrees and contacts opened doors for many of us. We are a privileged and special generation. Arriving on earth just before penicillin made it possible to treat infections, we benefited from dramatic advances in medicine that extended and improved the quality of our lives. Some of us served in Vietnam, but I cannot identify any classmate killed there, and with the draft ending in 1973, few if any of our children were forced to serve in the military. We were among the last cohort of our type—all male, almost entirely white, from middle-class backgrounds or above, predominantly Protestant, elite, educated—whose leadership and prominence seemed to go unchallenged. Born near the end of the Depression, many of us experienced the prosperity of the postwar period, with stock market and housing values rising dramatically during the course of our adult lives. We entered the job market before other groups rose to challenge the dominance of white men. We were also part of one of the smallest demographic cohorts in twentieth-century America, which meant there were fewer competitors for positions in prestigious graduate and professional schools.[17]

The Making and Unmaking of the American Class System

Our lives reveal major changes in the history of class privilege in America. Jack Heinz III and Jim Ottaway Jr. benefited from what Henry John Heinz II and James Ottaway Sr. achieved in ketchup and newspapers. In contrast, chance, poor decisions, or alcohol caused some classmates to fall from the social heights they occupied when they arrived at Yale. Yet scores of us rose from more humble—but not too humble—origins to achieve success beyond our wildest 1960 dreams. All of this meant that many of us experienced tremendous social mobility in the course of our lives.

If the *Forbes* list of the wealthiest is accurate, then Sam Heyman was the richest among us, with his net worth once standing at one and one half billion dollars. In the 1930s his father had launched Heyman Properties, which Sam helped develop into a commercial real estate empire. Sam grew up in Danbury, Connecticut, in an upper-middle-class household. He had a very strong academic record and earned his major "Y" on the tennis courts as what he jokingly called, given the skills of his more talented teammates, "the seventh player on a six-man roster." Jeremy Nahum, his roommate for their last three years at Yale, speculated about what explained his success. "Sam," he remarked shortly after Sam died in November 2009, "was driven, determined, dedicated, and directed." Never doubting that Heyman would succeed, Nahum pointed to his fierceness as a gambler while at Yale. "Every week he would bet carefully on a variety of professional and college sporting events, never letting his feelings rule. Perhaps," Nahum concluded, "this was a precursor to his high-stakes, steely-nerved willingness to risk a great deal in pursuit of his ends."[18]

It is easier to discover who in the class rose than who fell. Classmates tell me of peers who as legacies, sons of wealthy parents, and prep school graduates came to Yale with every possible advantage, but whose health problems, bad luck, alcoholism, and false starts caused them to end up way below where they began in the socioeconomic hierarchy. Their stories, along with those of classmates whose trajectory was upward, remind us of what Vilfredo Pareto called the circulation of elites. At Yale in the late 1950s, many of us lived in a world on the cusp between an overemphasis on pedigree and the often compulsive stress on credentials. In terms William Deresiewicz describes in *Excellent Sheep* (2014), we could still find a way to a meaningful life.[19]

Social class in higher education is as critical an issue today as it was in 1956.[20] In the late 1950s, a sociologist has written, Yale had "a trickle of students from low-income families, and a giant river of youths from high-income families."[21] With mixed success, I tried to track the lives of some of the wealthiest and poorest classmates. Doing the former was relatively easy. I focused on those who came to Yale from Greenwich, Connecticut, almost all of them from boarding schools and with legacies. With one notable exception (John Hawkins, the son of a minister, who became a librarian), all of them worked as executives for business corporations. Using Zillow.com and addresses listed in reunion books, I concluded that none of them ended up below the ranks of the upper middle class, although I suspect that at mid- or end career, some of them were much wealthier than in 1960 and others were comparatively less so. Because in the mid-1950s Yale had more interest in recruiting students from Greenwich than those who resided in impoverished inner cities or rural areas, tracking classmates whose lives began at the lower end of the social scale was more difficult. At Yale wealth was vastly more visible than poverty or modesty. So I can only hazard some informed guesses.

Today a higher percentage of Yale undergraduates come from families within range of the poverty line than was true for the class of 1960.[22] This is clear from discussions about allocation of scholarships funds that occasionally came to the fore. In spring 1959, Yale's admissions office responded to criticism in a *New York Times* article that relatively few poor students received scholarships. This came at a time when approximately 30 percent of Yalies received financial aid and getting into Yale College was significantly easier for applicants who did not receive it. "I'm tired of all this mythical-pooh about so-called 'able students' being deprived of a college education," remarked a Yale admission officer before going on to acknowledge that there was a "psychological barrier" against applying, especially to prestigious institutions. Later generations of admissions officers worked to overcome such obstacles by imaginatively recruiting applicants from diverse backgrounds, but he simply noted that Yale could not admit someone who did not apply.[23] In my junior year a vigorous debate erupted over Yale's bursary system, one that, unlike Harvard's, required all scholarship students to work on campus. Critics decried the program's compulsory nature and the requirement that all recipients of such aid endure "token sacrifice" by showing appreciation for Yale's generosity.[24]

Although I can identify some students who were working class or lower middle class, their parents often had middle-class aspirations. Most of those from modest backgrounds came to Yale from public schools. Some left Yale for financial reasons; one classmate, after watching his parents struggle with debt and not wanting to increase that burden by staying at Yale, transferred to complete his education. Then there is Ken Fujii, the only Japanese American in the class and someone from a modest background in California's San Joaquin Valley. The federal government had interned him and his family in the Rohwer War Relocation Center for seventeen months beginning in early June 1944; after Yale, Fujii earned an architecture degree and lived in a middle-class neighborhood in Fresno.

From what I can tell, almost all of those from relatively humble origins who graduated from Yale went on to earn higher degrees in science, law, or medicine, often launching themselves (sometimes with the help of a wife's profession or wealth) into the upper middle class. A study of the eighteen Italian Americans in our class, an easily identified ethnic group from relatively humble origins, provides ample evidence of social mobility. Compared with the class as a whole, there were significantly fewer legacies and graduates of private schools. Almost all of them were the first members of their families to graduate from college. Their parents' social position ranged from working to middle class. At Yale many of them had lives marked by achievement in the classroom and in extracurricular activities. Most went on to careers as lawyers and academics. About a third of them worked in the private sector, whether for small companies or in nonexecutive positions for large ones. At least two experienced significant social mobility: Caesar Naples, the son of a policeman, became vice chancellor of the California State University system, and Al Gillotti, the son of a factory worker, had considerable success as an international banker while successfully pursuing his ambition to become a novelist.[25]

The life of Bob Reynolds reveals why many from modest backgrounds chose professions over corporations. Growing up in "threadbare gentility" in a small Ohio town and encouraged by his mother's ambition for her children, he was a "scholarship boy" at Yale. As an outsider to the world of privilege and "overly studious," he went on to a highly successful academic career in medicine and information technology. He realized, he remarked retrospectively, that access to the corporate world was based on whom you knew, while entry into professions depended on merit.[26]

I found few if any cases of a rags-to-great-riches story that involved ascending into the upper reaches of the corporate world. To be sure, David Ball, from a modest background in Britain, arrived at Yale from Moody Bible College, joined Skull and Bones, and had a career as a Wall Street lawyer, an officer of a large multinational corporation, and a high-level federal government official. Growing up in a blue-collar family, Russ Tousley was what he called "a poor Catholic scholarship kid from New Haven" who dreamed of being an opera singer. In his first year at Yale he converted to Protestantism (the faith of his father's side of the family) and was active in an a cappella group. In his senior year he shifted from the choir at the Roman Catholic St. Thomas More to the Protestant one at Battell Chapel. Eager to get away from New Haven after graduation, he joined the navy, which sent him to the West Coast. Settling in Seattle, he married a Smith alumna he had known slightly in the late 1950s, earned his law degree at University of Washington, helped build a successful law practice, and assumed leadership positions at a Congregational church. He could not fulfill his dream of becoming a singer of arias, but he nonetheless ended up serving as president and chairman of the board of the Seattle Opera.[27]

What role Yale played in fostering social mobility specifically and social change more generally is hard to quantify, but some informed guesses are in order. At a time before need-blind admissions developed fully and when the admissions office had a constricted view of whom to recruit and admit, Yale's policies confirmed status more frequently than redistributed it. "Student experiences at college, and class trajectories at exit," two sociologists of higher education have written about a flagship public university in the Midwest in the early twenty-first century, "are fundamentally shaped by the structure of academic and social life on campus." While at Yale, the existence of multiple avenues to achievement, the opportunity for those who wanted it, and possibility to experience peers outside one's comfort zone all helped foster in many of us a sense that we could lead lives we knew nothing of before college. Yet several of my micro studies show clear patterns about our futures—shaped as much by the differential opportunities we perceived Yale opening to us as by the way academic and extracurricular activities fostered or impeded change.[28]

Liberal Education and the Democratic Ideal

This was the title of a 1959 book of Yale president A. Whitney Griswold. Education for democratic citizenship is an admirable goal, which the extracurricular world more adequately achieved than the curricular one. In spring

2013 Robert Rifkind, class of 1958, reminded me of other raisons d'etre for the liberal arts. "The primary purpose of a liberal education," he remarked, "is to rescue us from the provincialism with which we all start out—the taken-for-granteds of our village, family, clan—by getting us to engage with unfamiliar thought including that of other times, other places and even other room-mates." In addition, he commented, "a liberal education involved a critical exposure to a variety of disciplines by which men and women have attempted to impose order on aspects of their experience and thereby gain a sense of mastery over the flux."[29]

By that standard, how well did Yale do? For some of us, very well. Yale's distribution requirements meant that we had to take courses across a broad range of disciplines. In my first year, I studied and wrote poetry, struggled to understand both DNA and Nietzsche, strengthened my high school Spanish, and learned how political systems worked—though I doubt I understood the variety of disciplinary approaches that undergird these fields.[30] Even though as a major I focused on the nation I knew best, I confronted new and unfa-miliar aspects of it. Yet for me and for others there were limits to what we encountered. Absent a requirement that we study non-Western societies and given Yale's weakness in areas other than East Asia and the Soviet Union, few of us encountered unfamiliar cultures, although I suspect most of us learned about unfamiliar times. Yet limiting the range of what many of us encountered was not the gaps in the curriculum but the fact that many of my classmates did not take their formal education very seriously, choosing instead to devote time to sports, friendships, singing, drinking, and dating. As two sociologists in 2013 remarked, "a college—at least insofar as it offers real benefits—is less a collection of *programs* than a gathering of *people,*" although for me and some of my classmates the list of people would include professors who taught us. Mentors, they note, "can be invaluable, even life changing."[31]

In other ways, Yale had mixed success in rescuing many of us from the provincialism of our backgrounds. On the positive side, intentionally or not, the university avoided fostering any one set of student cultures and instead offered us widely divergent points of affiliation: athletics, fraternities, singing groups, residential colleges, majors, publications, and political organizations among them. While some of us aligned ourselves principally with only one choice, most assembled undergraduate lives with a rich mixture of commit-ments, which in combination made it possible to experience people and per-spectives unlike their own. Yet there were limits to how well we mixed. Some social locations had higher prestige than others: *Yale Daily News,* Skull and Bones, the Political Union, and Dwight Hall more than *Criterion,* unknown underground senior societies, the George Orwell Forum, the Society of King

Charles the Martyr, and the Mormon Desert Club. To the extent that we lived in silos, even multiple ones, we might encounter but not really get to know people unlike ourselves—though my best guess is that many of us were more successful than the current generation in developing friendships across political lines. The residential colleges did put us side by side with a variety of peers, but as the story of the Trumbull College Marble Team shows, groups often conflicted rather than intermingled. Bob Mallano, an Italian American from a modest middle-class background, could gain entry into DKE and Scroll and Key through his prowess as a football player, in a way that Raleigh Davenport with his dark skin could never have done. More significantly, Yale's admissions policy, which for the class of 1960 brought in a remarkably homogeneous group, placed sharp limits on how much any of us could interact with peers from diverse backgrounds.[32]

In the early twenty-first century, elite colleges and universities pride themselves on how well students mix with peers from different backgrounds and with interests other than their own, with roommate choice as one example. To test this for the class of 1960, I examined the senior roommate patterns, the only year for which data is publicly available, for two distinct and nonintersecting groups: the ten Junior Phi Beta Kappa members and the fifteen classmates in Skull and Bones. No one in the first group participated in varsity athletics and no one in the latter reached the academic top 10 percent in our junior or senior years. Academic excellence led to membership in the former; leadership, predominantly in varsity athletics, in the other. The two groups arrived at Yale from very different backgrounds. Junior Phi Betes: 50 percent Jews, 60 percent public high schools, 20 percent legacies; Skull and Bones, 0 percent Jews; 13 percent public high schools; 60 percent legacies. With relatively rare exceptions, members of both groups roomed with people who, from outward appearances, were like themselves, although this was less true of the Junior Phi Betes. Four members of Skull and Bones roomed with each other and one with his twin brother. In his first year, Bonesman David Dominick had roomed with two public high school graduates—Fritz Steele and me; as a senior he roomed with a prep school classmate. Not so different was the pattern among Junior Phi Betes, who tended to room with other academic achievers who were neither major athletes nor members of senior societies; in one case two of them, both math majors, roomed with each other. In my first year, I roomed with two people from backgrounds very unlike mine; for my junior and senior years, I roomed by myself.

Comparing these two groups also underscored the differential opportunities our futures held. From the ranks of the Junior Phi Betes came two medical doctors, one high school teacher, one lawyer with a major international firm, and one man about whom it is nearly impossible to find any information. The rest were professors or researchers in and outside the academy. The men from Skull and Bones by and large chose different paths: at midcareer ten of them worked for corporations; one was a professor of geology; one, a professor of community medicine; one, a lawyer; and two, artists. Liberals and high achievers probably chose the professions. Conservatives and the non-studious headed for corporate jobs principally because of familial aspirations and, more importantly perceptions of where merit or connections would lead us.

No Longer Dink Stover's Yale

Four other areas command our attention: finance, global reach, religion, and politics. In the late 1950s, room, board, and tuition, which by my senior year had risen to $2,300, was 41 percent of the national median family income; in 2010 that figure stood near or above 100 percent—although more generous financial aid lowers the real cost of a Yale education. Yale now prides itself on how little debt graduates carry and does so at a time when the comprehensive cost of a Yale education, adjusted for inflation, has grown 300 percent since 1960; few in my class graduated burdened by debt, in part because Yale then disproportionately recruited well-to-do students. Critics of higher education now complain that elite institutions shortchange undergraduates—with bloated administrative budgets, activities peripheral to the classroom, and highly paid faculty who focus more on research than on teaching all contributing to undermining a liberal arts education. I cannot judge the quality of a Yale College education now, but my own experience in the late 1950s underscores how remarkable and transformative the education was that Yale lavished on those of us eager to learn.

Yale now prides itself on being a global university, but in the late 1950s it was a remarkably provincial one. To get to the campus, about the same number of classmates traveled from their homes in the New Haven area as from abroad. Only a handful of us studied outside the country while undergraduates. Yet over the ensuing fifty years a very high percentage of us had extensive experience internationally; obviously as tourists but also as members of the armed services or diplomatic corps, as teachers and researchers, and as businessmen and professionals.

Before we arrived, William F. Buckley Jr. had lambasted Yale as a Godless place. As we have seen, William Sloane Coffin Jr. fought to change that, albeit not in ways Buckley approved. On campus in the late 1950s the religious options were relatively limited: you could be a Catholic, Protestant, or Jew—but in most cases quietly and within mainstream boundaries. The reunion books reveal a changed picture. Sam Heyman and Rich Epstein are the only two Orthodox Jews I can identify. In our class book Epstein did not mention membership in Hillel, the Jewish undergraduate organization. However, in our fiftieth reunion book, influenced by the teachings of Chabad-Lubavitch rebbes he first encountered in medical school, Epstein offered a more extensive discussion of his religious beliefs than any peer.[33] In contrast, as many as 50 percent of my Jewish classmates married non-Jews. For others, religious commitments were not unchanging: Jonathan Hufstadter announced in the spring of 1960 that he was going to become a Catholic priest and in 1968 earned a Licentiate of Sacred Theology in Rome. In 1986 he stepped down as headmaster of the Benedictine Portsmouth Abbey School, married a year later, earned his PhD at Harvard, and then became a faculty member in English at the University of Connecticut. His wife and two daughters are Jewish, and although he shares in their Jewish life, he remains unaffiliated. His life thus recapitulates much of the history of religion in America.[34] After graduation most of us remained publicly silent about our religious lives, but some presented their dramatic stories—finding Christ in the midst of a life crisis, discovering the compelling beauty of an Eastern religion, or learning how to communicate with the dead.[35] If for later generations social and sexual commitments were the problematic issues, for us it was more likely to be religious ones.

Buckley also claimed that Yale was too left-leaning. As undergraduates if we were political at all, most of us were Eisenhower Republicans or independents—and Yale changed few of us politically. My own sense is that although after 1960 some of us became more conservative, at least an equal number became more liberal. As I now read over reunion books and talk to classmates, a number of things are striking. Those on the left criticize American inequality and foreign policy, while conservatives decry fiscal irresponsibility and government interference with free enterprise. For those in the center, the most common political statements go something like this: Americans need to be less dogmatic and violent, and more tolerant and compassionate; we are witnessing the destruction of our environment, through some combination of greed, materialism, neglect, uncontrolled population growth; bitter partisan politics, poor leadership, and special interests prevent the nation from solving its problems and promoting the public good. Clearly, public issues matter to us now much more than they did in the late 1950s.

On the Cusp?

Before I began working on this book, I assumed there was a seamless connection between the rebellious stirrings I felt in the late 1950s and what happened in the ensuing decades. Now, having completed my research, I know that the historical change our class represented and, in some cases shaped, is more complex. Historians have tried to pin transitions to a single year—1959 or 1965, for example. But if we look at them from the micro level, changes from the past to the future appear subtle, halting, nuanced. There was no fluid continuity. Connecting past and present—childhoods, Yale in the late 1950s, and our futures—is a messy process. *Brown v. Board of Education,* the Montgomery Bus Boycott, the invention of the microchip, the launching of *Sputnik,* the assassinations of the Kennedys and King, the publication of Betty Friedan's *The Feminine Mystique,* the war in Vietnam, and the first Earth Day were historically transformative nationally. However, in lives lived day-by-day by a thousand Yalies—well, it's complicated.

First, let me make the case for how the experiences of my classmates reveal the ways the 1950s were different from the years after. Most of my peers were apolitical in the late 1950s, preferring to spend time drinking, dating, play-ing, or even studying over thinking about, much less engaging in, politics. For most of us, even the most politically minded, studying a problem or listen-ing to a lecture about it was more important that acting to solve it. Unlike those who later connected their identities to political action, key figures in my stories remained in the closet or separate, alone. In relatively isolated acts of rebellion, a few classmates took recreational drugs, read the radical *I. F. Stone's Weekly,* went to Manhattan to listen to jazz, or rode motorcycles. Reading reunion books and interviewing classmates has clarified for me that it was after graduation that major public events mobilized us: 1966 was a far cry from 1960, the early 1960s from the later Sixties.

On the other hand, there is plenty of evidence that we were on the cusp of a new era. In important ways, the late 1950s provided an opening that many of us took advantage of, even though it was not until the mid- to late 1960s that the world and our reaction to it turned decisively or clearly. Most of the issues that would command attention after we graduated were already percolating when we were undergraduates, but they were not yet prominent in our consciousness.

Our postgraduate transformations would draw on the racial, musical, religious, and familial experiences of our young adulthoods. Begin with race. The civil rights movement opened doors to my African American classmates. Moreover, I can think of notable instances where race lay in the background of several white classmates' lives, which inflected their later experiences. David Elliott's and Phip Hirsh's working alongside an African American farmhand on the family farm; John Ostheimer's having to sit in the balcony of a movie theater with African American household help; Dick Peace's high school friendship with an African American; Tom Miller's experiences with African Americans at the Farm School; my own trip to South Africa; and Lew Lehrman's challenge to Malcolm X—all these were formative experiences whose importance is clear in retrospect, even though at the time these seemed more isolated examples. Elements of the counterculture also pointed some peers forward. I do not think most of us who listened to folk music or jazz consciously understood the political or cultural meaning of what we experienced, but it was there to be drawn on later. Religion played a powerful role in transforming our lives as well.

The impact of Yale's Protestant leaders, Coffin especially, is palpable. Protestantism in general and Coffin specifically played major roles in political awakenings, even as such changes were rooted in our upbringing and in off-campus experiences. Coffin nudged, cajoled, and advised students across the religious spectrum in ways that had both short- and long-term consequences. In fact, Coffin's influence, based as it was on his commitments as a Christian, should caution us against concluding that by the 1960s nonbelief had become the overwhelmingly dominant established norm in American higher education. In looking at the transformative power of religion, I think not only of some of those who went to Africa but also of Ralph Bryant's Quakerism, Dick Peace's evangelical Christianity, as well as the Methodism of Dick Celeste and George McClain.[36]

Familial traditions also connected past and future. I think not only of my father's insistence of the contingency of my privilege but also of my grandmother's and mother's democratic socialism. Indeed, though evidence is scant, I suspect that for a good number of us our mother's politics shaped our commitments more than did our father's. Familial traditions worked their magic in other ways, seen in the long-term impact of Lehrman's Republicanism, Jared Lobdell's childhood reading on English literature, Sam Bowles commitment to public action and internationalism. Some of us, like Neil Herring and Sam Bowles, simultaneously fulfilled and challenged familial traditions. Two members of the John Dewey Society underscore how family traditions differed in their impact. Eric Walther turned away from the conservatism he learned growing up, while Jonny Weiss drew on his parents' liberal commitments.

What we read in the campus newspaper provides additional evidence that times were changing. In March 1957, when asked what were the leading topics of bull sessions, the *News* chairman replied that "we can rule out 'social reform,' whatever that means." Instead, he insisted that the most prominent issues under discussion were sex ("perennial number one"), our futures, and then "literature and art, ethics and metaphysics. . . . Politics has a place," he concluded, "but a relatively small one." Echoing influential 1950s social critics such as David Riesman and William H. Whyte Jr., he emphasized that the most urgent problem his peers faced after graduation was "maintaining some sort of creativity, individuality, aesthetic dimension," in the highly competitive and impersonal fields they entered.[37] When we arrived at Yale, the relationships between corporations, their workers, and labor unions were paramount in the pages of the *Yale Daily News* even if they did not command the attention of activists. As we were about to graduate, attention had shifted to race relations and to activism.

Additional signs of change are not hard to find. In fall 1956 Soviet-American relations dominated; by spring 1960 the nation's policies toward Africa were ascendant. Although what bracketed our time at Yale was the Soviet invasion of Hungary in our first semester and the shooting down of a CIA spy plane in our last, the Cold War was waning at home. When in our junior year Yale expressed serious reservations about taking federal funds for financial aid as long as students had to sign a loyalty oath, an editorial in the *Yale Daily News* stated, "We do not wish to go to college in the loyalty hunt atmosphere of the McCarthy days." When Jim Ottaway assumed the chairmanship of the *Yale Daily News* in late January 1959, he remarked, "We are against long cars, Communism, and the increasing volume of noise at Yale," in the process suggesting that opposition to communism had become a cliché.[38] In our first semester, Yalies revealed their anticommunist bona fides by protesting the Soviet invasion of Hungary; in our last semester some of us marched against racial segregation. Although the number of protestors was vastly larger in the fall 1956 rally than in spring 1960, nonetheless the shift in attention from Hungary to Greensboro, North Carolina, pointed forward to a new era.

"Emerging Movements of Change"

David Elliott may have sung "Eli Yale" as a Whiffenpoof during our senior year, a time when, as the song narrated, he indeed made good friends and studied only some. Three years later he unexpectedly embarked on a course that would transform him into a trenchant and learned critic of the war in Vietnam. In his analysis, offered at the beginning of this chapter, he was right when he said we were an "'in-between' generation" and that stereotypical pictures of the 1950s college student as a member of a silent generation provided "a thin veneer covering the emerging movements of change in civil rights, political orientation, and cultural attitudes that are now associated primarily with the decade of the 1960s. We were on the cusp of that decade," he concluded.

ABBREVIATIONS

25th RD	*Yale 60: Official 25th Reunion Directory* (New Haven: Yale Alumni Records Office, [1960])
30th RD	*Yale 60: 30th Reunion Directory* (New Haven: Yale Alumni Records Office, 1990)
35th RD	*35th Reunion Directory: Yale 1960* (New Haven: Office of Information Resources, 1995)
40th RD	*Yale 1960 40th Reunion Class Directory* (New Haven: Office of Information Resources, 1960)
Class Book 1960	*1960 Senior Class Book, Yale University* ([New Haven]: Yale Banner Publications, 1960)
Class of Its Own	*'60 . . . A Class of Its Own: Yale Class of 1960 50th Reunion Yearbook* (New Haven: Class Reunion Press, 1960)
DH/HLH	Daniel Horowitz and Helen L. Horowitz personal papers, Cambridge, MA
Schiffrin Papers	André Schiffrin Papers, Tamiment Library, New York University, New York, NY
SLID Papers	Student League for Industrial Democracy Papers, Tamiment Library, New York University, New York, NY
YAM	*Yale Alumni Magazine*
YDN	*Yale Daily News*
YUA	Yale University Manuscripts and Archives, Sterling Memorial Library, Yale University, New Haven, CT

NOTES

Preface

1. This and other biographical data comes from data in ancestry.com. In opening with the census, I am following Martha Sandweiss, *Passing Strange: A Gilded Age Tale of Love and Deception across the Color Line* (New York: Penguin, 2009), 1–3.

2. Mike Dickerson, telephone conversation, Jan. 30, 2014. Throughout the book, I distinguish between "telephone conversation" and in-person "conversation."

3. John Bing, conversation, Oct. 13, 2012.

4. Ted Stebbins, e-mail to author, Oct. 29, 2013.

5. John J. Black, Edward J. Coughlin, and Rudolph Kass, "Yale: For God, Country, and Success," *Harvard Crimson*, Nov. 25, 1950.

6. I rely here on Edmund Leites, telephone conversation, Jan. 20, 2014.

Introduction. On the Cusp in 1960

1. Throughout this book, I cite the class book and reunion books only if I am quoting or paraphrasing.

On Cold War consensus, see Wendy L. Wall, *Inventing the "American Way": The Politics of Consensus from the New Deal to the Civil Rights Movement* (New York: Oxford University Press, 2008).

2. Books that focus on one year and major events include Fred M. Kaplan, *1959: The Year Everything Changed* (Hoboken, NJ: Wiley, 2009); James T. Patterson, *The Eve of Destruction: How 1965 Transformed America* (New York: Basic, 2012); Christian Caryl, *Strange Rebels: 1979 and the Birth of the 21st Century* (New York: Basic, 2013).

3. Thomas Frank, *The Conquest of Cool: Business Culture, Counter Culture, and the Rise of Consumerism* (Chicago: University of Chicago Press, 1997) explores important connections between the two decades. For one of the many discussions of the relationships between 1950s and 1960s and of the long 1960s, see David Farber, review of *Freedom's Orator: Mario Savio and the Radical Legacy of the 1960s,* by Robert Cohen, *Reviews in American History* 39 (Dec. 2011): 712–17.

4. Otto Butz, ed., *The Unsilent Generation: An Anonymous Symposium in Which Eleven College Seniors Look at Themselves and Their World* (New York: Rinehart, 1958).

5. Peter M. Wolf, *My New Orleans, Gone Away: A Memoir of Loss and Renewal* (Harrison, NY: Delphinium, 2013), 90–148, captures key aspects of the class of 1957.

6. Richard Banbury, *YAM*, Jan./Feb. 2013, 83.

7. Kirke Wilson, conversation, Feb. 14, 2013.

8. Arthur Howe Jr., "Speech to Enrollment and Scholarship Convocation," Sept. 5, 1957, quoted in Joseph A. Soares, *The Power of Privilege: Yale and America's Elite Colleges* (Stanford: Stanford University Press, 2007), 55. I am relying here on suggestions from Maurice Isserman, conveyed to me in one of a series of e-mails in January 2014.

9. There are several genres pertinent to this study. Some works by historians combine the

personal and the scholarly, though not quite as I do: Lois W. Banner, *Finding Fran: History and Memory in the Lives of Two Women* (1998); Christopher Benfey, *Red Brick, Black Mountain, White Clay: Reflections on Art, Family, and Survival* (2012); Martin Duberman, *Cures: A Gay Man's Odyssey* (1991); Geoff Eley, *A Crooked Line: From Cultural History to the History of Society* (2005); Alice Wexler, *Mapping Fate: A Memoir of Family, Risk, and Genetic Research* (1995). I do not follow the most common path, revealed in too many books to list here, of how an author discovers some family secret. Nor do I do the genre blending represented by authors such as the novelist Michael Chabon or the anthropologist Ruth Behar. Several historians have written books on their lives but rarely use analytic techniques or original research to illuminate what they discuss: Jerold S. Auerbach, *Jacob's Voices: Reflections of a Wandering American Jew* (1996); John Morton Blum, *A Life with History* (2004); Morton Keller, *My Life and Times: A Historian's Progress through a Contentious Age* (2010). Among the exceptions are Gerda Lerner, *Fireweed: A Political Autobiography* (2002), and Henry F. May, *Coming to Terms: Study in Memory and History* (1987). Then there are two books that offer innovative takes on the juncture of history and memoir: Jack Metzgar, *Striking Steel: Solidarity Remembered* (2000), and Mark D. Naison, *White Boy: A Memoir* (2002). Three collections of essays successfully combine the personal and the scholarly: James M. Banner and John R. Gillis, eds., *Becoming Historians* (2009); Laura Lee Downs and Stéphane Gerson, eds., *Why France? American Historians Reflect on an Enduring Fascination* (2007); and Jeffrey Rubin-Dorsky and Shelley Fisher Fishkin, eds., *People of the Book: Thirty Scholars Reflect on Their Jewish Identity* (1996). For a thoughtful discussion of how historians write about their own lives, see Jeremy D. Popkin, *History, Historians, and Autobiography* (2005).

Several books focus on cohorts, but each in ways unlike what I do. Among them are Miriam Horn, *Rebels in White Gloves: Coming of Age with Hillary's Class—Wellesley '69* (1999); Michael Medved and David Wallechinsky, *What Really Happened to the Class of '65?* (1976); Sherry B. Ortner, *New Jersey Dreaming: Capital, Culture, and the Class of '58* (2003); Luisa Passerini, *Autobiography of a Generation: Italy, 1968,* trans. Lisa Erdberg (1996); Richard H. Pells, *War Babies: The Generation That Changed America* (2014); and Howard Gillette Jr., *Class Divide: Yale '64 and the Conflicted Legacy of the Sixties* (Ithaca: Cornell University Press, 2015). George E. Vaillant, *Adaptation to Life* (1977), is a longitudinal study of a group of Harvard graduates of classes from 1939 to 1944, which, although it has some socioeconomic data, as well as information on politics, social mobility, careers, and events, mainly focuses on the "adaptive mechanisms" these men use as they go through life. The essays in Kathleen Day Hulbert and Diane Tickton Schuster, eds., *Women's Lives through Time: Educated American Women of the Twentieth Century* (1993) present a series of model longitudinal studies of a series of cohorts of women.

10. In addition to Helen Lefkowitz Horowitz, *Campus Life: Undergraduate Cultures from the End of the Eighteenth Century to the Present* (New York: Knopf, 1987), here I am relying on Leonard H. Ellis, "Men among Men: An Exploration of All-Male Relationships in Victorian America" (PhD diss., Columbia University, 1982), 258–324.

11. Horowitz, *Campus,* 12–17 and 118–19, with quotes on 12, 14, and 16.

12. I use the term "major 'Y'" when that is the designation in the yearbook, even though I am not sure how this term differs from other designations, listed in various publications, for participation in varsity sports.

13. Bryant M. Wedge and James S. Davie, "The Psychosocial Position of the College Man," in *Psychosocial Problems of College Men,* ed. Bryant M. Wedge (New Haven: Yale University Press, 1958), 10–14.

14. James S. Davie, "Satisfaction and the College Experience," in Wedge, *Psychosocial,* 41 and 43; Horowitz, *Campus,* 149–50.

15. Gideon Gordon, "OCD Strategists Expect Usual Bladderball Victory," *YDN,* Nov. 1, 1958, 1; Gideon Gordon, "A Gentleman's Drinking Engagement," *YDN,* May 13, 1960, 4; "Trumbull Race Proves Waterloo for Umbawas," *YDN,* May 9, 1960, 1; David Gergen, "Requiem for a Geometer," *YDN,* May 20, 1960, 12.

16. Willis B. Boyer Jr., "Academia and the Old Blue," *YDN,* May 12, 1960, A-12.

17. "Inside Eli's," quoted in D. W. K. Sumner, "Inside Eli's Appears on Yale Scene to Mock Folly in Campus Activities," *YDN,* Nov. 1, 1956, 1; Calvin Trillin, *Remembering Denny* (New York: Farrar, Straus and Giroux, 1993), 7.

18. William Pollard Lamb Jr., "Senior Year," *Class Book 1960,* 34.

19. C. Howard Wilkins, letter to the editor, *YDN,* Dec. 5, 1858, 2; James H. Ottaway Jr., "Yale Fraternities Face a Future of Financial Crisis," *YDN,* Oct. 9, 1958, 4.

20. Monroe Price, "Undergraduate Yale," *YAM,* Dec. 1959, 28. On white fraternities nationally in the postwar period, especially how members discriminated against African Americans and Jews, see Nicolas L. Syrett, *The Company He Keeps: A History of White College Fraternities* (Chapel Hill: University of North Carolina Press, 2009), 229–61.

21. Gordon B. Chamberlain, "Among the Trumpets," *YDN,* May 7, 1959, 2.

22. Wedge and Davie, "Psychosocial," 11.

23. Saint Anthony Hall was a cross between a fraternity and senior society.

24. André Schiffrin and Michael G. Cooke, "If You Have the Time," *YDN,* April 18, 1957, 4; "Weiss Attacks, DeVane Defends Societies," *YDN,* May 1, 1957, 1; William Sloane Coffin Jr., quoted in Bruce Chabner, "Secret Societies Scored for Snobbery, Influence on Undergraduates' Values," *YDN,* April 23, 1959, 1. We will meet Schiffrin in a later chapter. Cooke may well have had multiple offers from aboveground senior societies despite his being an Afro-Caribbean: he was Class Day Poet, Scholar of the House, and All-American in soccer.

25. Wedge and Davie, "Psychosocial," 13.

26. Gerald Jonas, "Sound and Fury," *YDN,* Oct. 11, 1956, 2; Donald L. Robinson, "The Student Agencies: A Conspicuous Entity," *YDN,* Oct. 10, 1956, 2; and a series of articles by Robert G. Donnelley in *YDN:* "Service with a Pay Check," Oct. 23, 1958, 1 and 5; "Money: Scholarship and Otherwise," Oct. 24, 1958, 1 and 8; "A Double Standard of 'Self-Help,' " Oct. 28, 1958, 1 and 6.

27. In his senior year Schiffrin gave Aurelian new life by having it issue a report on intellectual apathy on campus after the administration blocked him and his colleagues from investigating the admissions office: "Aurelian Society Hits Yale Intellectual Apathy," *YDN,* April 19, 1957, 1; JHO [James H. Ottaway Jr.], "Honorable Apathy," *YDN,* Dec. 9, 1958, 2.

28. Peter M. Wolf, *New Orleans,* 131–32; Wedge and Davie, "Psychosocial," 11; James Sargent Campbell, "Academic History," *Class Book 1960,* 44–45.

29. Horowitz, *Campus,* 168.

30. George W. Pierson, *A Yale Book of Numbers: Historical Statistics of the College and University, 1701–1976* (New Haven: Yale University, 1983), 87, 98, 136, and 289. In discussing the composition of the class, I am relying heavily on the data gathering and analysis of Smith College student Emily Huesman.

31. Arthur Howe Jr., report to President and Corporation, Oct. 8, 1957, and "Statistics for Report to the President and Fellows," Oct. 1, 1957, Y31 + A13 1956–57, YUA.

32. Lee, *Class of Its Own,* 336; Ed Rhoads, e-mail to author, July 23, 2013; Dana Young, e-mails to author, Aug. 26 and 27, 2013. Lee, Young, and Oscar Tang had grandfathers who came to the United States with the Chinese Educational Mission, an effort Edward Rhoads chronicled in *Stepping Forth into the World: The Chinese Educational Mission to the United States, 1872–81* (Hong Kong: Hong Kong University Press, 2011).

33. Bill Garnsey, *Class Book 1960,* 417; *25th RD,* 49; *35th RD,* 68.

34. Lamb, "Senior," 35; Campbell, "Academic," 46.

35. Phip Hirsh, telephone conversation, Aug. 12, 2013.

36. A. Bartlett Giamatti, "Class Oration," *Class Book 1960,* 347–48.

37. Albert S. Pergam, "Class History," *Class Book 1960,* 350–51.

38. I am grateful to Jonathan Freedman of the University of Michigan for helping me puzzle out the meaning of "thinking Yiddish," which he did when he hosted my visit to Ann Arbor in the fall of 2012.

Chapter 1. Think Yiddish

1. For information on his years at Yale, see William Horowitz, interview by Geoffrey Kabaservice, May 7, 1991, Griswold-Brewster Oral History Project, RU 217, series 1, box 6, folder 74, YUA.

2. My discussion of admissions at Yale relies heavily on Jerome Karabel, *The Chosen: The Hidden History of Admission and Exclusion at Harvard, Yale, and Princeton* (Boston: Houghton Mifflin, 2005), 110–18, 200–226, 321–78, 412–27, 449–67, and 478–82, with the quote on 112. Still quite useful are Harold Wechsler, *The Qualified Student: A History of Selective College Admissions in America* (New York: John Wiley, 1977); Marcia G. Synnott, *The Half-Opened Door: Discrimination and Admissions at Harvard, Yale, and Princeton, 1900–1970* (Westport, CT: Greenwood, 1979), Dan A. Oren, *Joining the Club: A History of Jews and Yale* (New Haven: Yale University Press, 1985). Marcia G. Synnott, *Student Diversity at the Big Three: Changes at Harvard, Yale, and Princeton since the 1920s* (New Brunswick, NJ: Transaction, 2013), carries the discussion into the early twenty-first century and extends it beyond Jews to include homosexuals, the disabled, Latinos, African Americans, women, and students from outside the United States. The ideals of the humanistic Menorah Association were incompatible with my father's politics and religion: on this group, see Daniel Greene, *The Jewish Origins of Cultural Pluralism: The Menorah Association and American Diversity* (Bloomington: Indiana University Press, 2011); Seth Korelitz, "The Menorah Idea: From Religion to Culture, From Race to Ethnicity," *American Jewish History* 85 (March 1997): 75–100.

3. Karabel, *Chosen*, 110; Robert N. Corwin, "Memorandum on the Problems Arising from the Increase in the Enrollment of Students of Jewish Birth in the University," May 12, 1922, and "Limitation of Numbers," Jan. 9, 1923, quoted in Karabel, *Chosen*, 111 and 112.

4. Robert N. Corwin, report as chairman of Board of Admissions, in "Reports to the President of Yale University," *Bulletin of Yale University*, 21st series, no. 24, Sept. 1, 1925 (New Haven: Yale University, 1925), 5–16; A. Whitney Griswold, quoted in André Schiffrin, *A Political Education: Coming of Age in Paris and New York* (Hoboken, NJ: Melville House, 2007), 123.

5. "An Ellis Island for Yale," *YDN*, March 30, 1926, quoted in Karabel, *Chosen*, 115.

6. S. S. Snell, letter of recommendation, June 6, 1924, in author's possession. The figures come from George W. Pierson, *A Yale Book of Numbers: Historical Statistics of the College and University, 1701–1976* (New Haven: Yale University, 1983), 87.

7. Robert N. Corwin, "Memo on Jewish Representation in Yale," May 26, 1922, quoted in Karabel, *Chosen*, 112; Karabel, *Chosen*, 118.

8. My discussion of the Rostow family draws on David Milne, *America's Rasputin: Walt Rostow and the Vietnam War* (New York: Hill and Wang, 2008), especially 16–31, quote on 18.

9. Walt W. Rostow, *Concept and Controversy: Sixty Years of Taking Ideas to Market* (Austin: University of Texas Press, 2003), 7; award description is in the Wikipedia entry for Eugene Rostow. Karabel, *Chosen*, 210 discusses Rostow's 1945 call for a more meritocratic admissions policy in the wake of what World War II revealed about Hitler's racism.

10. Eugene Rostow, "The Jew's Position," *Harkness Hoot*, Nov. 23, 1931, quoted in Karabel, *Chosen*, 118. James Rowland Angell to Robert N. Corwin, Jan. 6, 1933, quoted in Karabel, *Chosen*, 119. On the treatment of Sapir, see Regna Darnell, *Edward Sapir: Linguist, Anthropologist, Humanist* (Berkeley: University of California Press, 1990), 400–402. Sapir was a member of the graduate faculty but not the faculty of Yale College, then an important distinction.

11. Will Herberg, *Protestant-Catholic-Jew: An Essay in American Religious Sociology* (1955; rev. ed., Garden City, NY: Doubleday, 1960), 178; Philip M. Klutznick with Sidney Hyman, *Angles of Vision: A Memoir of My Lives* (Chicago: Ivan R. Dee, 1991), 44. For my grandfather's job on the railroad, see Sol D. Chain, "The New Havener," *New Haven Info*, July 1965, 17. One of my father's sisters died when my father was young; the other one, Rose Horowitz Marks, had an education after high school, but hardly one that matched a BA from Yale.

12. Herberg, *Protestant*, 18. K. Healan Gaston, "The Cold War Romance of Religious Authenticity: Will Herberg, William F. Buckley Jr., and the Rise of the New Right," *Journal of American History* 99 (March 2013): 1133–58, captures the opposition to secularism and ethnic particularism of Herberg's 1955 book.

13. Card for William Horowitz, in "Yale College Student Records," RU 587, acc. 2002-A-003, box 22, YUA; Daniel Horowitz, "it is perhaps," autobiographical essay, academic year 1959–60, in author's possession.

14. My father described his tight finances in letters to his family dated Dec. 18, 1926, March 9, 1927, April 28, 1927, and May 7, 1928, DH/HLH. At the time, Yale had rates for dorm rooms that varied from $762 to $110; my father could only afford the least expensive: "The Undergraduate Schools," *Bulletin of Yale University*, 23rd series, no. 15, 225 and 229–35.

15. Joshua Zelinsky, "William Horowitz and Yale: Styles of Jewish Leadership in American History," Advanced Placement essay, April 8, 2002, 3 and 6, copy in author's possession, discusses my father's role in arranging the visit of Weizmann and more generally his outsider status at Yale.

16. Paul Mellon with John Baskett, *Reflections in a Silver Spoon: A Memoir* (New York: William Morrow, 1992), 68 and 109. For descriptions of Yale soon after my father graduated, see Gaddis Smith, "Life at Yale during the Great Depression," *YAM*, Nov./Dec. 2009.

17. Mellon, *Reflections*, 112, 115–16, and 117.

18. The evidence here is contradictory: the 1910 census has her born in New York, while the 1930 one lists Illinois; relying on stories she told me, I locate her first on Maxwell Street in Chicago and then on the Lower East Side. For general background information, see Jonathan D. Sarna, ed., *Jews in New Haven* (New Haven: Jewish Historical Society of New Haven, 1978).

19. David Laskin, *The Family: Three Journeys Into the Heart of the Twentieth Century* (New York: Viking, 2013), 25, calls my grandfather Hayim Yehoshua. For additional information on the family of my material grandfather I am relying on David Laskin, e-mail to author, March 28, 2012; David Laskin, telephone conversation, April 3, 2012.

20. S. B. Goodkind, *Eminent Jews of America: A Collection of Biographical Sketches of Jews Who Have Distinguished Themselves in Commercial, Professional, and Religious Endeavor* (Toledo: American Hebrew Biographical, 1938), 32–33. At its height, supported by government contracts in World War II and the Korean War, the company employed about one hundred people in Hamden, a similar number in Worcester, and a small number in Manhattan. On this and other issues, I am relying on Lainie Lipsher and Larry Lipsher, telephone conversation, Aug. 3, 2011. Further information is contained in Botwinik Brothers, "World Famous for Reliability and Service," pamphlet, c. 1950, DH/HLH. For general background, see Eli Lederhendler, *Jewish Immigrants and American Capitalism, 1880–1920* (Cambridge: Cambridge University Press, 2009). Jennifer Le Zotte discusses Jews as scrap dealers in the early twentieth century and the prejudice against this and other secondhand businesses in "From Goodwill to Grunge: Secondhand Consumerism in Twentieth-Century United States," PhD diss., University of Virginia, 2013, chaps. 1 and 2.

21. Laskin, *Family*, 317; www.eilatgordinlevitan.com/rakov/rakov.html.

22. Of my classmates, approximately 26 percent were Italian Americans; 20 percent Jews; 15 percent African Americans (some from the Caribbean); 6 percent Irish Americans; 3 percent Polish Americans: *The Elm Tree as Presented to the Class of 1956* (New Haven: Hillhouse High School, 1956).

23. Financial statement for William and Miriam Horowitz, July 15, 1955, in author's possession. Because he used the book value for his largest holding, he may have underestimated his net worth.

24. Robert Dahl, *Who Governs: Democracy and Power in an American City* (New Haven: Yale University Press, 1961), 74. It was indeed a small bank: in 1954, its total deposits were just above $1 million: General Industrial Bank, "Comparative Statement of Condition," for the year ending Dec. 31, 1954, in author's possession.

25. www.hartfordradiohistory.com/WBIB-FM.html says Sol Chain owned WBIB. My best recollection, confirmed by my father's interview with Kabaservice, is that Chain was the manager of WBIB but that the Botwinik-Horowitz group was the principal owners. A partial listing of his activities is given in "Horowitz, William," from *Who's Who in America*, mid-1970s, copy in DH/HLH; S. D. C. [Sol D. Chain], "William Horowitz, Yale Corporation Candidate," *Info*, June 1964, 10–11.

26. On the role my father played in helping to buy machine tools for the Haganah soon after World War II, see Leonard Slater, *The Pledge* (New York: Simon and Schuster, 1970), 41.

27. Florence B. Johnson, "The Treasurer Is a Lady," *Info,* July 1954, 9.

28. On the influence of James on Harlow, see S. Ralph Harlow, *Thoughts for Times Like These* (New York: Philosophical Library, 1957), 3.

29. Nothing better represents the political differences between my parents than their divergent reactions, late in their lives, to Joe Lieberman. In fall 1960 when he entered Yale College, Lieberman opened a bank account at General Industrial Bank. My father befriended him and helped him get his start in Connecticut politics. Lieberman reciprocated by naming my parents the godparents to his son Matthew. Later on, my father sustained his support for Lieberman while my mother dissented from Lieberman's opposition to the right to abortion and more generally from his increasing conservatism.

30. Dahl, *Governs,* 64 and 86.

31. Dahl problematically stated that African Americans were "not discriminated against in city employment; they have only to meet the qualifications required of white applicants to become policemen, fireman, school teachers, clerks, stenographers": Dahl, *Governs,* 293–94.

32. K. A. Cuordileone, *Manhood and American Political Culture in the Cold War* (New York: Routledge, 2005); James Gilbert, *Men in the Middle: Searching for Masculinity in the 1950s* (Chicago: University of Chicago Press, 2005); Barbara Ehrenreich, *Hearts of Men: American Dreams and the Flight from Commitment* (Garden City, NY: Anchor, 1983); Robert L. Griswold, *Fatherhood in America: A History* (New York: Basic, 1993); Michael Kimmel, *Manhood in America: A Cultural History,* 3rd ed. (New York: Oxford University Press, 2012); Elaine Tyler May, *Homeward Bound: American Families in the Cold War Era* (New York: Basic, 1988); E. Anthony Rotundo, *American Manhood: Transformations in Masculinity from the Revolution to the Modern Era* (New York: Basic, 1993).

33. David Riesman, *The Lonely Crowd: A Study in the Changing American Character* (New Haven: Yale University Press, 1950), 295; Gilbert, *Middle,* 3.

34. On some of the historical dimensions of these changes, see Lizabeth Cohen, *A Consumer's Republic: The Politics of Mass Consumption in Postwar America* (New York: Knopf, 2003).

35. Daniel Horowitz, letter, March 12, 1950, in possession of Benjamin Horowitz, Pleasanton, CA.

Chapter 2. Dress British

1. Noah Feldman, "The Triumphant Decline of the WASP," *New York Times,* June 27, 2010. Marcia G. Synnott, *Student Diversity at the Big Three: Changes at Harvard, Yale, and Princeton since the 1920s* (New Brunswick, NJ: Transaction, 2013), 299–302, discusses how many writers, including E. Digby Baltzell, have focused on the notion of a decline of a WASP elite. In *After Cloven Tongues of Fire: Protestant Liberalism in Modern American History* (Princeton: Princeton University Press, 2013), esp. 18–55, David A. Hollinger offers a different assessment by emphasizing how after 1945 mainline Protestants, although they conceded ground, profoundly shaped American thought and culture.

2. For the Ivy style at the height of its influence on campuses, see Patricia Mears, "Ivy Style: Heyday of the Mid-Century," in *Ivy Style: Radical Conformist,* ed. Patricia Mears (New Haven: Yale University Press, 2012), 93–111. See also Deirdre Clemente, *Dress Casual: How College Students Redefined American Style* (Chapel Hill: University of North Carolina Press, 2014); Rebecca C. Tuite, *Seven Sisters Style: The All-American Preppy Look* (New York: Rizzoli, 2014); Gabriel Goldstein and Elizabeth Greenberg, eds., *A Perfect Fit: The Garment Industry and American Jewry (1860–1960)* (Lubbock: Texas Tech University Press, 2103).

3. Patricia Mears, "Inter-War Years and the Birth of Ivy Style," in Mears, *Ivy Style,* 40–42.

4. Brooks Brothers, founded in 1818, was sold in 1946 to Julius Garfinckel and Co., founded in 1905 by the son of Jewish immigrants: John William Cooke, *Generations of Style: It's All About the Clothing* (New York: Brooks Brothers, 2003). On another Jewish clothing merchant, see Joshua Levine, *The Rise and Fall of the House of Barneys: A Family Tale of Chutzpah, Glory,*

and Greed (New York: William Morrow, 1999). It is also quite possible that Jews founded Jos. A. Banks. On how gentlemen should dress, see Jenna Weissman Joselit, *A Perfect Fit: Clothes, Character, and the Promise of America* (New York: Metropolitan Books, 2001), 75–99.

5. For a genealogy of stores offering the Ivy League style, see "The Art of Wearing Clothes," www.dandyism.net, and Richard Press, "Tradition and Change: The J. Press Interview, Part II," July 15, 2009, www.ivy-style.com. Also see "Golden Years: Introducing the Richard Column," April 15, 2011, and "Family Guy: The Richard Press Interview," March 28, 2011, at www.ivy-style.com.

6. Richard Press, "Golden Years: Shoe vs. Weenie," Sept. 8, 2011, www.ivy-style.com.

7. D. H. Marchman, *YAM*, 1942, quoted in Brooks M. Kelley, *Yale: A History* (New Haven: Yale University Press, 1974), 433. This is Kelley's citation, but I have been unable to locate the original article.

8. Fred Horowitz, e-mail to author, Oct. 27, 2012. In *Truth Comes in Blows* (New York: Norton, 1998), 251–53 and 278, Ted Solotaroff tells the story of his late 1940s interview for admission at Yale in which a combination of his feistiness about the Jewish quota and his distinctly non–Ivy League dress helped kill his chances.

9. "The Ivy League Look Heads Across U.S.," *Life*, Nov. 22, 1954, 70. This history relies on Richard Press, telephone conversation, Jan. 28, 2011; "Family Guy," ivy-style.com interview. See also Richard Press, "J. Press and Yale," talk before class of Jay Gitlin, Yale, fall 2011, copy in author's possession; Richard Press, "Family Guy: An Interview with Christian Chensvold," in Mears, *Ivy Style*, 75–91. For a discussion of dress at Yale in the mid-1950s, see Calvin Trillin, *Remembering Denny* (New York: Farrar, Straus and Giroux, 1993), 30–32.

10. George C. [Hutchinson] III, "'Getting There Is Half the Fun,'" *Yale Record*, Sept. 1956, 24.

11. Lisa Birnbach, ed., *The Official Preppy Handbook* (New York: Workman, 1980), 11, 121, and 152. For a precursor to the handbook, see Nelson Aldrich Jr., "Preppies: The Last Upper Class?," *Atlantic Monthly*, Jan. 1979, 56–66.

12. For the trans-Pacific circulation of styles, see Masafumi Monden, "Ivy in Japan: A Regalia of Non-Conformity and Privilege," in Mears, *Ivy Style*, 175–85.

13. "Family Guy," ivy-style.com interview; James Axtell, *The Making of Princeton University: From Woodrow Wilson to the Present* (Princeton: Princeton University Press, 2006), 312 and 320; Owen Johnson, *Stover at Yale* (1912; New York: Macmillan, 1968), 55.

14. Press, telephone conversation.

15. Cavlin Trillin, *Messages from My Father* (New York: Farrar, Straus and Giroux, 1996), 78.

16. Calvin Trillin, telephone conversation, May 21, 2014, insists that although he told my father of a relatively low grade in Latin and my father told him to apply to other schools as well as Yale, the stink-bomb story concerns one of Trillin's classmates, not Trillin himself.

17. Bryce E. Nelson, "Against Prep Schools: Toddlers in Tweeds," *Ivy Magazine* 2 (Dec. 1957): 8; Mike Thomas, "Against High Schools: The Suede Shoe Set," *Ivy Magazine* 2 (Dec. 1957): 11 and 12. Joseph A. Soares, *The Power of Privilege: Yale and America's Elite Colleges* (Stanford: Stanford University Press, 2007), 10–12 relies on Pierre Bourdieu to emphasize how elite universities protected their brand by emphasizing privilege.

18. Trillin, *Denny*, 39 and 41.

19. Charles Schmitz, "My Yale: Plan B," 2010, 2, copy in author's possession.

20. Because I cannot locate the report on my class, I am relying on statistics for the classes of 1959 and 1961: Harold B. Whiteman Jr., letter to A. Whitney Griswold, in *Report to the President*, July 31, 1956, 1–7; Arthur Howe Jr., reports on admissions and financial aid, *Report to President and Fellows* on class of 1961, Oct. 1 and Oct. 8, 1957.

21. Whiteman Jr., letter to Griswold, 3.

22. For figures for the class of 1961, see Whiteman, letter to Griswold, 4; for my own record, see Daniel Horowitz folder, box 160, Yale College Student Records for the Classes of 1904 to the Present, RU 587 acc. 1961-A-004, YUA. On how predictions of student accomplishment favored those from elite backgrounds, see Soares, *Privilege*, 27–33.

23. Robert N. Corwin to Francis Parsons, Oct. 1, 1929, quoted in Jerome Karabel, *The Chosen: The Hidden History of Admission and Exclusion at Harvard, Yale, and Princeton* (Boston: Houghton Mifflin, 2005), 117.

24. Charles Seymour, Inaugural Address, Oct. 16, 1937, quoted in William F. Buckley Jr., *God and Man at Yale: The Superstitions of "Academic Freedom"* (1951: Washington, DC: Regnery Gateway, 1986), 43.

25. Buckley Jr., *God and Man*, 30.

26. McGeorge Bundy, "The Attack on Yale," *Atlantic Monthly*, Nov. 1951, 50 and 52; William F. Buckley Jr., "The Changes at Yale," and McGeorge Bundy, "McGeorge Bundy Replies," *Atlantic Monthly*, Dec. 1951, 78, 80, 82, and 84. On Holden's role, see Wayne Thorburn, *A Generation Awakes: Young Americans for Freedom and the Creation of the Conservative Movement* (Ottawa, IL: Jameson, 2010), 7.

27. Henry Sloane Coffin to unidentified Yale alumnus, quoted in Buckley, Introduction to 1977 Edition, *God and Man,* xxi; Frank Ashburn, "'Isms' and the University,'" *Saturday Review of Literature,* Dec. 15, 1951, 45.

28. In *A Nation of Outsiders: How the White Middle Class Fell in Love with Rebellion in Postwar America* (New York: Oxford University Press, 2011), Grace E. Hale explores many dimensions of the romance of the outsider. Robert A. Burt, *Two Jewish Justices: Outcasts in the Promised Land* (Berkeley: University of California Press, 1988), 1 makes clear how different a situation Jews of my generation faced at Yale Law School.

29. In this discussion of the variety of Jewish experiences at Yale, I am relying on conversations with Jewish classmates, but especially on Fred Horowitz, telephone conversation, Oct. 30, 2012 and e-mails of Oct. 23 and Oct. 27, 2012.

30. There was relatively little discussion of Jews in the *Yale Daily News*. However, in the fall of 1956 a controversy erupted over the issue of the loyalty to America of Jews who were Zionists: "Dr. Weiss' Address," *YDN,* Oct. 2, 1956, 2; Mitchell C. Kur, letter to the editor, *YDN,* Oct. 4, 1956, 2; Jess Cook, letter to the editor, *YDN,* Oct. 6, 1960, 2.

31. Two other classmates, the cousins Fred and Joe Schwerin, had Jewish ancestry that they became aware of years after graduating from Yale.

32. Philip Hirsh, *Voices from the Hollow: What Happened When the Blue Bloods Met the Blue Ridge* (Buena Vista, VA: Mariner, 2005), 23; Phip Hirsh, telephone conversation, Aug. 11, 2013.

33. Monroe Price, *Objects of Remembrance: A Memoir of American Opportunities and Viennese Dreams* (New York: Central European University Press, 2009), 119.

34. In his 1953 talk to entering students, Professor Richard Sewall discussed Yale as "a stepping-stone to what we Americans fondly call 'success'": Sewall, quoted in Trillin, *Denny,* 50.

35. Bryant M. Wedge and James S. Davie, "The Psychosocial Position of the College Man," in *Psychosocial Problems on College Men,* ed. Bryant Wedge (New Haven: Yale University Press, 1958).

36. Lynda Glennon, "Yale: Reflections on Class in New Haven," *Yale Review* 67 (Summer 1978): 629 and 638; Schmitz, "My Yale," 3.

37. DH to HL, June 9, 1960. Correspondence with family members I cite throughout this book is in the author's possession.

38. "Education: Dean of Deans," *Time,* October 19, 1962, 37; William Sloane Coffin Jr., interview with Warren Goldstein, December 29, 1993, in Warren Goldstein, *William Sloane Coffin Jr.: A Holy Impatience* (New Haven: Yale University Press, 2004), 106–7.

39. Goldstein, *Coffin,* ix, 67, and 330. On his family and life, see alsoWilliam Sloane Coffin Jr., *Once to Every Man: A Memoir* (New York: Atheneum, 1977).

40. William Sloane Coffin Jr., Commencement Address, June 13, 1960, quoted in Goldstein, *Coffin,* 107–8.

41. J. Steven Renkert, "Intellectual Promise Not Enough to Assure Matriculation at Yale," *YDN,* Sept. 12, 1957, 21. In January 1959 Griswold publicly denied there was a quota for Jews but in May a student named Richard Weinert wondered if the heavy emphasis placed on interviews in the admissions process favored those with social poise rather than "imagination and creativity": "Harvard and Yale Deny Discrimination in Admissions," *YDN,* Jan. 7, 1960, 2; Richard Weinert, letter to the editor, *YDN,* May 19, 1960, 2.

42. James G. Hershberg, *James B. Conant: Harvard to Hiroshima and the Making of the Nuclear Age* (New York: Knopf, 1993), 80; Geoffrey Kabaservice, "The Birth of a New Institution:

How Two Yale Presidents and their Admission Directors Tore Up the 'Old Blueprint' to Create a Modern Yale," *YAM*, December 1999.

43. In telling the story of undergraduate admissions at Yale, I have relied on Dan A. Oren, *Joining the Club: A History of Jews and Yale* (New Haven: Yale University Press, 1985), 173–214 and on the relevant sections of Karabel, *Chosen*.

44. A. Whitney Griswold, quoted in Geoffrey Kabaservice, The *Guardians: Kingman Brewster, His Circle, and the Rise of the Liberal Establishment* (New York: Henry Holt, 2004), 155; Kabaservice, "Birth"; Alfred Whitney Griswold, "What We Don't Know Will Hurt Us: The Power of Liberal Education [1954]," in *In the University Tradition* (New Haven: Yale University Press, 1957), 24–25.

45. Trillin, *Denny*, 33 and 36; Trillin, quoted in Kabaservice, "Birth." For the numbers who came from these private schools, see Arthur Howe Jr., "Statistics for Report to the President and Fellows," Oct. 1, 1957, in Howe, "Report."

46. William Horowitz to A. Whitney Griswold, April 5, 1960, quoted in Oren, *Joining*, 191; A. Whitney Griswold, memo, April 5, 1960, quoted in Oren, *Joining*, 191–92.

47. Coffin, *Once*, 137–38. The article by Katherine Kinkead, discussed in Karabel, *Chosen*, 326–29, appeared in the Sept. 10, 1960, issue.

48. Karabel, *Chosen*, 336–37. As often happened, Yale was following in Harvard's footsteps, especially the 1960 report Admission to Harvard College: Karabel, *Chosen*, 248–93.

49. Leonard Doob, reported in Kabaservice, "Birth", "The Education of First Year Students in College," *YAM*, June 1962, 10; Oren, *Joining*, 204. On the composition of the class of 1967, see Kabaservice, "Birth."

50. For biographical information, I am relying on material provided by Sarah Hartwell at the Rauner Special Collections Library, Dartmouth College, including the form Doob filled out on matriculation, Sept. 14, 1925. On his identity as a Jew, my sources are Christopher Doob, telephone conversation, Jan. 16, 2012; Anthony Doob, telephone conversation, Feb. 23, 2012; Doob's FBI file, copy in author's possession. On his radicalism, see Leonard W. Doob, "Thomas and a Third Party," *Tomahawk*, Oct. 1928, 14. On the study of student politics, see Gordon W. Allport, "The Composition of Political Attitudes," *American Journal of Sociology* 35 (Sept. 1929): 229; Leonard W. Doob, "Political Opinion at Dartmouth," *Tomahawk*, June 1929, 8–9. Doob was a version of the Czech name Dub: Anthony Doob, e-mail to author, Feb. 23, 2012. After Dartmouth, Doob spent 1930–32 in Frankfurt, Germany, studying with Karl Mannheim and Max Wertheimer, and in early 1933 he learned that his Jewish mentors had fled into exile. Soon after he returned to America, he followed Allport to Harvard, where he earned his PhD, and in 1934 began more than four decades on the Yale faculty. On his views of the situation in Germany, see Leonard W. Doob to Ernest M. Hopkins [Oct. 1931], and Leonard W. Doob to Ernest M. Hopkins, Dec. 18, 1931, both in President Ernest M. Hopkins, folder on Fellowships, OP-11 (6911): G7, Rauner Special Collections Library, Dartmouth College, Hanover, NH.

51. Oren, *Joining*, 258; on the Sapir story, see 131–34. For the academic year 1950–51, three Jews were promoted to full professor: Doob, Erich Auerbach, and Bernard Bloch. In thinking about Doob's identity, I have benefited from talking to several people, especially Sidney Blatt, telephone conversation, Feb. 23, 2012, and a series of e-mails with Dan Oren, Feb.–March 2012. In addition to those cited elsewhere, I have learned from the telephone conversations with Thomas Achenbach, Feb. 17, 2012; Allan Wagner, Feb. 21, 2012; and Sidney Mintz, Feb. 8, 2012; and e-mails from Mintz of Feb. 16 and March 30, 2012. For the story of the appointment of Jews to the faculty, see Oren, *Joining*, 259–69. Doob surely knew that in *The Nature of Prejudice* (1954) his mentor Gordon Allport explored how contact with people from different backgrounds could reduce prejudice.

52. On the Chaunceys, Yale, Harvard, and the SAT, see Nicholas Lemann, *The Big Test: The Secret History of the American Meritocracy* (New York: Farrar, Straus and Giroux, 1999), esp. 3–10, 15–16, 57–70, 97–100, 140–53, and 183–84. On the changes Brewster and Clark wrought and the reactions against them, see Karabel, *Chosen*, 349–77, 412–27, and 449–67.

53. Karabel, *Chosen*, 478–82. On the limits to which Yale and other elite institutions embraced merit in undergraduate admissions, see Soares, *Privilege*, chaps. 1–4. William F. Buckley Jr.,

among others, led the protests against the directions in which Yale was headed: William F. Buckley Jr., "What Makes Bill Buckley Run," *Atlantic Monthly,* April 1968, quoted in Karabel, *Chosen,* 362–63.

54. Frederick Robert Shaw, class of 1955, letter to *YAM,* March 2000.

55. Pat McPherson, conversation, mid-August 2010.

56. William C. DeVane, "Report of the Dean of the College, Yale Report to the President, 1947–48," quoted in Oren, *Joining,* xiv; *Time,* quoted in Karabel, *Chosen,* 322. See Karabel, *Chosen,* 325, for concern at Yale over the university's standing vis à vis Harvard.

57. Karabel, *Chosen,* 326. On how institutions of higher education fared in producing leaders, see George W. Pierson, *The Education of American Leaders: Comparative Contributions of U.S. Colleges and Universities* (New York: Praeger, 1969). In 1959 parents of winners of National Merit Scholarships ranked Yale forth, way behind number one Harvard: "Parents of National Scholarship Winners Rank Yale Nation's Fourth Best College," *YDN,* Feb. 9, 1959, 2. At the time the campus newspaper reported that Yale was behind Harvard, MIT, Radcliffe, Caltech, and Stanford: Gideon Gordon, "Yale 6th Choice of Merit Scholars," *YDN,* Feb. 11, 1959, 1.

58. "Admissions III," *YDN,* Sept. 23, 1957, 2; "5 Yale Students Among 32 Winners of Rhodes Scholarships in Country," *YDN,* Jan. 5, 1960, 2.

59. http://rhodesscholars.wordpress.com/2007/07/13/leslie-epstein/; Leslie Epstein, *Class of Its Own,* 223.

60. George Akerlof, Peter Diamond, Murray Gell-Mann, Paul Krugman, and James E. Rothman were clearly identified as Jews. Alfred Goodman Gilman had a Jewish father, but he did not consider himself a Jew or participate in any organized Jewish activity: Alfred Gilman, e-mail to author, Jan. 10, 2012; see also István Hargittai, "Alfred G. Gilman," in István Hargittai, *Candid Science II: Conversations with Famous Biomedical Scientists,* ed. Magdolna Hargittai (London: Imperial College Press, 2002), 245–46. 239–51. On the relationship between the entrance of Jews into the professoriate, the enhanced role of science, and the decline of the Protestant establishment, see David A. Hollinger, *Science, Jews, and Secular Culture: Studies in Mid-Twentieth-Century American Intellectual History* (Princeton: Princeton University Press, 1996), 7.

61. From 1941 to 1966, Bronx High School of Science, Manhattan's Stuyvesant High School, and Brooklyn's James Madison High School produced among them fifteen Nobel laureates, almost all Jews. Many of them went to Ivy League institutions but none to Yale: see "Nobel Prize Laureates by Secondary School Affiliation" at http://en.wikipedia.org; this list is incomplete. For Jewish Nobels, see "Jewish Biographies: Nobel Prize Laureates" at www.jewishvirtuallibrary.org. Between 1950 and 1954, only 7 graduates of Bronx High entered Yale, while 275 from Andover did.

62. This summary of Yale's record relies on Roger L. Geiger, *Research and Relevant Knowledge: American Research Universities since World War II* (New York: Oxford University Press, 1993), 31, 82–90, 106, 108, 111 (quotation), and 116. In the funding from foundations for the social sciences from 1946–58, Yale ranked fourth, at a dollar level that was almost a third of Harvard's, which ranked number one. On the post–World War II emergence of federal funding of university research, see Rebecca S. Lowen, *Creating the Cold War University: The Transformation of Stanford* (Berkeley: University of California Press, 1997).

63. On the NSF, see Mark Solovey, *Shaky Foundations: The Politics–Patronage–Social Science Nexus in Cold War America* (New Brunswick: Rutgers University Press, 2013).

64. J. Merton England, *A Patron for Pure Science: The National Science Foundation's Formative Years, 1945–57* (Washington, DC: National Science Foundation, 1983), 204–6 and 231; Toby Appel, *Shaping Biology: The National Science Foundation and American Biological Research, 1945–1975* (Baltimore: Johns Hopkins University Press, 2000), 82. I am grateful to Marc Rothenberg, NSF agency historian, for helping me research this topic.

65. NSF grants to Yale with a start date of January 1, 1960, totaled $3.3 million; replacing that would require $66–80,000,000 in endowment or $500–610,000,000 million in 2011 dollars. For the figures, see www.nsf.gov/awardsearch. My calculations offer a range of figures, depending on the draw on the endowment.

66. Karabel, *Chosen,* 372; Pierson, *Yale Book,* 614.

67. Oren, *Joining,* 207.

68. Sam Chauncey, a member of the Yale administration knowledgeable about such matters, made clear that the nominating committee did not intentionally put my father against less than compelling candidates: telephone conversation, Dec. 21, 2011.

69. John C. Devlin, "Trustee of Yale Breaks Tradition: Horowitz, Jewish Executive, Is First Non-Protestant on University's Board," *New York Times,* June 21, 1965, 31. John Mortimer Schiff, class of 1925 and from a German Jewish banking family, had run unsuccessfully as an official nominee. William Horowitz served as an alumni trustee, not a successor trustee.

70. www.scribd.com/doc/44396826/Skull-and-Bones-Brochure. Among them Lindsay; Governor of Pennsylvania William Scranton; Secretary of State Cyrus Vance; PanAm founder Juan T. Trippe; Federal Reserve head William McChesney Martin; chair of Rockefeller Center J. Richardson Dilworth; president of Carnegie Institution Caryl Haskins; Assistant Secretary of State William Bundy; U.S. Commissioner of Education Harold Howe II; Episcopal Bishop of New York Paul Moore Jr.; Cummins Corporation head J. Irwin Miller; and art collector, media investor, and philanthropist John Hay "Jock" Whitney.

71. William Horowitz, "Yiddishkeit at Yale's Bradford College," *Jewish Digest,* November 1973, 54–56. On the larger story of ethnic pride, see Matthew Frye Jacobson, *Roots Too: White Ethnic Revival in Post-Civil Rights America* (Cambridge: Harvard University Press, 2006).

72. William Horowitz quoted in "Yale Student Petition Supports Brewster's Stand on Panthers," *YDN,* April 30, 1970, 1.

73. Bill Scranton and Bill Horowitz, handwritten note, in author's possession. In 1971, the Corporation chose Lance Liebman as the first Jew among the successor trustees and Hanna Holborn Gray as the first female among the successor trustees. On the broader story of the struggles over the opening up of American society, see John D. Skrentny, *The Minority Rights Revolution* (Cambridge: Harvard University Press, 2002).

74. Lance Liebman, telephone conservation, Jan. 2, 2012.

75. See Kabaservice, *Guardians,* 10–13 on how the northeastern elite understood it had to change and in doing so continue to provide leadership.

Chapter 3. In White America

1. "Faubus: A Man on the Spot," *YDN,* Sept. 19, 1957, 4; Jonathan J. Seagle, "Public School Segregation and Democratic Principles," *Rostrum* (Yale Political Union), Sept. 1960, 10 11.

2. Tuttle and officer quoted in "Montgomery: Tension in the Heart of Dixie," March 23, 1960, 1. The Salisbury article was probably "350 Negro Student Demonstrators Held in South Carolina Stockade," *New York Times,* March 16, 1960. See also e-mail from George Akerlof to Monroe Price, Aug. 31, 2011, copy in author's possession. For the articles in *YDN,* see George A. Akerlof and Monroe E. Price, " 'No Force Under the Sun," March 21, 1960, 1 and 4; "Two Cities Face Racial Problems," March 22, 1960, 1 and 4; "A Decision for the Split Peach State," March 24, 1960, 1 and 3; "Centennial of Protest," April 6, 1960, 1 and 4.

3. Robert M. Mallano, "Sophomore Year," *Class Book 1960,* 23. For statistics on the local African American population, see Tianna N. Terry, "Racial Residential Integration in Greater New Haven in the Post–Civil Rights Era," Yale Law School, Student Scholarship Papers, no. 50, May 11, 2007, 42.

4. Ralph C. Bryant III, "Junior Year," *Class Book 1960,* 32; Herschel E. Post Jr., "Oak Street Ghetto Sheds Squalid Past; Tenements Fall Before Renewal Plans," *YDN,* Oct. 2, 1959, 1, and "The Fine Art of Relocation," *YDN,* Oct. 6, 1959, 1. For the more typical coverage of urban renewal, see Robert B. Semple Jr., "Yale-Stevens Syndicate Submits Offer for Ten-Acre Oak Street Residential Site," *YDN,* May 1, 1957, 1. For one historian's assessment of urban renewal in New Haven, see Lizabeth Cohen, "Place, People, and Power: City Building in Postwar America," inaugural lecture, October 15, 2012, Radcliffe Institute for Advanced Study, Harvard, video available at www .radcliffe.harvard.edu/video/place-people-and-power-city-building-in-postwar-america.

5. Robert Penn Warren, *Segregation: The Inner Conflict in the South* (New York: Random House, 1956), 53 and 65–66. For reporting on how knowledgeable faculty looked at school

integration in the South, see Albert S. Pergam, "Faculty Views Integration Crisis," *YDN*, Sept. 25, 1958, 1.

6. Rollin G. Osterweis, *Romanticism and Nationalism in the Old South* (New Haven: Yale University Press, 1949), vii and 6; see also Rollin G. Osterweis, *The Myth of the Lost Cause, 1865–1900* (Hamden, CT: Shoe String Press, 1973).

7. John Dollard, *Caste and Class in a Southern Town* (1937; New York: Doubleday Anchor, 1957), 289 and 266. In "Southern Trauma: Revisiting Caste and Class in the Mississippi Delta," *American Anthropologist*, n.s. 106 (June 2004): 334–45, Jane Adams and D. Gorton offer a critical assessment of Dollard's book and show how Doob delayed the publication of a competing one, Hortense Powdermaker's *After Freedom: A Cultural Study in the Deep South* (1939), in order to amplify the impact of Dollard's.

8. For biographical information I am relying on the Robert A. Bone Papers, Rare Book and Manuscript Library, Butler Library, Columbia University, especially material in box 2 such as Robert A. Bone, telephone conversation with Leslie Herzfeld, March 29, 1984, and Robert A. Bone, "Finding the Center: Reflections on a Teaching Career," Oct. 20, 1991. In addition, I draw on Richard Courage, telephone conversation, June 27, 2012, and e-mail to author, July 15, 2014.

9. Robert A. Bone, *The Negro Novel in America* (New Haven: Yale University Press, 1958), vii. The African American scholars Sterling Brown, Hugh M. Gloster, and J. Saunders Redding among others had written on black literature.

10. Bone, *Negro*, 160–62, 166, and 168.

11. Leonard W. Doob, *Social Psychology: An Analysis of Human Behavior* (New York: Henry Holt, 1952), 276 and 468.

12. Dollard, "Preface—1957," *Caste and Class*, xi–xii.

13. Dollard, "Preface—1957," vii. For the results of his summer 1935 time in Mississippi, see Leonard W. Doob, "Poor Whites: A Frustrated Class," in Dollard, *Caste and Class* (1937 ed.), 445–84. At some point after they worked together on *Caste and Class*, the relationship between Doob and Dollard frayed, and Dollard did not include Doob's contribution in the 1957 edition.

14. An examination of "Undergraduate Couse of Study," *Bulletin of Yale University*, from 1956 to 1960, a source that does not necessarily convey everything covered, reveals that there was little attention to race. Those who wrote on African Americans did not appear to teach any course in which race was central. The sociologist Jerome K. Myers taught a lower-level course that included attention to race and nationality. John Eusden taught a course in religion on Christianity and social problems that paid some attention to race relations. As early as 1958–59 the course catalog listed as Race and Cultural Contacts and another called American Society: Racial Groups, but during my years at Yale neither of these courses was actually offered. In 1959–60, Jacob Cohen taught Race and Nationality in American History since 1800.

15. Harry J. Carman and Harold C. Syrett, *A History of the American People*, 2 vols. (New York: Knopf, 1952), 1:501, 503, and 648. Kenneth Stampp's *The Peculiar Institution* (1956) was among the first works of scholarship to challenge the widely held view of slavery, but there is no evidence regarding the impact of Stampp's views on what I was taught.

16. Carman and Syrett, *History*, 2:31.

17. David M. Potter and Thomas G. Manning, eds., *Nationalism and Sectionalism in America, 1775–1877: Select Problems in Historical Interpretation* (New York: Henry Holt, 1949); Thomas G. Manning and David M. Potter, eds., *Government and the American Economy, 1870–Present: Select Problems in Historical Interpretation* (New York: Henry Holt, 1950). It is possible that we also read some of the edited books in the series known as the "Amherst pamphlets."

18. Potter and Manning, *Nationalism*, 165 and 347; the second volume did offer the voices of ex-slaves recorded by the Federal Writers Project.

19. On Potter, see Daniel Horowitz, *Anxieties of Affluence: Critiques of American Consumer Culture, 1939–1979* (Amherst: University of Massachusetts Press, 2004), 79–100.

20. Howard R. Lamar, lecture notes for History 20, Jan. 11, 1957, and Jan. 16, 1957, WA MSS S-2639, box 11, folder titled "History 20A Lectures. History Survey—Yale before 1877. 1950s," Howard Lamar Papers, Beinecke Rare Book and Manuscript Library, Yale University. These lec-

ture notes are from a year before I took the course, but I am assuming what I heard pretty much followed what he said a year earlier. On Lamar, see Lewis L. Gould, "Howard Roberts Lamar," in *Clio's Favorites: Leading Historians of the U.S., 1945–2000,* ed. Robert Allen Rutland (Columbia: University of Missouri Press, 2001), 84–97.

21. Edmund David Cronon, *Black Moses: The Story of Marcus Garvey and the Universal Negro Improvement Association* (Madison: University of Wisconsin Press, 1955), xi–xii, 4, 27, and 203. Cronon understood how uphill a battle it was to counter the department's inbreeding, something marked by a preference for men with a Yale BA and a Harvard PhD: E. David Cronon, interview, tape 14, Aug. 23, 2004, University Archives, University of Wisconsin–Madison; see also David Cronon, interview with Judith Craig and Barry Teicher, Aug. 23, 2004, University of Wisconsin oral history project, interviews of David Cronon, first interview, tape 14, side 2, and obituary, Dec. 5, 2006, University of Wisconsin–Madison News, www.news.wisc.edu/13251. I am grateful to David Null for facilitating my use of this material. William Cronon has informed me that his father did not leave behind his lecture notes for this course: William Cronon, e-mail to author, June 28, 2012.

22. Martin Duberman, *Cures: A Gay Man's Odyssey* (New York: Dutton, 1991), 1. See also Paul A. Robinson, *Gay Lives: Homosexual Autobiography from John Addington Symonds to Paul Monette* (Chicago: University of Chicago Press, 1999), 339; Paul A. Robinson, "Becoming a Gay Historian," in *Becoming Historians,* ed. James M. Banner Jr. and John R. Gillis (Chicago: University of Chicago Press, 2009), 240–41; Jeremy D. Popkin, *History, Historians, and Autobiography* (Chicago: University of Chicago Press, 2005), 266–76.

23. Duberman, *Cures,* 56.

24. Duberman, *Cures,* 3.

25. Martin Duberman, *Charles Francis Adams, 1807–1886* (Boston: Houghton Mifflin, 1961), 43.

26. Martin Duberman, *In White America: A Documentary Play* (Boston: Houghton Mifflin, 1964). Duberman, *Cures,* 69–74, traces the play's impact on his career. Duberman came out in 1972 when he wrote about a faculty member who had to leave the college after being arrested for "crimes against nature": Martin Duberman, *Black Mountain, An Exploration in Community* (New York: Dutton, 1972), 232.

27. Daniel Horowitz, "The Reconstruction Period," 1–2, paper for History 20, Jan. 10, 1958, in author's possession.

28. Martin Duberman, comments on Horowitz, "Reconstruction," 3, 4, 10, and 13; Horowitz, "Reconstruction," 3, 4, 6, and 13.

29. Robinson, *Gay,* 335.

30. Yale was hardly alone in its lack of interest in recruiting African Americans: see William T. Bowen and Derek Bok, *The Shape of the River: Long-Term Consequences of Considering Race in College and University Admission* (Princeton: Princeton University Press, 1998), 1–3.

31. Bruce Ballard, telephone conversation, May 9, 2014. In 1961, Howe hired Charles McCarthy (Yale 1960, Skull and Bones) to direct a search for talented students, especially among African Americans, an effort other Ivy League schools soon copied: Dan Oren, *Joining the Club: A History of Jews and Yale* (New Haven: Yale University Press, 1985), 210. For parodies of admissions policy under Howe, see "Headshrinkers to Rule Brave New Policy of 'Eclectic' Admissions," *YDN,* May 11, 1957, 1; Alice Danzig, "Down with College Boards," *YDN,* May 14, 1960, 3. For an especially cogent critique of admissions under Howe, see Richard Celeste, letter to the editor, *YDN,* April 16, 1959, 2.

32. Davenport was the son of a worker on the C & O Railroad. Tignor's father was a high school principal. Puryear's father was a contractor, and Ballard's a medical doctor, while both of the parents of Moses taught at Hampton. For Davenport I am relying on ancestry.com; Richard Minear, conversation, Sept. 27, 2013; Tom Miller, e-mail to author, Sept. 28, 2013. Jonathan Bramwell, *Courage in Crisis: The Black Professional Today* (Indianapolis: Bobbs-Merrill, 1972), 4–5 and 49–55, written by an African American member who entered Yale College in 1957, describes his own elite background and offers a picture of the racism he experienced as an undergraduate.

33. Tignor's brother preceded him to Yale.

34. I am relying on Puryear, conversation and Bruce Ballard, conversation for information on these patterns of social interaction.

35. Greg Tignor, telephone conversation, May 13, 2014.

36. Alvin N. Puryear and Charles A. West, *Black Enterprise, Inc.: Case Studies of a New Experiment in Black Business Development* (Garden City: Doubleday, 1973), 28–29.

37. Greg Tignor, *Class of Its Own*, 489. On Moses, see obituary, http://alumninet.yale.edu/classes/yc1962/obituaries/moses.html; Jonathan A. Weiss, "William Henry Moses," *Class of Its Own*, 77. On Puryear, I rely on "Byron Puryear, Civil Rights Activist," August 8, 1991, *Hampton Daily Press*, http://articles.dailypress.com/1991-08-08/news/9108080094_1_hampton-institute-mr-puryear-big-brothers; Al Puryear, telephone conversation, April 3, 2012.

38. See, for example, Peter G. Platt, "Thurgood Marshall, Counsel for NAACP, Says Segregation Also Practiced in North," *YDN*, Feb. 18, 1957, 1; Seagle, "Segregation." Martha Biondi, *The Black Revolution on Campus* (Berkeley: University of California Press, 2012), 13–42, explores the racial situation in higher education during the early to mid-1960s; the rest of her book provides a contrast with what existed at Yale and elsewhere up to 1960.

39. Raleigh Davenport, "Segregation, North and South," *Criterion*, April 1959, 12–14. For information on racial discrimination in fraternities in these years, DKE especially, see "Fraternities and Discrimination," folder 26, box 21, RG 126, YRG–A, acc. 1964-A-003, YUA.

40. "The Negro at Yale," *YDN*, April 8, 1959, 2; Albert E. Stone, "Sex, Segregation, Science," *YDN*, April 8, 1959, 2.

41. David George Ball, *A Marked Heart* (Bloomington, IN: iUniverse, 2011), 61 and 62.

42. Martin L. King Jr., speech, *YAM*, May 1959, 12; publisher of *Ivy Magazine* quoted in Ball, *Marked Heart*, 74.

43. Ball, *Marked Heart*, 74 and 76.

44. David George Ball, "The Use of Pupil Placement Laws in the South as a Device to Avoid Integration," preface [p. ii] and 113–15, RU 118, series II, box 4, folder 17, YUA.

45. David Ball, *Class of Its Own*, 121; Ball, *Marked Heart*, 78; *30th RD*, 6.

46. John Bing, "Deerfield Integration," senior honors thesis in American studies, pp. b–c, 16, 50, and 77, RU 331, acc. 19ND-A-437, folder 14, box 3, YUA.

47. I can identify no other classmate who focused his career so significantly on civil rights for African Americans, although many focused on other groups, especially Native Americans and Latinos, including David Dominick, Neil Herring, Steve Kunitz, Dick Lee, William MacKinnon, Monroe Price, Robert Putsch, William Wiese, Kirke Wilson, and William Wroth. As far as I can tell, Conrad Cafritz is the only white classmate who married an African American.

48. Sydney Ahlstrom directed the thesis, a copy of which I have not been able to locate.

49. George McClain, *After-Words*, 47. As he approached graduation, McClain, having taken Harry Rudin's course on African history, was headed for a year in the Belgian Congo, a plan thwarted by political upheaval there. Instead he studied theology under Karl Barth in Switzerland on a Rotary Foundation Fellowship. He went to Union Theological Seminary in 1964 because of the presence of Paul Tillich and George Webber, who offered a vision of urban ministries in *God's Colony in a Man's World* (1960).

50. I rely here on George McClain, telephone conversation, Dec. 1, 2012, and e-mail to author, Dec. 12, 2012; "Introducing the New Executive Secretary," *Social Questions Bulletin* 64 (Jan. 1974): 1; George D. McClain, *Claiming All Things for God: Prayer, Discernment, and Ritual for Social Change* (Nashville: Abingdon, 1998); George McClain, quoted in "21 MFSAers Arrested in Protests," *Social Questions Bulletin* 75 (Jan.–Feb. 1985): 1.

51. Sally Train, telephone conversation, July 24, 2012. On his father, see obituary, *Savannah Morning News*, April 24, 1999.

52. John K. Train III, "Walter White: A Study of a Man and His Time," senior honors thesis in American studies, 153, 128–29, and 191, RU 331, acc. 19ND-A-437, folder 188, box 31, YUA. From discussions with many of Train's close friends it is clear that it is highly unlikely that he was the member of DKE who blackballed Davenport, and that the appreciation and sympathy he expressed in his thesis for White and more generally for both the plight and creativity of

African Americans circa 1960 were deeply felt: Steve Easter, conversation, June 24, 2012; Richard Minear, e-mail to author, June 24, 2012; Guy Stevens, telephone conversation, June 25, 2012.

Chapter 4. Africa

1. On how Americans in the 1950s and 1960s experienced Africa, see Fritz Fischer, *Making Them Like Us: Peace Corps Volunteers in the 1960s* (Washington, DC: Smithsonian Institution Press, 1998); Larry Grubbs, *Secular Missionaries: Americans and African Development in the 1960s* (Amherst: University of Massachusetts Press, 2009); Elizabeth Cobbs Hoffman, *All You Need Is Love: The Peace Corps and the Spirit of the 1960s* (Cambridge: Harvard University Press, 1998); Martin Staniland, *American Intellectuals and African Nationalists* (New Haven: Yale University Press, 1991); Jonathan Zimmerman, *Innocents Abroad: American Teachers in the Twentieth Century* (Cambridge: Harvard University Press, 2006). On the international dimensions of racial conflict and civil rights, see Thomas Borstelmann, *The Cold War and the Color Line; American Race Relations in the Global Arena* (Cambridge: Harvard University Press, 2001); Mary L. Dudziak, *Cold War Civil Rights: Race and the Image of American Democracy* (Princeton: Princeton University Press, 2000); Brenda Gayle Plummer, *In Search of Power: African Americans in the Era of Decolonization, 1956–1974* (New York: Cambridge University Press, 2013); Penny M. Von Eschen, *Race against Empire: Black Americans and Anticolonialism, 1937–1957* (Ithaca: Cornell University Press, 1997).

2. Richard F. Celeste, "Toward an African Personality: The History and an Analysis of Pan-Africanism and the Pan-African Movement," spring 1959, i, Records and Essays of the Scholars of the House Program, RU 143, acc. 19ND-A-382, box 10, YUA.

3. Celeste, "Toward an African Personality," 58, 90, 107, and 164.

4. Celeste, "Toward an African Personality," F-12, n. 7; F-13, n. 26; Celeste, telephone conversation, April 26, 2012. For his earlier essay, one that linked the situation with Africa and African Americans, see Richard Celeste—An African Analysis," *Criterion*, Oct. 1958, 10–13.

5. On the development of the study of Africa as a field at Yale, I am relying on William Foltz, e-mail to author, Sept. 28, 2011. Other faculty members in the late 1950s focused some attention on Africa, including Karl Deutsch, James Fesler, Karl Pelzer, and Lloyd Reynolds. On the development of African studies as a field, see David Newbury, "Africanist Historical Studies in the United States: Metamorphosis or Metastatsis?" in *African Historiographies: What History for Which Africa?*, ed. Bogumil Jewsiewicki and David Newbury (Beverly Hills, CA: Sage, 1984): 151–64; Robert I. Rotberg, "The Teaching of African History," *American Historical Review* 69 (Oct. 1963): 47–63.

6. For biographical information, see John M. W. Whiting, "George Peter Murdock (1897–1985)," *American Anthropologist*, n.s. 88 (Sept. 1986): 682–86. Later in his life, Murdock repudiated the approaches on which much of his life's work relied: George Murdock, "Anthropology's Mythology," *Proceedings of the Royal Anthropological Institute of Great Britain and Ireland*, no. 1971 (1971): 17–24.

7. Harry R. Rudin, *Germans in the Cameroons: 1884–1914: A Case Study in Modern Imperialism* (New Haven: Yale University Press, 1938), 9 and 11; John Bing, paraphrasing Harry Rudin's conversation, July 24, 1961, from Bing's typewritten notes, copy in author's possession. Among Rudin's essays are "The Continuity of Russian Imperialism," *Yale Review* 42 (Spring 1953): 342; "The Problem of Colonialism," *Current History* 30 (March 1956): 129–34; "The International Position of Africa Today," *Annals of the American Academy of Political and Social Science* 306 (July 1956): 50–54; "United States Policies toward Africa," *Current History* 32 (March 1957): 155–59; "Chaos in the Congo," *Current History* 40 (Feb. 1961), 98–104. On Rudin's outlook in the late 1950s, see Jonathan J. Seagle, "US African Policy Discussed, Analyzed," *YDN*, March 13, 1959, 1.

8. Leonard W. Doob, *Becoming More Civilized: A Psychological Exploration* (New Haven: Yale University Press, 1960), 231. His other book on Africa, *Communication in Africa: A Search for Boundaries* (1961), offered taxonomies of communication. Ellen Herman, *The Romance of American Psychology: Political Culture in the Age of Experts* (Berkeley: University of California

Press, 1995), 137–41, makes clear how problematic was Doob's analysis of the dichotomy of civilized/uncivilized.

9. George Peter Murdock, *Africa: Its Peoples and Their Culture History* (New York: McGraw-Hill, 1959), 7 and 39. Soon after the end of World War II, Murdock warned the FBI that radical anthropologists (nearly all of them Jews and students of Boas) were trying to take over the field's professional association: David H. Price, *Threatening Anthropology: McCarthyism and the FBI's Surveillance of Activist Anthropologists* (Durham, NC: Duke University Press, 2004), 70–93.

10. At least two others classmates, Sam Bowles and Bill Arnold, went to Africa while we were still in college: Bill Arnold, e-mail to author, Aug. 22, 2014.

11. DH to JK and LK, June 4, 159; DH to EB, June 18, 1959; DH to family, date unclear; DH to MBH and WH, July 20, 1959, and unidentifiable white guide, quoted in same; DH to EB, July 23, 1959. In the notes, JK is my sister Judy Katz; LK, her husband Len Katz; EB, my grandmother Esther Botwinik; WH, my father; and MBH, my mother.

12. DH to JK and LK, July 21, 1959.

13. J. C. G. Walker, "South Africa's Approach to Race Relations," *Rostrum,* Nov. 16, 1957, 8. For his views of apartheid then and now, I am relying on Jim Walker, telephone conversation, Aug. 6, 2013. The other classmate from Africa was Henri Louis Fraise, who came to Yale from an American prep school and in 1960 listed addresses in Tananarive, Madagascar, and Manhattan's Upper East Side.

14. DH to MBH and WH, Aug. 2, 1959; DH to MBH and WH, July 30, 1959. On the prominence of Jews in the battle against apartheid, see Gideon Shimoni, *Community and Conscience: The Jews in Apartheid South Africa* (Hanover, NH: University Press of New England, 2003), esp. 55–119.

15. I am grateful to Frances Suzman Jowell for e-mail exchanges on March 31, 2014, that clarified this situation.

16. On Lowenstein's work, see William H. Chafe, *Never Stop Running: Allard Lowenstein and the Struggle to Save American Liberalism* (New York: Basic, 1993), 134–45.

17. DH to EB, Aug 14, 1959; DH to MBH and WH Aug. 20, 1959.

18. DH for family, Aug. 14, 1959; DH to EB Aug. 17, 1959.

19. DH to family, Aug. 10, 1959. J. D. Shingler, quoted in caption to "A call goes to students," *Rand Daily Mail,* Aug.1, 1959, copy in author's possession.

20. DH to EB, Aug. 1, 1959, DH to family, July 31, 1959, DH to family, Aug 11, 1959, Aug. 12, 1959, DH to family, Aug, 22, 1959; DH to MBH, WH, JK, and LK Aug. 12, 1959; DH to family, Aug 11, 1959.

21. DH to family, c. Aug. 6, 1959; DH to JK and LK, Aug. 16 or 17, 1959; DH to family July 31, 1959; DH to JK and LK, Aug. 3, 1959; DH to family, Aug. 12, 1959; Cushing Strout to DH, summer 1959.

22. DH to family, Aug, 12, 1959, DH to JK and LK, Aug. 3, 1959, DH to family, Aug. 11, 1959, DH to family, Aug. 3, 1959; DH to family Aug. 16 or 17, 1959.

23. DH to JK and LK, Sept. 5, 1959. In my prediction I was closer to the view of Leopold's heirs than of knowledgeable American observers: see Adam Hochschild, *King Leopold's Ghost: a Story of Greed, Terror, and Heroism in Colonial Africa* (Boston: Houghton Mifflin, 1998), 301 and Melville J. Herskovits, *The Human Factor in Changing Africa* (New York: Random House, 1962), 334.

24. DH to EB, July 23, 1959.

25. "South African Students to Discuss Race Dilemma," *YDN,* May 3, 1960; "South African Student Panel Condemns Apartheid Policy," (including the quote from Burgert Roberts), *YDN,* May 4, 1960, 1 and 4. For Roberts's later opposition to apartheid and support for Nelson Mandela, see Burgert Roberts, "Quo Vadis, America?," Mtunzini, South Africa November 17, 2004, Yale Class of 1962 website, Features, http://alumninet.yale.edu/classes/yc1962/roberts1104.html.

26. [Ivor Schwartzman] to Miriam [Horowitz], *YDN,* May 3, 1960, 2 and accompanying editor's note.

27. There may be others. Shortly after graduation, John Curtis went to Ghana on Operation

Crossroads, but I lack sufficient information to include him here; in the late 1960s Sidney Baker served as a Peace Corps physician in Chad.

28. John O. Dwyer, *25th RD,* 38; John O. Dwyer, telephone conversation, Feb. 3, 2012; John O. Dwyer, "The Acholi of Uganda; Adjustment to Imperialism" (PhD diss., Columbia University, 1972).

29. Harvey M. Feinberg, *Africans and Europeans in West Africa: Elminans and Dutchmen on the Gold Coast during the Eighteenth Century* (Philadelphia: American Philosophical Society, 1989).

30. John Bing, resume; Bing, letters and essays covering the period from his stay in Nigeria in summer 1960 until his return to Evanston summer 1964; [John Bing], "Number 15," a three-page typed essay on "Political Development in Africa," "Civil Rights," and "Public Welfare," probably mid-1960s for graduate school. Copies of all in author's possession.

31. Owen Cylke, e-mail to author, July 25, 2012; Owen Cylke, telephone interviews by author, July 24 and 26, 2012.

32. Ed Elmendorf, e-mail to author, May 7, 2012. See also Ed Elmendorf, e-mails to author, May 7, 2012, and July 27, 2012; Ed Elmendorf, telephone conversation, May 7, 2012; c.v. of Ed Elmendorf, Sept. 2011, copy in author's possession.

33. Here I rely on Richard Peace, e-mails to author, Jan. 30, 2011, and Aug. 11, 2012; Richard Peace, conversation, March 9, 2011; "Richard V. Peace," Faculty Profile, Fuller Theological Seminary, www.fuller.edu/academics/faculty/richard peace.aspx, Richard Peace, *Noticing God in Mystical Encounters, in the Ordinary, in the Still Small Voice, in Community, in Creation and More* (Downers Grove, IL: Intervarsity Press, 2012), 95–96.

34. Judy Boppell Peace, *The Boy Child Is Dying: A South African Experience* (San Francisco: Harper and Row, 1986), 9, 14, 23, 42, 56–57, 65–66, and 88.

35. Peace, e-mail to author, Aug. 11, 2012.

36. *25th Reunion Directory,* 90; Peter Parsons, e-mail to author, March 10, 2012; see also *Class of Its Own,* 71–73, for essays on Marriott by Tim Light and Peter Parsons.

37. Karl Robinson, telephone conversation, Feb. 12, 2012; Karl Robinson, e-mails to author, Feb. 12, 2012, Feb. 13, 2012, Feb. 15, 2012, and June 27, 202, Karl Robinson, draft of "Prologue" to his book, dated Feb. 12, 2012, copy in author's possession.

38. Karl E. Robinson Jr., letter to the editor, *Christian Science Monitor,* Feb. 10, 1959, 16. Robinson continued to promote this idea: "Robinson Scores 'Colossal Waste' of Men," *YDN,* March 11, 1959, 1 and 4, and during February of our senior year when Congressman Henry Reuss visited Yale and promoted his own version of what would later become the Peace Corps.

39. Karl Robinson, telephone conversation, Feb. 12, 2012.

40. Alfred M. Lee, letter to the editor, *YDN,* May 14, 1957, 4; Alfred M. Lee, letter to the editor, *YDN,* Sept. 30, 1957, 3.

41. Al Lee, "How I Joined the Peace Corps and Found Mao," c. 1966, 1, 3, and 9–10, box 4, MsC861, Alfred M. Lee Papers, Special Collections and University Archives, University of Iowa, Iowa City. I am grateful to Jake Altman for helping me research Lee's papers. Also in box 4, MsC861, in the same collection is Al M. Lee, "An Amiable American," a 314-page manuscript that tells a story about the life of a young man in Africa. I am also drawing on Karen Lee, telephone conversation, March 27, 2012; Al Lee, *Time* (New York: Ecco Press, 1974); Al Lee, ed., *The Major Young Poets* (New York: World, 1971).

42. Lee, "Accra," 70–71; Jason Thatcher [pseud. for Al Lee], "Accra," *Partisan Review* 32 (Winter 1965): 70–71; Lee, "Joined," 4. Also influential in his radicalization was his friendship with Winston Mvusi: Karen Lee, conversation.

43. William Jameson Kunz, *Class of Its Own,* 324.

44. Jamie Kunz, telephone conversation, Oct. 28, 2012. In addition to these sources I am relying on Jamie Kunz, e-mails to author, Oct. 17, 19, and 28, Nov. 1 and 3, 2012. For a published version of some of these the events, see Paul Theroux, "The Killing of Hasting Banda [1971]," in Paul Theroux, *Sunrise with Seamonsters: Travels and Discoveries, 1964–1984* (Boston: Houghton Mifflin, 1985), 63–75.

45. Kunz, e-mail, Oct. 28, 2012.

46. On the senior Bowles, see Howard B. Schaffer, *Chester Bowles: New Dealer in the Cold War* (Cambridge: Harvard University Press, 1993); Richard P. Dauer, *A North-South Mind in an East-West World: Chester Bowles and the Making of United States Cold War Foreign Policy, 1951–1969* (Westport, CT: Praeger, 2005). On Chester Bowles's opposition to discrimination in college admissions, see Jerome Karabel, *The Chosen: The Hidden History of Admission and Exclusion at Harvard, Yale, and Princeton* (Boston: Houghton Mifflin, 2005), 211. For his views of Africa, see Chester Bowles, *Africa's Challenge to America* (Berkeley: University of California Press, 1956). It is important not to exaggerate the progressivism of his vision; like Rudin, he emphasized how important African minerals were to the United States and looked favorably on how Western nations, including Belgium, administered their colonies: C. Bowles, *Africa's Challenge*, 30. Of the classmates who went to Africa, Sam Bowles is the only one of those still living who has not responded to my requests for an interview.

47. My discussion relies on letters in the Chester Bowles Papers, YUA—MS 628, Part V, Series 1, folder 29, box 203 and MS 628, Part VI, Series 1, folder 64, box 271: Nancy Bowles and Sam Bowles, No. 1, Sept. 4, 1960; No. 2, Oct. 5, 1960, 5–6; No. 3, Dec. 21, 1960; No. 4, Feb. 10, 1961; No. 6, Aug. 11, 1961, and Aug. 13, 1961; No. 7, July 10, 1961; No. 8, March 23, 1962.

48. "U.S. Teachers in Africa . . . Busy Couple," *Look,* March 28, 1961, 51. The rest of the paragraph draws on the following letters: No, 1, Sept. 4, 1960; No. 3, Dec. 21, 1961; No. 4, Feb. 10, 1961.

49. Samuel Bowles, *Planning Educational Systems for Economic Growth* (Cambridge: Harvard University Press, 1969), 9–10 and 213–14; Samuel S. Bowles, "The Efficient Allocation of Resources in Education: A Planning Model with Application to Northern Nigeria" (PhD diss., Harvard, 1966). Both the Rockefeller Foundation and the USIA funded work on his thesis, through a grant to Harvard's Center for International Affairs. For a 1969 critique of the center by David Horowitz during his radical phase, see "Sinews of Empire," *Ramparts Magazine,* October 1969, 32–42. In fall 1969 Bowles participated in SDS protests against federal funding, expanding the critique of the emphasis on efficiency over equality that he wrote about in his 1969 book. For an assessment of modernization theory, which influenced many discussed in the chapter, see Nils Gilman, *Mandarins of the Future: Modernization Theory in Cold War America* (Baltimore: Johns Hopkins University Press, 2003). The earliest piece on American education I could find was Samuel Bowles and Henry Levin, "Economics of Educational Opportunity: A Critical Appraisal," 1967, unpublished paper, copy in Gutman Library, Harvard Graduate School of Education, Cambridge.

50. John Ostheimer, telephone conversation, April 25, 2012.

51. See the following works written or edited by John Ostheimer: "The Achievement Motive among the Chaga of Tanzania" (PhD diss., Yale, 1967); *Nigerian Politics* (New York: Harper and Row, 1973); *The Politics of the Western Indian Ocean Islands* (New York: Praeger, 1975); Nancy C. Ostheimer, *Life or Death—Who Controls* (New York: Springer, 1976); Leonard Ritt, *Environment, Energy, and Black Americans* (Beverly Hills, CA: Sage, 1976).

52. In addition to class and reunion books, I am relying on John Ostheimer, e-mails to author, Jan. 14, 2012, June 27, 2012, and June 29, 2012. On his family's background, see Ostheimers in England thread on RootsWeb, http://archiver.rootsweb.ancestry.com/th/read/OSTHEIMER/2008-06/1213048699.

53. Miller, *Class of Its Own,* 376. I am also relying on Tom Miller, e-mails to author, Feb. 10, 2012, June 23, 2012, June 24, 2012, and May 9, 2014; Tom Miller, conversation, Feb. 10, 2012; Tom Miller profile, Miller Washington & Kim, LLP, website, http://milwaki.com/our-staff/attorneys/tom-miller/.

54. Tom Miller, from article in *Tribune Magazine,* c. 1960–61, quoted in John Bing, talk in 1960–61, possibly a sermon at Evanston church, copy in author's possession.

55. For the comparative impact of the Peace Corps experience, I am relying on Fischer, *Making Them Like Us,* esp. 182–91.

56. William C. Weeden, "Initial Arrangements for 'Yale-in-Africa' Set by Coffin, Studds," *YDN,* May 7, 1959, 1.

57. D. Murray Last, letter to the editor, *YDN,* April 29, 1960, 2.

Chapter 5. Becoming an Academic Man

1. Counselor's Preliminary Report, Nov. 5, 1956; Counselor's Report, Feb. 18, 1957; Counselor's Final Report, May 26, 1957, folder for Daniel Horowitz, Yale College Student Records for the Classes of 1904 to the Present, RU 587, acc. 1961-A-004, box 160, YUA; John Knowles, "The Yale Man," *Holiday*, May 1953, 67.

2. "Prospectus for American Studies Program," Nov. 14, 1949, quoted in Michael Holzman, "The Ideological Origins of American Studies at Yale," *American Studies* 40 (Summer 1999): 84. See also Sydney E. Ahlstrom, "Studying America and American Studies at Yale," *American Quarterly* 22 (Summer 1970): 503–17; Liza Nicholas, "Wyoming as America: Celebrations, a Museum, and Yale," *American Quarterly* 54 (Sept. 2002): 437–65.

3. A. Whitney Griswold to William Robertson Coe, Nov. 27, 1951, quoted in Holzman, "Ideological Origins," 88; William C. DeVane to Charles Seymour, received May 16, 1949, quoted in Holzman, "Ideological Origins," 82–83; *New York Times*, May 30, 1954, 32.

4. Mike Thomas, "Looking Down," *YDN*, Jan. 16, 1958, 4; parody of undergraduate course of study, 1959–60, *Yale Record*, May 1959, 4.

5. The best history of the field is Gene Wise, "'Paradigm Dramas' in American Studies: A Cultural and Institutional History of the Movement," *American Quarterly* 31 (1979): 293–337; see also Leila Zenderland, "Constructing American Studies: Culture, Identity, and the Expansion of the Humanities," in *The Humanities and the Dynamics of Inclusion since World War II*, ed. David A. Hollinger (Baltimore: Johns Hopkins University Press, 2006), 273–313.

6. Linda Kerber, "Diversity and the Transformation of American Studies," *American Quarterly* 41 (Sept. 1989): 415–31.

7. Robin W. Winks, *Cloak and Gown: Scholars in the Secret War, 1939–1961* (New York: Morrow, 1987), 317; Norman Holmes Pearson, "The Nazi-Soviet Pact and the End of a Dream," in *America in Crisis: Fourteen Crucial Episodes in American History*, ed. Daniel Aaron (New York: Knopf, 1952), 326–48. The best source on Pearson is Winks, *Cloak*, 247–321; see also Doug Henwood, "Spooks in Blue," *Grand Street* 7 (Spring 1988): 212–19.

8. Robert Wheeler, "American Communists: Their Ideology and Their Interpretation of American Life, 1917–1939" (PhD diss., Yale University, 1952). On Wheeler, I am relying on Albert Stone to author, June 6, 1996; Dana White, e-mail to author, Aug. 23, 2012; Robert A. Paul, e-mail to author, Aug. 23, 2012; Matthew Mancini, telephone conversation and e-mail, both Aug. 24, 2012; and an Oct. 1, 2012, e-mail from a colleague of Wheeler's who chooses to remain anonymous.

9. John W. McCoubrey, *American Tradition in Painting* (New York: Braziller, 1963), 8–11. On his life, I used information provided by Nancy R. Miller of the University of Pennsylvania Archives: John W. McCoubrey, curriculum vitae; Nancy R. Miller, e-mail to author, Aug. 24, 2012. See also Sally A. Downey, "John Walker McCoubrey, 86, art history professor," obituary, *Philadelphia Inquirer*, Feb. 14, 2010.

10. On Strout, I have relied on DH to Al Stone, May 17, 1996, DH/HLH; Peter Novick, *That Noble Dream: The "Objectivity Question" and the American Historical Profession* (Cambridge: Cambridge University Press, 1988), 324; information from Linda Hall, an archivist at Williams College.

11. Cushing Strout, "The Twentieth-Century Enlightenment," *American Political Science Review* 49 (June 1955): 326; see also Cushing Strout, *The Pragmatic Revolt in American History: Carl Becker and Charles Beard* (New Haven: Yale University Press, 1958), 9–10.

12. Lawrence W. Chisolm, *Fenollosa: The Far East and American Culture* (New Haven: Yale University Press, 1963), ix, 4, 6, and 246–47. On Chisolm, I am relying on Patricia Donovan, "Lawrence W. Chisolm Dies at 69," April 30, 1998, University at Buffalo News Release, www.buffalo.edu/news/4114, and Michael Frisch, telephone conversation, Sept. 11, 2012.

13. Course description for American Studies 81, *Bulletin of Yale University. Undergraduate Course of Study*, series 54, no. 6, 41.

14. In discussing this course and others, I benefit the extensive notes John Bing took during classes, which focused solely on professors' statements and provide no information on what,

if anything, students contributed. Bing generously loaned me this material on the honors program, contained in two binders currently in my possession.

15. Syllabus for American Studies 81, 1958–59, Bing binder.

16. Bing, class notes, American Studies 81, Sept. 23, 1958, Oct. 21, 1958, and April [date not clear], 1959.

17. For example, Stone avoided wrestling with the issues raised by the essay with which he began the course, Henry Nash Smith, "Can 'American Studies' Develop a Method," *American Quarterly* 9 (Summer 1957): 197–208.

18. Bing, class notes, American Studies 81, Feb. 17, 1959 and Feb. 24, 1959.

19. For later interpretations of Whitman, influenced by Queer theory, see Byrne R. S. Fone, *Masculine Landscapes: Walt Whitman and the Homoerotic Text* (Carbondale: Southern Illinois University Press, 1992), 148; Michael Moon, *Disseminating Whitman: Revision and Corporeality in Leaves of Grass* (Cambridge: Harvard University Press, 1991), 45–49.

20. Syllabus for American Studies 82, 1958–59, Bing binder.

21. Bing, class notes, American Studies 82, Sept. 18, 1958.

22. Louis Hartz, *The Liberal Tradition in America: An Interpretation of American Political Thought since the Revolution* (New York: Harcourt, Brace, 1955), 5–7.

23. Bing, class notes, American Studies 82, Nov. 14, 1958; Jan. 15, 1959, discussion of "Reform and Protest" early in second semester, discussion in second semester of Oliver Wendell Holmes Jr.

24. Cushing Strout, "Liberalism, Conservatism, and the Babel of Tongues," *Partisan Review* 25 (Winter 1958): 101–2.

25. Bing, class notes, American Studies 82, final class, second semester.

26. Lewis Lapham, *Money and Class in America,* quoted in André Schiffrin, *A Political Education: Coming of Age in Paris and New York* (Hoboken, NJ: Melville House, 2007), 127; DH to HLH, June 8 and 9, 1960.

27. Cushing Strout to DH, Oct. 1965, in author's possession. On the image of the intellectual in these years, see Aaron Lecklider, *Inventing the Egghead: The Battle over Brainpower in American Culture* (Philadelphia: University of Pennsylvania Press, 2013), esp. 191–220.

28. A. Bartlett Giamatti, "To Make Oneself Eternal [1980]," in *A Free and Ordered Space: The Real World of the University* (New York: Norton, 1988), 195.

29. DH to MBH and WH, June 3, 1959, DH to JK and LK, June 4, 1959, DH to JK and LK, June 10, 1959.

30. DH to family, June 24, 1959, DH to JK and LK, June 4, 1959, DH to family, June 21, 1959, DH to MBH and WH, June 20, 1959.

31. DH to family, July 2, 1959.

32. DH to MBH and WH, July 9, 1959.

33. DH to family, June 12, 1959; DH to MBH and WH, June 24, 1959; DH to family, June 27, 1959.

34. DH to family, June 27, 1959, DH to MBH and WH, July 4, 1959.

35. DH to Stone, May 17, 1996.

36. Syllabus for American Studies 87, 1959–60, in Bing binder; Bing, class notes, American Studies 87, including a quotation from Pearson.

37. For readings, see Bing, binder for American Studies 88, 1959–60. I am also drawing on two syllabi that Michael Cowan provided, for American Studies 88 in 1958–59 ("Concepts of American Character," Wheeler and Chisolm) and American Studies 81 in 1957–58 ("American Institutions," Stone and Wheeler), copies in author's possession. I do not want to exaggerate the thoroughness of their breakthrough because they reinforced aspects of the anti-utopian and anti-Marxist message Strout had offered a year earlier.

38. Bing, class notes, American Studies 88, Feb. 10, 1960.

39. Bing, class notes, Feb. 10, 1960; "Is Capital Punishment a Wise Policy?" and "You Can't Live There!," in *Attorney for the Damned,* ed. Arthur Weinberg (New York: Simon and Schuster, 1957). For a retelling of the case, see Kevin Boyle, *Arc of Justice: A Saga of Race, Civil Rights, and Murder in the Jazz Age* (New York: Holt, 2005).

40. William F. Weidlich "Thomas Nast's Cartoons: A Dominant Factor in the Downfall of the Tweed Ring," American Studies Senior Essays, YRG 47-L, RU 331 19ND-A-437, YUA; Joel M. Jones, "The Economic Status of the Faculty Members of American Institutions of Higher Learning: What Was Their Status? What Is It? What Have Been the Factors Determining It?," 1, 88, and 154, American Studies Senior Essays, YRG 47-2, RU 331, ACCN 19-ND-A-421 box 6, YUA; Robert LeValley Church "The Novelist and His Public: The Career of John William DeForest," 3, 8, 17, and 142–43, American Studies Senior Essays, YRG 47, RU 331, ACCN 19ND-A-421, box 5, YUA. Jones was in our cohort only in our senior year. I cannot locate the thesis by Steve Phillips.

41. Daniel Horowitz, "American Art at International Fairs in Europe, 1851–1900," honors thesis in American Studies, May 2, 1960, iii, 26, 64, 100, and 101, in author's possession.

42. I am grateful to John Bullock, a Yale graduate and now faculty member, for his suggestion to think about the quality of the writing of my peers' theses.

43. Daniel Horowitz, "*The Jungle,*" paper for American Studies 87, Nov. 5, 1959, and Pearson's comment on same, in author's possession.

44. Daniel Horowitz, "Report on Kouwenhoven's *Made in America,*" paper for American Studies 88, March 9, 1960; Daniel Horowitz, "Henry Adams as a Cultural Historian," paper for American Studies 88, Oct. 1, 1959; Daniel Horowitz, untitled paper on Henry Adams, *History of the United States* for American Studies 88, undated [academic year 1959–60]; Daniel Horowitz, "The Political Thought of Irving Babbitt," paper for American Studies 82, May 7, 1958, 1 and 5, and Strout's comment on same, all in author's possession.

45. Paul A. Robinson, *Gay Lives: Homosexual Autobiography from John Addington Symonds to Paul Monette* (Chicago: University of Chicago Press, 1999), 339–40.

46. Daniel Horowitz, "it is perhaps," autobiographical essay, academic year 1959–60, in author's possession.

47. Daniel Horowitz, "Nathan Glazer: *American Judaism,* A Problem and a Search for a Solution," paper for Hans Frei, Religion 10b, March 4, 1958, in author's possession; Horowitz, "it is perhaps."

48. Horowitz, "Nathan Glazer," 6; DH to JHK and LK, July 24, 1959.

49. Daniel Horowitz, "*American Judaism,*" paper for American Studies 88, Dec. 6, 1959, 5, in author's possession.

50. Sam B. Girgus, "The New Covenant: The Jews and the Myth of America," in *The American Self: Myth, Ideology, and Popular Culture,* ed. Sam B. Girgus (Albuquerque: University of New Mexico Press, 1981), 105–24, explores how Jewish writers pondered the meaning of America.

51. David A. Hollinger, "Why Are Jews Preeminent in Science and Scholarship? The Veblen Thesis Reconsidered [2002]," in *Cosmopolitanism and Solidarity: Studies in Ethnoracial, Religious, and Professional Affiliation in the United States* (Madison: University of Wisconsin Press, 2006), 140.

52. Carl Bridenbaugh, "The Great Mutation," *American Historical Review* 68 (Jan. 1963): 322–23.

53. Thorstein Veblen, "The Intellectual Pre-eminence of the Jews in Modern Europe [1919]," in *The Portable Veblen,* ed. Max Lerner (New York: Viking, 1948), 475.

54. DH to HL, March 8 1960; DH to HL, June 11 1960.

55. DH to HL, June 11, 1960.

56. DH to family, June 16, 1959; Hans Frei to DH, Aug. 24, 1959.

57. DH to HL, May 17, 1960.

Chapter 6. Recasting Gender in a Masculine World

1. Jerome Karabel, *The Chosen: The Hidden History of Admission and Exclusion at Harvard, Yale, and Princeton* (Boston: Houghton Mifflin, 2005), 412. The literature on the history of masculinity, fatherhood, and the family helps illuminate but does not fully capture what I experienced growing up and coming into maturity: see K. A. Cuordileone, *Manhood and American Political Culture in the Cold War* (New York: Routledge, 2005); Babette Faehmel, *College Women in the Nuclear Age: Cultural Literacy and Female Identity, 1940–1960* (New Brunswick: Rutgers

University Press, 2012); James B. Gilbert, *Men in the Middle: Searching for Masculinity in the 1950s* (Chicago: University of Chicago Press, 2005); Robert L. Griswold, *Fatherhood in America: A History* (New York: Basic, 1993); E. Anthony Rotundo, *American Manhood: Transformations in Masculinity from the Revolution to the Modern Era* (New York: Basic, 1993).

2. John Knowles, "The Yale Man," *Holiday* 13 (May 1953): 58.

3. *Yale Class Book '97*, 42.

4. Quotations from Women at Yale, "Sterling Memorial Library: Linonia and Brothers Room," www.yale.edu/womenatyale/LinoniaBrothers.html.

5. Mark Alden Branch, "A Very Special Saloon," *YAM*, April 1999.

6. Sidney Mintz, telephone conversation, Feb. 8, 2012; Knowles, "Yale Man," 60.

7. Geoffrey T. Hellman, "Pies and Pasties at the Lizzie," *New Yorker*, March 7, 1959. On how agitation in the late 1960s led to the admission of more than token women into the Elizabethan Club, see Stephen Parks, *The Elizabethan Club of Yale University: A Centenary Album* (New Haven: n.p., 2011), 74–87.

8. "Whiffenpoofs of 1960," *Class Book 1960*, 312–14. Randy Ney, class of 1959, may well have been the first Jew in the Whiffs: David Elliott, conversation, Jan. 27, 2013.

9. "Alley Cats," *Class Book 1960*, 315.

10. Lyrics by Albert Von Tilzer, Irving Bilbo, and Leo Robin.

11. Lyrics by B. G. DeSylva and Lew Brown.

12. For the 1960 repertoire, see www.whiffalumni.com/whiffs/group.php?groupyear=1960. More generally for the Whiffenpoofs, see www.whiffalumni.com/. I am grateful to Barney Stewart for e-mails and CDs that helped me understand the songs. In an e-mail of Oct. 16, 2012, he wrote me that "Tear It Down" is no longer in the repertoire because of its "racial overtones."

13. I write about this change in pattern of friends in "it is perhaps," autobiographical essay, academic year 1959–60, DH/HLH.

14. DH to HL, Tuesday evening, late May 1960. For an essay on friendship written by a friend from the class of 1961, see Richard Munich, "Man's Need of Man Constitutes His Highest Perfection," *Criterion*, May 1960, 3–5.

15. "A Letter on Secrecy," spring 1959, in author's possession.

16. Schedule of events for my senior society, May 1959, in author's possession.

17. DH to HL, Aug. 18, 1960.

18. Helen Lefkowitz Horowitz, *Campus Life: Undergraduate Cultures from the End of the Eighteenth Century to the Present* (New York: Knopf, 1987), 222.

19. "Amidst Cascading Footballs, Men Still Play Marbles," *YDN* clipping from 1958–59, in author's possession; *Class Book 1960*, 168.

20. Paul [Pete] Magee, Editorial, *Trumbull Times*, Oct. 11, 1957, 2, Yja43 T71+ oversize, YUA.

21. *Trumbullian*, Nov. 7, 1958, Yja43 T7 1+ oversize, YUA. The articles were unsigned but those behind the issue were members of the Marble Team. The articles are "The Natural Order," p. 1; "Princeton Weekend Ape-Rape Highlights College Social Season," p. 1; "Editorial: The Problem," p. 2; "Opinion: In Laud of Lust," p. 3–4; notice of Tap Day, p. 4; ad for College Aides, p. 5; "Cotton Mill Blues," p. 6; "Do Not Pester the Fellows," p. 6. Two essays in *Criterion* advocated the restoration of sexual desire in our lives: William Cobb, "The Phenomenology of Desire," Dec. 1959, 16–18; T. K. Swing, "Sex in Existence or Existence in Sex?," April 1959, 5–10. On parietal rules, see "Two Students Apprehended for Neglect of Guest Rule, Suspended by Dean's Office," Dec. 17, 1959, 1; "Dormitory Visiting Hours," *YDN*, Feb. 23, 1960, 1.

22. Daniel Horowitz, essay on Trumbull College for the class book, fall 1959, in author's possession.

23. Leslie Epstein, conversation, Sept. 25, 2012.

24. John S. Nicholas to DH, Feb. 13, 1959, in author's possession.

25. SN to DH, Oct. 27, 1959; Daniel Horowitz, "To Members of the Rhodes Scholarship Committee," fall 1959, in author's possession.

26. *35th RD*, 25 and 120.

27. Henry Harper Hart, "Fear of Homosexuality in College Students," in *Psychosocial Problems*

of College Men, ed. Bryant M. Wedge (New Haven: Yale University Press, 1958), 200; "perverse sexual cravings" comes from Edward Kempf, *Psychopathology* (St. Louis: C. V. Mosby, 1920).

28. John Bing, "Okie," poem written c. 1955, copy in author's possession.

29. On homosexuality at Harvard in a later period, see Toby Marotta, *Sons of Harvard: Gay Men from the Class of 1967* (New York: William Morrow, 1982).

30. Sherwin Goldman, e-mail to author, July 20, 2014.

31. Calvin Trillin, *Remembering Denny* (New York: Farrar, Straus and Giroux, 1993), 183–84.

32. *Class Book 1960,* 283, 288, 298, 316, and 324.

33. *Class of Its Own,* 510.

34. All of these quotes from are from 1999 issues of *YAM.*

35. Course description for Sociology 30b, taught by Jack Buerkle, 1959–60 undergraduate catalog, 197; John Dollard, *Caste and Class in a Southern Town* (1937; New York: Doubleday Anchor, 1957), 137.

36. Harry J. Carman and Harold C. Syrett, *A History of the American People,* 2 vols. (New York: Knopf, 1952), 1: 494 and 496.

37. Judith Schiff, Sterling Memorial Library, Manuscripts and Archives, OIR W009, "Enrollment Milestones in the Education of Yale Women," http://oir.yale.edu/detailed-data. Bessie Lee Gambrill earned tenure in the graduate school's Department of Education in 1952.

38. *Class Book 1960,* 58.

39. Laurel Thatcher Ulrich, *Yards and Gates: Gender in Harvard and Radcliffe History* (New York: Palgrave Macmillan, 2004), 10.

40. *Women at Yale: A Tour,* www.yale.edu/womenatyale/.

41. Liena Vayzman, Ruth Vaughn, and Laura Wexler, "The Pioneers," *YAM,* Sept./Oct. 2012, 42–47.

42. Daniel Horowitz, "Love and Self-Knowledge," poem written for English 15, April 8, 1957, and unnamed professor commenting on same, in author's possession.

43. David S. Allyn, *Make Love, Not War: The Sexual Revolution, An Unfettered History* (Boston: Little, Brown, 2000), 94–95. For a picture of the dating scene at an Ivy League college, see J. D. Salinger, "Franny," in *Franny and Zoey* (1955; New York: Bantam, 1964), 3–44.

44. Eli S. Jacobs, "Yale College Action on 'She Is Coming' Contest Anticipated," *YDN,* Oct. 30, 1957, 1; R.F. A [llen] "A Jigger of Wry," *Yale Record,* Sept. 1956, 4; [D.]Watson and [William B.] Cudahy [Jr.], "Posture Photos," *Yale Record,* Oct. 1957, 13. For a fictional view of how some Yale undergraduates exploited women, see Richard Frede, *Entry E* (New York: Random House, 1958).

45. Not that everything was perfect ever after, with investigations, scandals, harassment, and even sexually related murders much in the news. Nathan Harden published *Sex and God at Yale: Porn, Political Correctness, and a Good Education Gone Bad* (New York: St. Martin's, 2012), the conservative bookend to William F. Buckley Jr.'s *God and Man at Yale.*

46. The 1962 Doob report raised the possibility of admitting women as undergraduates as a side issue, in part to take focus off its recommendations about student life and admissions: Karabel, *Chosen,* 412–14.

47. See the following from *YDN:* Bill Furlong and Ron Miller, letter to the editor, Sept. 24, 1958, 2; [Calvin Trillin], "Oh Save Us," Sept. 29, 1956, 2; William Calin, letter to the editor, Sept. 29, 1956, 2; Gerald Jonas, "J'Accuse," Sept. 29, 1956, 2; L. J. Lemisch, letter to the editor, Oct. 9, 1956, 2. For a thoughtful editorial on coeducation, see [Calvin Trillin?], "The Future of Co-eds," Oct. 1, 1956, 4. Throughout the book, I place the name of the chairman of the *Yale Daily News* in brackets as the author of editorials because the person in that position wrote most of them. However, caution is in order: Calvin Trillin says that when he was chairman, different staff members, including the chair, wrote the editorials on different days (telephone conversation, May 21, 2014); Jim Ottaway says that under his chairmanship, he wrote all but two or three (telephone conversation, May 20, 2014).

48. Charles Schmitz, "My Yale: Plan B," 2010, 2–3, copy in author's possession; for spoofs of dating practices, see John C. Wellington, "Why Get Shot Down Again?" *YDN,* May 11, 1960, 2; Gordon B. Chamberlain, "Among the Trumpets," *YDN,* Jan. 12, 1960, 2.

49. PB to DH, winter 57 58.

50. Susan Gillotti, telephone conversation, June 28, 2014; e-mail to author, July 8, 2014; Phip Hirsh, e-mails to author, July 10, 2014, Jacques de Labry, telephone conversation, July 8, 2015. In addition to Hirsh and de Labry, the other members were Jim Conzelman, Emory Olcott, and Dave Sellers.

51. DH to WH, Feb. 28, 1967.

52. Faehmel, *College Women,* 79; throughout, Faehmel also speaks to issues I focus on here, including the importance of introspection, the search for more egalitarian relationships, the norm of male sexual aggressiveness, and the gendering of intellectuality. For an exploration of alienation, existentialism, and authenticity in the New Left, see Douglas Rossinow, *The Politics of Authenticity: Liberalism, Christianity, and the New Left in America* (New York: Columbia University Press, 1998), esp. 2–8 and 298–99. On changing meanings of authenticity, see Abigail Cheever, *Real Phonies: Cultures of Authenticity in Post–World War II America* (Athens: University of Georgia Press, 2010).

53. MY to DH, spring and summer 1958.

54. Martin Buber, *I and Thou,* trans. Ronald G. Smith (1923; New York: Charles Scribner's Sons, 1937), 27–28; Allen Ginsberg, *Howl: For Carl Solomon* (San Francisco: Marthe Rexroth for Allen Ginsberg, 1956); J. D. Salinger, *Catcher in the Rye* (Boston: Little, Brown, 1951). See also Lionel Trilling, *Sincerity and Authenticity* (Cambridge: Harvard University Press, 1972).

55. The reference to Fromm's book appears in DH to HL Sept. 7, 1960. During my years at Yale, the *Yale Daily News* only occasionally contained a discussion of existentialism: for an example, see James S. Campbell, review of *Truth and Symbol* by Karl Jaspers, Nov. 18, 1959, 2.

56. William Barrett, *Irrational Man: A Study in Existential Philosophy* (Garden City, NY: Doubleday, 1958), 8, 12, 18, 20, and 25.

57. Barrett, *Irrational Man,* 28, 31, and 230; Barrett, *Irrational Man,* quoted in DH to HL, Aug. 11, 1960. On the importance of Barrett's book, see George Cotkin, *Existential America* (Baltimore: Johns Hopkins University Press, 2003), 144–47.

58. This paragraph draws on letters from women I knew. On the history of dating and mating, see Beth Bailey, *From Front Porch to Back Seat: Courtship in Twentieth-Century America* (Baltimore: Johns Hopkins University Press, 1988); Ellen K. Herman, *Hands and Hearts: A History of Courtship in America* (New York: Basic, 1984).

59. Alfredo Namnum, "The Relationship of Intellectual Achievement to the Process of Identification," in Wedge, *Psychosocial Problems,* 258.

60. DH to HL, Feb. 29, 1960; DH to HL, March 8, 1960; DH to HL, May 7 or 8, 1960; DH to HL, Sept. 2, 1960; DH to HL, Aug. 18, 1960.

61. HL to DH, April 22, 1960; HL to DH, Sunday, mid-May 1960; HL to DH, May 17, 1960; HL to DH, May 29, 1960; HL to DH, June 6, 1960; HL, quoted in DH to HL, Sept. 7, 1960.

62. DH to HL, Tuesday evening, late May 1960; DH to HL, June 7, 1960; DH to HL, July 6, 1960.

63. HL to DH, June 4, 1960; DH to HL, July 15, 1960.

64. DH to HL, June 23, 1960; DH to HL, June 21, 1960.

65. DH to HL, June 23, 1960; HL to DH, June 21, 1960; DH to HL, May 7 or 8, 1960; DH to HL, May 8, 1960; HL to DH May 27, 1960; DH to HL, May 29, 1960.

66. DH to HL, late May 1960; HL to DH July 9, 1960.

67. HL to DH, July 10, 1960.

68. DH to HL, Aug. 30, 1960.

Chapter 7. Political Engagement in an Apolitical World

1. "College Political Poll Shows Nixon Ahead; Stevenson Runner-Up," *YDN,* April 19, 1960, 1.

2. Martin Filler, "Real Cool," *New York Review of Books,* June 21, 2012, 40; *Class Book 1960,* 305.

3. Jared Lobdell, telephone conversation, Nov. 27, 2012. Lobdell has been indispensable as an

informant on conservatism at Yale in this period: conversation, Nov. 27, 2012; e-mails to author, esp. Nov. 19 and 20, 2012.

4. C. Wright Mills, *The Power Elite* (New York: Oxford University Press, 1956), 302.

5. [Scott Sullivan], "An Absolute Imperative," *YDN*, Feb. 27, 1957, 4; see also, Scott Sullivan, "We Fill Out a Poll," *YDN*, March 1, 1957, 2. Sullivan wrote a novel set at Yale in the 1950s: *The Shortest Gladdest Years* (New York: Simon and Schuster, 1962).

6. Jim Ottaway, "Albertus WHO?," *Class of Its Own*, 53–54; Jonathan Seagle, telephone conversations, Jan. 3 and 9, 2013; Jonathan Seagle, letter to author, Feb. 27, 2013, in author's possession. Their writings in the campus paper are extensive: for Robert Rifkind, see "Through the Looking Glass," Oct. 15, 1957, 2, and Nov. 12, 1957, 2; for Jonathan Seagle, see the article on segregation cited in "In White America" and "Beat-Russia Politics," Feb. 23, 1959, 2; for Michael Uhlmann, see letters to editor, Nov. 12, 1958, 4, and Dec. 15, 1958, 2 and 4, and "Ayn Rand: Individualism or Altruism, But Not Both," Feb. 17, 1960, 4.

7. Neil M. Herring in *YDN*: "Preacher-Reformer: Gandhi Style," Jan. 15, 1959, 1; "An Undogmatic Commitment to Ideology," Feb. 10, 1959, 2; "Stumbling Blocks at the Summit," March 13, 1958, 2; "David Wang Wields Anti-NAACP Axe, Hits Minority Groups in Harvard Talk," Feb. 17, 1958, 1; " 'Challenge' Program Outlines Plans for Talks, Discussions, Debates," Sept. 24, 1959, 1.

8. M. Stanton Evans, *Revolt on the Campus* (Chicago: Henry Regnery, 1961), 7–8 and 10. Jared C. Lobdell, "I Am the Martyr of the People," *National Review,* Jan. 28, 1969, 80. On the history of an important conservative campus organization, which apparently did not have a chapter at Yale in the late 1950s, see Lee Edwards, *Educating for Liberty: The First Half-Century of the Intercollegiate Studies Institute* (Washington, DC: Regnery, 2003).

9. Warren Means, telephone conversation, Sept. 30, 2013. Means was the third member.

10. The class book also listed Jim Porter, but my conversation with him made it clear how unreliable such listings are: not a joiner and never active in Party of the Right, Porter's political trajectory was from liberal Republican to Obama supporter. In talking of conservative undergraduate groups I am relying on Lobdell, telephone conversation, Nov. 27, 2012, and David Stuhr, telephone conversation, Oct. 2, 2013. From what I can determine, the Party of the Right had formed earlier in the 1950s when conservatives objected to Eisenhower's defeat of Taft Republicans, leaving the Conservative Party as more moderate than the Party of the Right.

11. Ray Cassidy, Dale Collinson, Christopher Cooley, John Haverly, Bill Stiles, David Stuhr, Doug Wagner. Cooley's membership, and perhaps that of some others, was short-lived: Christopher Cooley, letter to author, Nov. 29, 2013. Collinson seems to have become more moderate during his time at Yale: compare his defense of Senator Joseph McCarthy in his letter to the editor, *YDN*, May 13, 1957, 4, with his appreciative critique of William F. Buckley Jr. in his review of Buckley's *Up from Liberalism* in *YDN*, Sept. 29, 1959, 2.

12. Lobdell, e-mail to author, Nov. 20, 2012.

13. J. C. Lobdell, "Meet Them in St. Louis," *National Review,* Sept. 23, 1969, 949.

14. Robert M. Schuchman, "Libertarian Reflections on the Failure of Democracy," *Criterion,* Feb. 1960, 16–18. On Schuchman, see Stuhr, telephone conversation; Wayne Thorburn, *A Generation Awakes: Young Americans for Freedom and the Creation of the Conservative Movement* (Ottawa, IL: Jameson, 2010), 26–29 and 42; Evans, *Revolt,* 109, 110, 163, and 173–74. On Stuhr, see David Stuhr, letter to the editor, *YDN*, Dec. 13, 1957, 4. Schuchman died of a cerebral aneurysm at age twenty-seven.

15. Jared Lobdell, *England and Always: Tolkien's World of the Rings* (Grand Rapids, MI: W. B. Eerdmans, 1981), x–xiii.

16. Jared Lobdell, "Gloria in Excelsis," *Yale Literary Magazine,* Summer 1959, 61; telephone conversation, Nov. 27, 2012; Jared Lobdell, e-mail to author, Nov. 20, 2012.

17. Jared Lobdell, "The Wisdom to Know the Difference," *Criterion,* Feb. 1960, 19–21.

18. Monroe Price, "Insufficiency without Protest," *YDN*, Oct. 29, 1958, 4 and 8; David Finkle and William C. Weeden, "Out of Class: Up the Prestige Ladder," *YDN*, May 11, 1960, 1. In fall 1959, the *Yale Daily News* listed Newman and me as the people to contact about getting involved with *Criterion:* " 'Criterion' to Award $50 Lovett Prize; Mailing List, Format to be Expanded," *YDN*, Oct. 7, 1959, 1.

19. David Brooks, "The Sidney Awards, Part I," *New York Times,* Dec. 20, 2011, which drew on Robert Boyers, "A Beauty," *Agni 74* (2011): 179–89; Daniel Horowitz, "Charles Hamilton Newman Jr.," *Class of Its Own,* 78–79.

20. Charles H. Newman Jr., "A Romantic in the Modern World: Hutchins Hapgood, 1869–1944: An Intellectual Portrait," iii–v, 8, 60, 207, and 211, Yale Student Paper Collection, folders 122–23, box 22, RU 331, acc. 19ND-A-437, YUA. There is little in the thesis on Hapgood's *Spirit of the Ghetto.*

21. DH to HL, May 14, 1960; Aug. 2, 1960.

22. Richard Posner, "Yale, A Confusion of Values," *Criterion,* Oct. 1958, 14–16. Earlier, with biting wit, Posner had criticized the *Yale Daily News* and called on Yale to raise academic standards: Richard Posner, letter to the editor, *YDN,* March 3, 1958, 2 and 4; for a thoughtful response, see Winston Lord, *YDN,* March 6, 1958, 2 and 4. I am also relying on Richard Posner, telephone conversation, Jan. 2, 2014. For other critiques of Yale in *Criterion,* see Kaehao Swing, " 'Change Your Heart, and Everything Else Shall Take Care of Itself,' " Oct. 1958, 5–8; Edmund Leites, letter to the editor, Jan. 1959, 22; John Train, "Yale—An Unobjective Evaluation," Dec. 1959, 12–13; John Andrews, "Disillusionment Reconsidered: A Polemical Analysis," Dec. 1959, 14–15; Charles Newman and Richard Bernstein, "Reflections on Teaching: A Dialogue," May 1960, 25–32.

23. CHN [Charles Hamilton Newman], "Words . . . ," *Criterion,* Feb. 1960, 3. In addition to the essays discussed here, there were others published on politics during my senior year, but not by Yale undergraduates: Brand Blanshard, "Charles Van Doren and After," Dec. 1959, 5–7; George Lefcoe, "Education for What?," Feb. 1960, 8–10; Jerome Cohen, " 'The Third American Revolution,' " Feb. 1960, 26–31; Massimo Salvadori, "Concerning Ayn Rand," May 1960, 6–10; Barbara Branden, "An 'Objectivist' Reply," May 1960, 11–14.

24. David Caplin, "Perspective from Abroad," *Criterion,* Feb. 1960, 4–7.

25. Peter Paul Bergman, "Why I Am a Socialist," *Criterion,* Feb. 1960, 15. On his life, I am relying Peter Paul Bergman, telephone conversation, Dec. 3, 2011; *Peter Bergman's Radio Free Oz,* www.radiofreeoz.com/?s=yale.

26. Sherwin Goldman, "Liberalism: A Prologue," *Criterion,* Feb. 1960, 11–14. For his concern that students were not sufficiently committed to focusing of the problems on African Americans, see "Goldman 'Upset' by Today's Student in Report for Washington Meeting," *YDN,* March 16, 1960, 1.

27. Charles Blitzer, "Criterion Review," *YDN,* March 18, 1960, 2.

28. Classmates in United World Federalists were also active in these years, though not nearly with the public prominence of JDS or GOF.

29. Robert Herbert, telephone conversation, Nov. 13, 2012. It is somewhat difficult to find ample information on GOF. One exception is Richard Greeman (class of 1961), *Beware of Capitalist Sharks!* (lulu.com, 2012).

30. Neil Herring, telephone conversation, Nov. 12, 2012. Leddy came from a prosperous family in Taunton, MA. His politics seem to have derived from an eagerness, shared with his father, to be open to the world, an ability to associate with the widest variety of people, and a strong dislike of injustice: Tracy Leddy, telephone conversation, Feb. 1, 2014. In the chapter on Africa, I discuss GOF member Ed Elmendorf, who entered with our class but graduated in 1961.

31. Kirke Wilson, *Class of Its Own,* 522. Other biographical information is Kirke Wilson, telephone conversation, Nov. 19, 2012; Kirke Wilson, e-mail to author, Feb. 23, 2013; Kirke Wilson, conversation, Feb. 14, 2013. See also Kirke Wilson, "Riots! There Have Been Some Great Ones," *Ivy Magazine* 2 (March 1958): 9–13, which treats riots in elite colleges as driven by a desire for fun and psychological relief.

32. *Class of Its Own,* 522.

33. A. J. Leddy, Charles Newman, Robert Laird, Richard Koffler, Richard Greeman, and Richard Posner, letter to the editor, *YDN,* Nov. 11, 1958, 2. [Robert B. Semple Jr.], "More on Pasternak," *YDN,* Nov. 11, 1958, 2. For a forceful reply, see A. J. Leddy, Charles Newman, Richard Posner, letter to the editor, *YDN,* Nov. 6, 1958, 2. For Robert Bone's defense of the GOF position, including his long-standing anticommunism and his hope that he could make Semple a more

effective anticommunist, see Robert A. Bone, letter to the editor, *YDN*, Nov. 7, 1958, 3. Semple has not responded to my repeated requests for information on who wrote editorials for the *News* when he was its chairman.

34. John W. Powell to Dean Richard Carroll, June 5, 1961, in the files of William C. DeVane, RU 126, acc. 1964-A-003, folder 38, box 22, YUA. On Powell's job with the FBI, see "Griswold Names FBI Agent Powell Associate Dean, Security Director," *YDN*, Feb. 23, 1960, 1. Williams did not show up because he had fled to Cuba and his lawyer spoke instead. On FBI surveillance of the George Orwell Forum, see John Rodden, *George Orwell: The Politics of Literary Reputation, The Making and Unmaking of 'St. George' Orwell* (New York: Oxford University Press, 1989), 410. Sigmund Diamond, *Compromised Campus: The Collaboration of Universities with the Intelligence Community, 1945–1955* (New York: Oxford University Press, 1992), 204–42, explores how Yale cooperated with the FBI in the investigation of students and faculty. In the spring of 1961, those on the executive committee of GOF were Bergman and Greeman from the class of 1961; Herring, then at Yale Law School; from the law school Eleanor Holmes (Norton); Jonathan Spence, then a Clare fellow studying Chinese history; and faculty adviser Robert Herbert; "Program and Structure of the George Orwell Forum," undated document, but probably spring 1961, in RU 126; acc. 1964-A-003:folder 38, box 22, YUA. Under GOF's auspices Bone organized a conference in May 1959, welcoming New England students interested in the positions *Dissent* took. Among the speakers were Michael Walzer, Lewis Coser, and Seymour Melman: notice for "Dissent Student Conference," *Dissent* 6 (Spring 1959): 170.

35. André Schiffrin, *A Political Education: Coming of Age in Paris and New York* (Hoboken, NJ: Melville House, 2007), 122; André Schiffrin, telephone conversation, Nov. 14, 2012; André Schiffrin, "The Student Movement in the 1950's: A Reminiscence," *Radical America* 2 (May–June 1968): 26–40.

36. For early discussions at Yale and nationally about a name change, see material dated Feb. 1957 in folder labeled "LID," box 1, Schiffrin Papers; "Name Change 1959," folder 9, box 7, SLID Papers. Kirkpatrick Sale, *SDS* (New York: Random House, 1973), 15, says that in the late 1950s there were three chapters of SLID—Yale, Columbia, and Michigan; however, Haber, conversation, claims that in the late 1950s André Schiffrin failed in his effort to persuade members of Michigan's Political Issues Club to affiliate with SLID. The material in box 10, SLID Papers, and Jonny Weiss, conversation, Dec. 17, 2012, make it clear that there were more chapters than those at Yale, Columbia, and Michigan. Nonetheless, for very early years of SDS I do rely on Sale, *SDS*, 15–27.

37. André Schiffrin, typescript, probably spring 1957, unmarked folder, box 1, Schiffrin Papers. For a negative view of the predominance of Jews, see Tom Hayden, *Reunion: A Memoir* (New York: Random House, 1988), 29–30. Among the early members were Jesse Lemisch, one of the few of my Yale contemporaries who bridged Old and New Left as did Greeman, class of 1961. For lists of members, see Feb. 8, 1957, list, unmarked folder, box 1; "John Dewey Society Membership," probably fall 1956, brown folder, box 2; "John Dewey Society of Yale University, Membership—1955," brown folder, box 2, all in Schiffrin Papers. In *If I Had a Hammer . . . The Death of the Old Left and the Birth of the New Left* (New York: Basic, 1987), Maurice Isserman shows the continuity and connections between the two movements. With Schiffrin's impending departure, leadership passed for 1957–58 to Rifkind: Robert Rifkind, telephone conversation, Nov. 14, 2012.

38. Schiffrin, *Education*, 134. I can identify one classmate, Stephen Kunitz, who came from an Old Left background. His father Joshua Kunitz, wrote *Russia: The Giant That Came Last* (New York: Dodd, Mead, 1947) and was expelled from the Communist Party in the early 1940s because he preferred autonomy to authority. He was blacklisted from academic positions. On Joshua Kunitz, see also Daniel Aaron, *Writers on the Left* (1961; New York: Avon, 1965), 236–40. Steve Kunitz grew up in Greenwich Village, went to progressive private schools, and in Manhattan encountered rich, cosmopolitan cultures and politics. Apolitical at Yale, Kunitz in his professional life as a medical doctor both followed his parents' commitments to social justice and distanced himself from their belief in the inevitability of progress: Steve Kunitz, telephone conversation, Aug. 16, 2014; Steve Kunitz, memoir, copy in author's possession.

39. André Schiffrin to Jim [Farmer], Dec. 7, 1953, folder 17, box 10, SLID Papers. Soon after, James Farmer, who coordinated SLID's efforts from the New York office, left to lead the Congress of Racial Equality. Others were somewhat more open about their goals for JDS: see Charles Van Tassel, "Dear Friend," mimeographed letter, March 27, 1958, folder 19, box 10, SLID Papers.

40. "Report of Activities—Spring Term, 1954," May 1954, folder 19, box 10, SLID Papers.

41. On Vietnam, "Report of Activities—Spring Term, 1954," folder 19, box 10, SLID Papers; on Aptheker, André Schiffrin, e-mail to author, June 13, 2013; material in folder 21, box 10, SLID Papers.

42. My interviews with classmates active in JDS make clear that Jonny Weiss played a key role in persuading many to join. I had known him in high school when he stayed at our house, his mother deceased and his father traveling. The list of JDS members in the class book is hardly complete, and the SLID papers contain membership lists for JDS that included Les Aspin, Ned Cabot, and Oscar Tang: "JDS Membership Mailing List," probably 59–60, folder 18, box 10, SLID Papers, and "Membership, Yale J.D.S., 3/26/59," folder 18, box, 10, SLID Papers. My name does not appear on any list, though I know that I attended meetings of JDS. More generally membership lists hardly contain all of the classmates on the left. For example, Bill Cobb read *I. F. Stone's Weekly* and Cobb's close friend Bob Stone often went to Manhattan to listen to jazz and in 1959 went to Cuba: David Elliott, conservation, Dec. 27, 2013.

43. Eric Walther, telephone conversation, Nov. 15, 2012.

44. "'I Love Ludwig' Promoter to Edit Publication; Literary Magazine, 'Angst,' Will Appear May 6," *YDN,* April 29, 1957, 1.

45. "Leites of 'Ludwig' Fame Scores Yale Intellectuals; Plans New Discussions," *YDN,* Oct. 10, 1957, 1.

46. Jon Borgzinner, "Allen Ginsberg Reads Poetry," *YDN,* Nov. 25, 1958, 1; Edmund Leites, e-mail to author, Feb. 3, 2013. It is possible to read Edmund Leites, *The Puritan Conscience and Modern Sexuality* (New Haven: Yale University Press, 1996), as a call on Yale to remember an earlier, more capacious attitude to sexuality: Edmund Leites, e-mail to author, Jan. 23, 2014.

47. Edmund Leites, "Report of Education Vice President," *SLID Voice,* Sept. 1958, copy in unidentified folder, box 1, Schiffrin Papers. Leites is not listed specifically as author but because this was the report of an office he held, I assume he wrote it.

48. Sale identified Weiss as someone from Antioch College, but Weiss, Walther, and Haber make it clear that this is Yale's Jonny Weiss. For what he has written on his experiences at Yale, including on JDS, see Jesse Lemisch, "A Dissenting View: Bushes 'R' Us," *Class of 1957 50th Reunion Book* (New Haven: Office of Information Resources, 2007), 75–80.

49. *Venture,* 2 (Sept. 1960): 2 (list of officers) and 27–29 (Caplin essay), unidentified folder, box 3, Schiffrin Papers. The other two officers were Al Haber and Carol Weisbrod. She has been unwilling to talk to me about her work at SLID as it transformed into SDS.

50. The materials on the Yale chapter (folders 17–21, box 10, SLID Papers) are far more extensive than those for any other chapter. In addition to classmates who were officers, Charlie Van Tassel and Michael Rosenbaum served as SLID presidents: see "SLID Officers, 1958–59," folder 13, box 6, SLID Papers; "1960 S.D.S. Convention," folder 11, box 7, SLID Papers.

51. In addition to these three, I would mention as philosophy majors who were on the left Tom Miller, Kirke Wilson, Bill Cobb, Howard Richards, Burt Rutledge, and Edward Schieffelin.

52. Edmund Leites, conversation, Dec. 17, 2012.

53. "Undergraduate Course of Study, 1958–59," 155; parody of undergraduate course of study, 1959–60, *Yale Record,* May 1959, 15. Richard Bernstein, telephone conversation, Jan. 7, 2013 discussed the course on Marxism. Hendel voted for the appointment of Weiss, although he worried about him as someone whose lowly social origins impelled him to be too assertive. On Hendel's concerns about the Weiss appointment, see Dan A. Oren, *Joining the Club: A History of Jews and Yale* (New Haven: Yale University Press, 1985), 263. On the philosophy department, I am relying on Alex Mourelatos, telephone conversation, Feb. 12, 2013; Bruce Kuklick, "Philosophy at Yale in the Century after Darwin," *History of Philosophy Quarterly* 21 (July 2004): 313–36. See also Karsten Harries, e-mail to author, Feb. 4, 2013; Edmund Leites, telephone conversation, Feb. 3, 2013.

54. Edmund Leites, Eric Walther, and Jonny Weiss, conversation, Dec. 17, 2012.

55. Tim Light, e-mail to author, March 5, 2014. Light's story suggests Ludwig was Wittgenstein but the articles in the *Yale Daily News,* as well as information from Leites, cited above, refer to Beethoven.

56. "Hirshorn Wins Screen Producers Film Award," *YDN,* Jan. 28, 1960, 1 and 9; "Local Insurance Exec Was Hollywood Producer," *Chestnut Hill Local,* Oct. 20, 2010, http://chestnuthilllocal. com; [Ralph] Hirshorn, "Screen Sketches," *YDN,* Oct. 6, 1959, 3. Though less countercultural, also influential were the music reviews by my classmate Jonathan Hufstadter and Robert Kimball, class of 1961.

57. Coburn Britton, "Odetta," *YDN,* Oct. 21, 1957, 2. On the festival, see "Expanded Schedule of Folk Music Set for Current Year," *YDN,* Oct. 24, 1959, 1. On folk music at Yale more generally, see Gideon Gordon, "Folk Music: Escape from 'Shoeness,' Desire for Permanence," *YDN,* Oct. 23, 1959, 8.

58. "Novelist Mailer to Relate 'Beatnicks,' Negro Culture," *YDN,* Dec. 8, 1958, 1; Stephen A. Lefkowitz, review of *The Subterraneans* by Jack Kerouac, *YDN,* Feb. 26, 1958, 2; Stephen A. Lefkowitz, review of *Selected Poems* by Kenneth Patchen and *A Coney Island of the Mind* by Lawrence Ferlinghetti, *YDN,* May 16, 1958, 4 and 7; Leslie Epstein, "A Poet Reads His Work," *YDN,* March 12, 1959, 7; R. W. B. Lewis, quoted in Albert M. Chambers Jr., "R. W. B. Lewis: A World of American Studies," *YDN,* March 4, 1960, 2.

59. Daniel Horowitz, "To the members of the Rhodes Scholarship Committee" and "To the Woodrow Wilson National Fellowship Foundation," fall 1959, in author's possession; Edmund Leites, telephone conservation, Feb. 3, 2013.

60. DH to family, June 27, 1959; DH to parents, July 4, 1959.

61. DH to parents, June 24, 1959; DH to family, Aug. 22, 1959.

62. DH to HLH, Feb. 15 and 29, 1960, June 8 and 9, 1960, July 14, 1960.

63. DH to HLH, June 2, 1960; also DH to HLH, Tuesday evening, June 7, 1960, and Aug. 13, 1960.

64. Jeremy Nahum, Joel Finer, and Neil Glazer, conversation, Nov. 13, 2013

65. Kirke Wilson, conversation, Feb. 14, 2013. In addition, Edward Schieffelin combined left politics with countercultural experiences.

66. Lemisch, "Dissenting," 77; Dick Celeste, telephone conversation, Nov. 19, 2012.

Chapter 8. It All Comes Together

1. Benjamin Fine, " 'Silent Generation' Regains Voice on Major Problems," *New Haven Register,* March 13, 1960, copy in author's possession. Challenge had also begun to attract some visitors who would emerge in the 1960s as major figures in progressive student movements. Al Lowenstein attended at least one of its meetings. Al Haber, the first president of SDS, came to New Haven for the March 1960 program and then returned to Ann Arbor for the initial conference of SDS, held on the first weekend of May. On Lowenstein's presence, I am relying on Kirke Wilson, telephone conversation, Nov. 9, 2012; on Haber, Al Haber, telephone conversation, Oct. 17, 2012.

2. "Mock UN Session Planned; To Convene Here in April," *YDN,* Oct. 12, 1957, 1 and 6; "Model UN Convenes Today with Speech by [Chester] Bowles at North Haven High School," *YDN,* April 11, 1958, 1. Among the others were classmates Rod Marriott, Peter Seed, Peter Kirchner, Guy Stevens, Brian Jensen, Howard Richards, William Rockefeller, and Louis Tharp.

3. "Sound and Fury: At Yale . . ." *YDN,* Feb. 10, 1958, 2.

4. [Robert B. Semple Jr.], "Yale's Discussion Process: Politics," *YDN,* Feb. 27, 1958, 2, surveyed the scene and wondered where innovation in student politics would come from. For one of many of examples of the problems at the Political Union, see "Rightists Stymie 4th Party Movement, Outmaneuver Constitutional Unionists," *YDN,* April 29, 1960, 1. On the merger of the Undergraduate Lecture Committee and Challenge, which really was a takeover by the latter, see "Challenge, ULC Pool Resources in an Attempt to Better Programs," *YDN,* Oct. 2, 1959, 1. On the origins of the Undergraduate Lecture Committee in Fence Club, see Herschel E. Post Jr., "A Spark of Light Amidst the Political Gloom at Yale," *YDN,* Sept. 23, 1958, 4.

5. Dick Celeste, telephone conversation, April 26, 2012.

6. Challenge letterhead, in author's possession. The budget figures are from Stephen Kass, "Challenge: A New Concept in Student Organizations," *YAM*, Feb. 1960, 11.

7. The discussion of leaders and supporters draws on Steve Kass, e-mail to author, Dec. 2, 2011, who also emphasized the role that Joel Fleishman played; Celeste, conversation, April 26, 2012; Bryant, conversation, Nov. 25, 2011. In addition to Bowles and Bryant, in the class book the following classmates listed Challenge among their activities: Neil Herring, Howard Kirshbaum, Andrew Logue, James Porter, Monroe Price, Richard Seidman, Jonny Weiss, and Kirke Wilson.

8. I am relying on Celeste, conversation, April 26, 2012, and telephone conversation, Nov. 19, 2012.

9. Ralph Bryant, letter to the editor, *YDN*, March 13, 1959, 2. On rooming with an African American: Ralph Bryant, conversation, Nov. 25, 2011. It was a common practice for Yale to make sure a white would not object to having an African American roommate; Yale contacted Jim Porter, and he also agreed and roomed with Bruce Ballard: Jim Porter, telephone conversation, Nov. 13, 2012. On Bryant, see Ralph Bryant, letters to editor, *YDN*, Nov. 15, 1958, 2; Jan. 18, 1960, 2 (with Sam Bowles). For the attacks, see Michael A. Doyle, letter to editor, *YDN*, Nov. 11, 1958, 2; Ted Sheldon, letter to editor, *YDN*, Jan. 20, 1960, 2.

10. Ralph C. Bryant III, "Junior Year," *Class Book 1960*, 25–32.

11. Celeste, conversation, April 26, 2012.

12. Posters, "The Challenge of American Democracy" and "The Challenge of the Nuclear Age," and letterhead for "Challenge," in author's possession.

13. "*Challenge:* The Idea," undated document, probably spring 1959, folder 20, box 10, SLID Papers.

14. "Yale Colloquium Explores the Challenge of the Nuclear Age," Dec. 1959, 4-page typescript, in author's possession.

15. "challenge* . . . THE IDEA," brochure announcing the academic year's programs, probably early fall 1959, in author's possession. In another, less public, document, the organizers articulated their commitments more clearly when they affirmed the importance of greater efforts at disarmament and "positive integration in all phases of society" as the "minimum demand of freedom": "The Ideology of *Challenge*," undated document, 1958–59 academic year, folder 20, box 10, SLID Papers.

16. Virginia Tansey, " 'Challenge' Conference at Yale Draws 1300 Regional Students," *Wellesley College News*, Dec. 10, 1959, 3, in author's possession.

17. On Frank, "Challenge: Third Progress Report," in author's possession; on Warburg and Berns, see "Yale Colloquium Explores." Originally, there were to be three programs, but the organizers collapsed "The Future of Non-Western Revolutions," and "Racial Integration: American Society Tomorrow" into one: "Challenge: Tentative Outline of Program," undated document, 1958–59 academic year, folder 20, box 10, SLID Papers.

18. "Yale Colloquium Explores."

19. "Challenge of American Democracy."

20. Celeste, conversation, April 26, 2012.

21. Daniel Horowitz, "To the Woodrow Wilson National Fellowship Foundation," fall 1959, in author's possession.

22. Charles Schmitz, "My Yale: Plan B," 2010, 8, copy in author's possession; Kass, e-mail. Steve Kass and Peter Paul Bergman led Challenge in 1960–61. For a somewhat apolitical statement of the goals of Challenge, see Kass, "Challenge," 11.

23. Tansey, " 'Challenge' Conference."

24. William Pollard Lamb Jr., "Senior Year," *Class Book 1960*, 35.

25. Advertisement, *YDN*, Dec. 4, 1959, 5.

26. Charles Blitzer, "Innocence and Indifference," *YDN*, April 7, 1959, 2; [Herschel E. Post Jr.], "The Unsanitary Generation," and Loren N. Divinsky, "Yale and the 'Antiseptic Generation,' " *YDN* (special edition), May 12, 1960, 2 and A5, respectively.

27. Richard B. Stewart, "Brought Forth in Folly," *YDN*, March 10, 1960, 2. For the debate

over Challenge, see Van V. Burger, "Commitment for Challengers," *YDN*, Dec. 7, 1959, 1 and 9; [James H. Ottaway Jr.], "They Cannot Wait for Us," *YDN*, Dec. 7, 1959, 2; [Herschel E. Post Jr.], "The Attack from Within," *YDN*, March 14, 1960, 2. Stewart came to Yale from University High School in Cleveland. At Yale he joined a fraternity, Torch, and Elihu, was junior Phi Beta Kappa and summa cum laude, and feature editor of the *News*; after Yale he headed for Oxford on a Rhodes, followed by a degree from Harvard Law School and a career as a professor of law, principally at Harvard and NYU.

28. Tansey, " 'Challenge' Conference."

29. Information on how Bryant, Kass, and Bergman took different positions on disarmament is found in "Challenge* Disarmament: One of the Vital Questions for College Youth," *Yale Reports* radio program, Jan. 24, 1960, DH/HLH.

30. On the transformative and political power of folk music, see Judith Smith, *Becoming Belafonte: Black Artist, Public Radical* (Austin: University of Texas Press, 2014); Robert Cantwell, *When We Were Good: The Folk Revival* (Cambridge: Harvard University Press, 1996). In contrast, one contemporary emphasized not the political dimensions of folk music but its importance as "a cultural treasure and an art": Christopher Cory, "Folk Singing," *Ivy Magazine* 4 (Dec. 1959): 13.

31. "Four Subjects Selected for Challenge Talks; Response 'Excellent,' " *YDN*, March 2, 1960, 1.

32. On the problems Challenge posed to conservative groups, see "Bozell Will Represent Conservative Viewpoint in Calliopean Lecture," *YDN*, Dec. 3, 1959, 5; "Calliopean Society," *YDN*, Dec. 5, 1959, 4; "Conservatives to Speak to Calliopean Society during Coming Weeks," *YDN*, March 10, 1960, 1; caption of photograph, in Dennis Koromzay, "Challenge*," *Ivy Magazine* 4 (Dec. 1959): 17.

33. [Ottaway Jr.], "They Cannot Wait"; Richard Flacks, "Who Protests: The Social Bases of the Student Movement," in *Protest! Student Activism in America*, ed. Julian Foster and Durward Long (New York: Morrow, 1970), 152–53; Ruth Feldstein, *How It Feels to Be Free: Black Women Entertainers and the Civil Rights Movement* (New York: Oxford University Press, 2013), 55; see also Ryan Irwin, *Gordian Knot: Apartheid and the Unmaking of the Liberal World Order* (New York: Oxford University Press, 2012). In fall 1959, protests developed against discrimination in housing faced by graduate students from Africa, Asia, India, and the Caribbean: William G. Bardell, "Discrimination against Foreign Students Disrupts Yale Graduate Housing," *YDN*, Oct. 6, 1959, 1 and 5.

34. Monroe Price, "Undergraduate Yale," *YAM*, May 1960, 25.

35. "Eight Yale Students Picket Downtown Woolworth Store; Five of Group Apprehended by City Police Officers," *YDN*, Feb. 22, 1990, 1, 4, and 12.

36. "Eight Yale Students"; "Harvard Picketers Protest Woolworth's Discrimination in Chain's Southern Stores," *YDN*, March 1, 1960, 1; Bowles, Leddy, Bryant, and James Turner [a Yale Law School student], letter to editor, *YDN*, March 18, 1960, 2; "Freedom Fund Plans to Ask Contributions at Meeting Tomorrow," *YDN*, March 22, 1960, 2; "Graduate Students Formally Protest Discrimination in New Haven, South," *YDN*, March 23, 1960, 1; "Students Circulate Segregation Letter; Hometown Papers to Receive Copies," *YDN*, May 17, 1960, 1.

37. Barry Loncke, telephone conversation, Jan. 7, 2014; Donald A. Downs, *Cornell '69: Liberalism and the Crisis of the American University* (Ithaca: Cornell University Press, 1999), 5 and 194–95. After law school Loncke worked for a corporate law firm in Los Angeles, then moved to Sacramento for a state government job, and eventually served as a judge for twenty years on the Sacramento Superior Court. On his career, see Mark Starr, Dennis A. Williams, and Aric Press, "A Look Back at Anger," *Newsweek*, April 23, 1984, 3.

38. Charles Keil, "Afterword: Postscripts," in *Urban Blues* (1966; Chicago: University of Chicago Press, 1991), 225; Keil, *Urban Blues*, viii. On Keil, I rely on Robert Christgau, "Up from Darien: Charles Keil," *Village Voice*, 1998, available at www.robertchristgau.com/xg/bkrev/keil-96.php, and Charles Keil, telephone conversation, Jan. 10, 2014.

39. Charles Keil, Barry Loncke, Isiah Baker, and Nelson Kasfir, letter to editor, *YDN*, Feb. 18, 1960, 2. See also "NAACP at Yale," *YDN*, Feb. 15, 2012, 2; Barry Loncke, letter to editor, *YDN*,

March 1, 1960, 2; "Yale NAACP Branch Encourages Negroes to Seek Admission," and "NAACP Group Plans Program to Encourage More Negro Applicants," *YDN*, April 11, 1960, 1. Two African Americans from the class of 1961 who joined Loncke in the Yale NAACP are Baker and Theodore S. Ledbetter.

40. "Group to Aid Natives Combatting Apartheid Established at Yale," *YDN*, April 18, 1960, 1; "Organization to Aid Jailed South Africans Joins National Drive," *YDN*, April 20, 1961, 1; Murray Last, letter to editor, *YDN*, April 29, 1960, 2. Two Yale Law School students also played crucial roles in the anti-apartheid protest: James R. Turner and Joel Fleishman.

41. [Herschel Post Jr.], "Make Room for the Martyrs," *YDN*, Feb. 22, 1960, 2; [Herschel Post Jr.], "Chase Those Windmills," *YDN*, Feb. 26, 1960, 2; English Showalter, letter to editor, *YDN*, Feb. 29, 1960, 2; Jonathan J. Seagle, "On Civil Rights," *YDN*, March 23, 1960, 2; [Herschel Post Jr.], "Oblivion Road" and "Freedom Fund," *YDN*, March 24, 1960, 2.

42. Paul N. Klotz and Robert M. Schuchman, letter to editor, *YDN*, Feb. 26, 1960, 2; John David Maguire, letter to editor, *YDN*, April 13, 1960, 2.

43. "NAACP at Yale"; Keil, Loncke Baker, and Kasfir, letter to editor.

44. Kevin P. Buckley, "The Curious, the Convinced," *YDN*, April 7, 1960, 1 and 5.

45. *YDN*, March 23, 1960, 1.

46. Information from Bill Arnold, telephone conversation, Aug. 21, 2014, and e-mails to author, Aug. 21, 22, and 23, 2014. "Expanded Schedule of Folk Music Set for Current Year," *YDN*, Oct. 24, 1959, 1. Arnold relied on classmate John Burgis to carry out the practical aspects of these folk music endeavors. After graduation Arnold opposed the war in Vietnam; in the late 1960s decided he was gay; built and then sold a company; and became involved in HIV/AIDS activism, first in New York's Hudson River valley and beginning in 1995 in Washington, DC.

47. For the scholarship on student activism, most of it focusing on the 1960s and those on the left, see Richard Flacks, "The Liberated Generation: An Exploration of the Roots of Student Protest," *Journal of Social Issues* 23 (July 1967): 52–75; Richard Flacks, "Social and Cultural Meanings of Student Revolt: Some Informal Comparative Observations," *Social Problems* 17 (Winter 1970): 340–57; Flacks, "Who Protests," 134–57; Virginia P. Lacy, "Political Knowledge of College Activist Groups: SDS, YAF, and YD," *Journal of Politics* 33 (Aug. 1971): 840–45; Milton Mankoff and Richard Flacks, "The Changing Social Base of the American Student Movement," *Annals of the American Academy of Political and Social Science* 395 (May 1971): 54–67; Riley Dunlap, "Radical and Conservative Activists: A Comparison of Family Backgrounds," *Pacific Sociological Review* 13 (Summer 1970): 171–81. Kenneth Keniston, *The Uncommitted: Alienated Youth in American Society* (New York: Harcourt, Brace and World, 1965) and *Young Radicals: Notes on Committed Youth* (New York: Harcourt, Brace and World, 1968), focus on a somewhat but significantly later period.

48. David Stuhr, telephone conversation, Oct. 2, 2013, has helped me understand these dynamics, as did Jared Lobdell, telephone conversation, Nov. 10, 2013.

49. In the *Yale Daily News* I could find no mention of the JDS after February 1963 and of the GOF after April 1964. The Calliopean Society persisted well into the 1960s but not with the prominence it had in our years. Students for a Democratic Society barely struggled on until its revival in 1965. Challenge went on for a while and then like the other organizations, it disappeared—with Joe Lieberman, class of 1964 and future senator from Connecticut, reporting its demise in 1962. *Criterion* had a longer life, but with a final issue in 1968, it too died. On the waning of political activism in the early 1960s, see Joseph I. Lieberman, "Organized, Neutral, Spectacular," *YDN*, Feb. 8, 1962, 1; "Challenge," *YDN*, Feb. 12, 1963, 2; "The Freshman in Politics," *YDN*, Sept. 17, 1963, 23.

50. Clinton J. Najarian, "House Un-American Sub-Committee Begins Local Communist Hearings," *YDN*, Sept. 24, 1956, 1.

Chapter 9. Postpartum Politics

1. Saul Pett and Hugh Mulligan, *Cedar Rapids Gazette*, June 5, 1960, 8; Jim Ottaway and Charles Sorrels quoted in same.

2. "Fesler Stresses Vietnam Importance; Credits Diem with Country's Success," *YDN,* Dec. 3, 1956, 2; David Chandler, "Paul Mus (1906–1969): A Biographical Sketch," *Journal of Vietnamese Studies* 4 (Winter 2009): 149–91.

3. Mike Dickerson, telephone conversations, Jan. 29 and 30, 2014; Michael Dickerson, *Class of Its Own,* 198.

4. Rob Hanke, telephone conservation, Feb. 10, 2014.

5. Matt Gardner, *25th RD,* 49; Richard H. Minear, correspondence with author, Nov. 4 and 5, 2013; Richard H. Minear, *Victor's Justice: The Tokyo War Crimes Trial* (Princeton: Princeton University Press, 1971), xi.

6. Peter Karsten (with seven students), "'Professional' and 'Citizen' Officers: A Comparison of Service Academy and ROTC Officer Candidates," in *Public Opinion and the Military Establishment,* ed. Charles C. Moskos Jr. (Beverly Hills, CA: Sage, 1971), 42, 56, and 57; Peter Karsten, "The 'New' American Military History: A Map of the Territory, Explored and Unexplored," *American Quarterly* 36 (1984): 389–418; Peter Karsten, ed., *The Military in America: From the Colonial Era to the Present* (New York: Free Press, 1980); Peter Karsten, "Anti-ROTC: Response to Vietnam or 'Consciousness III,'" in *New Civil-Military Relations: The Agonies of Adjustment to Post-Vietnam Realities,* ed. John P. Lovell and Philip S. Kronenberg (New Brunswick, NJ: Transaction, 1974), 111–27; Peter Karsten, telephone conversation, Jan. 23, 2014. Tim Light helped run Clergy Concerned About Vietnam from Union Theological School for several months in 1966: Tim Light, telephone conversation, March 4, 2014.

7. Miller, *35th RD,* 126. On the work of Miller and Barsky, see Terrence Smith, "Vietnam Clinic Aids War-Maimed Children," *New York Times,* Oct. 10, 1969.

8. Miller, *25th RD,* 98–99.

9. Martha Gellhorn, "Open Arms for the Vietcong" [original, 1966, *The Guardian*], in Martha Gellhorn, *The Face of War* (New York: Atlantic Monthly Press, 1986), 243. See also David W. P. Elliott, *Changings Worlds: Vietnam's Transition from Cold War to Globalization* (New York: Oxford University Press, 2012).

10. Jonathan Mirsky, "Wartime Lies," *New York Review of Books,* Oct. 10, 2003.

11. David W. P. Elliott, *The Vietnamese War: Revolution and Social Change in the Mekong Delta, 1930–1975,* 2 vols. (Armonk, NY: M. E. Sharpe: 2003), 1:xv.

12. Mai Elliott, *RAND in Southeast Asia: A History of the Vietnam War Era* (Santa Monica, CA: Rand, 2010), 250. Information on David comes from Mai's book and from multiple conversations and e-mails with them both beginning in late December 2012.

13. Elliott, *Vietnamese,* 1:xiii, 4, and 5, and 2:1382.

14. Duong Van Mai Elliott, *The Sacred Willow: Four Generations in the Life of a Vietnamese Family* (New York: Oxford University Press, 1999), 19, 28, 36, 69, and 98.

15. Elliott, *Sacred Willow,* 227.

16. Elliott, *Sacred Willow,* 276, 289, and 291.

17. Elliott, *Sacred Willow,* 316–17, 319, 323, and 334.

18. Sam Bowles, quoted in Joel R. Kramer, "The Voices of Dissent," *Harvard Alumni Magazine* March 25, 1967, 24. Aside from Bowles perhaps the most important radical from our ranks was Howard Richards. He left Yale after two years and sustained his radicalism from before his days at Yale to the present. For information on Richards, I am relying on Howard Richards, e-mails to author, Feb. 2 and 3, 2013; Howard Richards, Professor of Peace and Global Studies, and Philosophy, Earlham College, website, www.howardri.org; Kirke Wilson, e-mail to author, Feb. 3, 2013; Edmund Leites, e-mail to author, Feb. 3, 2013.

19. Samuel Bowles and Herbert Gintis, *Schooling in Capitalist America: Educational Reform and the Contradictions of Economic Life* (New York: Basic Books, 1976), 14–17, 28, and 288. Earlier Bowles had begun to explore the issues raised in the Coleman Report: Samuel Bowles and Henry M. Levin, "The Determinants of Scholastic Achievement—An Appraisal of Some Recent Evidence," *Journal of Human Resources* 3 (Winter 1968): 3–24; Samuel Bowles, "An Explanation," *Phi Delta Kappan* 50 (Oct. 1968): 108.

20. Samuel Bowles, "Hardly a Surprise," *Harvard Crimson,* Feb. 27, 1973; Samuel Bowles and Herbert Gintis, *A Cooperative Species: Human Reciprocity and Its Evolution* (Princeton: Princ-

eton University Press, 2011). On the situation at Harvard, see Richard Parker, *John Kenneth Galbraith: His Life, His Politics, His Economics* (New York: Farrar, Straus and Giroux, 2005), 506–10.

21. For this discussion of his life, I am relying on Neil Herring, telephone conversation, Nov. 12, 2012. Kirke Wilson, *40th RD*, 144.

22. On the racial, artistic, and commercial issues connected with the Houston Grand Opera's revival of *Porgy and Bess* in the late 1970s, see Ellen Noonan, *The Strange Career of Porgy and Bess: Race, Culture, and America's Most Famous Opera* (Chapel Hill: University of North Carolina Press, 2012), 284–300.

23. William Schott, review of *New Axis* by Charles Newman, *Life*, July 1, 1966, copy in author's possession.

24. Among Carol Brightman's books are *Venceremos Brigade: Young Americans Sharing the Life and Work of Revolutionary Cuba* (New York: Simon and Schuster, 1971), co-edited with Sandra Levinson; *Writing Dangerously: Mary McCarthy and Her World* (New York: Clarkson Potter, 1992); *Sweet Chaos: The Grateful Dead's American Adventure* (New York: Clarkson Potter, 1998); *Total Insecurity: The Myth of American Omnipotence* (New York: Verso, 2004).

25. For his celebration of Schuchman, see Jared Lobdell, "A Time to Mourn," *Insight and Outlook*, March–April 1966, 7.

26. See, as examples, the following essays by Lobdell in *Insight and Outlook*: "Mimeocracy," Jan. 1962, 19 and 21; "Subject and Sovereign," Nov. 1962, 14; "A Bold Amusing Instinctive Thing to Do," Sept.–Oct. 1964, 9–10; "With Friends Like These," July–Aug. 1965, 14–15; "Washed by the River, Blest by the Suns of Home" and "Mason-Dixon," Sept.–Oct. 1965, 10 and 13; "Who Shall Overcome?," Nov.–Dec. 1965, 14–15; "For Conscience Sake," Jan.–Feb. 1966, 7; "All Aboard!," Spring 1967, 7; "Hier, Stehe, Ich," Summer–Fall 1967, 7; "Some Points of Issue," Fall 1967, 11–12; "The First Ten Years," anniversary issue 1969, 4–9. I am grateful to Daniel Hummel for helping me research Lobdell's essays in Madison, WI.

27. Jared Lobdell, "Neighborhood America," Oct. 27, 1972, 1191; "The Old Acheson and the New," Dec. 30, 1969, 1330; "Meet Them in St. Louis," Sept. 23, 1969, 949, "I Am the Martyr of the People," Jan. 28, 1969, 80, all in *National Review*. For another statement on how to reconcile traditionalist and libertarian strands of conservatism, see Jared Lobdell, "Conservatism: Think and Clear," *National Review*, March 8, 1985, 37. For information on his career, see Yale Political Union, Alumni Board, http://theypu.com/alumni/ypu-alumni-board.

28. See these publications by Jared Lobdell: *A Tolkien Compass*, ed. Jared Lobdell (LaSalle, IL: Open Court, 1975); C. W. Larison, *Sylvia Dubois: A Biografy of the Slav Who Whipt Her Mistres and Gand Her Fredom*, ed. Jared Lobdell (New York: Oxford University Press, 1998); *The Scientifiction Novels of C. S. Lewis: Space and Time in the Ransom Stories* (Jefferson, NC: McFarland, 2004); *This Strange Illness: Alcoholism and Bill W.* (New York: Aldine de Gruyter, 2004); *The World of the Rings: Language, Religion, and Adventure in Tolkien* (Chicago: Open Court 2004); *The Rise of Tolkienian Fantasy* (Chicago: Open Court, 2005). I am also relying on Jared Lobdell, e-mail to author, Oct. 29, 2013. He published essays in the libertarian *Agorist Quarterly* from the 1970s to the 1990s, in *New Libertarian*, and in *Regulation*, a publication of the American Enterprise Institute, where he worked from 1972 to 1984.

29. Jared Lobdell, telephone conversation, Nov. 10, 2013.

30. Dave Stuhr, telephone conversation, Oct. 2, 2013; on Hinish, see *Class of Its Own*, 280–82. Doug Wagner is a possible exception to the patterns of persistence: in his e-mail to author, Oct. 8, 2013, he discusses his eventual turn to the Democratic Party.

31. Lewis Lehrman, telephone conversation, July 3, 2012.

32. Lewis Lehrman to Martin Duberman, March 15, 1962, folder "Correspondence, 1962. J-O," box 4, Martin Duberman Papers, Manuscripts and Archives Division, New York Public Library.

33. Samuel G. Freedman, *The Inheritance: How Three Families and America Moved from Roosevelt to Reagan and Beyond* (New York: Simon and Schuster, 1996), 356 and 373. His remarks on Freedman's book appear in Lewis Lehrman, e-mail to author, March 24, 2013. Mark Oppenheimer, "Jewish Converts Offer a Window on Conservative Christianity," *New York Times*, May 25, 2013. On Lehrman's public career, see also Brian Domitrovic, *Econoclasts: The Rebels Who Sparked the Supply-Side Revolution and Restored American Prosperity* (Wilmington, DE: ISI,

2009), 119–22. In 1980 Ronald Reagan seriously considered Lehrman for the position of secretary of the treasury.

34. See the following articles by Lewis Lehrman: "How to Decide about Strategic Defense," *National Review*, Jan. 31, 1986, 32–37; "For the Reagan Doctrine," *New York Times*, Jan. 21, 1987; "Faith and the Future of Capitalism," *Wall Street Journal*, April 16, 1993; "Romneyeconomics; Good but Incomplete," *American Spectator*, July 23, 2012.

35. For his major writings, see the following by Lewis E. Lehrman: "The Creation of International Monetary Order," in *Money and the Coming World Order*, ed. David P. Calleo (New York: New York University Press, 1976), 71–120; with Ron Paul, *The Case for Gold: A Minority Report of the U.S. Gold Commission* (Washington, DC: Cato Institute, 1982); *Real Money: The Case for the Gold Standard* (New York: Random House, 1982); *Lincoln at Peoria, The Turning Point: Getting Right with the Declaration of Independence* (Mechanicsburg, PA: Stackpole, 2008); *The True Gold Standard*, 2nd ed. (New York: Lehrman Institute, 2012); *Lincoln "by littles"* (New York: Lehrman Institute, 2013); *Money, Gold, and History* (New York: Lehrman Institute, 2013). For access to some of his essays, see http://lehrmaninstitute.org/economic-policy/essays.asp. On his call for Reagan and Romney to more fully embrace a conservative agenda, see Lewis Lehrman, "A New Conservatism," *American Spectator*, Jan. 1984, 28–29, and "Romneyeconomics." Conversations with Lois Horton (April 30, 2013) and David Blight (in 2011 and 2012) make clear that Lehrman supports research and teaching regardless of ideological considerations.

36. Lewis Lehrman, e-mail to author, March 16, 2013.

37. Lehrman, *True*, 120. On his commitment to Rueff's works, I rely on Lewis Lehrman, e-mail to author, March 14, 2013. In *Face Value: The Entwined Histories of Money and Race in America* (Chicago: University of Chicago Press, 2012), esp. 3–10 and 203–7, Michael O'Malley argues that for many libertarian advocates of the gold standard, there was a connection between the intrinsic value of gold and racial differences. I find no such parallel in Lehrman's work; in fact, what is striking is that Lehrman advocated both for the gold standard and for expanding opportunity for African Americans.

38. Lehrman, *True Gold Standard*, 9.

39. Lehrman, *Lincoln at Peoria*, 264 and 265. For information on his interest in Lincoln, I am relying on Lewis Lehrman, e-mail to author, March 14, 2013; also see the following essays by Lehrman: "The Right to Life and the Restoration of the American Republic," *National Review*, Aug. 29, 1986, 26; "The Declaration of Independence and the Right to Life," *American Spectator*, April 1987, 22, "'Work Is the Main Thing," *Wall Street Journal*, Feb. 10, 1998; "The Party of Lincoln: The Legacy of the First Republican President," *Weekly Standard*, Feb. 16, 2004, 21–22.

40. This list includes prominent classmates involved in politics, but hardly all of them. Among classmates are several ambassadors and high-ranking federal officials, including Ben Erdreich, a five-term congressman from Alabama.

41. Ferdinando Fasce, *An American Family: The Great War and Corporate Culture in America*, trans. Ian Harvey (Columbus: Ohio State University Press, 2002), 95–96.

42. Porter Goss, telephone conversation, June 26, 2012.

43. John Negroponte, telephone conversation, June 23, 2012.

44. For full story of his career, see George W. Liebmann, *The Last American Diplomat: John D. Negroponte and the Changing Face of American Diplomacy* (London: I. B. Taurus, 2011). For books by his wife, see Diana Villiers Negroponte, *Seeking Peace in El Salvador: The Struggle to Reconstruct a Nation at the End of the Cold War* (New York: Palgrave Macmillan, 2012); ed., *The End of Nostalgia: Mexico Confronts the Challenge of Global Competition* (Washington, DC: Brookings Institution Press, 2013).

45. Ted Stebbins, "Henry Jack Heinz, III," *Class of Its Own*, 67.

46. In writing on Aspin, I am relying on his brother Jim's e-mails to author, Feb. 10 and Feb. 11, 2013.

47. Clint Brooks, "Leslie Aspin, Jr.," *Class of Its Own*, 62–63.

48. Leites, conversation, Dec. 17, 2012. At our commencement, Griswold remarked that "it is by what you are and by what you make of yourselves that your country will be judged": A. Whitney Griswold, "Baccalaureate Address," *YAM*, July 1960, 9.

49. On the relationships between college and political trajectories, see Neill Gross, *Why Are Professors Liberal and Why Do Conservatives Care?* (Cambridge: Harvard University Press, 2013).

Conclusion. Looking Backward

1. James Atlas, "Between the Lines of Harvard's Red Book," *New York Times,* April 15, 2012. I will leave to someone else the task of discussing the testimonials in "The 1960 Confessionaire," *Class of Its Own,* 533–61, anonymous (and in some cases fabricated) rendering of transgressive and scandalous behavior. The life of Joel Finer provides evidence of what reunion books obscure: from his childhood through his career as a medical doctor, he committed himself to progressive positions on race for which the reunion books provide no evidence: Joel Finer, telephone conversation, Nov. 26, 2013.

2. Andrew Wexton, "Yale Mourns Death of President Giamatti: Friends Recall Warmth, Eloquence, Sharp Wit," *YDN,* Sept. 6, 1989, 1 and 4.

3. A. Bartlett Giamatti, quoted in Edward B. Fiske, "Lessons," *New York Times,* Sept. 6, 1989. Here I am relying on A. Bartlett Giamatti: *The Earthly Paradise and the Renaissance Epic* (Princeton: Princeton University Press, 1966); *The University and the Public Interest* (New York: Atheneum, 1981); *A Free and Ordered Space: The Real World of the University* (New York: Norton, 1988). See also Edward B. Fiske and A. Bartlett Giamatti, "Yale's MVP Learns New Signals—and Sends Some," *New York Times,* May 27, 1979; William E. Geist, "The Outspoken President of Yale," *New York Times Magazine,* March 6, 1983; Roger Angell, "The Sporting Scene: Celebration," *New Yorker,* Aug. 22, 1988, 50–60; Anthony Valerio, *BART: A Life of A. Bartlett Giamatti by Him and about Him* (New York: Harcourt Brace Jovanovich, 1991); Kenneth S. Robson, ed., *A Great and Glorious Game: Baseball Writings of A. Bartlett Giamatti* (Chapel Hill, NC: Algonquin Books, 1998); and Robert P. Moncreiff, *Bart Giamatti: A Profile* (New Haven: Yale University Press, 2007).

4. Giamatti, "To Make Oneself Eternal" (1980), in *Free and Ordered Space,* 193.

5. Giamatti, "The Academic Mission" (1987), in *Free and Ordered Space,* 36.

6. Angell, "Sporting Scene," 50.

7. William Borders, quoted from *YAM* 1989, in *Class of Its Own,* 66.

8. I rely here on the following e-mails: Leslie Epstein, Aug. 7, 2014; Tom Miller, Aug. 7, 2014; Bob Mallano, Aug. 7, 2014; Gwen Jensen, Aug 8, 2014; and on Carol and Sandy Schreiber, conversation, Aug. 13, 2014, and John A. Wilkinson, conversation, Aug. 15, 2014.

9. Paul Alpers, "Giamatti's Spenser," *Aethlon: The Journal of Sports Literature* 14 (Spring 1997): 91–93; the quote is from A. Bartlett Giamatti, *Play of Double Senses: Spenser's 'Faerie Queene'* (Englewood Cliffs, NJ: Prentice-Hall, 1975), 49.

10. A. Bartlett Giamatti, "The Problem of Evil and The Restoration of Paradise," speech to class of 1960, *30th RD,* xi; for a somewhat different version, see A. Bartlett Giamatti, "Ruminations of University Presidency," in *Free and Ordered Space,* 17–30; original is in folder 215, box 10, RU65, accession 1988-A-054, YUA.

11. Giamatti, "Problem of Evil," x–xvi.

12. Borders, *Class of Its Own,* 66.

13. Tom Miller, *30th RD,* 109.

14. Lewis Lehrman, *Class of Its Own,* 65–66.

15. Sharon Olds, once married to classmate David Olds, won the 2013 Pulitzer Prize for Poetry for *Stag's Leap* (New York: Knopf, 2012), which the prize committee described as "unflinching poems on the author's divorce that examine love, sorrow and the limits of self-knowledge": www.pulitzer.org/citation/2013-Poetry.

16. The following discussion draws on William T. Bowen and Derek Bok, *The Shape of the River: Long-Term Consequences of Considering Race in College and University Admissions* (Princeton: Princeton University Press, 1998); Andrew Hacker and Claudia Dreifus, *Higher Education: How Colleges Are Wasting Our Money and Failing Our Kids—And What We Can Do about It* (New York: Times Books, 2010); Andrew Delbanco, *College: What It Was, Is, and*

Should Be (Princeton: Princeton University Press, 2012); Elizabeth A. Armstrong and Laura T. Hamilton, *Paying for the Party: How College Maintains Inequality* (Cambridge: Harvard University Press, 2013); Neil Gross, *Why Are Professors Liberal and Why Do Conservatives Care?* (Cambridge: Harvard University Press, 2013); William J. Bennett and David Wilezol, *Is College Worth It? A Former United States Secretary of Education and a Liberal Arts Graduate Explore the Broken Promise of Higher Education* (Nashville: Thomas Nelson, 2013); Jeffrey J. Selingo, *College (Un)Bound: The Future of Higher Education and What It Means for Students* (Boston: Houghton Mifflin Harcourt, 2013).

17. For a statement of these advantages, see Jack Latona, *Class of Its Own*, 330.

18. Sam Heyman and Jeremy Nahum, in *Class of Its Own*, 69.

19. Vilfredo Pareto, *The Rise and Fall of Elites: An Application of Theoretical Sociology* (1901; Totowa, NJ: Bedminster, 1968). William Deresiewicz, *Excellent Sheep: The Miseducation of the American Elite and the Way to a Meaningful Life* (New York: Free Press, 2104).

20. See Marcia G. Synnott, *Student Diversity at the Big Three: Changes at Harvard, Yale, and Princeton since the 1920s* (New Brunswick, NJ: Transaction, 2013), 299–323, for a summary of continuing debates over admission to elite universities. For a provocative essay suggesting that by the early twenty first century the era of high-achieving Jews was waning, see Ron Lund, "The Myth of American Meritocracy: How Corrupt are Ivy League Admissions?," *American Conservative*, Nov. 28, 2012.

21. Joseph A. Soares, *The Power of Privilege: Yale and America's Elite Colleges* (Stanford: Stanford University Press, 2007), 66.

22. In 2014, 15 percent of Yale undergraduates received Pell grants, the federal program for students from families with low to moderate incomes and the widely accepted measure of educational access: David Zax, "Wanted: Smart Students from Poor Families," *YAM*, Jan./Feb. 2014, 47. This percentage is the lowest in the Ivy League except for Princeton and lower than that for Amherst, Smith, Vassar, Wellesley, and Williams.

23. Donald K. Walker, quoted in "Scholarship Distribution Examined," *YDN*, April 13, 1959, 1.

24. James T. B. Trip, "Bursary System: Unique Program," *YDN*, April 30, 1959, 1.

25. This discussion relies on material in the class book and reunion books, as well as the following e-mails and telephone conversations: Al Gillotti, Aug. 12, 2013; Jack Latona, July 19, 2013; Bob Mallano, July 24 and 25, 2013; Russ Mancini, July 24 and 25, 2013; Bob Porfirio, July 25, 2013. My list of eighteen does not include Giamatti because of his mother's elite background. Gillotti's wife has written of her family: Susan Gillotti, *Women of Privilege: 100 Years of Love and Loss in a Family of the Hudson River Valley* (Chicago: Academy, 2013). For Al's most recent novel, see A. F. Gillotti, *George Evans* (Chicago: Academy, 2013).

26. Robert Reynolds, telephone conversation, Aug. 7, 2013; Robert Reynolds, "Notes of Personal Story," early Aug. 2013, copy in author's possession. Data on scholarships policies and practices for the class of 1960 is hard to come by, but my guess is that Yale's system was in transition, at the time imperfectly providing talented students with financial aid packages that would not come even close to leveling the playing field. On the development of systems and policies, see Rupert Wilkinson, *Aiding Students, Buying Students: Financial Aid in America* (Nashville: Vanderbilt University Press, 2005), esp. 111–28. A 1958 Yale study confirms Reynolds's judgment: academic overachievers came from high schools and did not expect help from family or friends of family in getting their first job after college: Ralph M. Rust, "Personality and Academic Achievement," in *Psychosocial Problems of College Men*, ed. Bryant M. Wedge (New Haven: Yale University Press, 1958), 60.

27. Russ Tousley, *Class of Its Own*, 492; Russ Tousley, telephone conversation, July 24, 2013.

28. Armstrong and Hamilton, *Party*, 3. Data on who dropped out of Yale is difficult to tease out, but my guess is that the departed included those from privileged backgrounds who left because a combination of excessive partying, less-than-ideal aptitude, and the need to reconsider their choices, as well as more talented and less privileged classmates who found themselves in an environment that was inhospitable. In the class of 2017 more than half come from public high schools; 10 percent from abroad; 12 percent will be the first in their families to graduate from a four-year college; 15 percent are recipients of Pell grants; 37 percent of the class identi-

fied themselves as students of color. Amy Wang, "Class of 2017 Boasts Socioeconomic, Racial Diversity," *YDN*, Aug. 30, 2013.

29. Robert Rifkind, e-mail to author, June 4, 2013. In *Forms of Intellectual and Ethical Development in the College Years: A Scheme* (New York: Holt, Rinehart and Winston, 1970), William G. Perry relies on studies of Harvard and Radcliffe students of the late 1950s and early 1960s to chart how as undergraduates they moved from absolutism, through uncertainty and the contextual, to commitment and responsibility.

30. The distribution requirements included two courses each in English, the social sciences, history (including history, history of art, and history of music), a foreign language, math or science, and classical civilization, religion, or philosophy.

31. Daniel F. Chambliss and Christopher G. Takacs, *How College Works* (Cambridge: Harvard University Press, 2014), 5 and 155.

32. For entry into the literature on the educational benefits of student diversity, see Patricia Gurin, Eric L. Dey, Sylvia Hurtado, and Gerald Gurin, "Diversity in Higher Education: Theory and Impact on Educational Outcomes, *Harvard Educational Review* 72 (Fall 2002): 330–67; Dan Berrett, "Encounters with Diversity, on Campuses and in Coursework, Bolster Critical-Thinking Skills," *Chronicle of Higher Education,* Nov. 19, 2012. On the impact on prejudice of contact with roommates from different backgrounds, see Colette Van Laar, Shana Levin, Stacy Sinclair, and Jim Sidanius, "The Effect of University Roommate Contact on Ethnic Attitudes and Behavior," *Journal of Experimental Social Psychology* 41 (July 2005): 329–45.

33. Richard Epstein, *Class of Its Own,* 223–25; Richard Epstein, telephone conversation, October 30, 2012.

34. Jonathan Hufstadter, e-mail to author, Nov. 7, 2013.

35. Brian H. Jensen describes how Jesus came to him as he lay in the hospital: *30th RD, 79;* on communicating with the dead, see Bill Guggenheim's After-Death Communication website, www.After-Death.com.

36. All this provides a useful corrective to George M. Marsden, *The Soul of the American University: From Protestant Establishment to Established Nonbelief* (New York: Oxford University Press, 1994). On the shift in higher education from morality to a split between fact and value, see Julie A. Reuben, *The Making of the Modern University: Intellectual Transformation and the Marginalization of Morality* (Chicago: University of Chicago Press, 1996).

37. Scott Sullivan, "We Fill Out a Poll," *YDN*, March 1, 1957, 1.

38. [James H. Ottaway Jr.], "Old Order Changeth," *YDN,* Jan. 28, 1959, 2; "Student Loyalty," *YDN,* Feb. 2, 1959, 2.

INDEX

DANIEL HOROWITZ is the Mary Huggins Gamble Professor of American Studies Emeritus at Smith College. He graduated from Yale in 1960, magna cum laude in American studies, and later earned a doctorate in history at Harvard. From 1966 until he retired from teaching in 2012, he taught American studies and U.S. history, mostly at women's colleges, often with his wife, Helen Lefkowitz Horowitz, who holds a PhD in the History of American Civilization from Harvard.

Horowitz's work has focused on the history of consumer culture and social criticism in the United States during the twentieth century. Among his publications are *The Morality of Spending: Attitudes toward the Consumer Society in America, 1875–1940* (1985); *Betty Friedan and the Making of* The Feminine Mystique: *The American Left, the Cold War, and Modern Feminism* (1998); *The Anxieties of Affluence: Critiques of American Consumer Culture, 1939–1979* (2004), winner of the Eugene M. Kayden Prize for the best book published in the humanities in 2004 by a university press; and *Consuming Pleasures: Intellectuals and Popular Culture in the Postwar World* (2012).

He has held fellowships from the National Endowment for the Humanities; the National Humanities Center; the Schlesinger Library at Radcliffe College, Harvard; and the John Simon Guggenheim Memorial Foundation. In 2003 the American Studies Association awarded him its Mary C. Turpie Prize for "outstanding abilities and achievement in American Studies teaching, advising, and program development at the local or regional level."

Dan and Helen live in Cambridge, Massachusetts. Their daughter, Sarah, is an associate professor of history at Washington and Lee University. Their son, Ben, is a software engineer in the San Francisco Bay Area.